PREHISTORIC WORLD

Artists

John Barber
Ray and Corinne Burrows
Jim Channell – (Linden Artists)
Thomas Crosby-Smith
Peter Crump
Drawing Attention (Rhoda and Robert Burns)
Gay John Galsworthy
Kim Ludlow
Tony Morris (Linda Rogers Associates)
Oxford Illustrators
Linda Parry
Eric Robson
George Thompson
Maurice Wilson
Mike Youens

PREHISTORIC WORLD

Richard Moody
B.Sc Ph.D F.G.S.

CHARTWELL
BOOKS INC.

Endpapers Coelurosaur footprints from the Triassic, Australia

The author wishes to thank Dr David John and Dr David Wright for their help with the preparation of the manuscript, Linda Parry for contributing greatly to the artwork and David Bayliss for providing many of the photographs.

DEDICATED TO THE MEMORY OF MORAG JONES.

For copyright reasons this edition
is only for sale within the U.S.A.

Published in the United States by
Chartwell Books Inc.,
A Division of Book Sales Inc.,
110 Enterprise Avenue
Secaucus
New Jersey 07094
Copyright © The Hamlyn Publishing Group Limited 1980
ISBN 0-89009-362-8
Library of Congress Catalog Card No. 80-66357

Phototypeset by Filmtype Services Limited, Scarborough, England
Printed in Italy

Contents

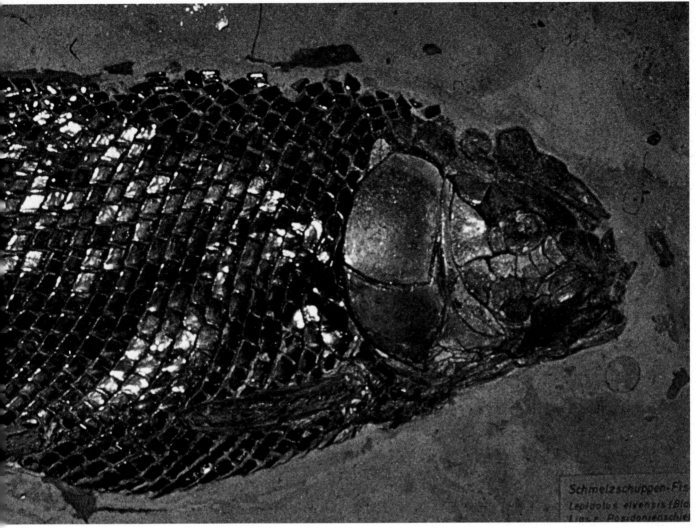

Schmelzschuppen-Fis
Lepidotus elvensis (Bl
Lias f. Posidonienschie

Measurements given in this book are metric, but the imperial units
can be found by noting the metric measurement and using the
following conversion table

Length	Mass
1 millimetre (mm) 0·039 inches	1 gram (g) 0·035 ounces
1 centimetre (cm) 0·39 inches	1 kilogram (kg) 2·2 pounds
1 metre (m) 3·2 feet	
1 kilometre (km) 0·6 miles	

For conversion of temperatures from centigrade to Fahrenheit
multiply by $\frac{9}{5}$ and add 32.

Introduction

Life on Earth began approximately 3·5 billion years ago. It followed
a long period of chemical synthesis and an even longer period
during which the solar system was born and the Earth condensed
into the layered planet we now recognize. As far as we know the
Earth is the only planet with a well-developed biosphere and it is
certainly the only one on which we can trace the succession of life.
In the last 3·5 billion years, life has developed from simple organic
molecules to the structured human communities of the present time.
At first the development of the earliest organisms was painstakingly
slow, but once animals and plants were able to reproduce sexually
and to pass on hereditary characters, the progress of evolution
speeded up dramatically. The record of this and of subsequent
extinctions and radiations, is a variable one and we should
remember that the sample we obtain from the rocks is limited by
various biological and geological factors. However, the sample is
still a valuable one and from it we are able to reconstruct the
relationships that existed between an animal and its environment
and to establish the role the animal played within the community.
The fossil sample is constantly being added to and as our knowledge increases so we are able to offer improved theories and
interpretations on the evolution and ecology of extinct organisms.
Prehistoric World is an attempt to bring together in a popular form
the latest researches and theories in this constantly changing and
exciting branch of science.

The birth of the solar system

To many people the questions of 'How old is the solar system?', and 'How was it formed?' are amongst the most intriguing. They are fundamental questions. The answer to the first of these questions is derived from the analysis of meteorite fragments, whilst a definitive answer for the second is denied us because of inadequate knowledge of the processes that have, and still are, taking place within the solar system. The figure of 4·6 billion years, plus or minus 100 million years, for the origin of the solar system is arrived at by counting the atoms of the various *noble gases* trapped in fragments of extra-terrestrial materials.

This theory was formulated long before man had a knowledge of dynamics and it has been questioned on details such as the relative rotational speed of the condensed sun. Other theories include the collision of a massive proto-sun with another body; the planets being formed from a large mass that broke away to spin around the parent body. In more recent theories scientists, such as Fred Hoyle, have suggested that a magneto-hydro-dynamic force was inherent in the formation of the solar system, with the proto-sun contracting, increasing in temperature and developing strong magnetic fields. This resulted in gases and even

Stages in the formation of the solar system

These fragments represent the remains of large bodies that crystallized and then disintegrated during the birth pangs of the universe. The bodies in question, were born at the same time as the planet Earth; the birth of which has intrigued man for hundreds of years.

One of the more acceptable theories of origin was presented by Pierre Simon Laplace, whose *nebular hypothesis* involved the separation of cloud masses from a rotating and collapsing proto-sun.

solids at first trailing and then rotating around the 'mother' sun. According to many experts the next stage after the spin off of the cloud masses, from the central solar body, was the accretion of matter into mini-planets. These continued to rotate around the sun over a period of 100 million years, with frequent collisions and gravitational attraction reducing their numbers to that of the surviving planets.

Included amongst this number was the Earth,

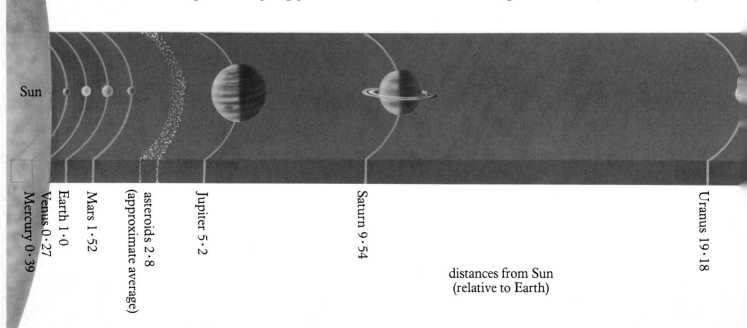

Sun

Mercury 0·39
Venus 0·27
Earth 1·0
Mars 1·52
asteroids 2·8 (approximate average)
Jupiter 5·2
Saturn 9·54
Uranus 19·18

distances from Sun (relative to Earth)

Our diagram is an attempt to illustrate the important stages in the formation of the Earth. The first stage represents the cloud of gas and dust that accumulated in the outer regions of the swirling nebula. The remainder shows various stages in the condensation and contraction of the cloud to form our planet. Chemical differentiation led to the formation of the core and mantle and, later still, a primitive crust. Approximately 3·7 billion years ago large-scale convection currents began to develop within the mantle. These affected the crust and are thought to be important to the process of plate tectonics.

Pierre Simon Laplace (1749–1827)

which itself grew as a result of the accumulation of mini-planets or planetesimals. Each planetesimal added heat on impact with the proto-planet and continuous accumulation and compression gave the newly-born planet an internal temperature of approximately 1000°C. With the increase in temperature iron in the outer region of the early Earth melted and moved towards the centre,

where it formed a liquid core. The formation of the core was the first stage in differentiation, which finally resulted in the zonation of our planet into core, mantle and crust. As far as we can tell, this differentiation took place approximately 4·5 billion years ago, which is a date which coincides with that provided by meteorites. The oldest rocks on Earth are dated by radiometric methods which are based on the constant rate of decay of radioactive elements.

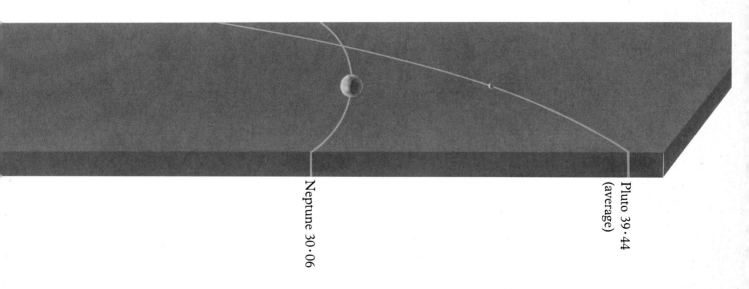

Neptune 30·06

Pluto 39·44 (average)

Planet Earth

From space it is possible to see the relationships that exist between the physical zones known as the *atmosphere*, *hydrosphere* and *lithosphere*. Our appreciation of the beauty of the planet has been enhanced by the skills of our space scientists, and through space photography we are able to witness the dramatic movements of the atmosphere and hydrosphere. The atmosphere comprises the thin gaseous layer that envelops the Earth, the most obvious features of which are the white, swirling clouds, whose patterns provide evidence of atmospheric circulation. The hydrosphere includes the oceans, seas, lakes and rivers, which in total cover just under 80 per cent of the Earth's surface. The movements of air and water are obvious to us all, but we should also be aware of the motion of the rocky crust of the Earth known as the lithosphere which, through geological time, has resulted in the splitting and drifting apart of the continental masses. According to some scientists the Earth is expanding at an accelerating rate and we are now assured that our world is not as perfectly round as was once believed.

Apart from the physical zones noted above, the Earth is also characterized by a unique biosphere, an organic realm recognized from space by the distribution of the great forests of the tropical regions. The plants and animals that live within the biosphere are adapted to the climatic conditions that prevail in the environment, in much the same way as the style and variety of land forms depends on the amount of rain, sun, ice or wind that prevails in certain latitudes.

Our section through the Earth and its atmosphere shows clearly the layered or zoned nature of the planet. In the centre is the *core* or central mass which has a diameter of approximately 7 000 kilometres and with an average density of 10·72. This is almost twice that of the mantle and whereas the core has only 16 per cent of the Earth's volume, it accounts for 32 per cent of the Earth's mass. The core is composed of nickel and iron with a solid inner core and a liquid outer core.

The layer that surrounds the outer core is called the mantle. It is rich in dark silicate minerals and as a layer it accounts for over 80 per cent of the Earth's volume. Above the mantle, the asthenosphere and the rigid lithosphere occupy the outer 300 kilometres of the Earth's radius. The asthenosphere is soft or partially melted and because of this is capable of flow; with circulating convection cells within the layer acting as the mechanism for continental drift. The cells which rise to the upper surface of the asthenosphere cause the rigid lithosphere to arch and fracture. An expression of this deep-seated activity is the opening of oceanic and continental rift systems which are usually recognized by zones of volcanic and earthquake activity.

The continental blocks float on the denser, lower lithosphere. They are made up essentially of lighter granitic rocks with sedimentary and metamorphic rocks providing a unique characterization. The lithosphere is like the shell of an egg, beyond which are the outer layers including the thin biosphere which has been so affected by the major changes that have taken place in the physical zones during the passage of geological time.

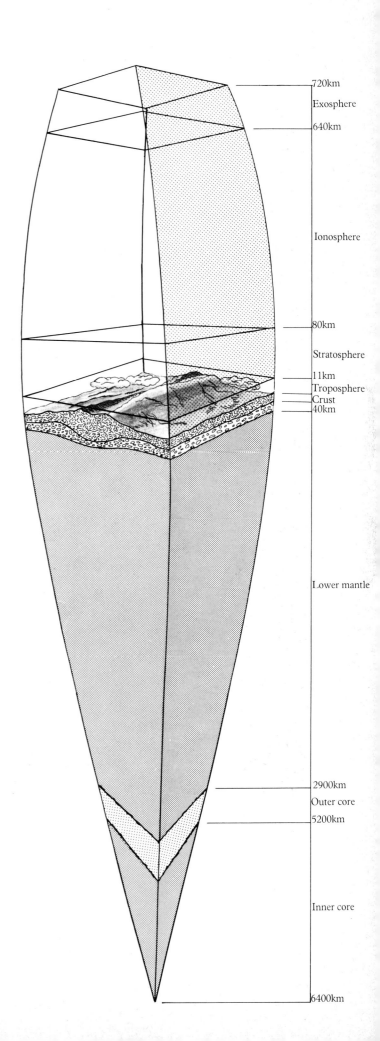

The building of the continents

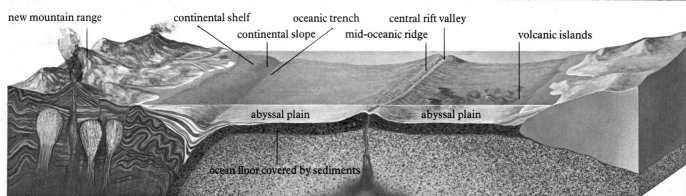

new mountain range   continental shelf   oceanic trench   central rift valley

continental slope   mid-oceanic ridge   volcanic islands

abyssal plain   abyssal plain

ocean floor covered by sediments

Surely life on the surface of the primeval planet, was 'hell on Earth'. Lavas poured out over the surface to form a thin crust and clouds of steam rose into an atmosphere rich in carbon dioxide, hydrogen sulphide and hydrogen dioxide. The emission of lava and water at the surface was linked with the differentiation that was taking place within the early planet: the heavier nickel and iron was moving towards the centre, the lighter materials, including lavas and trapped waters, were moving to the surface. In the earliest stages the crust resembled a rocky 'mush' and the amount of free water was minimal. With time, however, the crust thickened and pools of water formed on the Earth's surface. Rain waters, the product of transpiration and precipitation, began to erode the newly developed rocks and gradually a thin veneer of sediments covered areas of our planet. The crust was often fractured by deep-seated forces and both the igneous and sedimentary materials were baked and altered to form metamorphic rocks. On many occasions whole sections of the early crust would have been altered or even absorbed into the developing asthenosphere. The processes described above were continuous and over a long period of time the various rock types came to form the ancient nucleus of the emerging continents. Repeated crustal disturbances would affect this nucleus, but the final outcome was the accretion of more and more materials until the continents as we know them came to float on the surface of the lithosphere. The lithosphere itself had thickened and cooled and major fractures had formed marking the boundaries of large oceanic and continental plates. Unlike their continental counterparts the oceanic plates are the true surface of the solid Earth, they may have a surface covered by deep water sediments but the true ocean floor is composed of basalt, usually less than 150 million years old.

Below left:
A photograph of the Red Sea and the Gulf of Aden taken from 620 kilometres from the spacecraft Gemini 11. This is one of the most recent seaways and is formed by the drifting of the continents of Africa and Arabia.

Below
In the Atlantic Ocean the presence of a mid-oceanic ridge is evidence of splitting and continental drift. The ridge is several hundred kilometres wide and its high, rugged relief is evidence of basaltic magma accretion at the plate margins. A study of the basalts added to the margins, over the last 80 million years, has revealed that the Earth's magnetic field has been reversed frequently. The evidence for the reversals is actually preserved in the iron minerals within the basalt, each successive basalt being magnetized according to the polarity that prevailed during its extrusion. The changes in magnetic polarity are reflected on either side of the oceanic ridge with the parallel matching strips of normal and reversely magnetized basalts providing evidence that the sea floor is spreading.

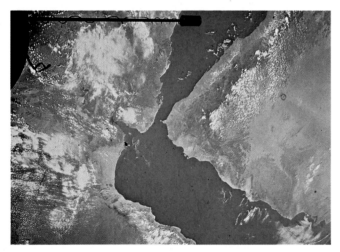

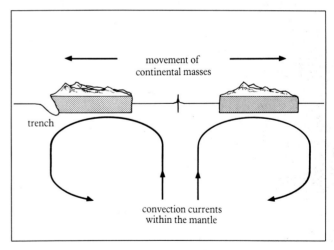

Left
The theory of plate tectonics has become one of the great unifying themes of geology, or more specifically of the Earth's dynamic system. It accounts for the building of the continents, for the origin of the oceans and for the formation of mountain chains and oceanic trenches. The surface evidence for plate movement and of the dynamic system that affects our planet, includes folds and faults in ancient rocks, volcanoes, and the tremors and destructive power of earthquakes. When oceanic and continental plates collide, the oceanic one is inevitably pushed downwards to form a deep trench and the descending lithosphere is gradually absorbed into the asthenosphere. The overriding continental plate, on the other hand, is uplifted and its margin broken and folded. Mountain ranges, volcanoes and earthquakes are the result with granite magmas moving upwards, from depth, into the folded and faulted regions.

Earth materials

limestone

granite

metamorphic rock

feldspar

quartz

All things on Earth, and those in the universe, are composed of elements such as oxygen (O), silicon (Si), and aluminium (Al). Elements are the building blocks of both inorganic and organic substances, and although most substances are combinations of elements, native or single elements, such as silver and gold, also exist. Like these, other naturally occurring inorganic solids with a definite chemical structure are called minerals and the silicate minerals, which are mostly made up of silicon and oxygen, account for over 95 per cent, of the volume of the Earth's crust. By x-ray techniques it is possible to identify the crystal structure of such minerals, and in the case of silicates, x-rays have revealed that the basic unit is the silicon-oxygen tetrahedron. In this the single, small silicon atom and four large oxygen atoms form a four-sided pyramid. Variations and combinations of this model, result in a number of mineral groups within the silicates: quartz, and the feldspars being of great importance in the composition of many rock types. The abundance of the silicates contrasts greatly with that of the metallic or ore minerals, which form only a minute part of the Earth's crust. Copper, tin, nickel and other metallic minerals are often associated with the intrusion of magmas, with plate margins representing an ideal environment for the generation of ores.

Rocks

Geologists recognize three main types of rocks within the Earth's crust. These are igneous rocks, which are the product of the cooling and crystallization of a magma; sedimentary rocks, the products of erosion and precipitation; and metamorphic rocks which are the result of the deformation and recrystallization of an existing solid rock. Magmas are rich in silicate minerals and are known to rise from the depths of the asthenosphere and the lower mantle. In some examples the percentage of quartz is over 66% and the magma is termed acidic but in others the silica percentage is between 45 and 55% and the magma is described as basaltic. At depth, a magma is like a hot gas-rich slush and when it cools, large crystals may develop to give it a characteristic texture. Igneous rocks crystallizing at depth are called 'intrusive', whilst those that break through to the surface are called 'extrusive'. The eruptions of volcanoes are a spectacular testimony to the dynamics of the Earth's interior, being linked at depth to a magma chamber.

The erosion of granites, basalts and other rocks, causes the breakdown of the original structure and the loose particles or sediment, are often transported into a new area. The degree of rounding, the size of the particles and mineralogy is a good indication as to the maturity of the sediment; with coarse grained sedimentary rocks, such as breccias (angular) and conglomerates (rounded), generally having travelled less than a fine-grained sandstone. Some sediments may be the result of the precipitation of chemicals dissolved in the waters of lakes or seas, whilst others represent the remains of dead animals and plants.

The intrusion of magmas, the folding of strata during mountain building and even the impact of meteorites may cause solid rocks to be altered. The rocks may originally be of igneous or sedimentary

During a series of traverses across an area, a geologist would collect samples and record the field relationships that exist between the various rock types. In time, after an analysis of his samples and a synthesis of the data collected, he would be ready to construct a map, a cross section and a history of the events that had taken place. From our hypothetical section, it is apparent that the geologist has recognized the intrusion of a granitic magma into the original country rock and that contact metamorphism has resulted in a distinct aureole being formed. Uplift and erosion has taken place since the intrusion of the granite and this is now exposed as rounded 'tors'. An encroachment of the sea in more recent times has resulted in the deposition of a sequence of sediments over both the granite and country rocks, and a final uplift has raised the sediments to a new position above sea-level.

The processes of magma intrusion, contact metamorphism, erosion and deposition are all contained with the sequence of events that have taken place. They are central to the formation of the three main rock types found in the Earth's crust.

granite tor

heathland

woodland

sedimentary rock

Igneous intrusion

metamorphic rock

origin, but the alteration of their mineral composition or texture transfers them to the metamorphic suite. Pressure and temperature changes are the main causes of metamorphism and such changes may occur on either a local or regional scale.

Organic substances

Elements as well as being the building blocks of minerals are also the basis of the biological compounds associated with life. Amino acids and proteins are stages in the evolution of life, occurring somewhere between the simplest aggregations of elements and the first fermenting bacterium. Beyond this come the 'true' plant and animal cells, the former being tightly bound by box-like, cellulose cell walls.

Oil, coal, natural gas and organic limestones

In the search for resources, native elements such as gold, silver and platinum are highly prized, whilst the oxides and sulphides of iron and other minerals provide the essential raw materials for many industries. However, these minerals, like many rocks, are the products of inorganic processes whereas coal, natural gas, oil and some limestones have an organic origin. Apart from natural gas, these substances are intrinsically the remains of living organisms which have died and have subsequently been buried beneath layers of sedimentary rocks. Organic limestones are mostly the remains of preserved skeletons of plants or animals whilst coal is composed of the tissues of various plants. Oil and gas, on the other hand, are largely derived from microscopic organisms via chemical transformation. In these days of rapid resource depletion the irrational use of these fossil fuels is a cause of great concern.

plant cell

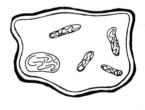

animal cell

Plant cells are rather box-like structures bounded by a distinctive cellulose wall. The inner contents consist of the cytoplasm and a nucleus. The cytoplasm is made up of amino acids and its form and functions are controlled and coordinated by the nucleus. In contrast to the plant cell, the animal cell is bounded by a thin flexible membrane. It contains no cellulose, and the chloroplasts typical of most plant cells are invariably absent.

Geological time

For the majority of us the concept of time is usually restricted to our everyday life and to recent history and this reality is put to the test when we are asked to relate to events that happened millions and thousands of millions of years ago. To the geologist, however, the concept of time is much broader and the measuring devices, or 'clocks', that he uses are natural ones.

Natural clocks, including the beat of our hearts or menstruation, are basic to man's appreciation of the concept of time and the successive deposition of layers of sedimentary rocks and the change in the succession of life are essential clues to the dating of rock outcrops. These help us determine an order of events for the last 570 million years. The geological time scale is divided into four eras, the last three of which are subdivided into eleven periods. The uses of sedimentary sequences and fossils as timing devices is somewhat restricted, for they provide only a *relative age* for each of the various rock units. Absolute dating or timing is only possible with the aid of radiometric dating.

Dating geological events

Absolute dating is achieved by the measurement of the rates of radioactive decay. This process involves the loss of particles from the nucleus of an element and the formation of a 'daughter' element. The process is one of disintegration and the rate is fixed. It is measured in terms of half-lives, for half of the original atoms decay during each time-interval or half-life. Some elements have short half-lives whilst other have half-lives that measure tens of millions of years. The decay of a radioactive isotope, which is one of several possible forms of the same element, is essentially the ticking of a nuclear clock and in some cases as when uranium^{235} decays to give lead^{207} the timing of half life, i.e. 713 million years, is thought to be accurate to plus or minus 14 million years.

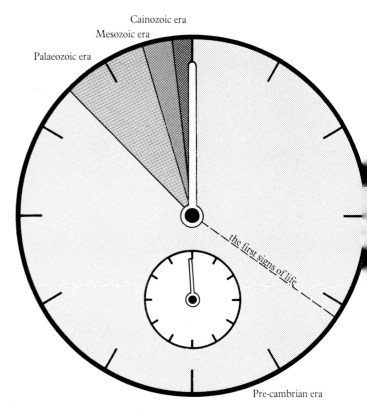

Cainozoic era
Mesozoic era
Palaeozoic era
the first signs of life
Pre-cambrian era

Mid-day on your wrist watch can be taken to represent the birth of our planet approximately 4·6 billion years ago. At three o'clock the first signs of life appeared, and by ten minutes past four o'clock blue-green algal colonies were commonplace. Animals with hardparts suddenly appeared at twenty minutes past ten o'clock. This also marked the dawn of the Palaeozoic era which was to last until twenty-five minutes past eleven o'clock. The Mesozoic and Cainozoic eras account for only thirty-five minutes or so of 'geological time', and on the small dial the indication is that *Homo sapiens* appeared only a second or so before midnight.

Stratigraphic record

The stratigraphic record is known to geologists throughout the world. It is concerned with the last 570 million years of time, and begins with the appearance of highly organized animals in the Cambrian Period and continues today through the age of man. In our look at geological time we saw that this phase of the Earth's history was divided into three eras and eleven periods of time. The eras are the Palaeozoic, the age of 'ancient life'; the Mesozoic or 'middle life'; and the Cainozoic, the era of 'new life', characterized by the evolution of the mammals. Each of the individual periods may be divided into Early, Middle or Late and, each is characterized by a sequence of rocks or a group of fossils.

In recent years geologists who are particularly interested in sediments and in the ecology of fossils have presented detailed reconstructions of the ancient environments in which the fossiliferous rocks of the stratigraphic column were originally deposited.

The stratification of rocks and the basic rudiments of a stratigraphic clock were noted by Nicolaus Steno as long ago as 1669. Steno's *Principles of Original Horizontality and Superimposition* were the product of his own observations on the horizontal sedimentary rocks near Florence. In

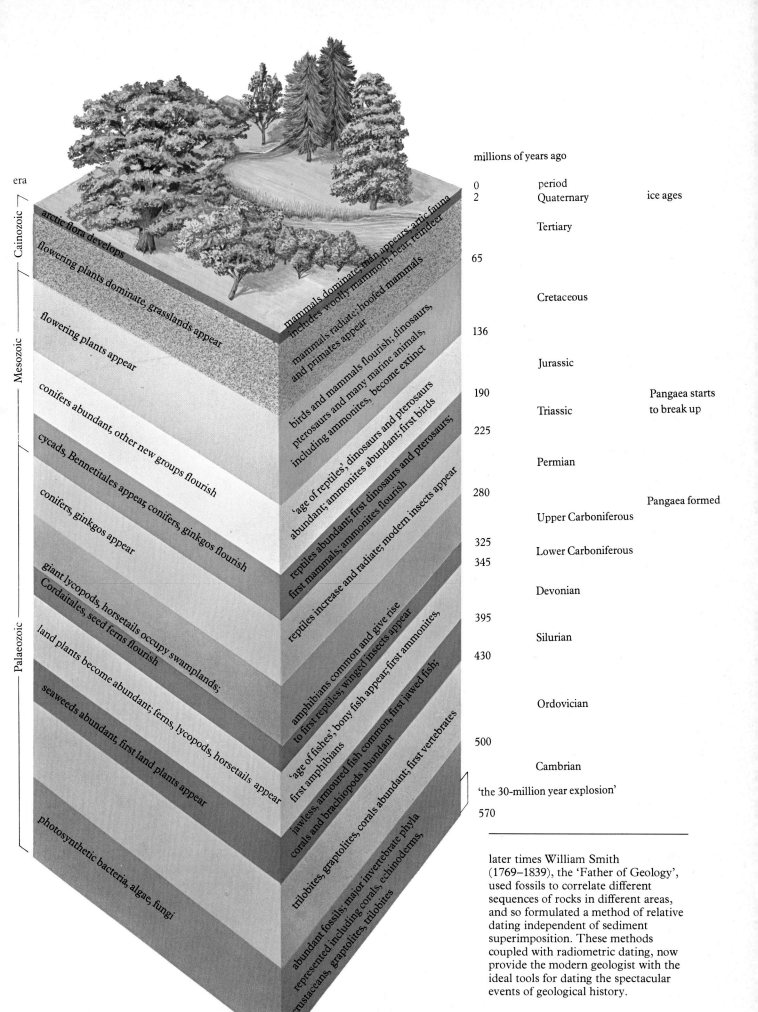

era

Cainozoic

Mesozoic

Palaeozoic

millions of years ago

0	period	
2	Quaternary	ice ages
	Tertiary	
65		
	Cretaceous	
136		
	Jurassic	
190		Pangaea starts
	Triassic	to break up
225		
	Permian	
280		Pangaea formed
	Upper Carboniferous	
325		
345	Lower Carboniferous	
	Devonian	
395		
	Silurian	
430		
	Ordovician	
500		
	Cambrian	

'the 30-million year explosion'

570

arctic flora develops

flowering plants dominate, grasslands appear

flowering plants appear

conifers abundant, other new groups flourish

cycads, Bennetitales appear, conifers, ginkgos flourish

conifers, ginkgos appear

giant lycopods, horsetails occupy swamplands;
Cordaitales, seed ferns flourish

land plants become abundant; ferns, lycopods, horsetails appear

seaweeds abundant, first land plants appear

photosynthetic bacteria, algae, fungi

mammals dominate; man appears; arctic fauna includes woolly mammoth, bear, reindeer

mammals radiate; hoofed mammals and primates appear

birds and mammals flourish; dinosaurs, pterosaurs and many marine animals, including ammonites, become extinct

'age of reptiles'; dinosaurs and pterosaurs abundant; ammonites abundant; first birds

reptiles abundant, first dinosaurs and pterosaurs; first mammals; ammonites flourish

reptiles increase and radiate; modern insects appear

amphibians common and give rise to first reptiles; winged insects appear

'age of fishes'; bony fish appear; first ammonites, first amphibians

jawless, armoured fish common, first jawed fish; corals and brachiopods abundant

trilobites, graptolites, corals abundant; first vertebrates

abundant fossils; major invertebrate phyla represented including corals, echinoderms, crustaceans, graptolites, trilobites

later times William Smith
(1769–1839), the 'Father of Geology',
used fossils to correlate different
sequences of rocks in different areas,
and so formulated a method of relative
dating independent of sediment
superimposition. These methods
coupled with radiometric dating, now
provide the modern geologist with the
ideal tools for dating the spectacular
events of geological history.

The Pre-cambrian

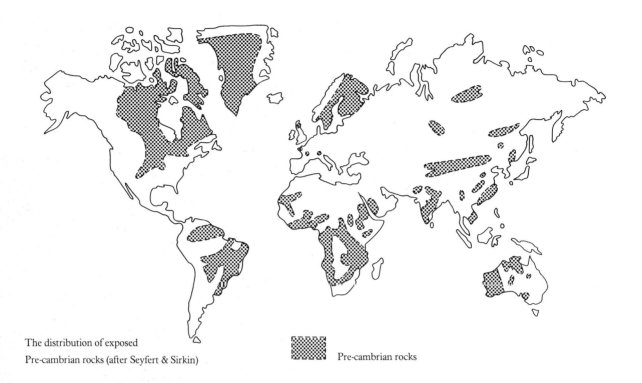

The distribution of exposed
Pre-cambrian rocks (after Seyfert & Sirkin)

Pre-cambrian rocks

Geological time is divided unequally into two eons, the Cryptozoic and Phanerozoic. The first, the age of 'hidden life', lasted approximately 4000 million years or five-sixths of geological time. The more common term used by geologists for the rocks formed during this eon is *Precambrian*, which literally refers to those materials formed before the dawn of the Cambrian Period, 570 million years ago. Rocks of Precambrian age are often altered due to the effects of heat or pressure generated during mountain building movements, when intense folding occurred and granitic magmas rose into the crustal layers. Sedimentary rocks laid down in Precambrian seas are preserved in various parts of the world and it is likely that one day geologists will establish for them a detailed sequence similar to that already constructed for those of the Phanerozoic eon. Rocks of the Precambrian are known from all continents, and often they outcrop as great *shields* or blocks which have resisted change since early geological time. In some regions the rocks are found as *cratons* or stable blocks which have a cover of younger sedimentary rocks. These Precambrian massifs often form the core of the present day continents.

What the rocks tell us

A study of the various rocks attributed to the Precambrian period reveals that the 'eon' is divisible into three long-term cycles which were completed 3000, 2100 and 1000 million years ago. These cycles involved periods when the rocks were folded and thrust-faulted, with one block moving over another. The emplacement of granite magmas and the degree of baking and deformation is important in the recognition and dating of the various rocks of the Precambrian, but absolute dates can only be determined by the use of the 'nuclear clocks'.

Precambrian life

For the first billion years of its existence the planet Earth was devoid of any form of life. Space probes from other planets would have reported that the primitive world possessed an atmosphere containing little or no free oxygen, but that the mixture of various gases present was capable, with the right energy sources, of producing the basic building blocks of life. In time these reports would have

proved correct, for the first single celled organisms
appeared approximately 3300 million years ago.
These organisms which lack a nucleus, are called
prokaryotes and it is likely that the first to appear
were completely intolerant of oxygen. Fortunately
this was an essential pre-requisite to further
development, for if the early atmosphere had been
rich in oxygen it is likely that many of the chemicals needed for life would have been destroyed by
oxidation. In time a whole range of prokaryotes,
some of which used oxygen in their metabolism,
evolved in the primordial soups of the planet's
surface. These prokaryotes, known as the *cyanobacteria*, were capable of photosynthesis, a process
where sunlight, water and carbon dioxide are
employed to manufacture carbohydrates. Oxygen
is a by-product of this process.

Gradually the increase of green photosynthetic
organisms gave the evolving planet a new colour
pattern and an oxygen-rich atmosphere. Within
the oxygenated waters of the planet, new forms of
life were also to appear with nucleated cells, called
eukaryotes with multicelled, soft-bodied animals
appearing between approximately 3·0 billion and

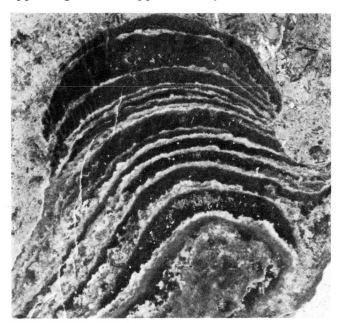

3·7 billion years after the origin of the solar
system. In terms of simple percentages the step
from one-celled prokaryotes to multicelled
organisms appears to have been a difficult one,
which took twice as long as that from the synthesis
of the first living organism. The 'hows' and 'whys'
of chemical evolution and the development of
multicelled organisms warrant separate
consideration.

Chemistry for life

The early atmosphere was rich in carbon dioxide and hydrogen sulphide. Boiling water provided oxygen and hydrogen and lightning the vital spark needed to fuse together the chemicals of life.

One often visualises the conditions on the surface of the early Earth as something akin to those of a fetid, enclosed cess pool. The early phases of chemical evolution were well advanced and amino acids, fatty acids and urea were all present within the primordial soup. Lightning flashed through the ammonia rich atmosphere and together with ultraviolet light from the sun and heat from volcanic eruptions provided a source of energy for the synthesis of additional chemicals. The life of these chemicals was assured as no free oxygen was present to degrade them.

In these conditions monomers, such as amino acids, sugars and fatty acids, could be welded together to form polymers. This reaction is termed polymerization and it involves the linking of monomers into elongate chains. Evaporation of pools of the soup may have helped in the con-centration of the simpler substances and aided polymerization to take place. Gradually polymer or protein-rich solutions formed along coastal stretches and it was within these that the first protein spheres formed. These spheres or coacervates, had a well-developed membrane which must have helped in the control of the internal environment. In time certain coacervates were to contain their own polymers and were able to manufacture energy. Their survival time increased and when they became too large they divided into 'daughter' units. The coacervates were not living organisms but soon, by some speculative action, such structures received catalysts that would set up a machinery to deal with the complex coding and replication of genetic information. The structures were the first living organisms, the catalysts were nucleic acids.

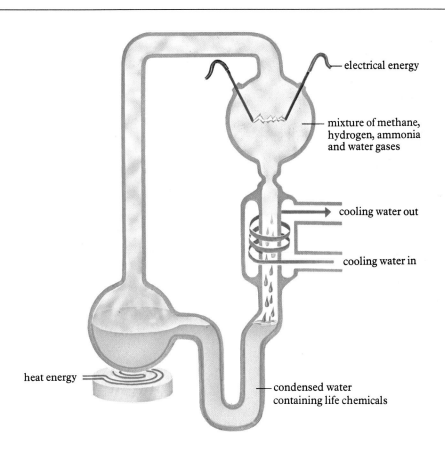

- electrical energy
- mixture of methane, hydrogen, ammonia and water gases
- cooling water out
- cooling water in

heat energy

- condensed water containing life chemicals

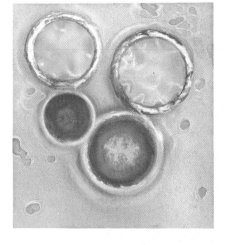

Stanley Miller and Harold Urey, two scientists from the University of Chicago in North America, designed the apparatus illustrated above in order to simulate the conditions in which they thought the first organic compounds were formed. Essentially the apparatus was a closed circuit: a mixture of gases, introduced through the left hand valve, was driven into the spark flask by steam rising from the boiling water. The electrical discharge was to simulate lightning and the water and gases were to simulate the primitive atmosphere. Miller and Urey's experiment produced four of the amino acids found in proteins and clearly demonstrated a probable stage in the evolution of life.

Amino acids are the building blocks of proteins. Glycine was one of the four amino acids produced during Miller and Urey's experiment.

- ● carbon
- ○ hydrogen
- ○ oxygen
- (N) nitrogen

Another experiment involved the heating of amino acid mixtures. This produced microscopic spheres which have a shape similar to living cells and some spheres appeared to have a double-layered membrane like that found in bacteria. The spheres are not living organisms, however, for they lack the internal structures of true cells.

glycine

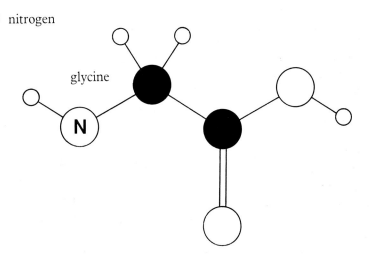

The present is the key to the past

The recent discovery of living stromatolites in Australia and the West Indies has provided palaeontologists with an insight on the form and structure of some of the earliest communities.

Fossil stromatolites. The first stromatolitic mounds were recorded by Charles Walcott from Precambrian rocks of western North America. The mounds were formed by the prokaryotic cyanobacteria in much the same way as those found today in Shark Bay, Australia. The concentric laminations are the result of the trapping of sediment on the mat-like surface of the community – hundreds of mounds preserved on the bedding planes of Precambrian rocks suggest that stromatolite reefs were once a common feature of coastal environments. In section many of the mounds exhibit a pillar-like structure.

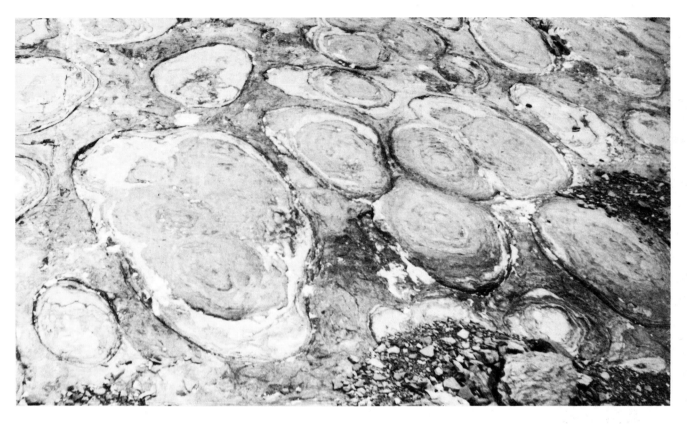

In 1785, James Hutton, the originator of several of the fundamental principles of geology, proposed that the Earth had evolved as a result of the same processes that operate today. This infers that the laws of nature remain unchanged throughout geological time and that continuity and constancy are all important. Hutton termed his principle *Uniformitarianism*, and other great scientists such as Charles Lyell (1797–1875) and Charles Darwin (1809–1882) were to use it as the foundation of their own works.

Uniformitarianism has been translated by many to mean 'the present is the key to the past', and although this definition is broadly acceptable it is in itself an oversimplification. Processes have varied in importance through time, with the great glaciations of the Permo-Carboniferous and the Pleistocene providing irrefutable proof of fluctuation. Uniformitarianism does, however, provide us with a logic essential to the interpretation of the past. Geologists therefore study present day processes in order to understand the records preserved in the rocks. Naturally the further we go back in time, the more difficult is the task of direct comparison. It is often impossible to relate features in ancient rocks to recent processes.

However, many features provide an excellent documentation of past events; for example, we automatically assume that ancient ripple marks were formed by the action of waves or currents. Coral reefs are also thought to have developed under similar conditions as today, and when discovered are considered to be indicators of warm, shallow and and well-oxygenated waters. Individual fossils themselves can be compared with living representatives and, in the case of *Lingula*, an inarticulate brachiopod, the animal and its mode of life have remained unchanged for hundreds of millions of years.

Another outstanding example of uniformitarianism occurs in the plant kingdom where the simple stromatolitic algae can be traced back over 2000 million years. At the present time stromatolitic mounds are best known from Shark Bay, Australia, where they occur in salty coastal habitats. These mounds are protected from grazing invertebrates by the high salinity of the water and elsewhere their occurrence is severely restricted. This was not true of earlier times, however, for in the Precambrian the circular, laminated stromatolite mounds had a worldwide distribution. They indicate the presence of similar environmental conditions to those that now prevail in Shark Bay, and their distribution is proof of the absence of invertebrate grazers.

Towards many-celled animals

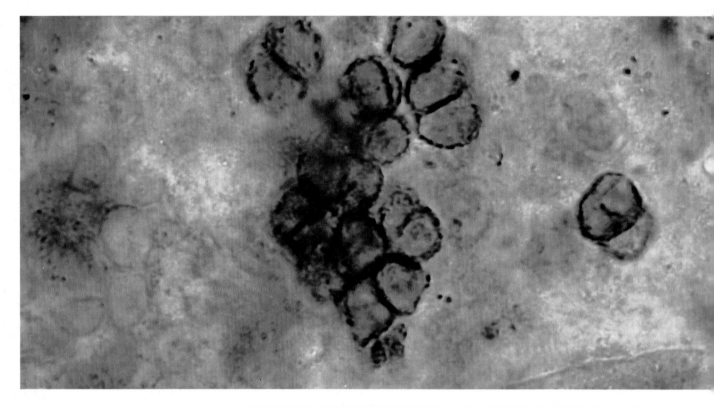

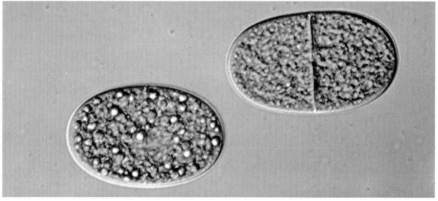

Above
Above are shown fossilized prokaryotic cells dividing, from the base of the Amelia Dolomite, McArthur Group, Northern Territory, Australia – approximately 1600 million years old.

Right
The two prokaryotic organisms belong to the blue-green algae or cyanobacteria, one cell has formed a cross wall and the contents of the cell have divided into two halves. Simple splitting is also characteristic of many single-celled animals, including *Amoeba*.

The appearance of the first multicelled animals is recorded in 700 million year old rocks. Their appearance is one of the most significant events in the record of life and one should remember that almost 2000 million years had passed since the evolution of the first prokaryote. The vast majority of animals and plants we can see with the naked-eye are multicellular, and it is no surprise to know that these organisms are much more efficient than their single-celled ancestors. To achieve internal physiological balance alone would have required a great deal of time and it is likely that the evolution of mulitcelled creatures passed through several stages.

Evidence for some of these stages has, miraculously, been preserved in ancient rocks, which also tells us of changes in the Earth's atmosphere. At first the atmosphere contained little or no free-oxygen but eventually the appearance of the photosynthetic bacteria and of the blue-green algae led to a change in the global environment. Free oxygen was essential for aerobic conditions

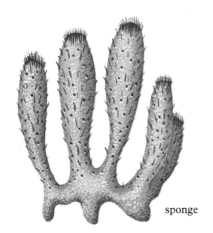
sponge

The sponges are the simplest of the multicelled animals (Metazoa). They are much larger and more complicated than any of the single-celled eukaryotes and the presence of different cells has improved the functional efficiency of the animal. The sponges are the only metazoans thought to be directly descended from a single-celled ancestor. The first sponge probably appeared around 700 million years ago.

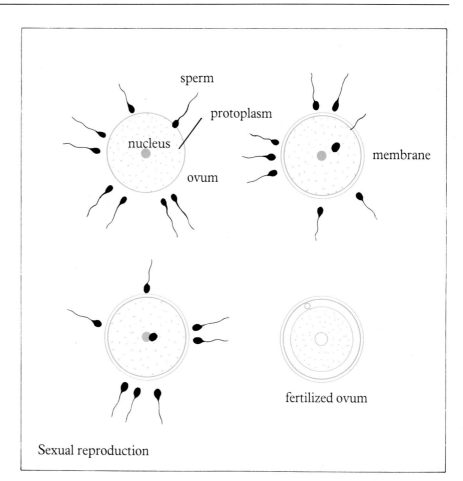

sperm

protoplasm

nucleus

ovum

membrane

fertilized ovum

Sexual reproduction

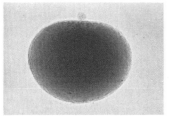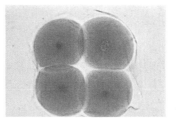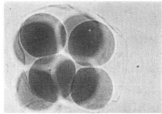

Sexual reproduction began over 1000 million years ago. It involved the production of sex cells which then fused to form a new cell. In some algae the sex cells may be identical but in others the cells are of different sizes with a large 'female' and small 'male' cell. This condition is similar to that of higher organisms where the two cells, carrying genetic information from the parent producers fuse to form a single cell which then divides rapidly. The advent of sexual reproduction led to increased diversity and was essential for the evolution of multicelled organisms. Above are shown the early stages in the development of a sea-urchin.

which in turn were needed for the evolution of the eukaryotes. These were larger than their predecessors and new methods of reproduction, including sexual reproduction, led to a sharing of characters and a greater diversity within the group. Sexual reproduction was well established at approximately 1000 million years BC and together with increased competition and predation, led to the evolution of new forms of life, including the first multicelled creatures. It is possible that the first multicellular creatures evolved by chance with the continued division 'after reproduction' of a large 'daughter' eukaryote. It is also possible that numbers of different eukaryotes aggregated to provide a greater functional efficiency, the resultant aggregation having some likeness to that of a simple sponge. According to many scientists the sponges arose directly from a eukaryote ancestor, whereas all other multicelled animals or metazoans arose from metazoan ancestors. The first sponges probably appeared around 700 million years ago.

The first communities

In the biological sense the word community is used to describe associations of populations, in terms of spacial distribution, and interaction with regard to feeding and energy transfer. Palaeontologists are the biologists of the geological world and many are interested in the reconstruction of ancient communities. Unfortunately much of the information that is needed for a complete reconstruction is often missing and to some extent the final interpretation is hypothetical. The further one goes back in time the less data one has to use, and for Precambrian communities the data is very restricted indeed. One locality, however, has produced a wealth of information, with sufficient fossil material being preserved to enable the reconstruction of a sea-shore community of Late Precambrian age.

The locality in question is in the Ediacara Hills of South Australia, where outcrops of medium-grained, quartz sandstones reflect the presence of a shallow water environment some 680 million years ago. All of the fossils found at this locality, belong to soft-bodied animals, such as worms, jellyfish and soft corals related to the modern sea-pens.

Worm trails and burrows have also been found and the fauna as a whole, suggests that these early many-celled organisms had become adapted to different modes of life. It is likely that sponges and sea-weeds were also present within the community, although no trace of their presence has actually been discovered.

The preservation of the animals as moulds and casts in sandstone, is unusual for these rocks often indicate a high energy environment. It is likely therefore, that this preservation is secondary with the sands infilling the original casts left by the animals in soft surface muds. This suggests that the environment in which they lived was a coastal one, with the dead organisms being stranded inshore on the surface of mud patches which stretched across a sandy beach. The jellyfish were free floaters, with one fossil having an appearance similar to that of the Portuguese Man-o-war. The worms on the other hand included free swimmers, burrowers and surface crawlers which either ingested mud or filtered their food from the enclosing waters.

The majority of animals in the Ediacara fauna

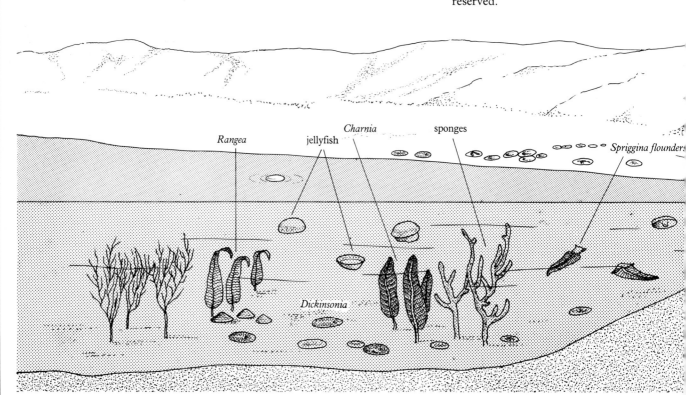

Rangea   jellyfish   Charnia   sponges   Spriggina flounders

Dickinsonia

fed on microscopic organisms although predation by the larger jellyfish cannot be ruled out.

The Ediacara fauna is not the only evidence for many-celled animals in the late Precambrian and other remains have been found as far afield as Newfoundland in Canada, and the Charnwood Forest in England. Once again, the evidence is of jellyfish, worms and soft corals and it is likely that these organisms had a worldwide distribution at this time. Their remains are always preserved as moulds or casts, however, and only the impressions of the needle-like spicules of sponges indicate the presence of skeletal materials. No doubt sponges and the soft corals did use organic or mineral compounds for support but the earliest recording of skeletal tissues does not occur until the dawn of the Phanerozoic. The nature of the fossil record is, particularly in the Precambrian, a sketchy affair with rare fossils occurring as the result of ideal conditions of preservation. In the Cambrian and later periods the record does improve dramatically, but the delicate nature of many organisms and the great forces that have affected ancient rocks make sure that the fossil record is one full of imperfections.

Medusina mawsoni is a classic example of a late Precambrian jellyfish, it is preserved as a cast in the red, quartzitic sandstones of the Ediacara formation.

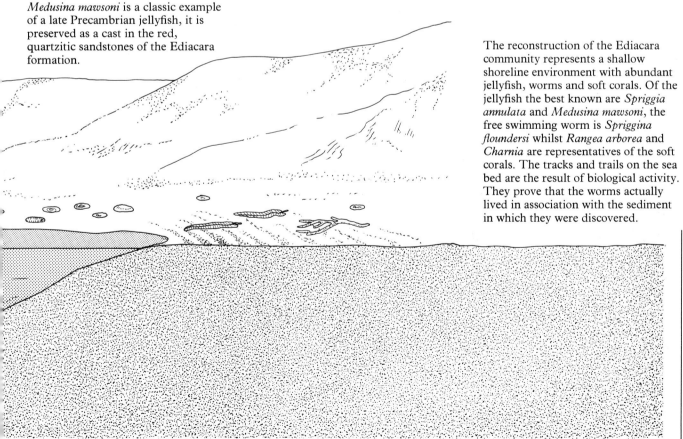

The reconstruction of the Ediacara community represents a shallow shoreline environment with abundant jellyfish, worms and soft corals. Of the jellyfish the best known are *Spriggia annulata* and *Medusina mawsoni*, the free swimming worm is *Spriggina floundersi* whilst *Rangea arborea* and *Charnia* are representatives of the soft corals. The tracks and trails on the sea bed are the result of biological activity. They prove that the worms actually lived in association with the sediment in which they were discovered.

The evidence for evolution

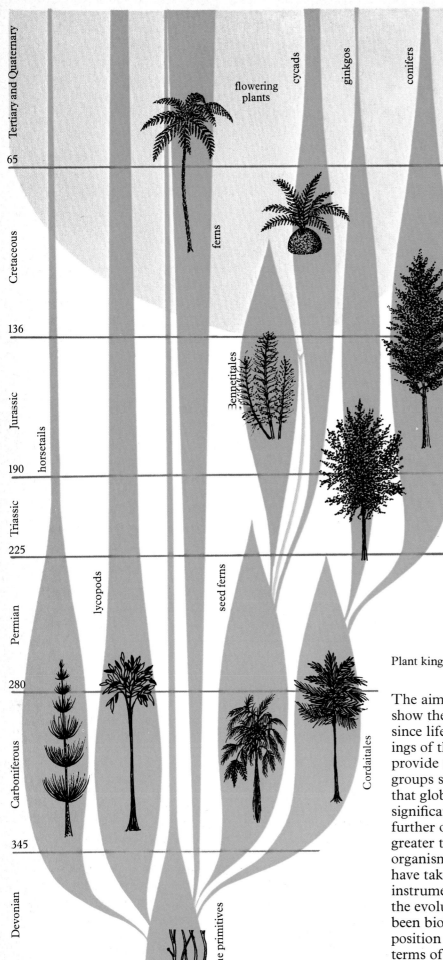

Tertiary and Quaternary — 65 — Cretaceous — 136 — Jurassic — 190 — Triassic — 225 — Permian — 280 — Carboniferous — 345 — Devonian — 395

millions of years ago

flowering plants · cycads · ginkgos · conifers · ferns · Bennetitales · horsetails · lycopods · seed ferns · Cordaitales · the primitives

Plant kingdom

The great kingdoms

The plant and animal kingdoms include all the single-celled organisms (Protista) as well as the far more complex organisms such as the giant redwoods and larger mammals. The histories of both kingdoms are closely linked, with the plants being the essential tie between the inorganic world and the animal kingdom. This is because the majority of plants utilize inorganic compounds as nutrients to create living matter. The appearance of photosynthetic plants in the seas of the world was essential for the evolution of animals, and the colonization of land by insects and vertebrates would have been an impossible task without the evolution of a 'water-proof' epidermis in the seed ferns and horsetails.

The aim of the diagrams on these two pages is to show the great diversification that has taken place since life began. They show the important groupings of the plant and animal kingdoms and provide some indication of the success of the groups since the late Precambrian. It is apparent that global communities or biotas have changed significantly with the passage of time and that the further one ascends the stratigraphic column the greater the differences between ancient and living organisms. From this we may deduce that changes have taken place, and that these changes were instrumental in the extinction of some forms and the evolution of others. The changes may have been biological in the sense of the genetic composition of a given population, or ecological in terms of responses to temperature, salinity or even predation.

The fossil record is proof of an increase in the

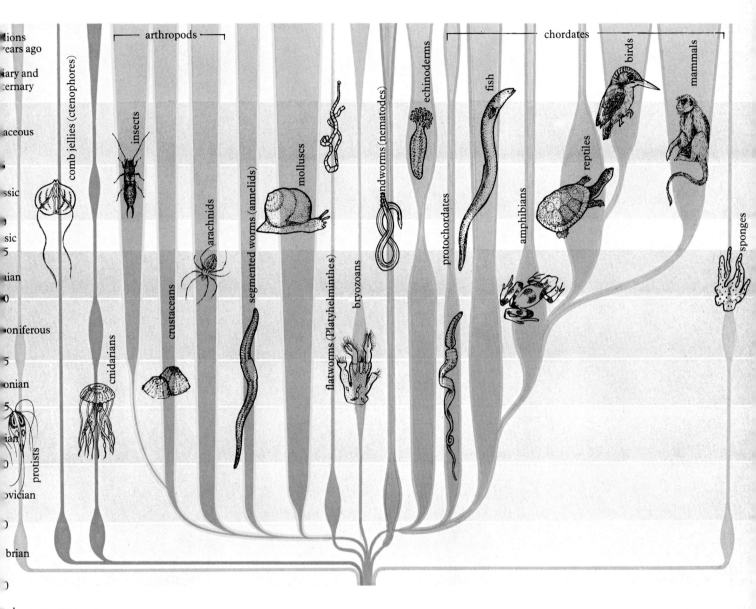

Animal kingdom

genetic pool through time, with more complex forms of life appearing at intervals. This episodic change in the heirarchy of life is directly linked to ecology, with continental drift causing major changes in the configuration of land masses, niche variety and climatic conditions. In times of continental fragmentation the seas tended to rise to new levels and shallow water environments spread over the continental platforms. This invasion correlates with species diversity when new forms evolve to occupy new niches. The opposite model exists for periods of continental accretion, for then the depths of the oceans are increased and the seas withdraw from the continental platforms. This increases the unstability of shallow water environments and reduces both niche and species numbers. During these episodes in the Earth's history it is the least specialized organisms that survive. These in Darwinian terms are the 'fittest', for their tolerance of difficult conditions enables them to exist whilst most organisms that need stable environments, with regard to temperature and food availability, die out. When the seas return a new diversification begins, with the survivors acting as the root stock for a new burst of evolution.

Hard parts and preservation

Apart from the casts of a limited number of sponge spicules in the Ediacara fauna, little or no evidence exists for the presence of skeletal hard parts in Precambrian rocks. The appearance of animals and plants with mineralized hard parts is one of the great phenomena of geological history and their sudden abundance coincides with the dawn of the Phanerozoic. Understandably the appearance of numerous groups with skeletons, often of a very advanced nature, has bewildered palaeontologists for many decades and no universally accepted, or definitive, explanation has, as yet, been presented. The theories proposed include the idea of the skeletons developing as protection against radiation and also one which entails more calcium carbonate being available for the construction of shells at the beginning of the Cambrian. Whatever the explanation, the abundance of fossil hard parts in the rocks of the lower Cambrian is an incredible happening and from the

Skeletal materials

Both minerals and complex organic compounds are utilized by organisms in the production of protective or support structures. The main materials used are illustrated below.

Chitin – this is a complex organic substance ($C_{32}H_{54}N_4O_{21}$). It is fibrous and acellular, waterproof and able to withstand corrosion by both weak acids and digestive juices. Chitin is an important component of arthropod, sponge, hydrozoan and bryozoan skeletons.

Calcium carbonate – this is one of the most common minerals used in the building of shells and other supporting structures. Calcium carbonate occurs as two distinct crystalline forms namely calcite and aragonite. The latter is unstable and rarely occurs in rocks older than those of the Cainozoic. It is often replaced by a more stable low magnesium calcite.

Silica – as a primary skeletal substance, silica is essentially restricted to the protists (Radiolaria) and the glass sponges. It is however, a very common alteration mineral. The silification of wood tissues and the opalization of gastropods and fish vertebrae result in extremely beautiful fossils.

Calcium phosphate – the bones of most vertebrates are composed of calcium phosphate and proteins. In fossil bones the protein constituents are mostly lost but the inorganic minerals may remain unaltered for great periods of time. Pyritization is often associated with the preservation of bones from the various periods.

organic skeletal compound (*Orthograptus*)

aragonite (modern mollusc shells)

silica (sponge spicules)

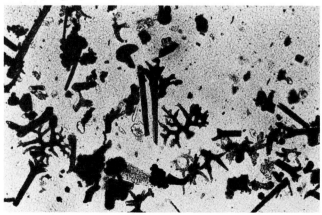

calcium phosphate (Dodo metatarsus bone)

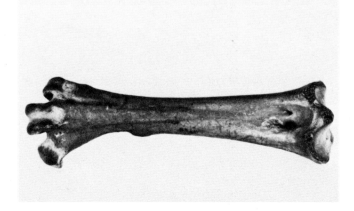

Fossilization sequence

For preservation to take place it is necessary that the animal is buried rapidly under layers of sediment. This protects it from disarticulation by scavengers or water currents and from the slow but sure destruction wrought by bacterial action.

very beginning it is obvious that certain criteria had to exist for the preservation of these hard parts to take place. These criteria include rapid burial, limited transportation and an environment free from scavenging and bacterial action.

The illustrations on these two pages show the variety of materials utilized by organisms, living and fossil, in the construction of protective or support structures. They also provide a visual account of how an animal would become fossilized and portray the types of preservation that may occur as a result of alteration since burial. Not all fossils represent actual bodily remains and the term *trace fossil* is given to the tracks and trails, burrows and borings created by ancient animals during their everyday life. Both body and trace fossils are essential clues in the reconstruction of ancient environments.

Above replacement (*Paraspirifer acuminatus*)

After burial, percolating ground waters carrying minerals in solution may invade the pores of the fossil. This often results in the crystallization of new minerals within the original structure and an increase in the weight and size of the specimen. This process has been termed permineralization or petrifaction. In some cases the original remains of the organism may be removed by solution. The natural mould that results is only one of many kinds of moulds and casts that occur in sedimentary rocks. The processes involved in the production of moulds and casts are dealt with in more detail overleaf.

One of the most common methods of preservation is where the original remains of the organism are replaced by minerals such as silica or iron pyrites. The original structure of these organisms is frequently destroyed, but the overall beauty is often enhanced.

Left
recrystallization (*Nautilus*)

Right
carbonization (leaf)

Fossil plants and graptolites are often found as thin carbonaceous films on the surface of rocks. The fossils are a result of the process of carbonization, in which only the carbon content of the original tissues survives distillation.

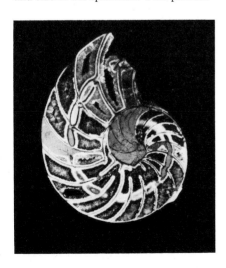

Moulds, casts and mummification

Moulds and casts of ancient species are common throughout the stratigraphic column. Often they are the only source of information on individual organisms or communities, and their presence in the rocks should never be ignored. Moulds are formed in two ways with pressure and solution acting as the governing processes. In the first case the pressing of an organic structure into soft sediments will result in a distinct impression, which can also be interpreted as an external or natural mould. This type of mould is quite common but the majority are the result of burial and solution. In this case the impression of the organism is formed in the enclosing sediment and the subsequent solution of the shell material results in a perfect external mould.

This type of structure only preserves the features of the external surface and as a mould it may be infilled by minerals or sediment. The result is a natural replica or external cast of the original. It is possible for the infilling by minerals or sediments to precede the solution of the shell, the result being that the infill records the internal surface structures of the original organism. The infill is correctly termed a core or steinkern (rock-kernel). Our illustration is an attempt to explain the ways in which these various structures are formed.

Field and laboratory workers often manufacture their own replicas of original specimens by pressing plasticine or pouring rubber solutions into the original moulds. The product frequently provides as much information as would be obtained from the actual shell.

Whereas the formation of moulds and casts may be placed amongst the 'bread and butter' modes of preservation, the results of mummification, can be ranked amongst the most spectacular. Mummification refers to the preservation of complete or almost complete organisms, with bones, skin and even hair surviving the passage of time. The process involves the rapid burial of an animal in a suitable medium such as brine saturated sediments, peat bogs or the muds of a glacial lake. The action of chemicals or intense cold prevents decay and thus unrivalled data on the form of prehistoric dinosaurs, pterosaurs, mammoths and bison is preserved in the fossil record.

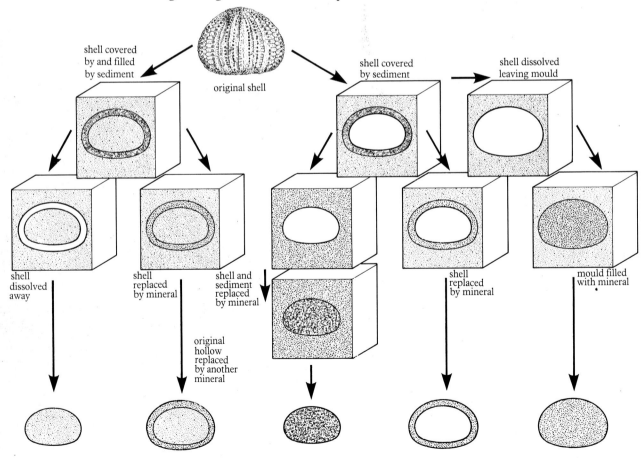

Diagram to show the various methods by which fossils may be formed (after Cox, 1975)

Below
A baby mammoth, believed to have been frozen in the ground for at least 9000 or 10 000 years, was recently dug up in a mummified condition in the north-east Soviet Union.

Bottom
A mummified duck-billed dinosaur, *Anatosaurus* from the Upper Cretaceous of North America.

Unaltered remains are rare in rocks older than 600 million years, the classic examples include the frozen mammoths of Siberia, but gastropods or bivalves composed of the primary carbonate mineral aragonite are amongst the more common discoveries.

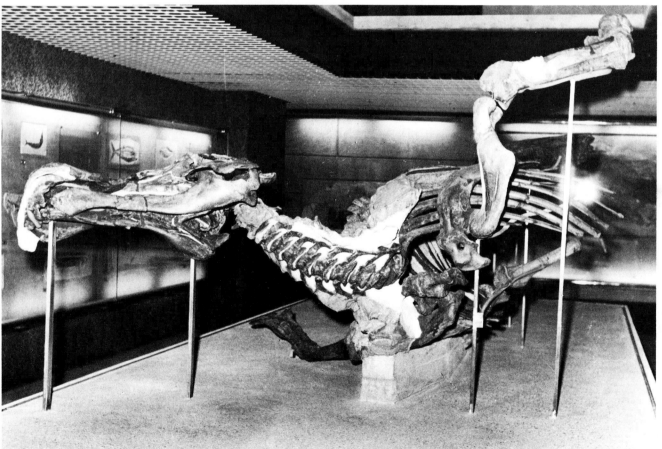

The need for classification

No biologist or palaeontologist could be satisfied with simply naming organisms, living or fossil. For this could create chaos and involve the specialist in the learning of thousands and even millions of names. Therefore for practical reasons he divides the named organisms into groups and so limits the amount of data he has to store mentally for the maximum retrieval of information. The ordering of organisms into groups is termed classification, and it is based on the obvious similarities and relationships that exist between animals or plants.

Aristotle (384–322 BC) was the founding father of biological classification. For long before the birth of Christ he had recognized major groups such as the birds and insects and had referred animals to two- or four-footed categories. Carolus Linnaeus (1707–1778) was a firm believer in the application of Aristotelian logic to classification. He also formulated a number of general principles of classification in his own right and was the first scientist to designate two descriptive latinized names to various organisms.

The two names are given to the genus and species to which an individual belongs, for example, with *Tyrannosaurus rex* aptly describing the 'King of the terrible lizards'. A species constitutes a group of organisms which have breeding potential, whilst a genus is made up of a number of related species. After this the groupings become larger by definition; a number of genera making up a family, families grouping into orders, orders into classes and classes into phyla. The trilobites are used as an illustration of the hierarchical system proposed by Linnaeus.

The theories and practice of classifying organisms is termed taxonomy and in recent years taxonomists have employed several approaches in an attempt to find the most useful method of classification. In a way these symbolize a revolt against the classic evolutionary system in which fossil evidence was deemed important.

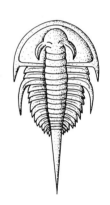

O. lapworthi

species

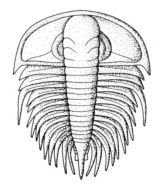

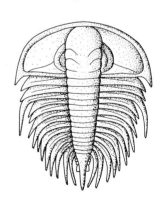

Classification of *Olenellus thompsoni*

Olenellus thompsoni

O. thompsoni

One such approach is termed *cladistic taxonomy* in which structural similarity is all important and the presence of early or primitive characters is used to place the organism in its correct evolutionary cluster. This theory has been the cause of great controversy and like *numerical taxonomy* has tended to gather a number of zealous disciples. The latter is really classification by computer, with numerical counts and the measurements of observable characteristics used to the exclusion of ecological and biogeographical factors.

order Redlichiida　　　　**class Trilobita**　　　　**sub-phylum Trilobitoidea**　　　　**phylum Arthropoda**

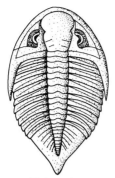

Dalmanites

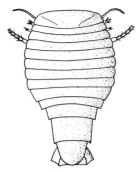

Sidneyia

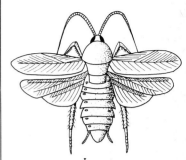

Insecta

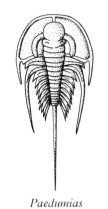

Paedumias

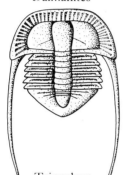

Trinucleus

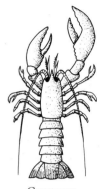

Crustacea

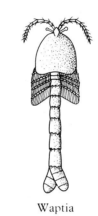

Waptia

Holmia

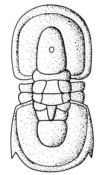

Agnostus

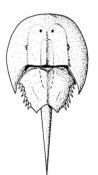

Merostomata

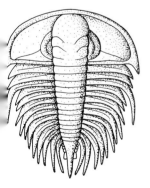

Olenellus

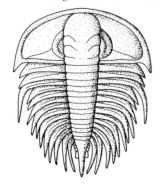

Redlichiida

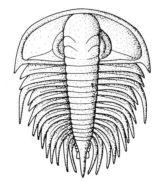

Trilobita

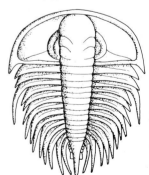

Trilobitoidea

The Cambrian

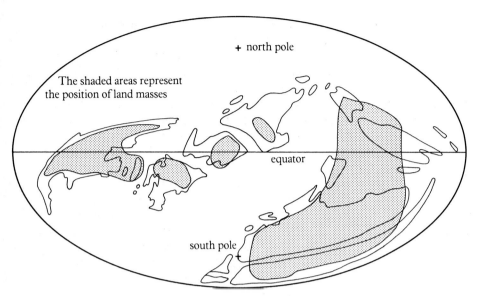

The shaded areas represent the position of land masses

+ north pole

equator

south pole +

A reconstruction of the continents during the Cambrian shows that those of the northern hemisphere were more fragmented than those in the southern. It is also noticeable that the equator passed through Antarctica and to the north of Greenland and northern Europe.

The Palaeozoic era

This, the first era of statigraphic time, lasted approximately 345 million years. It comprises the Cambrian, Ordovician, Silurian, Devonian, Carboniferous and Permian periods and is noted for the appearance of several groups of advanced organisms at its lower boundary. During the various periods numerous new groups of animals and plants arose, with land plants, fish, amphibians and reptiles warranting a special mention.

The appearance of advanced organisms is but one of several significant events that took place during the era; others include the great Caledonian and Variscan earth building movements and the Permo-Carboniferous glaciation of the southern continents.

The Cambrian period is the lowest time unit of the Palaeozoic era. It represents 70 million years of geological time and in many parts of the world its basal sediments rest unconformably on rocks of the Precambrian. The dawn of the Cambrian period is marked by a shallowing of the oceans and the spread of shallow seas over continental platforms. The seas provided ideal conditions for the diversification of life.

The chart illustrates the appearance of numerous complex organisms during the Cambrian period. Climatic change, irradiation and increased predation are amongst the theories put forward to explain the sudden appearance of organisms with hard-parts at the beginning of the Cambrian.

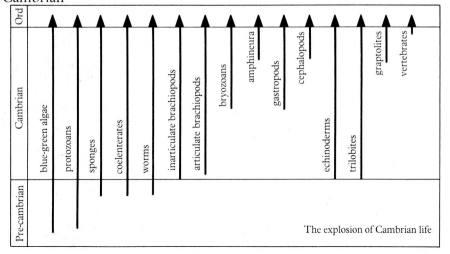

The explosion of Cambrian life

Cambrian Life

In contrast to the unfossiliferous rocks of the Precambrian, those of the early Cambrian provide fossil evidence of the appearance of the trilobites, inarticulate brachiopods, echinoderms, molluscs and archaeocyathids. Trilobites account for over half the recorded Cambrian fossils and certain genera are used to divide the period into lower, middle and upper units.

The appearance of the five groups noted above supplements the worms, soft corals, sponges, jellyfish and algae already known from Precambrian rocks. In the early Cambrian the needle-like spicules of sponges are well known although their presence is somewhat overshadowed by the occurrence of the conical archaeocyathids. The latter have a rigid skeleton and a double-wall structure but the presence of spicules and pores suggest an evolutionary link with the sponges. Archaeocyathids are cosmopolitan in their distribution and in some areas existed in reef gardens. It has been suggested that a mutual or symbiotic relationship, similar to that between certain reef dwelling fishes and deadly stinging corals, existed between the archaeocyathids and some trilobites.

Many of the first inarticulate brachiopods were rather small and somewhat insignificant, with individual genera, such as *Kurtogina*, and measuring only a few millimetres in length. In many parts of the world the larger inarticulate brachiopod *Lingulella*, a relative of the living lamp-shell, *Lingula*, is found in association with the trilobite trace fossil *Cruziana*, and together they are thought to be diagnostic of a shallow water environment. It is likely that the early echinoderms also inhabited these conditions, for *Helicoplacus*, from the Lower Cambrian of North America, has a flexible, spirally pleated test, which would be well adapted to withstand a limited degree of water turbulence. Trilobites existed in both shallow and deeper water environments and we shall analyse the reasons for their success.

As time progressed, new families appeared and the diversification of existing stocks increased. New phyla, classes and orders also evolved during the Middle and Upper Cambrian with representatives of the cephalopods, bivalve molluscs, articulate brachiopods, crinoids, ostracodes, graptolites and others appearing before the end of the period. During the Cambrian the initiation of new forms of life and the development of new ecological niches seems to have moved hand in hand, with bottom dwellers, free swimmers and floaters appearing within specific stocks. It would also appear that animals such as the trilobites occurred in faunal associations with each grouping providing evidence for the existence of a distinct faunal province.

The appearance of the graptolites in the upper most levels of the Cambrian provides evidence for the evolution of the chordate line and it is possible that the first fish also originated in this, the first period of stratigraphic time.

Aysheaia pedunculata is a fossil from the Middle Cambrian Burgess shale deposit of British Columbia. It bears a remarkable resemblance to the living onychophoran *Peripatus*.

Peripatus is a rather caterpillar-like creature which inhabits moist places in tropical forests. By contrast *Aysheaia* lived in a marine environment.

Trilobites and their allies

The appearance of the trilobites and several associated arthropod stocks in the Lower Cambrian is one of the mysteries of palaeontology. As arthropods they have elongate, segmented bodies which are encased in a chitinous exoskeleton. They also have jointed limbs and many have compound eyes, made up of numerous, closely-packed lenses. The origin of such complex organisms, surely occurred in the Precambrian but little or no direct evidence exists to support this hypothesis. Naturally, the very complexity of the individual organisms, would suggest a long period of evolution, with the Precambrian evidence indicating an ancestral tie with the segmented worms.

Both the trilobites and, the so called 'same-footed' arthropods, the homopods, were marine animals. The homopods are well known from the Middle Cambrian Burgess shale and individual genera such as *Sidneyia* and *Burgessia* look more like king crabs than trilobites. This variation in form is an indication of the diversification that had already taken place in arthropod stocks, and shows that their advanced structure enabled them to dominate many Lower Palaeozoic communities. The early arthropods had solved the problems of locomotion; the development of a durable outer skeleton changing the mechanics of movement from that of a series of rhythmic body contractions to a lever-like movement of the jointed limbs. This together with the development of gills and a specialized feeding mechanism ensured their superiority over contemporary invertebrates.

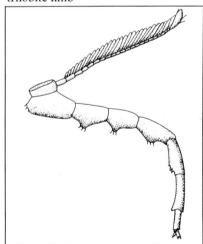

Trilobite dorsal view

free cheek fixed cheek · glabella
cephalon (head)
furrow
eye
facial suture
genal angle
thoracic segment
thorax
axis (axial lobe)
pleuron (segment)
length
width
pygidium

trilobite limb

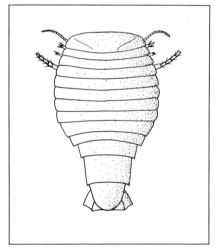

The limbs of the trilobites heralded a major advance in locomotion, they were jointed and were controlled by powerful muscles. Each limb was divided into two units with the telepodite functioning as a walking leg and the exite or exopodite serving as a gill and possible swimming organ. In the anterior region of the body the limbs may be modified, with the first pair functioning as antennae.

Sidneyia, a homopod or trilobitomorph arthropod from the Middle Cambrian.

Vision in trilobites is an intriguing research subject and the presence or absence of eyes has been interpreted as an indication of specific modes of life. This in itself is simplistic, as work on the structure and distribution of lenses and the plotting of visual fields is much more demanding in the scientific sense. Trilobite eyes may be

holochroal eye

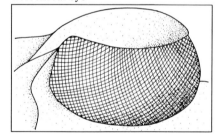

schizochroal eye

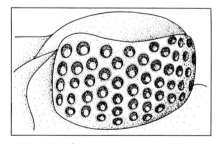

either holochroal (closely packed hexagonal lenses) or schizochroal (lenses rounded in aggregate) in character. The thickness and distribution of the lenses is associated with the collection of light and it is possible that trilobites with thick-lensed eyes were either nocturnal or the inhabitants of muddy waters.

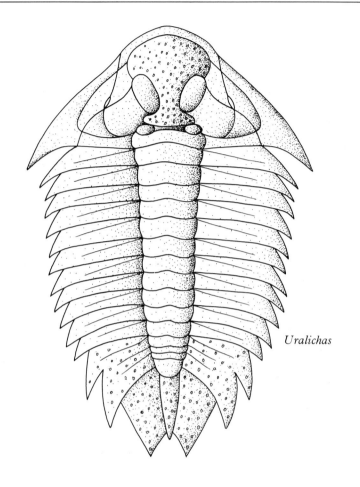

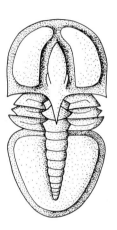

Uralichas and Eodiscus represent the opposite ends of the size spectrum in trilobites. Individual specimens referred to Uralichas measure up to 70 centimetres in length, whilst eodiscids rarely exceed 2 centimetres.

Uralichas

Eodiscus

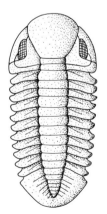

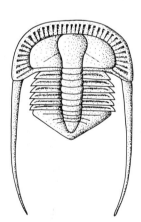

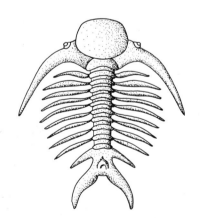

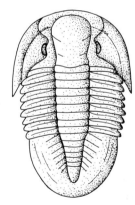

Phacops

Trinucleus

Deiphon

Ogygiocaris

The eyes of *Phacops rana* are extremely well developed, but *Trinucleus* is a blind trilobite.

The structure of different trilobites is an indication of their former life styles. In the case of *Deiphon* the stalked eyes and spinose segments suggest a free floating existence whereas the rounded, streamhead *Ogygiacaris* was a surface crawler.

Cambrian life

Any reconstruction of Cambrian life would be dominated by the presence of trilobites. In our panorama the importance of the early arthropods is fully recognized and an attempt is made to show that genera such as *Olenellus*, *Paradoxides* and *Olenus* were restricted to specific sub-periods. Their association with other organisms is also important and in several areas of the world, palaeontologists can recognize the presence of recurrent associations or communities. In the Lower Cambrian, *Olenellus* and its relatives were common as far as northwest Scotland, Greenland, parts of western Canada and the United States, whilst the form *Callavia* occurred in the Welsh Borderlands, Scandinavia, eastern Newfoundland and New England. This distribution is indicative of distinct communities, with *Olenellus* existing as a surface crawler.

Paradoxides is a Middle Cambrian trilobite, and its elongate genal spines and spiny tail are diagnostic characters. Some species grew to 30 centimetres in length and hundreds of individuals are known to have occurred in restricted geographic areas. *Paradoxides* is often found in association with the inarticulate brachiopod *Lingulella* and the gastropod-like *Hyolithes*. This group of animals lived in marine shallow water environments. In the Upper Cambrian *Olenus* is the important trilobite from the stratigraphic viewpoint. It is found in fine-grained sediments, along with the first of the graptolites and the surface-dwelling bellerophontid gastropods. Diminutive agnostid trilobites which swam just above the sea floor also occur in this association and the whole is representative of an offshore deeper water community.

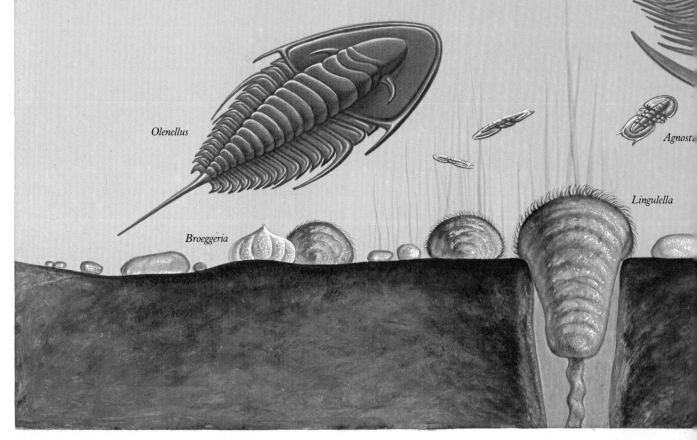

Olenellus

Agnost

Lingulella

Broeggeria

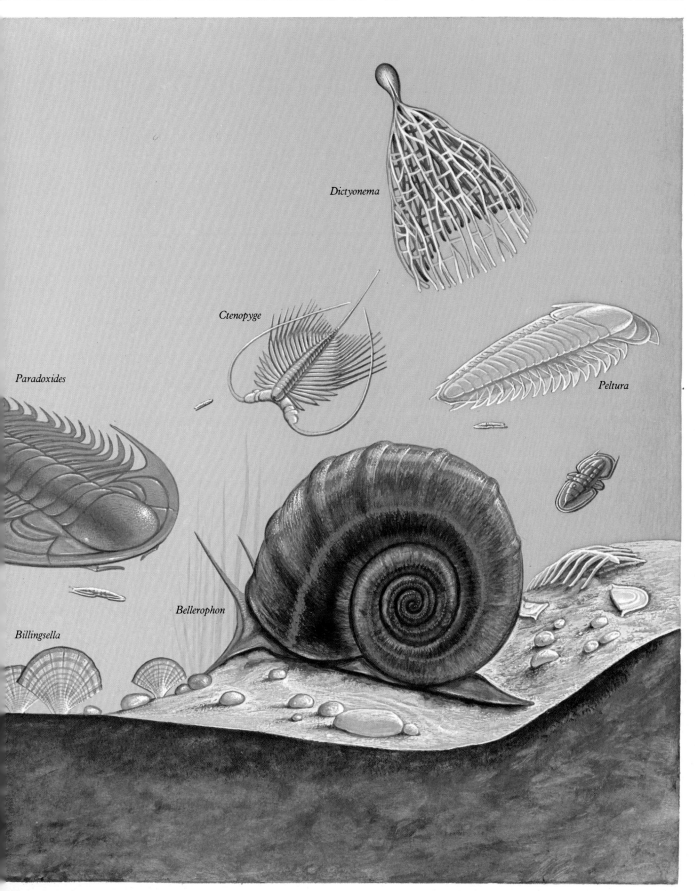

Dictyonema

Ctenopyge

Paradoxides

Peltura

Bellerophon

Billingsella

Symbiosis

Biologists use the word symbiosis to describe the intimate and often necessary association of two organisms. Often the relationship is beneficial but certain parasitic associations can also be termed symbiotic. The development of the two organisms concerned may involve co-evolution, where the origin of one is dependent on the evolution of the other. At the present time numerous examples of symbiosis can be recognized. Some associations involve two organisms of either the plant or the animal kingdom but others associate animal with plant. One of the classic cases of symbiosis, or mutualism, is the association of the modern stony-corals with the microscopic algae, zooxanthellae. In this the algae utilize the waste products of the coral during photosynthesis. The coral therefore benefits by their removal, particularly that of carbon dioxide, and also uses the algae as a source of some of its food.

In the fossil record examples of symbiosis are difficult to recognize as most associations relate to the organism and not the skeleton. The possible association of the tabulate coral *Aulopora* and the brachiopod *Spirifer* is, however, preserved in the fixed arrangement of the hard parts; the coral skeleton encrusting the upper surface of the brachiopod shell. This arrangement suggests that the coral benefited from the food and waste expelled by the brachiopod and that the brachio-pod itself was protected by the stinging cells of its ally. Many associations involve feeding and protection from predation and it would appear

that such a relationship existed between certain trilobites and the archaeocyathids. The latter possessed a cone-shaped, porous skeleton, the structure of which shows affinities with both the sponges and the stony corals. Soft parts of the archaeocyathids are unknown but reconstructions usually infer a coral-like appearance. Representatives of the phylum are known throughout the world in the Lower and Middle Cambrian and their abundant remains suggest that they existed as 'reef gardens'. It was here that trilobites sought protection from predators and where they in turn 'cleansed' the archaeocyathids of waste materials. The evidence for this association is based on the recurring presence of the archaeocyathids and trilobites, and one should be aware that any description of archaeocyathids with defensive stinging cells would be pure conjecture.

It should be mentioned here that some associations in the fossil record infer a relationship where one species benefited and the other was unaffected. Such a relationship is termed commensalism and it often refers to small creatures seeking protection on or within a larger organism. Within the fossil record evidence exists to show that small brachiopods attached themselves high up on stems of sea-lilies (crinoids), protecting themselves from bottom dwelling predators and placing themselves in food carrying currents.

Archaeocyathids and trilobites. In the Lower and Middle Cambrian archaeocyathid 'reef gardens' had developed in many parts of the world. Their frequent association with certain trilobites is interpreted as being of mutual benefit or symbiotic.

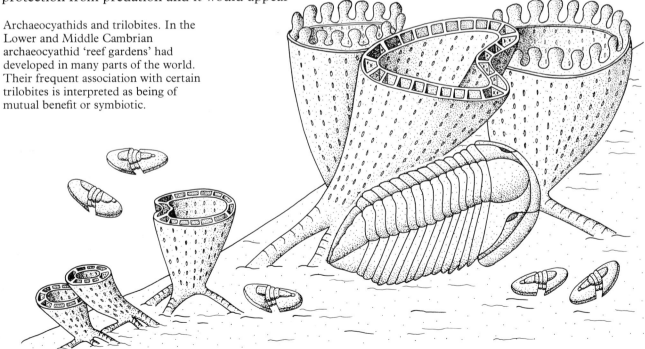

Double-walled archaeocyathids from
the Cambrian, Australia.

double-walled archaeocyathid

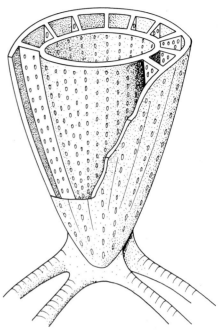

The cone-shaped porous skeleton of an
archaeocyathid is different to that of
any other known organism. It is made
up of coarse calcareous needles and the
majority of forms are double walled.
The walls are connected by both
horizontal and vertical partitions which
resemble similar structures in the stony
corals. It is believed that the actual
animals existed between walls and that
they had little tolerance of muddy
waters. A conspicuous rooting
structure is present in many species.

Single-walled archaeocyathids such as
Monocyathus are found in Lower and
Middle Cambrian deposits.

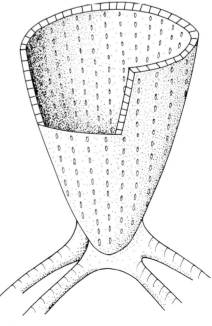

single-walled archaeocyathid

The Ordovician

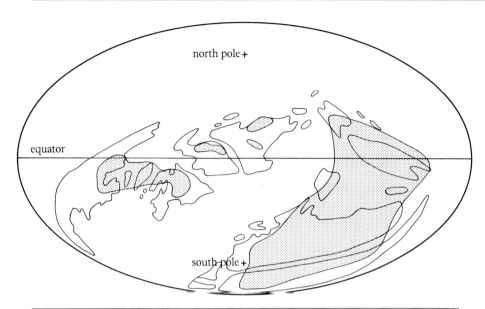

The palaeogeographic reconstruction of the continents during the Ordovician, indicates the coming together of the northern land masses. The south pole had migrated south-eastwards from its Cambrian position and is now positioned in the southern region of Algeria. Great ice sheets surrounded the pole and during the Ordovician the general movement of ice was to the west-north-west. America, Greenland and Europe lay to the south of the equator during these times and the eastern coastline of the North American continent was characterized by the presence of an elongate, depositional trough. It has been estimated that the accumulation of sediments within this trough was at the rate of 13 metres per million years; this accumulation of thousands of metres of sediment has provided tremendous data on the environments of deposition and the diverse nature of Ordovician life. In Europe thick sequences of sediments were also deposited and the correlation of strata between regions is made possible by fossils such as graptolites and brachiopods.

The complex growth of the graptolite colony is determined during the initial stages of growth. The diagram shows a leptograptid budding pattern.

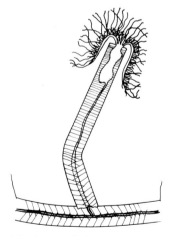

Rhabdopleura, a living 'tongue-worm' or hemichordate. The structure of its skeleton is similar to that of the graptolites.

Stratigraphy

Stratigraphy is the study of layered sedimentary or volcanic rocks, with special reference to their sequence in time, composition and fossil content. Steno and William Smith were early stratigraphers and their work on correlation was the cornerstone of modern studies. The history of stratigraphic study is closely linked with the development of geology in the British Isles and many of the names given to various rock and time units are derived from those of ancient British tribes, or localities where the individual rock unit or formation was first studied. The study of a local section is in itself relatively easy, but to follow it across country or to correlate it with a time equivalent on another continent is much more difficult. To do this the geologist, in a well-exposed and limited area, would simply walk the outcrop in poorly exposed areas and between discontinuous outcrops, he would have to employ more sophisticated methods.

The first of these would be to analyse the characteristics of the sediment and rely on their presence to correlate from outcrop to outcrop. This by itself is limited as different rocks, deposited in different environments may represent the same stratigraphic time unit. Stratigraphic time is mostly based on fossil evidence, with the same fossils or groups of fossils often having an intercontinental distribution and a short time range. These are called zone or guide fossils. In recent times radiometric dating and palaeo-magnetic measurements have improved the accuracy of the more classic methods.

Graptolites

To most people the first look at a graptolite fossil is an uninspiring event, which is unlikely to stir the imagination or turn them into dedicated palaeontologists. Graptolites, however, are complex and intriguing organisms that have now been placed with the simplest of chordate stocks. This links the group with the evolution of the vertebrates and ultimately with the origin of *Homo sapiens*.

The majority of graptolites are poorly preserved, but even poor specimens reveal that the animals were colonial. Their skeletons consist of one or more saw-like branches or stipes, with the teeth of the saw representing the cups or thecae in which tiny, individual animals lived. The whole colony is termed the *rhabdosome* and its shape, and the presence or absence of a floatational device, is indicative of the mode of life of the colony. Some shrub-like graptolites were bottom-dwellers whilst others with a reduced number of branches were adapted to free swimming and planktonic modes of life.

Palaeontologists recognize a two-fold division within the graptolites. The many-branched forms with three types of thecae are called dendroids whilst those with a low number of branches and large autothecal cups are called graptoloids. For many years the graptolites were linked with the corals or bryozoans, but detailed work on their structure has revealed that they are linked with the living 'tongue-worms' or Hemichordata.

The photographs on this page show some of the main forms of graptolites found during this period.

Bryograptus, a dendroid graptolite.

Tetragraptus, a graptoloid with four branches.

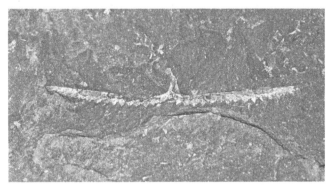

Didymograptus, a two-stiped graptoloid

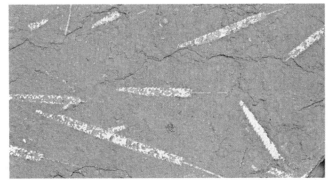

Orthograptus, a diplograptid showing thecae arranged on both sides of a single stipe.

Rastrites, a coiled single-stiped graptolite

Graptolite modes of life

Having noted the appearance of the graptolites in the Late Cambrian and Lower Ordovician and their probable link with chordate animals, it is worthwhile investigating the form and life styles of these strange creatures. To do this we can study samples prepared from muddy limestones by acid techniques, and the beautiful three-dimensional fossils formed when pyrite replaces the original organic skeleton. Both samples are of value to the palaeontologist although the first are more informative as they present us with the original skeletal materials.

The skeleton of a graptolite consists of two distinct layers. The fusellar or inner layer having an interlocking half ring structure similar to that of some living hemichordates. Outside this is a cortical layer which has a loose weave-like texture. In life these layers were common to both the thecal and main branch components of the skeleton and it is interesting that only the graptolites, of the hemichordates, possess cortical tissue. Spaces within the cortical layer suggest the presence of oil or fresh water droplets and indicate that the layer contributed to a floating or free-swimming mode of life. The droplets and the floatational devices, discovered with many fossil graptolites, contributed much to the overall bouyancy of the colony.

Further analysis of specimens reveals that the shrub-like dendroid graptolites had three types of cup, of which two were exposed to the external environment. These cups were of different sizes and it is believed that the animals within them performed different functions. The larger cups or autothecae contained animals which are thought to have carried out the feeding and reproductive functions of the colony, whilst the small bithecal organisms kept the colony free of falling sediment. In free-living dendroids it is possible that the animals moved rhythmically to maintain the stability of the colony.

The colonies of numerous diplograptids have been found attached to a large float structure. This 'multiple' colony is termed a synrhabdosome and it is thought that it floated within the surface waters of Lower Palaeozoic seas.

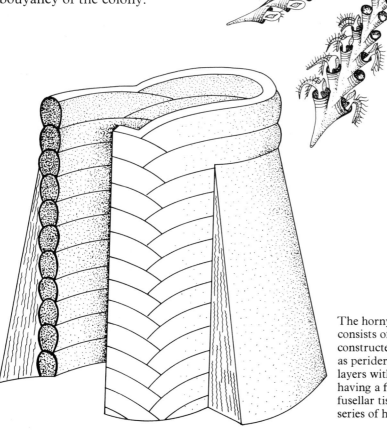

The horny skeleton of the graptolites consists of a series of hollow tubes constructed of a horny material known as periderm. This is divided into two layers with the outer or cortical tissue having a fibrous texture and the inner fusellar tissue being made up of a series of half-rings.

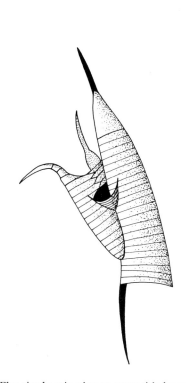

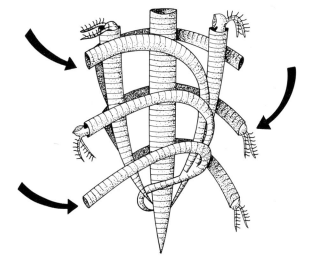

Bryograptus was a shrub-like, dendroid graptolite. The initial cup is called the sicula and its flattened base suggests a fixed mode of life. This may have involved attachment to pebbles on the sea bottom or to floating organic materials.

Dictyonema is one of the best known of the dendroid graptolites and its beautiful net-like skeleton is known from the Upper Cambrian to the Carboniferous. It had a distinct bell-shaped colony with the many branches held firmly together by numerous horizontal structures called dissepiments. *Dictyonema* possessed a small float structure and it is thought to have been planktonic in habit.

The single-stiped monograptids have been described as free swimming. Each colony had few individuals, but these were large enough and strong enough to create sufficient movement for the animal to stay within the surface waters where microscopic food was abundant.

In recent years it has been suggested that graptolites were active swimmers. They apparently swam with the initial cup or sicula pointing downwards and with the individual thecae inclined in such a way as to create strong feeding currents over the whole colony. The theory of graptolite automobility is the brainchild of Dr Nancy Kirk of the University of Aberwrystwth in Wales.

The organization of the 'true' graptolites is different, however, and apart from having fewer branches, only autothecal units have been identified. Many scientists believe that the graptoloids were purely planktonic in life-style but others believe that the size and organization of the colonies is indicative of the free-swimming mode of life. It should be noted that in the diplograptid stock, numerous single-branched colonies share the same large float structure. It is possible that the extinction of the graptoloids in the Upper Palaeozoic was linked with the radiation of surface-feeding fishes. Most graptolites lived in open sea environments and their remains are usually associated with the finer deeper water sediments of the Lower Palaeozoic.

New forms of life become established

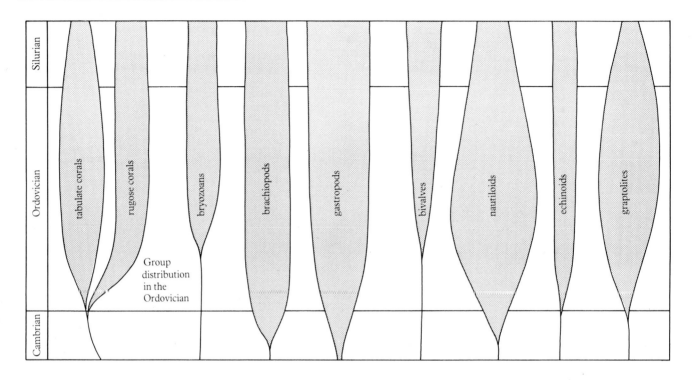

Group distribution in the Ordovician

Although overshadowed by the great extinctions of the Late Permian and Upper Cretaceous, those that took place at the end of the Middle Cambrian and the Upper Cambrian were to have a very significant effect on the world's biota. The late Middle Cambrian extinction affected the archaeocyathids, and their disappearance left the task of reef building to the blue-green algae. At the end of the Upper Cambrian a mass extinction affected the trilobites, with approximately two-thirds of the known families disappearing by the end of the sub-period. The demise of these families, like that of the archaeocyathids, left numerous niches unoccupied. These and many new ones were eventually occupied during the Ordovician when the appearances of new groups of organisms, at various levels, reached an extraordinary peak. The number of new phyla that appeared was restricted to the bryozoans and the true chordates but at family level the new additions totalled over 170.

The diversification of groups such as the corals, bryozoans, brachiopods, cephalopods and graptolites at specific level is even more spectacular. Almost 600 species of bryozoans are recorded for the first time from the Ordovician and even this large number fares rather badly when compared with the 1200 or so new species of nautiloids. These figures, and those noted for other groups, indicate waves of diversification which were without doubt linked to ecological factors. We have already mentioned that many niches had

been left unoccupied and naturally as these offered living space without the necessity of exhaustive competition, they were soon filled. Other organisms that had developed, however, were capable of occupying new niches where the food resources had been hitherto untapped. And in the Ordovician one of the most significant events was the appearance of many new suspension feeders. This had the effect of increasing the variety within bottom-dwelling communities and new intimate associations were to develop. Included amongst these was that between the algae and the stony corals, which was to result in the development of complex reef communities.

The increasing complexity of bottom-dwelling communities was in itself to add to potential food supplies and no doubt encouraged the diversification of larger scavengers and carnivores such as the cephalopods. The increase in the diversity of bottom-dwelling communities was not confined to shallow waters. Throughout the Ordovician the improved feeding mechanisms developed by suspension feeders, such as the brachiopods and bivalves, enabled them to inhabit the deeper regions of the shelf seas. In the surface waters of those seas the graptolites were abundant throughout the Ordovician. They were free-floaters and their abundance was probably linked with a general increase in microscopic plankton, although little or no direct evidence for this exists.

Of the various new families of trilobites that appeared during the Ordovician one of the most important was the Trinucleidae. A typical representative of which was the form *Cryptolithus* known from Europe and North America.

Amongst the many bryozoans that appeared during the Ordovician was *Fenestella*, a so-called 'lace bryozoan'.

Ordovician communities

Although far more advanced than their Pre-cambrian equivalent, the communities of the Cambrian are considered simple when compared with those of the Ordovician and other periods within the Palaeozoic. Many of the animals that lived during the Cambrian were of a generalized type, adapted to withstand any variations that may have occurred within an unstable environment. By the Ordovician, animals such as the archaeo-cyathids, several groups of inarticulate brachiopods, many trilobite families and various echinoderms had become extinct. These extin-ctions indicate that the generalized animals were incapable of diversifying into other niches and when challenged by more specialized forms, including new predators, were unable to respond.

The new forms of life included additional trilobite families, the graptolites, nautiloids and articulate brachiopods. Some of these were mud-grubbers or filter-feeders but others, including many nautiloids, were specialized as predators. By mid-Ordovician time the first of the stony corals had appeared and their association with algae and

Onnia superba – trilobite

Trilobites

In the Ordovician new families of trilobites evolved to replace the Cambrian olenellids, eodiscids and paradoxidids. Overall the trilobites were still numerous but their importance as zone fossils diminishes. Several distinct trilobite provinces can be recognized in the Ordovician, with the majority of species living in shallow seas that bordered the great southern continent of Gondwanaland and the proto-continents of North America and Northern Europe.

Reuschella semiglobata – brachiopod

Modiolopsis – bivalve

Brachiopods

Articulate brachiopods are character-ized by the presence of a hinge line with teeth and sockets. Six orders are known, and three of these appear for the first time during the Ordovician. Of the inarticulate brachiopods *Lingulella* persists as a burrower, a role it, or its relatives have filled for over 450 million years. The articulates are more varied with the small, ribbed orthids and the flat, broad stropho-menids having representatives in many communities. Many orthids and strophomenids rested on the surface of the sea-floor, but other orthids developed a strong pedicle by which they attached themselves to the substrate or on to other organisms.

Bivalves

The living oysters and clams are representatives of the Bivalvia. The group is distinct in that the two valves of the shell are alike; both shell and soft parts exhibiting bilateral symmetry. In Mesozoic and Cainozoic stocks the development of syphons and other features indicates diversification, but in the Cambrian and Ordovician the bivalves were rather primitive. Some, such as *Nucula* and *Modiolopsis*, were shallow burrowers but ribbed forms like *Ambonychia* were attached to the surface by thin byssate threads.

bryozoans led to the construction of reefs. Established forms such as the gastropods still occupied the role of sea-floor dwelling scavengers, whilst their bivalve cousins adapted to both deposit and suspension feeding. In shallow waters stalked crinozoan echinoderms were common. As with the Cambrian Period it is possible to recognize a number of associations between various Ordovician species. Some of these communities have worldwide distribution and the information they provide as to the depth of the seas and the environment is invaluable.

The discovery of the first fragments of fish in the Lower Ordovician adds a new dimension to the communities of this period. The majority of these fragments occur in near-shore deposits and there is a question as to whether the earliest fish were marine or fresh water in origin. It is likely, for reasons of body chemistry, that the first agnathans or jawless fish lived in the sea and invaded the lakes and rivers in later times. Within the shallow water environments the agnathans were essentially bottom dwellers ingesting muds and organic matter through their sucker-like mouths. Heavy armour was an essential prerequisite for protection against more agile predators.

During the Ordovician groups such as the nautiloids and graptolites showed a number of evolutionary trends. The nautiloids varied considerably in shape and size, and some endoceratid nautiloids are known to have exceeded 4 metres in length. In the graptolites the main evolutionary trend was a reduction in the number of branches and by the end of the Ordovician, deep-water communities were characterized by the presence of the single-stiped diplograptids.

Echinoderms

The origins of the Echinodermata or 'spiny-skinned' animals are lost in the Precambrian. A typical echinoderm has well-developed nervous, digestive and respiratory systems and a thick calcareous skeleton that is formed in the middle of the three layers of the body wall. The group is frequently divided on the basis of life style but recent studies suggest a four-fold division into the Crinozoa (crinoids or sea-lilies and related groups), the Asterozoa (starfish), the Echinozoa (echinoids) and the Holmalozoa (sea-cucumbers). In the Ordovician the crinozoans were important members of shallow-water communities and in some parts of the world the skeletons of the cystoid *Echinosphaerites* accumulated to form limestones. The first echinoids appeared in the Ordovician with the majority of forms having a flexible test. In numerical terms the echinoids were poorly represented in Ordovician communites.

Cephalopods

Modern representatives of the Cephalopoda include the *Nautilus*, the squid and the octopus. The *Nautilus* has a coiled shell but the last two are naked. A well-formed head surrounded by muscular tentacles is a characteristic feature of the class and one assumes that the same organs occurred in fossil representatives. In the Ordovician the nautiloids were the sole representatives of the Cephalopoda and several hundred species swam in the seas of the world at that time.

Gomphoceras – nautiloid

Anatolepsis – an early Ordovician fish; details of scale covering (x 300) from Spitzbergen. (Palaeontological Museum, Oslo)

Mesopalaeaster – starfish

The Silurian

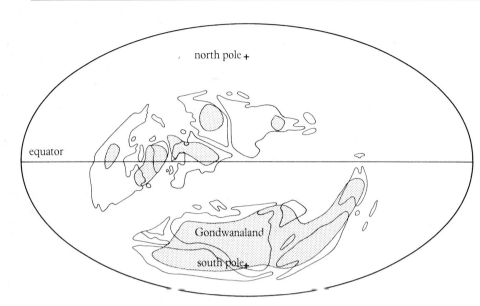

north pole +

equator

Gondwanaland

south pole +

By the beginning of the Silurian Period, 430 million years ago the northern continents had according to some experts almost amalgamated to form a single land mass. Much of this lay to the north of the equator, whilst the great southern continent of Gondwanaland lay to the south of the 30°S latitude. The south pole had migrated to a location approximating to the present-day position of Namibia in South West Africa and glacial deposits have been recorded from South Africa and Boliva during the Silurian Period. Depositional troughs surrounded the northern and southern land masses and marine life flourished in both shallow and deeper water environments. On land the first plants and animals set out on the long road to successful colonization.

Reef builders

One of the significant advances in marine life that occurred with the advent of the Silurian was the development and diversification of the stony corals.

By the Silurian both tabulate and rugose stocks were well established and both were major contributors to the construction of the coral reefs. Well known tabulates such as *Favosites* and *Halysites* typified the colonial character of the group. Unlike the rugose corals, the tabulates were small with well-formed, horizontal partitions (tabulae) being the major internal feature of the skeleton. The rugose corals also possessed tabulae, but radial partitions (septa) and the development of large solitary and colonial species distinguishes them from their tabulate cousins. Horn-shaped solitary corals were typical representatives of the Rugosa in reef and other shallow-water communities during the Silurian.

Apart from the stony corals, massive bryozoans such as *Hallopora* and lace bryozoans like *Fenestella* were also important reef builders and binders.

Silurian brachiopods

The bryozoans are also colonial organisms but their individual cups are very small and the actual animals have affinities with the Brachiopoda. Calcareous algae and the stromatoporoid coelenterates played important roles in Silurian reef assemblages with numerous brachiopods and molluscans occupying subsiduary niches. Trilobites, nautiloids and primitive fish filled the roles of scavengers and predators.

Syringopora reticulata
a tabulate coral

Fistulipora
a massive bryozoan

The sea floor or benthic communities of the Silurian were dominated by the articulate brachiopods. Strophomenids and orthids were still numerous but more specialized forms are indicative of a new faunal richness. In northern Europe palaeontologists have identified a number of communities that are characteristic of certain environmental conditions; most communities being named after a component brachiopod. The environments range from inshore lagoons and coastal waters to the deeper waters beyond the continental shelf. Articulate brachiopods flourished in waters between 10 and 100 metres in depth; the greatest variety occurring in the lime-rich sediments that depict warm waters and an abundance of food.

Salinity was a controlling factor in the colonization of the lagoonal and coastal waters, and the relative abundance of *Lingula* to that of articulates is a useful indicator. In low salinity environments *Lingula* was dominant, but in normal marine conditions articulates, including the small, coarsely ribbed and biconvex rhynchonellids, flourished. Seawards the role of the articulates increased and large strophamenids and several species of spiriferid and rhynchonellid brachiopod, dominated the sandier substrates. *Eocoelia* is an example of a rhynchonellid from this environment, whilst *Eostropheodonta* represents the strophomenids. In the lime-rich muds of the Silurian shelf the thick, biconvex shells of the petamerids were associated with the spire bearers *Atrypa* and *Whitfieldella* and the unique rhynchonellid, *Spaerirhynchia*. These brachiopods were of subsiduary importance in the reef community but they flourished in both fore and back reef environments. Away from the reef, and on into deeper waters, the density of the brachiopods declined. Smaller individuals including *Clorinda* were characteristic and because of the stability of the deep water realm the specific diversity was often greater. Beyond the continental shelf the graptolites became the dominant group.

Sphaerirhynchia wilsoni – an articulate brachiopod

above left
Cyrtia exporecta –
an articulate
brachiopod

above right
Atrypa reticularis –
an articulate
brachiopod

left
Leptaena depressa –
an articulate
brachiopod

right
Pentamerus –
an articulate
brachiopod

The Silurian sea floor

Fossiliferous blocks, like the one opposite, are amongst the most informative pieces of data available to the palaeoecologist. The surface shown represents a bedding plane, which in itself denotes the position of an ancient sea-floor within the Wenlock Limestone Formation. Different groups of invertebrates are well represented, their beauty and detail being enhanced by the removal of sediment by percolating ground waters. These waters follow joints and bedding planes within the limestone and gradually, through the accumulation of carbonate ions, act as a dilute acid. The accumulated material on the sea floor and the sediment in which it is buried provide clues as to the environmental conditions that once existed.

The fine calcium rich sediment of the specimen indicates a fairly low energy environment, characterized by warm waters and an abundance of food. The density of fauna supports this hypothesis, although one should realise that accumulations of fossils may be the result of current action the strength of which may be determined by both sedimentary structures and the degree of abrasion suffered by the fossil material. In our sample the degree of fragmentation and abrasion is limited and it is likely that the fossils accumulated in close proximity to the area in which they lived.

The abundance of stony corals, bryozoans and crinoids suggest that the fauna is a reef assemblage, whilst the brachiopods, trilobites and branching bryozoans indicate that the specimen represents a reef front. A reconstruction of the reef depends on a detailed analysis of the slab and associated materials, and any palaeoecological synthesis requires study of the individual fossils, the relationships between species and the density and diversity of contributing stocks. Comparisons with living reefs may also have merit, but to some extent the final reconstruction will always be hypothetical. This is particularly true for the reconstruction of soft parts as no direct evidence of their shape and function remains. The reconstruction of fossil communities is a relatively new and exciting innovation and in time additional data will add to our knowledge of past life and contribute to a greater understanding of the marine and terrestrial ecosystems.

D. V. Ager has warned, however, that the palaeoecologist must never forget that he is studying not the living inhabitants of the village, but only the bodies in the churchyard, and then only after many visits by grave robbers!

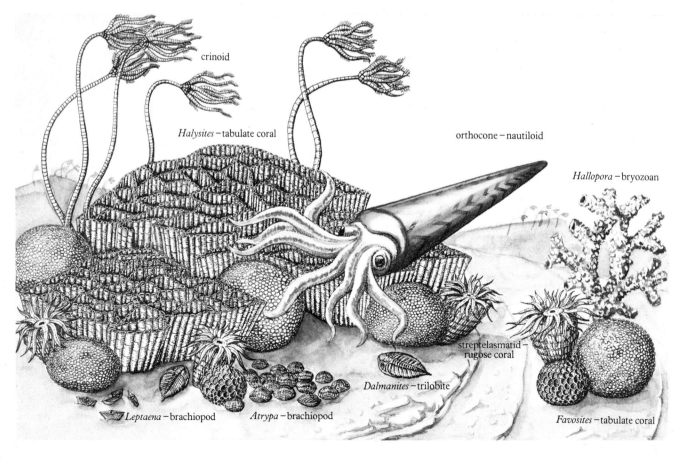

crinoid

Halysites – tabulate coral

orthocone – nautiloid

Hallopora – bryozoan

streptelasmatid – rugose coral

Dalmanites – trilobite

Leptaena – brachiopod   *Atrypa* – brachiopod

Favosites – tabulate coral

The richly fossiliferous bedding planes of the Wenlock Limestone (Silurian), provide the palaeontologist with an ideal opportunity to reconstruct an ancient community. The type of sediment, the variety of organisms as well as their state of preservation are important clues, and from the evidence available this fossil assemblage can be reconstructed as a reef as shown on the opposite page (after McKerrow, 1978).

Nautilus and its ancestors

Our account of Ordovician faunas commented briefly on the origin of the nautiloid cephalopods and the fact that the living *Nautilus* is the sole surviving genus of a once great stock. The shell of the *Nautilus* is beautifully constructed but its simple form and limited distribution in the Pacific Ocean, belittles the history of a group that once filled the seas of the Lower Palaeozoic. Internal deposits of calcite were used by the Palaeozoic nautiloids to maintain their feeding position, and it should be noted that no such deposits are present in extant *Nautilus*.

The variety of deposits found in the early nautiloids serves as an indication of group diversity, which is only fully appreciated when one studies the hundreds of genera within the Nautiloidea. Ancient nautiloid shells exhibit almost every shape between tightly coiled and perfectly straight and the shell is an excellent indicator of mode of life. Reconstructions of the soft parts of ancient nautiloids naturally resembles those of the living representative but differences in the shape of the living chambers and in the position of the syphonal tube, between the inner chambers, suggest that some species were, at least, physically different. Externally the shells of many fossil

The straight or orthocone shell is typical of several orders of the Nautiloidea. Shell ornament and internal structures separate the orders and both features have a functional importance. The shell illustrated is that of an actinoceratid nautiloid, representatives of which occurred throughout the Palaeozoic, from Lower Ordovician to Permian times.

Below
Nautilus, the only living nautiloid

The actinoceratids have wide siphuncles in which large doughnut-like calcareous deposits occur. During life the deposits grew and almost filled the siphuncular region, their weight helping to counter balance the increased size of the animal itself.

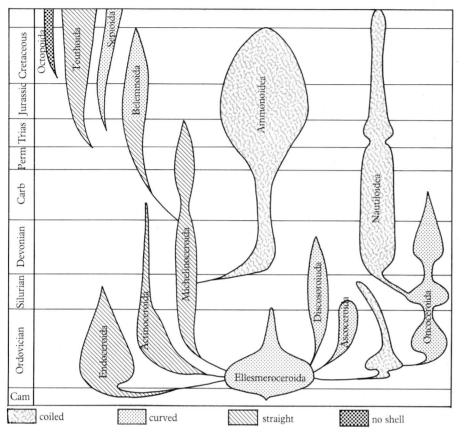

| | | coiled | curved | straight | no shell |

Chart labels (left axis, bottom to top): Cam, Ordovician, Silurian, Devonian, Carb, Perm Trias, Jurassic, Cretaceous

Group labels within chart: Octopoida, Teuthoida, Sepioida, Belemnoida, Ammonoidea, Michelinoceroida, Actinoceroida, Endoceroida, Ellesmeroceroida, Discosoroida, Ascoceroida, Nautiloidea, Orthoceroida

Legend: coiled · curved · straight · no shell

Nautiloids

The first nautiloids were small and lacked internal deposits. Their remains have been discovered in North America and Asia and their appearance in rocks of the Upper Cambrian, heralds the beginning of an incredible success story. The nautiloids have existed for over 500 million years and for a considerable portion of that time they were the rulers of the open seas. Both coiled and straight varieties reached dramatic sizes for invertebrates, and their varied morphologies indicate that they occupied a whole host of ecological niches.

Modes of life

Although effective, the deposition of siphonal and chamber deposits was not the only way nautiloids solved the problems of counter balancing or positional stability. In *Ascoceras* the problem was solved by the shedding of the early 'normal' shell followed by the development of an inflated adult shell, with asymmetric, air-filled chambers, enabling the animal to live an active free-swimming mode of life.

It is likely that most straight nautiloids swam horizontally or hovered over the sea bottom in a sub-vertical position. Open-coiled forms such as *Tritarthiceras* would have experienced difficulties as an active swimmer and it is likely that it grazed across the surface of the sea-bottom. Other grazers included the short, stubby forms such as *Phragmoceras* from the Silurian, whilst active swimmers included the tightly coiled *Tarphyceras*.

nautiloids were marked with a concentric or longitudinal ornament, growth lines, nodes and spines. This shell ornament may be linked with environmental factors and protection. Colour banding is an obvious surface feature of *Nautilus* and colour banding has been discovered in *Geisonoceras* and *Crytoceras* from the Lower Palaeozoic. In nautiloids the banding appears to reflect their swimming stance, with the area of colour banding facing towards the surface of the sea. In forms with a circular banding, the tip of the shell pointed upwards.

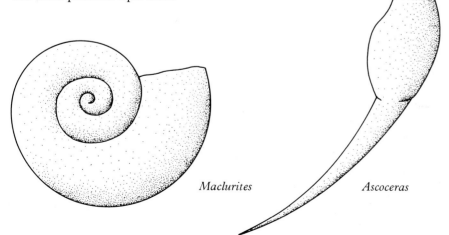

Maclurites

Ascoceras

Orthocone

Giant jointed-limbed animals

Apart from the trilobites and their close relatives other groups of arthropods arose during the Lower Palaeozoic. These included the ancestors of the crabs and lobsters, as well as those of the scorpions and spiders, king crabs and eurypterids. Of these, only the eurypterids have no living representatives; the last of the group appearing in rocks of the Permian. The eurypterids were spectacular creatures, however, and during the Silurian and Devonian numerous species occupied the roles of scavenger and predator within benthic communities.

The body of the eurypterid is long and streamlined and covered by a thin chitinous, external skeleton. The body is divided unequally into a small head-region (prosoma) and an elongate abdomen, both of which are segmented. Six pairs of limbs occur on the ventral side of the prosoma. The limbs were modified to perform various functions and the development of the last pair as large paddle-like, swimming organs gave the eurypterids a unique appearance. Two large cresentic eyes occur on the dorsal surface of the prosoma.

The majority of eurypterids were less than 30 centimetres in length but some giants such as *Pterygotus* grew to over 1·8 metres long and even 3 metre monsters have been recorded from the Silurian rocks of Buffalo, New York State.

The remains of early eurypterids have been discovered in marine sediments and it has been suggested that this was their natural habitat in those times. In the Silurian and Devonian, however, the eurypterids are known only from brackish water sediments and the idea of a Late Ordovician migration from marine to lagoonal or even river environments has been proposed. This may be so, but it is just as likely that the earliest specimens were carried seawards after death. This would take them away from their natural environment and cause them to be mixed with other organisms, with which they had no true association.

Eurypterus lacustris is a typical example of a eurypterid or giant water-scorpion. It is the most common eurypterid discovered in brackish water, Silurian deposits around Buffalo, New York State, U.S.A.

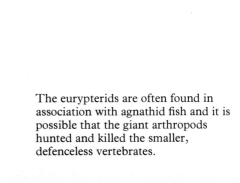

The eurypterids are often found in association with agnathid fish and it is possible that the giant arthropods hunted and killed the smaller, defenceless vertebrates.

Towards a life on land

During the Silurian a number of fossils indicate that both the plant and animal kingdoms were sending out front runners to explore and colonize the great terrestrial realm. To be successful these early colonists needed to protect themselves from dessication, a problem that hardly concerned their water-dwelling compatriots.

The first true land plant *Cooksonia*, is recorded from Silurian rocks. It is the first of a group of

The first animals to venture out of the sea were arthropods, with the ancient scorpion *Palaeophonus*, like *Cooksonia*, appearing in the Upper Silurian. It is not so surprising that the first terrestrial animals should arise from this lineage as the origin of the eurypterids in the Ordovician, had already heralded the invasion of lagoons and rivers. The arthropod skeleton is an ideal protective unit, and only slight modifications, to it

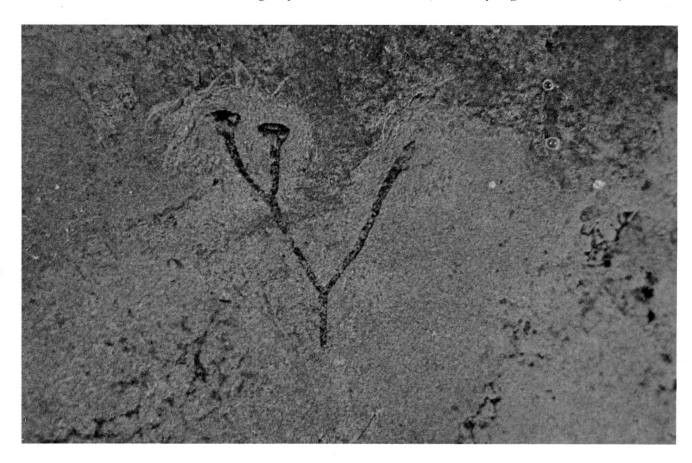

primitive vascular plants, called the Psilopsida, and its discovery traces the history of the group back over 400 million years of geological time. *Cooksonia* is known only by the remains of its reproductive sporangia and these indicate a close likeness to the living genera *Psilotum* and *Tmesipteris*. Through comparison it is therefore likely that *Cooksonia* was an erect plant with strong supportive tissues, and an underground rooting system known as the rhizome. It is also probable that it possessed a protective layer to prevent water loss and pores or stomata essential to the exchange of gases and water. Effectively the earliest psilopsids were still restricted to areas with standing water but their appearance was an irreversible step towards the colonization of land.

A fossil of *Cooksonia*, notice reproductive sporangia at the end of the forked stem

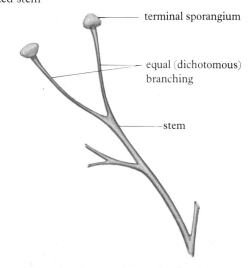

terminal sporangium

equal (dichotomous) branching

stem

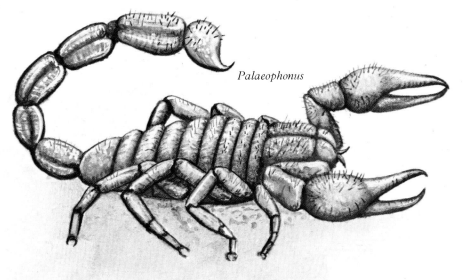

Palaeophonus

The first terrestrial animal was *Palaeophonus* a Silurian scorpion. Structurally it was very similar to living species, although variations in the number of body segments and the size of the pincers are noticeable. The record of arthropods in terrestrial sediments is not good, however, and it is only when unusual, albeit ideal, conditions prevail that their remains are preserved. Classic examples, such as the impressions of Carboniferous or Jurassic dragonflies, and the numerous insects in the Oligocene ambers of the Baltic, reflect the importance of arthropods in many terrestrial communities.

The fishes multiply

Although the discovery of *Anatolepis heintzi* and various scales and bone fragments places the origin of fishes firmly in the Lower Ordovician, the real expansion of the fishes was to wait some 50 million years with the advent of the Upper Silurian. Agnathans flourished at this time and several orders were well represented in marine and fresh water environments. *Tyriaspis* and *Poraspis* are typical of the thickly armoured agnathans of the time, but *Jamoytius*, a scaled anaspid, is most unusual, as its lightly ossified skeleton makes it more like the living lamprey than its ancient contempories.

The earliest true-jawed fishes also appear in the Upper Silurian, with the small ancanthodians as the first representatives. Few of these were as heavily armoured as the agnathans and as a result most, if not all, swam and fed in surface waters. The record of other fish stocks, including the bony fishes and their heavily armoured,

Jamoytius

placoderm cousins, may also be traced back into the Upper Silurian, but in their case the material is extremely limited. In the Lower Devonian these stocks diversify and the period as a whole is recognized as the 'Age of the Fishes'.

and the respiratory apparatus, would have been necessary. In fact, *Palaeophonus* is remarkably similar to its living relatives.

From the Silurian onwards the evolution of land-dwelling animals, particularly the vertebrates, was closely linked with the evolution of the vascular plants.

By the beginning of the Devonian three other orders of arachnids had joined the scorpions on land. These included the first mites, ticks and spiders, the remains of which occur in the silicified sediments of the Rhynie district of Scotland. Psilopsids are also known from these sediments and time equivalent discoveries in Central Europe, North America and Australia indicate that these vascular plants were already cosmopolitan.

Pteraspis, an early agnathan

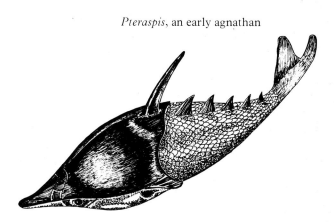

The Devonian

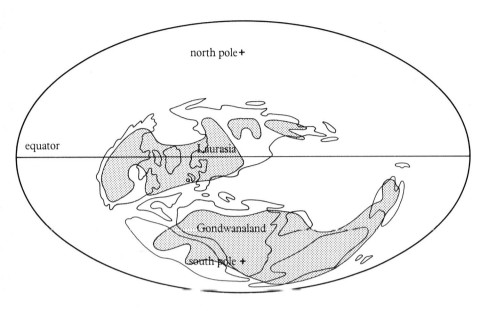

equator

north pole +

Laurasia

Gondwanaland

south pole +

The dawn of the Devonian period marks the beginning of the Upper Palaeozoic. In terms of evolution and tectonic activity this was to be one of the most dynamic sub-eras of geological time. Continental collision and uplift was to transform the great depositional troughs of the Ordovician and Silurian into massive mountain chains. Changes in the environment and climate also took place and new groups of animals and plants inherited the Earth. The Devonian saw the continued moving together of the northern continents which as Laurasia moved in an irreversible southward direction to eventually collide with Gondwanaland, and form the super continent Pangaea. In Europe, the Devonian period was essentially characterized by the deposition of two distinct sedimentary formations, one marine and the other terrestrial. Marine environments encircled many of the proto-continents and the south pole had migrated several hundred kilometres south-east of its Silurian position.

Reconstruction of an ancient land/sea scape

South-west England is one of the most beautiful regions of the British Isles, with rugged cliffs and moorlands, dominated by granite tors. Today, the woods and heathlands are filled with flowering plants and animals, including birds and mammals. Beneath the soil and along the shore, however, rocks of Devonian age provide data of a time when the region bordered the great Old Red Sandstone Continent. The shoreline ran approximately east-west from Ilfracombe to the Quantock Hills, with sea to the south and a high mountain range in the north.

Deep water environments occurred in South Devon and Cornwall and muddy sediments strewn with pebbles covered the sea floor. A fauna of small goniatites, the ancestors of the Mesozoic ammonites, had effectively replaced the graptolites in the upper waters but trilobites, bivalves and brachiopods continued to occupy benthic or sea floor niches. To the north, shallower water communities flourished and in some areas coral reefs fringed volcanic islands. Stony corals, bryozoans and other colonial organisms formed the main reef structure whilst brachiopods and bivalves dotted the calcareous muds of the sea bottom. The stony corals were represented by both tabulate and rugose species and it is likely that their tentacular soft parts gave vivid colour to these shallow Devonian seas. Trilobites and nautiloids lived as scavengers and predators within the community.

In the relatively shallow seas, away from the reefs, spire-bearing brachiopods (spiriferids), lace bryozoans and sea lilies were common. The spiriferids, and the goniatites of the deeper water environments, are the zone fossils of the marine Devonian.

Lakes and swamps bordered the shoreline of the northern land mass and fish, primitive plants and various arthropods thrived in and around the edges of their waters. The plants were mostly similar to *Cooksonia* from the Upper Silurian, but the genus *Asteroxylon* was one of the first lycopod pteridophytes. Mites,

spiders and shrimp-like branchiopods represented the arthropods, and it is likely that most of these were dependent in some way on the plants for food.

In the Devonian fresh water environments fishes were common, with various stocks dominating different stratigraphic horizons. In the Lower Devonian, the agnathans flourished but by the Middle Devonian the ancanthodians and bony fishes reigned supreme. Beyond the lakes and swamps the mountains were barren, as no life, except possibly the odd scorpion, had ventured onto their arid slopes. In the Devonian the northern region of the south-west peninsular was very different to the verdant pastures of the present day.

Space window on the Devonian world

Stories of time-machines and journeys through time have fascinated mankind for generations, and many geologists would admit to day-dreaming about the possibility of visiting a specific period of geological time. For the specialist the visit would hold many surprises and several of his or her favourite theories might be destroyed. As a scientist, however, he would settle to the task of recording data and, like a latter day Captain Cook, return to a modern world thirsting for knowledge.

Our reconstruction of the planet Earth during the Devonian is an attempt to illustrate a sighting from an approaching time-machine. The reconstruction is the equivalent of a space photograph and it clearly shows the three physical realms. The most noticeable difference to a current NASA photograph is the form of the lithosphere, with a large northern land mass filling our view. No tropical rain forests straddle the equatorial region and the only green is to be seen at the edges of the continental mass. On land the green marks the gradual spread of the vascular plants, whereas in the sea it is evidence of the continuing presence of the algae. Swirling clouds move high over the land and light-coloured patches mark the movements of the oceans over shallow coastal platforms.

The invention of a time-machine may never happen but the reconstruction of the Devonian world has been made possible by the collection of data from several continents. These include the occurrence of 'red beds': sediments in which the iron bearing minerals have been oxidized in hot arid conditions. Such deposits have been recorded from Siberia, Northern Europe and North America and in many areas the close proximity of marine sandstones and reef limestones mark the ancient shoreline. Volcanic deposits occur in many areas and submarine lavas mixed with deep sea sediments may indicate the presence of a plate boundary.

Corals as palaeontological clocks

Fossils tell us many things about evolution and about the ancient environments in which they lived. They also provide us with a tool for stratigraphic correlation and since 1963 certain fossils have been used as palaeontological clocks.

As we have seen earlier, natural clocks may include animal heart beats or menstruation and, in the case of plants, we can use the growth rings of trees. This last example plots the age of a tree with considerable accuracy, in much the same way as growth bands in modern stony corals record daily growth rates. Stony corals were common in the Devonian and their calcium carbonate skeletons display distinct horizontal ridges. These are thought to represent growth lines, with the more prominent ridges correlating to annual growth. Finer, closely-spaced lines are associated with daily growth and the average of numerous counts has provided us with a figure of

Ancient rugose corals from the Devonian period make ideal palaeontological clocks. The reconstruction is of a solitary coral and its skeleton, the outer wall of which is ornamented with horizontal, circular growth lines. The lines are formed by the deposition of the mineral, calcium carbonate, and each of the finer lines represents a day's growth. The major or prominent lines correspond to annual increments and in some specimens it is possible to divide each year's growth into monthly units. Because of the difficulty in counting individual daily bands we have enlarged a single year's growth and divided it according to the data available.

The two columns represent the divisions of a recent sidereal year and its Devonian equivalent. The latter is divided into 13·04 lunar months and each month into 30·6 days.

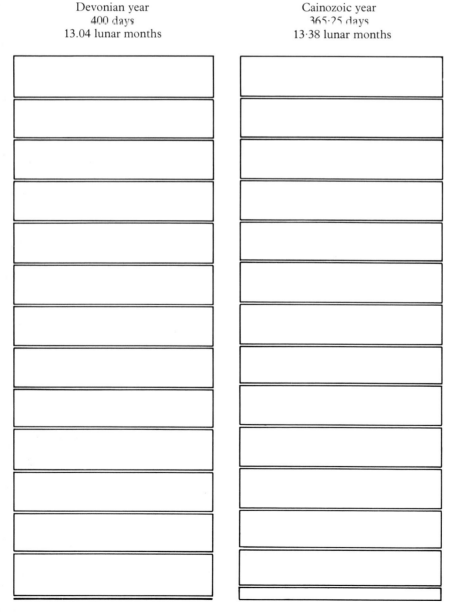

Devonian year
400 days
13.04 lunar months

Cainozoic year
365·25 days
13·38 lunar months

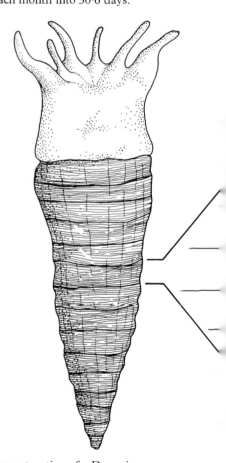

reconstruction of a Devonian rugose coral

400 days for a Devonian year. Palaeontologists have also recognized monthly groupings on the coral skeleton and it is now thought that each grouping represented a lunar month. This period, between new moons, lasted 30·6 days. Simple mathematics tells us therefore that each year consisted of 13 lunar months*.

In an attempt to validate the use of corals as indicators of time, scientists have employed geophysical and astronomical calculations. Surprisingly these prove that the corals are extremely accurate, and the suggestion is that tidal friction has been an important factor in increasing the length of each day. Calculations of tidal friction indicate that a Cambrian year had as many as 425 of the shorter days. Tidal friction alone appears to have been responsible for the gradual slowing down of the Earth's rotation.

one year's growth
13.04 lunar months

one month's growth
30·6 days

Devonian communities

The high angled cross-bedding illustrated is an indication that sandstones in which it occurs were deposited under arid conditions.

Several early vascular plants are represented in the reconstruction of a Devonian swamp community, *Rhynia*, the primitive psilopsid in the foreground, averaged approximately 20 centimetres in height. It had a smooth surface and terminal spore capsules, whereas *Asteroxylon* the early lycopod was characterized by the star-shaped arrangement of the conducting tissues and the tightly packed leaflets that surrounded its stem. Numerous tiny arthropods lived in the protective waters of the swamp (after McKerrow, 1978).

As we have seen from the introduction to Devonian faunas and from the reconstruction of a Devonian landscape, palaeontologists are able to recognize the existence of several communities during this period. These include the first well-defined terrestrial association of organisms, with the early vascular plants and fresh water arthropods as the major representatives of the plant and animal kingdoms. This community developed in lake or swamp environments bordering the arid continents. Inland the hills were barren with great thicknesses of 'red beds' being deposited across the flood plains of larger rivers. Seawards from the swamp large areas of the coast, in regions such as western Canada, were covered with layers of mineral salts, with halite, gypsum, anhydrite and sylvite representing the evaporation of sea water in a shallow restricted basin.

In some areas rivers constructed broad deltas with side branches of the main stream forming distributaries. Sand deposits marked the main line of a distributory as it flowed seawards but at the sides fine muds and silts accumulated to provide a suitable substrate for a coastal deltaic community. The sediments exhibit cross lamination

Rhynia

Asteroxylon

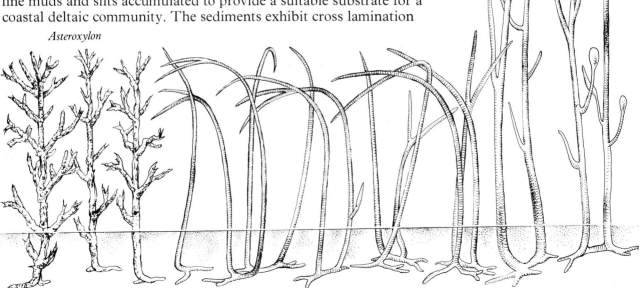

and together with scouring this indicates an increase in river flow due to heavy rains.

Owing to the conditions that prevailed the community was rather restricted in variety and was dominated by burrowing organisms such as worms and small arthropods. Some bivalves and the ubiquitous *Lingula* occurred in the bays that bordered the deltas. On the shelf beyond the influence of these deltas, shallow water marine communities flourished. The predominantly sandy sediments still bore evidence of the proximity of land, but the fauna was more diverse with starfishes, brachiopods, bivalves, trilobites, bryozoans

The shallow water deltaic communities of the Devonian were dominated by burrowing worms and arthropods. Some bivalves and inarticulate brachiopods may have colonized the area around the mouth of a distributory, but in general terms the variety of organisms was very restricted (after McKerrow, 1978).

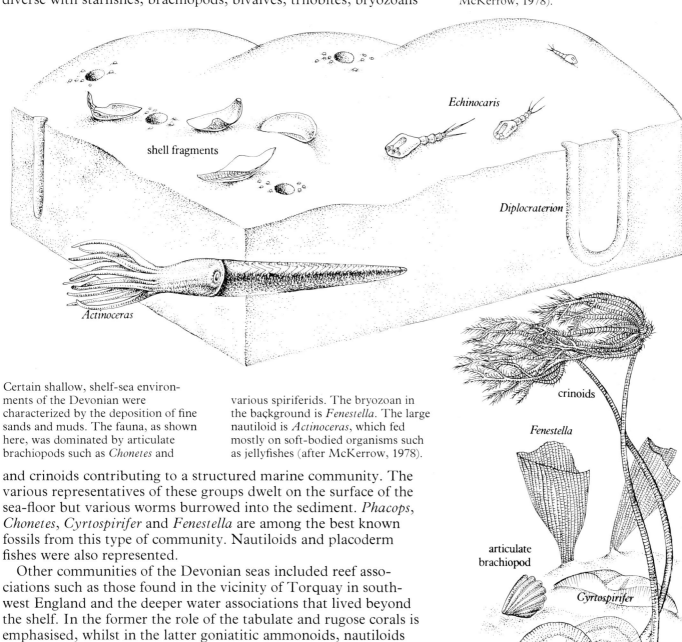

Certain shallow, shelf-sea environments of the Devonian were characterized by the deposition of fine sands and muds. The fauna, as shown here, was dominated by articulate brachiopods such as *Chonetes* and various spiriferids. The bryozoan in the background is *Fenestella*. The large nautiloid is *Actinoceras*, which fed mostly on soft-bodied organisms such as jellyfishes (after McKerrow, 1978).

and crinoids contributing to a structured marine community. The various representatives of these groups dwelt on the surface of the sea-floor but various worms burrowed into the sediment. *Phacops*, *Chonetes*, *Cyrtospirifer* and *Fenestella* are among the best known fossils from this type of community. Nautiloids and placoderm fishes were also represented.

Other communities of the Devonian seas included reef associations such as those found in the vicinity of Torquay in south-west England and the deeper water associations that lived beyond the shelf. In the former the role of the tabulate and rugose corals is emphasised, whilst in the latter goniatitic ammonoids, nautiloids and spiriferid brachiopods were very important. Most of the reef communities developed within 30° of the Devonian equator although some, such as those of north-western India, flourished well outside that latitude.

Brachiopod modes of life

By the beginning of the Devonian period all of the major orders of brachiopods were well established. The dominant stocks were the spiriferids and strophomenids and within their numbers individual species were adapted to specialized modes of life. To interpret the latter, palaeontologists analyse the form of the shell, the positions of the internal muscle scars and the construction of the feeding organ support structures. Shape and ornament are good indicators of environment and the form of the internal skeleton helps in the interpretation of the mechanics of feeding. To confine our study of brachiopod life styles to the spiriferids and strophomenids would be restrictive, particularly as other brachiopods provide important data on environments. Fortunately most of our examples can be found entombed in Devonian rocks.

Once again *Lingula* was a typical member of Devonian shallow coastal communities and many specimens have been found in their original position of life. *Lingula* lived in a tube-like burrow; the actual shell being fixed to the base by means of a thick flexible thread (pedicle). The living *Lingula* is rather like a fingernail in shape and, in fact, most of its growth is at the front of the shell. Obviously this is ideal for a burrowing mode of life. *Lingula* is, and was, a suspension feeder and it opens and closes its valves by means of a complex set of muscles. Its survival through time is a testament to its conservatism and tolerance.

Other inarticulates, including *Crania*, lived attached to different organisms on the sea floor. The craniid shell has a rather flattened conical shape and it obtained its food from currents that entered the shell from either side.

Amongst the articulate brachiopods the orthids and pentamerids survived into the Devonian but

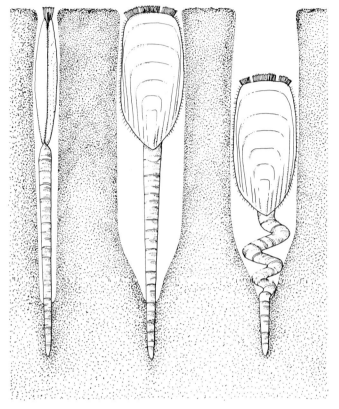

Lingula

their presence was overshadowed by more specialized forms. These included the strophomenids, with *Productus* and *Chonetes* occurring as bottom-dwelling representatives. Both forms developed spines to stabilize their position on the sea floor but *Productus* was much larger than its cousin, and many species lived in areas characterized by stronger currents. The two valves of the productid shell were of unequal size and the lower, larger and spinose one was mostly buried in the sea-floor sediment. The productids included some rather bizarre forms with the spiny *Prorichtofenia* from the Permian, having a shape similar to that of a solitary stony coral.

The spiriferids were probably the most important group of Devonian brachiopods. They were rather unique in form, with a very long hinge line and a distinct trilobate division of the shell. Internally the support structures for the feeding organ were extended as spirals parallel to the hinge line. These developed three streams of water with the lateral ones carrying food and oxygen into the body cavity. The third was used to expel waste products. The form and function of the spiriferid shell suggests that they lived on soft sediments; the elongate hinge line aiding stability.

Crania

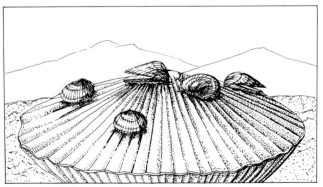

Of the remaining articulate brachiopods, the rhynchonellids and terebratulids show their own particular adaptations to the environment. The terebratulids were the newest addition to the brachiopod family-tree and although their numbers were limited, it has been found that the early forms, like their living relatives, were attached to the substrate by a strong pedicle. The small rhynchonellids rested unattached on the sea floor; the presence of a sharply folded anterior opening preventing large particles of sediment from entering the body cavity.

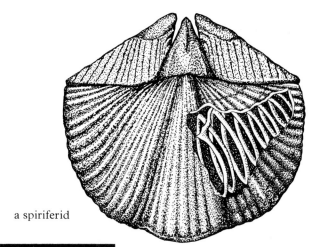

a spiriferid

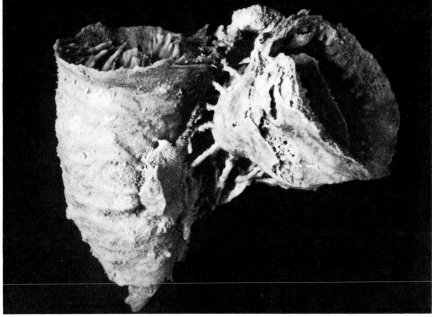

A coral-like brachiopod from the Permian, Glass Mountains, Texas.

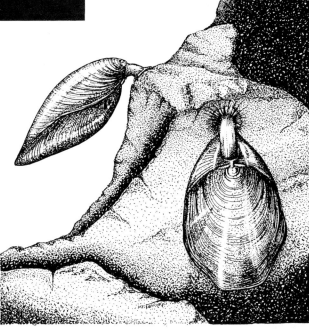

a terebratulid

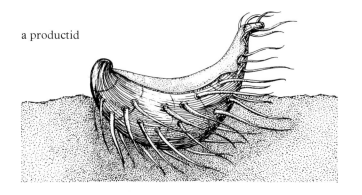

a productid

The age of fishes

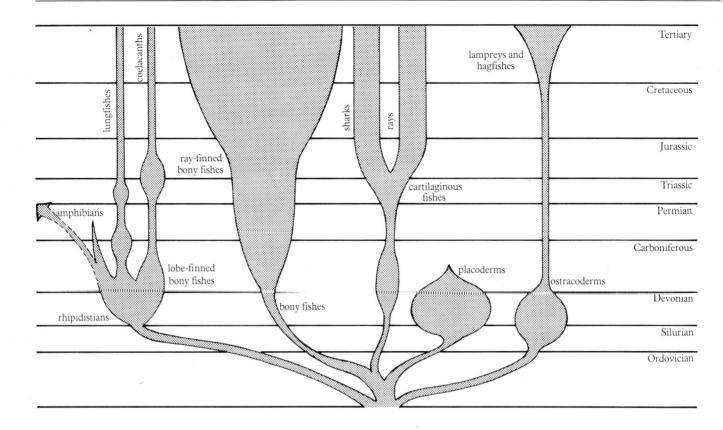

The evolution of the fishes can be traced back almost 500 million years but the great diversification of fish stocks was to wait until the end of the Silurian period. Our chart suggests that the agnathan (jawless) and gnathostome (jawed) fishes evolved from a common ancestor.

The evolution of the fishes gathered impetus in the Lower Devonian, with the jawed or gnathostome groups appearing in numbers. These fishes were well armoured and adapted for specific roles within marine and fresh water environments. Their appearance was somewhat sudden but it is likely that most can be assumed to have had Silurian or even Ordovician ancestry. In the Lower Devonian the jawless agnathans also increased in numbers and they remained the dominant group of fishes for several million years. It is unlikely that the first gnathostomes competed with the well-established agnathans for a particular niche. This diversification of the fishes was one of the most significant events of the Palaeozoic era and the phrase the 'Age of Fishes' is often used to describe the Devonian Period.

The evolution of jaws in the fishes is, itself, one

of the most important changes in the evolution of the group. In the earliest agnathans the mouth was sucker-like and terminal in position, and the gill arches were all identical. The latter extended forwards to the mouth, and were fixed dorsally to bones of the skull. In the gnathostome fishes the number of gill arches is reduced and the first two gill bars appear to have been modified to form jaws. If this modification is accepted then a 'missing link' probably occurred between agnathan and gnathostome stocks. Some experts doubt this hypothesis, however, and argue that a detailed study of the embryos of living forms, and the specialized nature of the two groups, argues for a common ancestry back in the Ordovician. This theory would not need the 'missing link' postulated above and would suggest an independent evolution for the two stocks.

Modes of Life

The variation in body form amongst the fishes is a good indicator of different modes of life. This is as true for fossil fishes as it is for living species, and those of the Devonian are no exception.

The flattened nature of many of the early agnathans suggests that forms such as *Tremataspis* and *Anglaspis* were bottom dwellers. In time, modifications to the body and the fins allowed various genera to occupy different niches. *Cephalaspis* is thought to have lived in fresh water streams, living a life comparable with that of the recent catfishes. Other agnathans, including various species of *Pteraspis*, became surface water feeders, whilst the descendants of *Jamoytius*, soft bodied anaspids, lived by scraping algae from the surface of rocks or shells.

Amongst the gnathostomes many forms evolved during the Devonian, with the acanthodians, the first 'true jawed fishes', swimming in mid and surface water zones. The streamlined shape of many Devonian bony fishes is indicative of a free-swimming mode of life, whilst lung-fishes closely resemble their modern day relatives. Burrows in Devonian sediments suggest that the lung-fishes were already capable of breathing air. Finally the reconstruction of the cartilaginous fish *Cladoselache* from the Upper Devonian reveals the presence of sharks and their predatory habits.

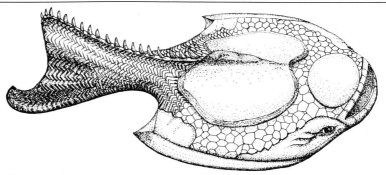

Drepanaspis

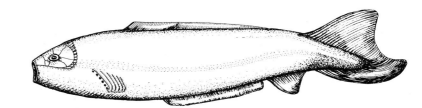

an early anaspid

Dipterus

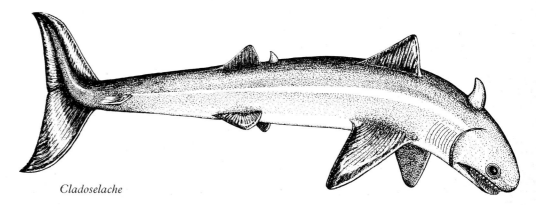

Cladoselache

Jaws, armour-plating, cartilage and bone

The development of jaws in fishes enabled them to attack and eat larger prey. Jaws are characteristic of four subclasses of the fishes, each of which showed spectacular diversity during the Devonian Period. The following accounts provide information on these subclasses and on some of the interesting developments that took place within their Devonian ranks.

Climatius

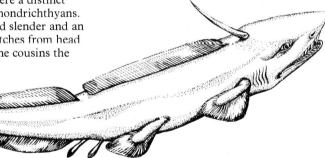

The acanthodians – the 'spiny sharks'

The acanthodians were rather small fishes with few individuals exceeding 20 centimetres in length. In general they were shark-like and possessed paired fin-spines. *Climatius* is a typical 'spiny-shark' and our reconstruction shows that it had a streamlined shape and a heterocercal tail. This last, is common to many primitive fishes and occurs when the backbone curves upwards and the greater part of fin development takes place below it. The body of *Climatius* was covered with small square and closely fitting scales. It is likely that *Climatius* possessed an airbladder and that it swam in an eel-like manner. Palaeontologists have suggested that the sharp fin-spines of the acanthodians were primarily protective in function; their fixed, elongate nature making *Climatius* and many other acanthodians unpalatable prey.

The chondrichthyans – cartilaginous fishes

The chondrichthyans include the sharks, rays and dogfishes. They have a cartilaginous internal skeleton and their representation dates back to the Lower Devonian. The early history of the group was confined to the cladoselachians or earliest sharks. *Cladoselache* is the best known representative of this stock, with individuals exceeding 2 metres in length. As in the acanthodians the body is streamlined but there are no paired fin-spines and the tail has a symmetrical outline. High cusped teeth are typical of many modern sharks and those of *Cladoselache* have a somewhat similar outline. The chondrichthyans, as a group, rarely occur in fresh water environments and *Cladoselache* was an open sea predator. The fossilized gut contents of this early shark indicate that it fed on other fish including many of its own kind.

In the Upper Devonian the xenacanthid 'sharks' were a distinct group of fresh-water chondrichthyans. *Xenacanthus* is long and slender and an elongate dorsal fin stretches from head to tail. Like their marine cousins the xenacanthids were predators; a well-developed sense of smell helping in the hunt for food.

The cladoselachians were replaced by more advanced sharks in the Lower Carboniferous but the xenacanthids continued through until the Triassic.

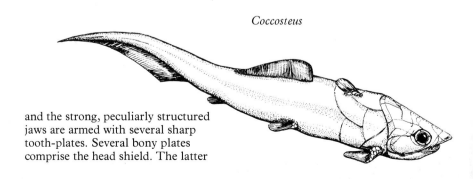

Xenacanthus

Coccosteus

The placoderms – armoured fishes or 'plated-skins'

Many fish experts believe that the ancient 'plated-skin' fish, the placoderms, are related to the living sharks and skates. The group is unique and very diversified. Most individuals have a rather flattened form and distinct head and 'chest' shields. The genus *Coccosteus* typifies the group and several species flourished in the Middle Devonian. Overall the fish has a streamlined shape, with the body tapering into a heterocercal tail. The head is rather square, in front view, and the strong, peculiarly structured jaws are armed with several sharp tooth-plates. Several bony plates comprise the head shield. The latter

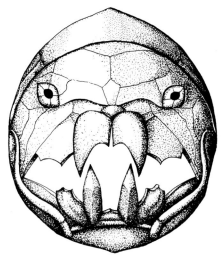

Dunkleosteus

articulates with the 'chest shield' and together they afforded the animal considerable protection. *Coccosteus* was a fresh-water dweller but other placoderms migrated into marine environments. Most were bottom living. Some placoderms fed on shell-

fish but others were active predators, darting after their prey with eel-like movements. The placoderms evolved rapidly in the Devonian to fill various niches, but by the end of the period they were being rapidly replaced by the more efficient sharks.

Dunkleosteus, a huge placoderm fish from the Upper Devonian of Europe and North America. The large tooth-like structures are in fact modifications of mineralized plates that covered the margins of the jaws.

The osteichthyans – the bony fishes

The first well recorded radiation of the bony fishes took place in the Middle Devonian, with numerous representatives appearing in fresh and seawater environments. Characteristically these had a skeleton of bone and an airbladder. This may have acted as a lung, or been modified into an organ that would have enabled the fish to hold its position in water without a great expenditure of energy. For the first time, fishes evolved with the capability of emerging from the water and making the first deliberate crawl over land. This action may have been the result of intense competition between the emerging bony fishes: a modified fin and the development of lungs enabling groups such as the lungfishes and rhipidistians to live in shallow pools around the edges of lakes and swamps.

Two major groups of bony fishes had appeared before the Middle Devonian with the lungfishes and rhipidistians having 'tassel' or 'lobed' fins and the palaeoniscids a 'ray-finned' structure.

Ray-finned fishes, or actinopterygians, are thought to represent the primitive condition, even though living species clearly outnumber their 'tassel-finned' relatives. *Cheirolepis* a palaeoniscid, is an early actinopterygian and our reconstruction clearly illustrates the diagnostic characters of a single dorsal fin and bony rays within the paired fins.

The lungfishes and the coelacanth are living representatives of the 'tassel-finned' or crossopterygian fishes. Their paired fins are fleshy and the supporting bones of these fins have been reduced in number. In most forms, including the early examples *Osteolepis* and *Holoptychius* from the Devonian, a pair of dorsal fins are present. These may be modified in more advanced crossopterygians but in general their presence is an additional character which separates the group from the 'ray-finned' fishes.

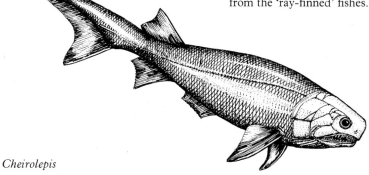

Cheirolepis

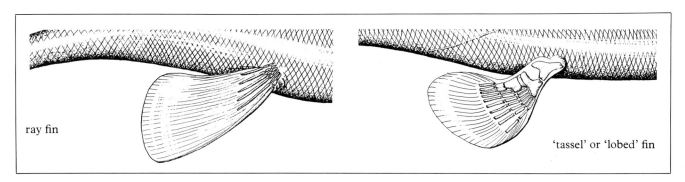

ray fin

'tassel' or 'lobed' fin

Fish in the Devonian seas

Vertebrate life in the seas of the Upper Devonian was ruled by gigantic 'plated-skins' such as *Dunkleosteus* and early sharks, like *Cladoselache*. *Dunkleosteus* was an arthrodire and therefore a member of the largest group of the placoderm fishes. It was a monster, with the head characterized by the presence of small eyes and powerful jaws. The jaws possessed a number of large, tooth-like picks, some of which measured half a metre in height. *Dunkleosteus* grew to over 9 metres in length; the head and the anterior armoured region measuring just over 3 metres. In life this huge fish swam in the mid-waters, between the sea floor and the surface. There it lurked in waiting for its prey, which probably consisted of any large

holocephalans

Cladoselache

organism unfortunate enough to attract its attention. The early sharks were no match for *Dunkleosteus*, as the various species of *Cladoselache* averaged less than 1 metre in length. All were predators, and it is likely that they fed on other sharks, small fishes and invertebrates. *Cladoselache* had a stream-lined shape and in life it had all the normal shark-like habits.

Although, it would appear that the structure of their teeth and jaws forced them to swallow their food whole. Another Devonian shark was *Diademodus*, which by comparison with *Cladoselache* was a poor swimmer and sought its food on the sea bottom. *Diademodus* had a well-developed snout region and, as in modern sharks, a good sense of smell helped it in its search for food.

Brachiopods and other shelled invertebrates were common in the sea floor communities of the Upper Devonian and it is likely that several species of ray-like holocephalans had evolved to plunder a rich harvest by the end of the 'Age of Fishes'.

Dunkleosteus

Towards a walk on land

Eusthenopteron a typical rhipidistian fish, lived in shallow fresh-water environments during the Upper Devonian.

The incredible variety of fishes present during the Lower and Middle Devonian sub-periods suggests that the competition for food and territory was fierce. Large predators such as *Dunkleosteus* ruled the seas, and the lakes and rivers were full of meat-eating arthrodires and bony fishes. To avoid predation, or perhaps to secure their own source of food many fishes came to inhabit the shallow waters at the edges of ponds and lakes. These included several crossopterygian stocks in which the development of lungs and strong, rounded fins were to prove ideal adaptations. Arid climatic conditions coincided with the movement of the 'tassel fins' into shallow waters, and their ability to gulp air and possibly to move over the surface of a drying pond with the aid of their strong fins, would have proved of great value in times of drought. Environmental change, coupled with intense predation, may have encouraged one of the crossopterygians to leave the safe keeping of the ancient environment for ever.

The fresh-water crossopterygians of the early Devonian included the lungfishes, coelacanths and rhipidistians and it is to these groups that we look for a likely amphibian ancestor. Of the three, the lungfishes and coelacanths have living repre-

The fin of *Eusthenopteron* is similar to that of other 'tassel-finned' fishes, but the reduction in the number of bones and the development of the humerus, radius and ulna, represent a significant step in the evolution of a walking limb. The limb of *Eryops*, an early amphibian is shown for comparison.

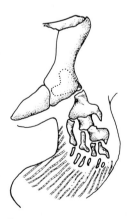

Eusthenopteron

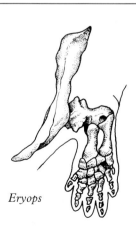

Eryops

sentatives and therefore we can analyse their form and life styles for clues of tetrapod ancestry. In the case of the lungfishes, the comparison indicates that little structural change has taken place, and the discovery of lungfish burrows in Devonian strata proves that their mode of life was the same then as it is now. Recent lungfishes live in tropical and subtropical regions, where the ponds, in which they dwell, dry out in drought conditions. To counter this change in their environment the fishes cocoon themselves in a flask-shaped burrow and await the return of the rains. The fishes survive by going into a state of aestivation, with air being drawn into the burrow by the movement of the lung. This mode of life was an ideal adaptation to the conditions that prevailed on the Devonian continents, but the passing of geological time has suggested that it was a 'stop-gap' adaptation with little evolutionary potential.

Unlike the lungfishes the living coelacanth *Latimeria*, also, structurally similar to its ancient relatives, has adapted to a new mode of life. It is no longer a fresh-water fish and the lung, characteristic of its relatives, has been lost. *Latimeria* now lives in the deep waters off the Comoro Islands in the Indian Ocean. Although its life style has changed the coelacanth still retains the four fleshy, paired fins of its ancestors. These are now used purely during swimming, but it is not difficult to imagine that once they had a sup-

portive or 'walking' function. Unfortunately, the coelacanth sought the seclusion of marine waters and, anyway, an analysis of its skull bones excludes it from the role of amphibian ancestor.

It is therefore necessary that we turn to the rhipidistians as our final hope of finding the 'missing link'. Unfortunately the group has been extinct since the Lower Carboniferous but certain features suggest that they were closely related to the proto-amphibian we are looking for. The rhipidistians were active predators and it is likely that their fleshy limbs supported their bodies whilst they rested or lurked, waiting to rush after passing prey. The structure of the rhipidistian fin is unique as the number of bones is greatly reduced and 'arm' bones, analogous with those of higher vertebrates, are discernable. The skull roof of the typical rhipidistian, *Eusthenopteron* also has a structure somewhat similar to that of a labyrinthodont amphibian and this, and other evidence, suggests that an animal not far removed from this 'tassel-finned' fish took the most important 'walk' in the history of evolution.

The first amphibian, *Ichthyostega*, appeared in the Upper Devonian. It measured 1·5 metres in length and its short, strong limbs enabled it to crawl about on land. A flattened skull was also an adaptation to life out of water, as it was easier to support, but the strong 'fishy' tail belied its probably crossopterygian ancestry.

The plants solve many problems

The emergence of the primitive vascular plants, the psilopsids in the Upper Silurian – Lower Devonian, marked an important step in plant evolution. Our reconstruction of *Cooksonia* clearly demonstrated that the early psilopsids had developed terminal organs called sporangia to protect their spores, and it is likely that the spores themselves were able to withstand dessication. Once evolved, these features were available for transfer to descendant stocks of a more advanced nature.

The life cycle of the extant tropical *Psilotum* is probably little changed from that of its Palaeozoic relatives. It involves the shedding of spores and their distribution by the wind over a large area. The spores then develop, in damp conditions, into tiny root-like structures that live below ground and feed on rotting substances. At this stage the plant is termed the prothallus and it is in this structure that the sex cells develop. Numerous male cells are held in the organ called the anthe-

ridium and when conditions are right they are released into the water that surrounds the prothallus. They then swim to the female organ, the archegonium, and enter and fertilize the single large egg contained therein. Fertilization is followed by the development of sporophyte which grows into a mature *Psilotum* with sporangia.

The ferns, horsetails and club mosses inherited the reproductive habits of the ancestral psilopsids, and primitive forms such as *Zosterophyllum* and *Horneophyton* still have their sporangia in the terminal position. These plant groups are collectively termed pteridophytes and their reproductive cycle is said to involve an alternation of generations (i.e. spore bearer – prothallus – spore bearer). Living examples of pteridophytes represent a long line of evolution but it is still essential that their reproductive phase occurs in water. Advances are obvious, though, and one of the more noticeable is the movement of the sporangia away from the tips of the stems. This followed a

Life-cycle of *Psilotum*

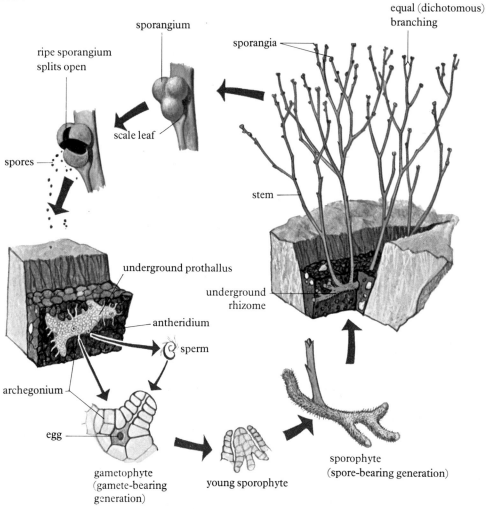

sporangium

ripe sporangium splits open

scale leaf

spores

equal (dichotomous) branching

sporangia

stem

underground prothallus

underground rhizome

antheridium

sperm

archegonium

egg

gametophyte (gamete-bearing generation)

young sporophyte

sporophyte (spore-bearing generation)

Illustrations 1 and 2 represent the early pteridophytes which have their sporangia in the terminal position. In 3 and 4 the presence of leaves leads to the movement of the sporangia to the underside of the leaves. In 5 and 6 the development of protective cone-like structures, as in *Selaginella*, was an important development in their adaptation to life on land.

Advances in sporangia protection

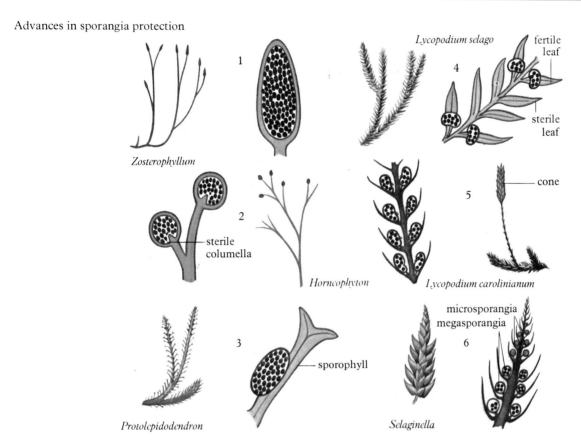

logical progression, with the sporangia first moving to a lateral position on the stem, and then, as the pteridophytes developed leaves, to ventral positions beneath the leaf. These stages are visible in the living club mosses and it would be safe to say that comparable conditions existed in several of their Devonian–Carboniferous ancestors. Small cone-like structures containing sporangia are also common to the living club moss, *Selaginella*, and their appearance must have represented a critical stage in the protection of spores and the development of plants truly adapted to a life on land.

The advances in sporangia protection and the development of a more complex overall structure enabled the pteridophytes to occupy new niches and grow to incredible sizes. The first ferns, horsetails and lycopods appeared in the early Devonian. By the middle of that period they were widespread and the first forests contained *Eospermatopteris*, a tree fern and *Protolepidodendron*, a lycopsid. In the Carboniferous the horsetails, with *Calamites*, grew to over 10 metres tall and some lycopods, including *Lepidodendron*, reached over 30 metres in height.

The characteristic of each of the various groups were well established by the Carboniferous period. The lycopods were massive and covered with tightly packed leaves. These gave the tree a reptilian appearance and they are commonly called scale trees. Like modern trees the lycopods increased the thickness of the stem by the addition of layers of woody tissue in the outer region. In the Upper Palaeozoic the horsetails were represented by the sphenopsids, which were also characterized by jointed stems and a whorled arrangement of the leaves. In *Calamostachys* cone-like reproductive organs had already appeared. True ferns of the Carboniferous already possessed the elaborately branched leaves typical of living genera. *Ptychocarpus* had well-formed sporangia on the under-surface of its leaves.

The swampland conditions of the Carboniferous were ideal for the various pteridophytes. Their position as 'top plants' was no longer safe, however, as the more advanced seed ferns, cordaitales, true conifers and ginkgoes had already appeared. In fact, the seed ferns and cordaitales were extremely common in the coal-forming forests and by the Late Carboniferous they were the dominant plants. As their name suggests the seed plants had evolved beyond the spore forming stage and the development of the seed was as an important a breakthrough, biologically speaking, as was the shelled egg of the reptiles.

The Carboniferous

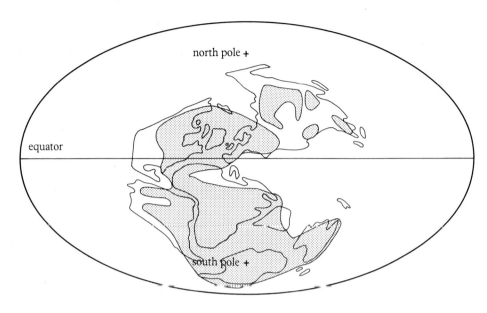

In terms of time the Carboniferous period lasted 65 million years, from 345 to 280 million years ago. The period takes its name from the huge coal-forming swamps, that developed in palaeo-equatorial regions during the upper part of its time span. The continental plates had moved closer together and the south pole had migrated into Antarctica. During the early Carboniferous much of Europe and North America was characterized by shallow water marine environments, but by the end of the period uplift had encouraged the spread of terrestrial conditions. On the southern continents a great ice sheet had developed by the Late Carboniferous and glacial deposits were common to South Africa, South America, India, Australasia and Antarctica.

From a palaeobiological point of view the period is of considerable interest, as significant changes took place in the representation of various groups of organisms. We shall see that the early part of the period was important with regard to the rugose corals and brachiopods but it was also a time of extinction. For it was then that the dendroid graptolites and several groups of echinoderms were to vanish from the fossil record. The uplift of land at the end of the Lower Carboniferous led to the withdrawal of shallow water marine communities from specific areas but in

An idealized reef community during the Lower Carboniferous (after McKerrow, 1978).

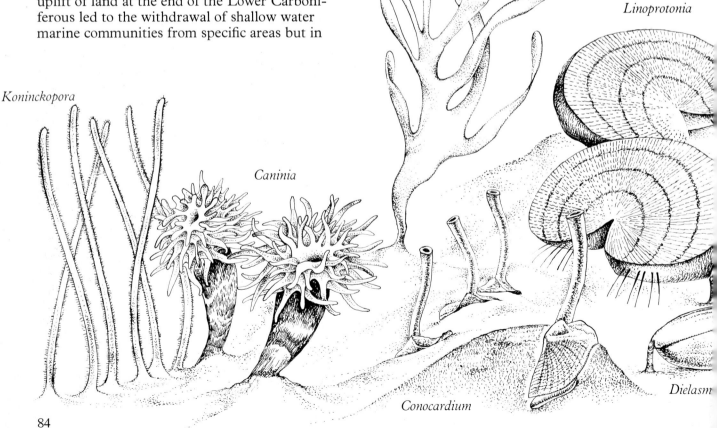

turn it encouraged the spread of many new plant species and the diversification of early tetrapod stocks. The Upper Carboniferous was essentially the 'Age of Amphibians' with the damp, tropical forests providing an ideal environment for the radiation of these water dependent creatures. The forests themselves saw the development of the first tree-sized plants and the Upper Carboniferous was noted for the abundance of the giant pteridophytes and the seed ferns.

A typical scene from the Lower Carboniferous would depict a reef community, with numerous organisms flourishing in the warm clear waters of a shallow sea. Rugose corals formed a major part of the reef structure with colonial genera occupying the core of the reef and large single corals the reef slopes. Large brachiopods such as the productids and strophomenids occurred within the community, as did the delicate colonies of the lace-like bryozoan *Fenestella*. Numerous species of bivalve flourished on the reef slopes and it is likely that some small trilobites occurred on the calcium-rich substrate. Algae and crinoids completed the benthic fauna but in the open waters around the reef, nautiloids, goniatites and bony fish fed on an abundance of organic debris. In the upper zones strong wave and current action would have brought about the natural selection of more hardy species. Whilst in deeper waters the variety of organisms would be greater as a response to a more stable environment.

Caninia was one of the largest rugose corals. It was a solitary form, with strong radial septa and numerous dissepiments in the outer areas of the elongate, calcareous skeleton.

Pustula pustulosa. During the Lower Carboniferous numerous productids such as this were present in shallow water communities. Some like *Gigantoproductus* grew to enormous size and probably lived like the great clams of the present day.

Corals galore

The fossil record of the rugose, stony corals, shows that by the Carboniferous period they had already experienced several phases of diversification and contraction. These may have been linked with ecological conditions and often the changes in representation meant the appearance of more specialized organisms. In the Lower Carboniferous, shelf seas advanced over low lying regions and their warm, shallow waters presented an ideal environment for a new burst of coral evolution. Many genera of the Carboniferous were characterized by the presence of a solid or complex, web-like structure in the centre of their skeletons, and it is thought that this development provided the soft parts with a more secure hold. Both compound and solitary species flourished at this time.

No rugose corals occurred on the tidal flats of the Carboniferous coastlines and this environment was left to the persistent and tolerant stromatolitic algae. Offshore, however, the corals were important components of many communities and different genera can be used as indicators of depth and general environment. Large

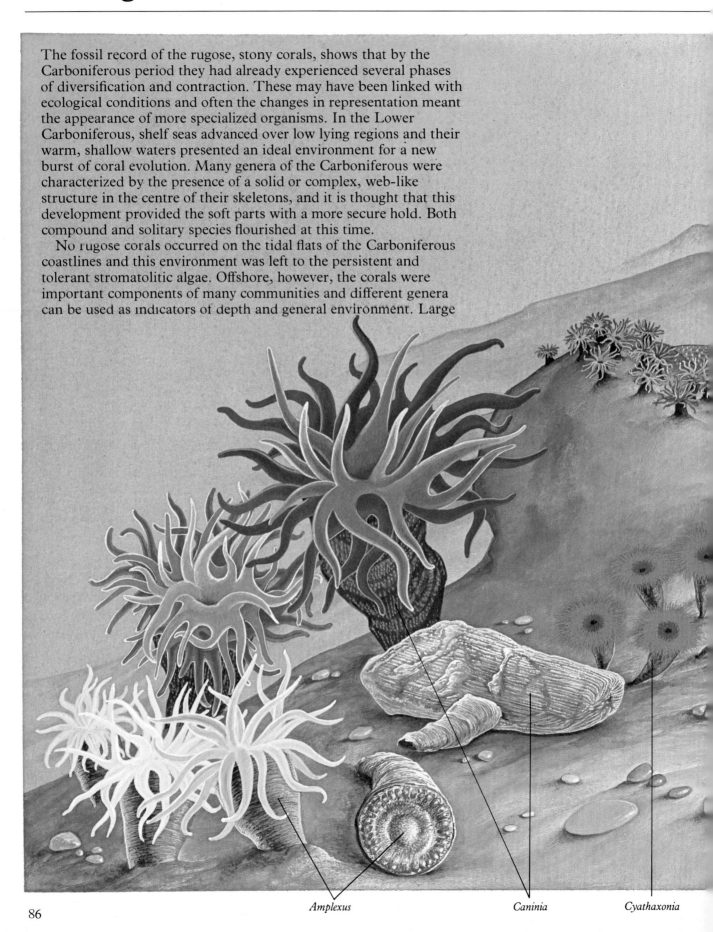

Amplexus   *Caninia*   *Cyathaxonia*

These corals are typical representatives of Lower Carboniferous communities and although they did not necessarily occur within exactly the same time zone, they do represent the variety that existed during the sub-period. They also give a good indication of the relationship between form and environment. Temperature, food abundance, wave and current action and sediment type were all factors in the distribution of specific genera.

solitary forms are good indicators of very shallow water and reef slopes, whilst the larger compound corals are mostly found in reef associations. In deeper waters the presence of small horn-shaped corals may reflect difficulties in obtaining food supplies. Apart from the rugose corals, various tabulates such as *Syringopora* were also common to the reef communities.

stomatolite domes

Michelinia

Palaeosmilia

Lithostrotion

Lonsdaleia

Lithostrotion

Dividing the Carboniferous

In terms of absolute time the Carboniferous period lasted 65 million years, from 345 million to 280 million years ago. Geologists in Europe divide the period into Lower and Upper sub-periods, whilst their American colleagues apply the names Mississippian and Pennsylvanian respectively to strata of roughly the same age. The Carboniferous of Europe is noted for the occurrence of three major sedimentary units, in which the general characteristics of the rocks indicate marine, deltaic and swamp environments. The marine environments are represented by the shallow-water limestones and shales of the Lower Carboniferous. This is sub-divided on the basis of the corals, brachiopods and goniatites that thrived in the seas which transgressed over large areas of the continental land mass. The deposits of the deltaic and swamp environments constitute the Upper Carboniferous sub-period, in which the corals and brachiopods are replaced first, by goniatites and then, by plants and non-marine bivalves, as the important zone fossils.

In many areas of eastern North America, geologists can recognize the presence of similar conditions to those that prevailed in Europe during both the Lower and Upper Carboniferous. But in some western and central regions of that great continent marine environments characterized much of the Pennsylvanian period. In these areas single-celled protozoans and other marine organisms assumed importance as major zone fossils. Marine conditions also existed in parts of Asia, at this time, and once again zonation of sub-division is based on the use of protozoans.

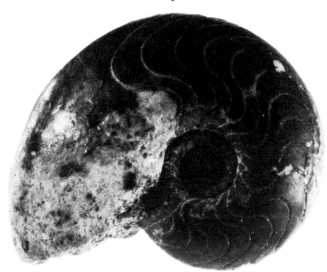

Goniatitic ammonoids are characterized by the presence of a septal suture line which is folded into forward-directed saddles and receding troughs or lobes. *Mantioceras* and other goniatites are used in the sub-division of the Namurian and Lower Westphalian rocks of Europe.

Below
Non-marine bivalves such as *Carbonicola* are important zone fossils in the Upper Carboniferous – Westphalian – Stephanian of Europe.

The Carboniferous is divided into two major sub-periods the Lower (Mississippian) and the Upper (Pennsylvanian). In many areas of Europe and North America the Lower Carboniferous is noted for the deposition of marine limestones and shales, whilst the Upper Carboniferous is known for deltaic and coal measure swamp deposits. These environments supported different faunas and floras, important representatives of which are used for zonation and correlation. The column on the left-hand side of the diagram lists the various sub-divisions of the Carboniferous in Europe whilst the other columns indicate the important zone fossils.

| Age | Period | Series | Marine animals | | Non-marine animals |
			Corals Brachiopods	Goniatites	Non-marine bivalves
280	Upper Carboniferous (Pennsylvanian)	Stephanian			
290		Westphalian		Gastrioceras	Anthracosphaerium Anthracosia Carbonicola
315 325	Lower Carboniferous (Mississippian)	Namurian		Gastrioceras Reticuloceras Homoceras Eumorphoceras	
360		Dinantian	Dibunophyllum Seminula Caninia Cleistopora Zaphrentis	Posidonia Beyrichoceras	

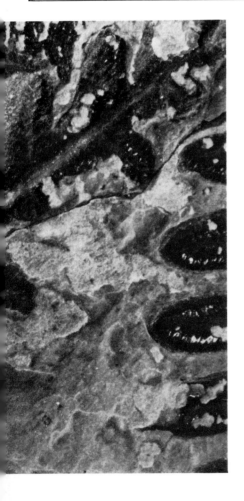

Left
A coal measure plant – *Alethopteris* – plants are used in the sub-division of the Upper Carboniferous Westphalian – Stephanian.

Above
Dibunophyllum, a medium to large size solitary coral which is easily recognizable because of the complex nature of its axial area. It is a relatively short-lived genus and a useful stratigraphic tool.

Swampland forests

The swampland forests of the Carboniferous were probably stratified in much the same way as the great tropical forests of Borneo today. The upper levels of growth were dominated by *Lepidodendron*, a scale tree, whilst *Calamites* and other horsetails occupied the next layer. True ferns, seed ferns and smaller horsetails provided a dense cover in the drier regions of the swamps. The likely acidic nature of the peat-rich substrate probably suited the great pteridophytes but one wonders whether or not it increased to such concentrations that would have ultimately led to their extinction! Coniferales, such as *Cordaites*, were also part of the swampland flora.

Lithomantis, a member of the Palaeodictyoptera

Sigillaria, a scale tree

Lepidodendron, a giant scale tree which produced large spore-producing structures. These are known independently as *Lepidostrobus*.

Ptychocarpus, a true fern.

A cockroach (Blattodea).

Sphenophyllum, a horsetail, in which the leaves were carried in whorls. The smaller horsetails filled a niche similar to that occupied by the modern day rushes.

Eogyrinus, was a large, rather primitive amphibian that flourished in the waters of the swamps. Individuals attained lengths of up to 4·5 metres. *Eogyrinus* had a long fish-like tail and rather short limbs.

Meganeura, a giant flying insect which closely resembles the living dragonflies.

Cordaites, ancestrial to the true conifer.

an early arachnid

Hylonomus, a small captorhinomorph reptile.

The formation of coal

Many of the major coal fields of the world are a reflection of the great swampland forests that dominated the upper part of the Carboniferous period. The swamps developed mostly along flat-lying coastlines where rivers had formed broad estuaries and large deltas. An accumulation of plant debris took place in the waters of the swamp, which were rather stagnant and with little free oxygen. The decay of the plant material was therefore incomplete and many leaves and stem fragments retained much of their original character. Many compounds disintegrated or responded to fermentation, however, and gradually a peat was formed. Often the accumulation of plant materials was arrested by a change in conditions brought about by an incursion of a river or sea waters, consequently covering the peat with deltaic or marine sediments. In time the flood waters would recede and a cover of vegetation would gradually edge its way back across the poorly drained and barren lands. Between the deposition of the flood deposits and the development of a new peat, a soil cover essential to plant growth, would have developed. In many areas these can be identified by their friable texture and the presence of *in situ* roots.

The accumulation of peat and the deposition of deltaic and marine deposits was cyclic and gradually a great thickness of sediments would build up. The first formed peats would be buried deeper and deeper and subjected to gradual increases in both temperature and pressure. Water within the peat would be driven out and the deposits consolidated. Over a long period of time this would result in the first-formed 'soft' coals such as lignite, continually changing in rank, becoming harder with a higher carbon content. The highest ranked coals are the anthracites and these are characterized by their vitreous appearance and a conchoidol fracture.

The incursion of the sea over the coal-forming swamps is reflected in the deposition of fine-grained shales and siltstones. These form distinct horizons, usually referred to as 'marine bands', which contain a restricted fauna of mainly bivalves, goniatites and inarticulate brachiopods.

The coal seam itself represents the accumulation of plant material over a long period of time. Often it is possible to recognize the remains of leaves and stem fragments in the familiar domestic 'house' coals.

Seat-earths, ganisters and fire-clays are terms applied to the fossil soils found in association with coal seams. Whereas the coal itself represents the accumulation of plant debris, the seat-earth marks the former position of the swamp floor.

The deltaic component of a coal cycle is reflected in the deposition of essentially barren sands and grits. Often the deltaic sediments fill large channels cut into the lower-lying sediments and are characterized by cross-stratification.

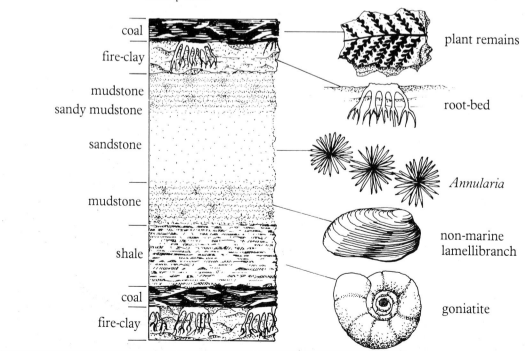

coal — plant remains
fire-clay

mudstone
sandy mudstone — root-bed

sandstone

— *Annularia*

mudstone

— non-marine lamellibranch

shale

coal

fire-clay — goniatite

Bottom
Gastrioceras.
A Palaeozoic ammonoid of the sub-order Goniatitina. The species *G. listeri* and *G. cumbrience* are used as zone fossils for the Namurian of north west Europe.

Below left
Annularia, a sphenopsid plant from the Upper Carboniferous.

Below right
Calamites, a jointed-stem plant is commonly found in Carboniferous coal measures.

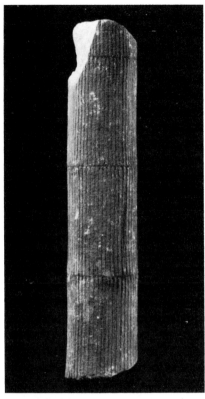

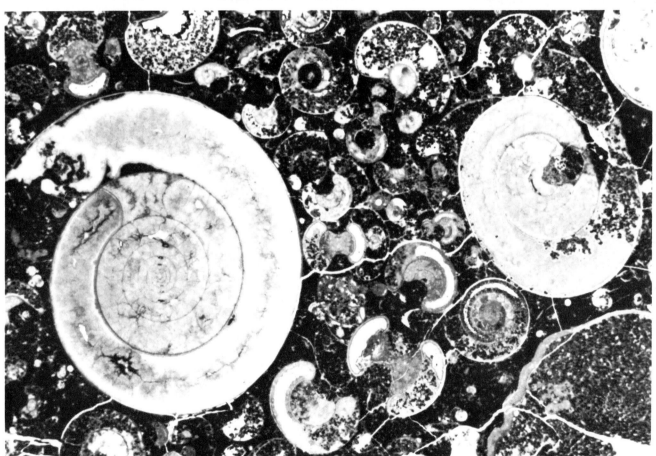

The age of amphibians

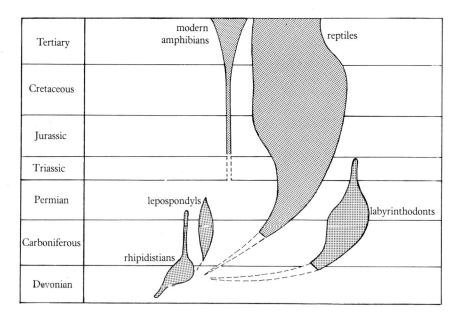

Tertiary	modern amphibians		reptiles
Cretaceous			
Jurassic			
Triassic			
Permian	lepospondyls		labyrinthodonts
Carboniferous	rhipidistians		
Devonian			

The various ancestral links between the rhipidistian, lobe-finned fishes and the amphibians are shrouded in the mists of time. It is likely that the two major amphibian stocks arose independently from a *Eusthenopteron*-like ancester and, strangely, either group could have provided the ancestors for both the modern amphibians and the reptiles.

Although *Ichthyostega* appeared in the Upper Devonian, the real radiation of the amphibians is not recorded until Upper Carboniferous times. The amphibian story during the Lower Carboniferous is obscured due to the transgression of the shallow seas over the continental margins and the absence of swampland and other terrestrial deposits in the stratigraphic record of this sub-period. Some discoveries in North America and southern Scotland do provide evidence of a continuing presence, with *Otocratia* having a similar skull structure to the first amphibian. Another representative of the amphibians in the Lower Carboniferous was *Pholidogaster*, one of the earliest recorded anthracosaurs. *Pholidogaster* was an aquatic form with small limbs and a strong tail which was used during swimming. It grew to just over a metre in length and is thought to have been the ancestor of the many anthracosaurs that flourished in the Late Carboniferous and Permian. The small and snake-like lepospondyls were also represented in the Lower Carboniferous.

By the Upper Carboniferous the seas had withdrawn from many areas and large deltas and swamps characterized the ancient shorelines of North America and Europe. In these new environments the amphibians flourished with many species growing to large sizes. The anthracosaurs were now divided into two major groups with *Diplovertebron*, a small animal, representing the ancestral stock and *Eogyrinus (Pteroplax)*, a large aquatic form, a more specialized side branch. *Eogyrinus* grew to over 4·5 metres in length and it filled the role of a major predator. Other large swamp dwellers included *Loxomma* and *Megalocephalus*, which were characterized by the labyrinthine structure of their teeth. *Megalocephalus* was a heavily built creature, with a broad skull and strong limbs. It fed along the edges of the swamps, where it also laid its 'spawn'.

Ophiderpeton, *Sauropleura* and *Microbrachis* represented the small lepospondylon amphibians

---

Amphibians need water!

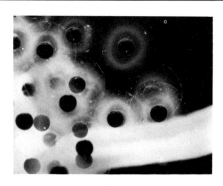

Although many modern amphibians have perfected methods of protecting both eggs and young they are still 'primitive' when compared with either the reptiles or the mammals. Most amphibians must lay their eggs in water, where they hatch into tadpoles or larvae with feathery external gills. In time the tadpoles develop legs and lungs and lose their long fish-like tails and gills. The change is termed metamorphosis and it results in a tiny, but well formed, frog, toad or newt. The spawn of the female amphibian is also usually fertilized in water and therefore the dependency of these animals on what is essentially a protective medium, really does earn them the title of the 'sham conquerors', which was attributed to the group by an eminent zoologist.

during the Upper Carboniferous. *Ophiderpeton* had a snake-like body in which the limbs had been completely lost, it grew to 0·7 metres in length, and up to 200 vertebrae were present in the backbone. *Sauropleura* bore a superficial resemblance to *Ophiderpeton* but unlike its cousin it retained some vestiges of very reduced limbs. Both animals swam with eel-like movements of the body, with the smaller *Sauropleura* (16 centi-

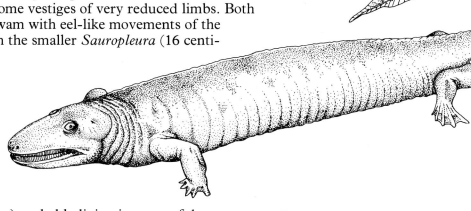

metres long) probably living in areas of dense vegetation. *Sauropleura* was related to the grotesque horned amphibian *Diplocaulus* of the Permian which was a pond dweller with strongly developed limbs. In *Microbrachis* the limbs were small but well formed and it is likely that this tiny (12 centimetres long) lepospondyl spent much of its time hiding under stones and in the broken stumps of trees. Some amphibians of the Upper Carboniferous possessed external gills like those of the *Axolotl*, but unlike this modern amphibian the 'branchiosaurs' were found to be the larval stages of labyrinthodont animals.

Eogyrinus or *Pteroplax*, as it is frequently called, was one of the major predators of the Upper Carboniferous swamplands. It grew to over 4·5 metres in length and its long weak-limbed body was pushed through the water by the side to side movements of the tail. Like many Carboniferous amphibians *Eogyrinus* had labyrinthodont teeth similar to those found in some of the lobe-finned fishes.

Microbrachis, a tiny miscrosaurian lepospondyl from the Upper Carboniferous (Pennsylvanian) of Europe. The microsaurs possessed only three fingers on each hand. Strangely, the name means 'little lizards'.

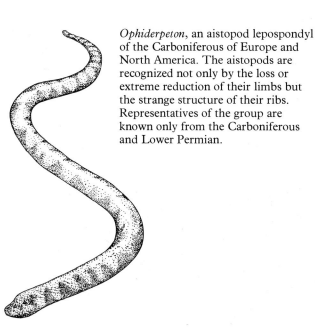

Ophiderpeton, an aistopod lepospondyl of the Carboniferous of Europe and North America. The aistopods are recognized not only by the loss or extreme reduction of their limbs but the strange structure of their ribs. Representatives of the group are known only from the Carboniferous and Lower Permian.

The first reptiles

There is little doubt that environmental changes and competition are key factors in evolution. They encourage modifications which sooner or later lead to the origin and diversification of new forms of life. Some modifications may be painstakingly small and of little apparent significance but others herald the arrival of major groups such as the fish, amphibians and reptiles. In the case of the last of these, the initial scene was acted out in swampland environments of the Early Carboniferous and the competition was between different groups of amphibians. The struggle was for food and territory and, naturally, the larger or more voracious forms were dominant. Small amphibians were forced to take shelter in the drier marginal regions of the swamps and, because of this, they developed a method of protecting their eggs against dessication. This protection took the form of a strong membrane or shell which allowed the embryo to develop within a controlled environment; the yolk providing an essential source of food.

The first animal to lay such an egg was the earliest reptile and it is likely that it had also lost the soft moist skin of the typical amphibian. The amniote egg and scaly skins are typical reptilian characters but their discovery in the fossil record is a rare occurrence. The identification of the first

reptile is therefore based on the bones of its skeleton. The reduction in the number of skull bones and changes in the structure of limbs and girdles are important clues. One of the oldest known reptiles is *Hylonomus*, a small rather lizard-like creature from the Middle Carboniferous of Nova Scotia, Canada. *Hylonomus* has been discovered in the fossilized tree trunks of the Joggins formation and it would appear that this association actually represented their normal habitat. This was similar to that projected for the proto-reptile mentioned above and it is possible that in this case, the egg had actually moved onto land before the animal!

The conquest of the land was made possible only by the significant advances in form and function witnessed in the reptiles. These included the development of a scaly skin to prevent dessication, fertilization inside the body of the female and the evolution of the amniote egg. The latter enabled the young to develop within its own watery environment. It contained its own food store, the yolk, and was enclosed within a protective shell.

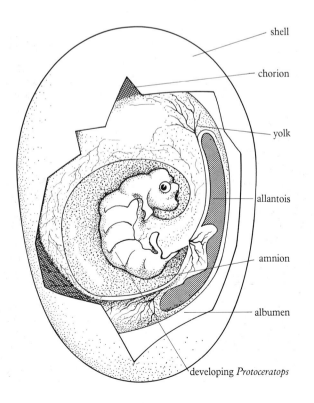

shell

chorion

yolk

allantois

amnion

albumen

developing *Protoceratops*

Hylonomus is found in association with other reptiles and it would appear that two major groups had already separated from a common ancestral stock. *Hylonomus* was the forerunner of the anapsid reptiles, a group characterized by a simple skull; the bony cover of which was only pierced by the holes of the eyes and the nostrils. The only living representatives of the anapsid line are the turtles and tortoises, but in the Permian the stem reptiles or cotylosaurs were a dominant group.

Hylonomus was a small stem reptile from the Middle Carboniferous, individuals grew to approximately 20 centimetres in length.

Some of the descendents of *Hylonomus* were still small but others such as *Scutosaurus* attained a length of 2 to 3 metres. It was a pareiasaur and like many of its relatives it was a huge, lumbering creature with a grotesque facial appearance. It seems strange that a creature such as this should have to lay eggs in some secluded area!

When disturbed the Bearded Lizard from Australia will expand its scaly frill as a defensive display. In the hot arid regions where it lives the frill or beard may also serve as a cooling device.

Ancient glaciers and warm-blooded animals

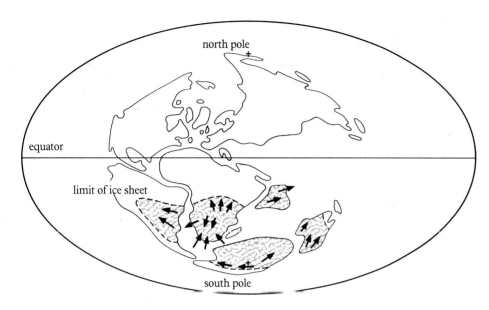

During the Upper Carboniferous – earliest Permian a large area of Gondwanaland was covered by ice-sheets. The Permo-Carboniferous south pole is indicated and the arrows indicate the general directions of ice movement.

The ice-sheets of the Late Carboniferous and Permian of Gond-wanaland covered most of Antarctica, Australia and India, as well as the southern areas of the great African and South American continents. The ice-sheets were comparable in area with those of the last ice age and evidence exists for the centres of origin being in south-west Africa and the eastern region of Antarctica. As a result glacial deposits are widespread over large areas of the southern continents. These consist of classic glacial tillites or unstratified sediments often with a clay matrix and a poorly sorted pebble-boulder fraction. Other evidence for glaciation includes the polished surfaces of Precambrian basalts plus striations caused when rock fragments within the ice are dragged over rock surfaces. Roche moutonnées were also formed when the ice moved away from the

The evidence for glaciation during the Permo-Carboniferous includes glacial striations, polished rock surfaces, roche moutonnées and thick deposits of the unstratified, poorly sorted sediments known as tillites.

tillite

98

centres of origin, across regions with resistant rock masses. These were smoothed and rounded on the up-valley side to give a gentle slope whilst on the down-valley side the rocks were shattered and broken to give an irregular surface. The glaciation of Gondwanaland reached a maximum in the earliest Permian and by late Permian times coal-forming swamps covered great areas of the southern part of the super-continent.

The mammal-like reptiles of the Late Permian of Gondwanaland possessed a bone microstructure similar to that of the mammals. The communities in which they lived also had a low predator-prey ratio compared with those of earlier or contemporary tropical reptilian associations and the argument is that animals such as *Anteosaurus* and other therapsids were warm-blooded.

The climatic changes from Late Carboniferous – earliest Permian glacial, to Late Permian sub-tropics was to affect the distribution of vertebrate faunas. No large vertebrates have been discovered in the early Permian rocks of the glacial regions of Gondwanaland, for the evidence of a sail-backed pelycosaur/amphibian communities is restricted to the, then, tropical regions of south-western North America and Europe. In the Upper Permian large reptile faunas were still confined to the tropics, but evidence for mammal-like reptile communities exists in South Africa and Zambia. According to some experts the climate was still quite cold in these regions and the presence of the mammal-like reptiles proves that these animals had acquired some mechanism for controlling their body temperature. The bones of their skeletons, like those of mammals, had many blood vessels passing through them and evidence exists for a hairy coat which prevented heat loss. This, in association with a low predator-prey ratio within the communities, argues for these creatures being the first truly warm-blooded animals and it is likely that the great glaciations of the Permo-Carboniferous were instrumental in their evolution.

The Permian

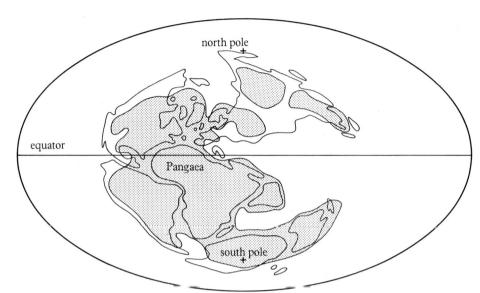

The palaeogeographic reconstruction of the Permian world shows the presence of the supercontinent Pangaea, originally named by Alfred Wegener in 1915. The coming together of the continental masses resulted in a deepening of the oceans and a withdrawal of the shallow marine seas from the continental margins. As a result the Permian terrestrial climates were more severe than those of earlier periods. Mass extinctions were the result of both marine regression and climatic change.

In his book, *The Origin of Continents and Oceans* published in 1915, the German meteorologist Alfred Wegener proposed that all the continents were once joined as a single land mass. Wegener named the supercontinent Pangaea and dated its existence as pre-Mesozoic. His theory was based on palaeontological and geological data and although the publication and subsequent translation of the book into English caused a great furore, Wegener's ideas successfully laid the foundations for the now sophisticated study of continental drift. Some scientists doubt the existence of Pangaea, claiming that the evidence supports the concept of two separate land masses: Gondwanaland and Laurasia. However, similarities between the Triassic faunas of Laurasia and Gondwanaland support the theory of a link or bridge between the two and it would appear that the connection was actually made in Permian times. Pangaea lives! From a geographical viewpoint, the south pole was sited in southern Antarctica throughout the period and the equator cut across Mexico, Florida and north Africa.

Permian life

With the formation of the supercontinent, the oceans of the world increased in depth and the seas withdrew from the edges of the land. Around the equator, many terrestrial regions were characterized by deserts and evaporitic basins, whilst to the south and north great forests flourished in various regions at different times. On Gondwanaland the general trend was for the forests to spread south with time; the great *Glossopteris* flora of the Early Permian of Argentina, migrating into South Africa and Antarctica during the upper part of the period. The plants of the *Glossopteris* flora were wet-land dwellers with sharp differentiations in their growth rings indicating that they were also adapted to cold environments. To the north, in Siberia, the Angaran flora exhibited similar adaptations, whilst the Euamerian flora of the equatorial regions was adapted to warm, equable, all-year-round conditions. Sail-backed pelycosaurs, cotylosaurs and amphibians thrived in the equatorial belt, whilst the warm blooded therapsids evolved to meet the challenge of the colder southern lands. Around the equator limestones and evaporites were deposited in shelf seas and in coastal basins, with some regions showing a cyclic succession of marine and evaporitic sediments. In northern Europe the Zechstein sea lay east of Britain and across Holland and north Germany. It was highly saline and apart from an early barrier reef community in the earliest part of the period the fauna was extremely restricted. In western and central North America and parts of Australia normal marine conditions prevailed for much of the Permian period. The communities in these regions were, to some extent, extensions of those of the Carboniferous, although certain invertebrate stocks including the coral-like brachiopods and crinoids reached new peaks of diversity. Many Palaeozoic stocks were missing from these communities, with the tabulate stony corals and the stromatoporoids having little or no representation in some of the great reefs that developed.

It is difficult to illustrate in diagrammatic form the true nature of the mass extinctions that took place during the Permian. The groups shown here are of various taxonomic levels (i.e. families or orders) and therefore little justice can be done to the true record of the hundreds and thousands of genera and species that vanished during the last 32 million years of the Permian period. The end of the Permian and the mass extinctions of the various organisms mark the close of the Palaeozoic Era.

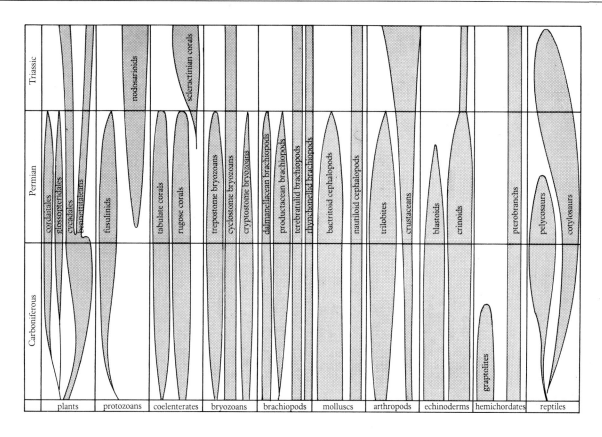

Mass extinctions

The demise of the tabulate corals and the stromatoporoids was part of a much greater happening, in which the number of marine invertebrate families was halved between the beginning and the end of the Permian period. This decimation of a significant fraction of the world's marine life represents one of the greatest mass extinctions of all time, with little or no selection involved. Many causes have been suggested for the disappearance of various organisms but it is probable that this mass extinction was indubitably linked with the withdrawal of shallow marine seas from the continental margins. It has been calculated that by the end of the Permian, these seas had been reduced to almost a third of their original Early Permian coverage. This had the effect of reducing the habitats available for occupation and therefore of increasing competition and predation. Linked with isolation this would have presented many families with insurmountable problems and the probability of extinction was greatly increased. Some of the more archaic stocks were already poorly represented in the Carboniferous and the dramatic changes of the following 55 million years were to prove too much. The withdrawal of the seas also reduced the supply of food from the

near-shore regions and as a result breaks in the food-chain would naturally have a great effect on the primary consumers and predators. By the end of the Permian the major groups that had disappeared included the tabulate and rugose stony corals, the stromatoporoids and the trilobites, the fusulinid protozoans, many bryozoans (trepostomes and cryptostomes), the productid brachiopods and large numbers of crinoids and ammonoids. Considering the importance of the productids and crinoids in the Permian reef communities their extinction must have been quite sudden; new replacements for the extinct groups did not appear until an expansion of the shallow marine seas occurred in the Triassic.

The withdrawal of the seas from the continental margins also changed the terrestrial climate with humidity and temperatures showing considerable fluctuation. Ice-sheets and deserts characterized the Permian world and, in many ways, the extinctions of large numbers of amphibians and reptiles can be linked with the changes in sea level. Significant changes in flora also took place during the Permian and once again the extinction of several plant groups can be related to the harmful biological effects which occurred as the result of continental accretion.

Truly fit for the land

Approximately 300 million years ago, or 90 million years after the appearance of the primitive *Cooksonia*, the gymnosperms or 'naked-seed' plants had begun to dominate world floras. Seed-ferns, cordaitales, ginkgoes and true conifers were present with the last two truly representing a further step in the conquest of the terrestrial environment. The cordaitales as we know had existed since Upper Devonian times and they were to reach the acme of their development in the Upper Carboniferous. They were the ancestors of the conifers and ginkgoes and in some ways it is difficult to separate certain specialized cordaitales from their descendants. As in the advanced lycopods, including the living *Selaginella*, the cordaitales and true conifers produce two types of spores, the smaller of which, in the gymnosperms, is carried in the wind as grains of pollen. Unlike *Selaginella*, the spores of the cordaitales and true conifers were developed in separate male and

female cones, with the fertilization of the 'egg' depending on the arrival of the microscopic pollen grain. In the cordaitales, the male and female cones consisted of a main axis bearing two distinct lines of leaf bracts, whereas those of the more advanced conifers have a definite spiral arrangement. Their female cones of the conifers are distinctly woody with the individual scales resulting from leaf modification. Cordaitalean seeds were also of a more simple construction than those of the true conifers although limited evidence for the existence of a living and of flotational devices does exist. The seeds are the result of the division and growth of the fertilized 'egg' and in the living conifers we can observe that the seed with its own food store and wind dispersal mechanism, must have been a major advance over the more primitive 'alteration of generations' characteristic of the lycopods, horsetails and ferns.

The more advanced cones and seeds of the

In the Upper Palaeozoic conifers and ginkgoes had become important components of most floras and they existed alongside their cordaitalean ancestors. New adaptations related to reproduction and overall structure were to prove of immense value to the 'new' gymnosperms in a changing world. By the end of the Permian they had totally replaced their more 'primitive' ancestors.

The reproductive methods of the conifers are clearly a major advance over those of the psilopsids, ferns and lycopods. The development of a seed with its own food store and wing, for wind dispersal, were important steps in the true colonization of the terrestrial environment.

Reproductive cycle of a conifer

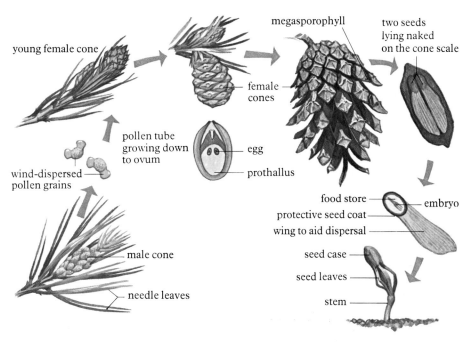

the huge, silicified tree trunks discovered in Upper Permian have in the past been associated with this genus. Unfortunately little evidence for this exists and it is likely that *Noeggerathiopis* had vanished from the southern continents by the end of the Lower Permian. Unlike the cordaitaleans the branches of these early conifers were not arranged in a crown at the top of the tree and this may have been an important factor ensuring that 100 per cent pollination took place. The wood of the early conifers was similar to that of their ancestors but a well-developed root structure ensured that their 'step' onto land was not an insecure and temporary one.

conifers must have given them a similar advantage over their cordaitalean ancestors. For, by the end of the Carboniferous, they were beginning to replace their more archaic ancestors in world floras. All cordaitaleans were extinct by the end of the Permian whereas the conifers were to undergo a considerable radiation and emerge with the ginkgoes as one of the dominant plant group of Triassic, Jurassic and early Cretaceous floras.

In the Late Palaeozoic the conifers were already separated into geographic groupings with the ancient Tethyan ocean acting as a natural barrier. Experts recognise two groupings based on generic membership, with the northern Laurasian group being characterized by the presence of *Lebachia* and *Ernestiodendron* and the Gondwana group by *Buriada*, *Walkomiella* and *Noeggerathiopis*. In the Late Palaeozoic three distinct floras have been recognized and it would appear that the conifers had or were adapting to a whole range of climatic conditions. Of the genera mentioned above *Lebachia* and *Ernestiodendron* have been likened to the living Norfolk Island Pine – *Araucaria heterophylla*, in that their branches occurred in whorls of five or six around the main trunk. The leaves of the ancient genera were unique, however, in that their tips were divided into two. Both male and female cones were borne on the same plant. *Noeggerathiopis*, a southern conifer, possessed large leaves with a parallel variation and many of

The first ginkgoes are recorded from strata of Permo-Carboniferous age. Unlike the conifers the branches of mature ginkgoes were arranged in open, spreading crowns and the leaves were usually broad and fan-shaped with a delicate, regularly branching variation. It is assumed that, like the conifers, they evolved from cordaitalean ancestors and that together they represent two distinct lines of evolution. In *Ginkgo biloba* palaeobotanists have a rival to the changeless *Lingula*, as the species has remained the same for almost 200 million years. As with the conifers, the ginkgoes were to thrive in Mesozoic floras until a rapidly changing world and the expansion of the flowering plants was to restrict their representation to the persistent *G. biloba*.

Small but extremely useful

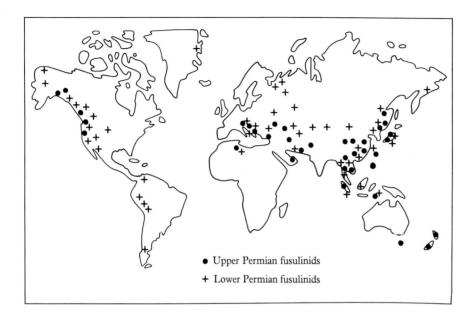

The distributions of specific fusulinids in Permian sediments, have allowed palaeontologists to reconstruct possible faunal provinces and migration routes that existed over 225 million years ago (after Hallam, 1973).

● Upper Permian fusulinids

+ Lower Permian fusulinids

Although the ancestry of the single-celled animals (protozoans) can be traced back into the Cryptozoic or the 'age of hidden life', their representation in the early and middle periods of the Palaeozoic era is somewhat restricted. In the Upper Carboniferous and Permian this changed with the appearance of several new groups of protozoans with calcareous skeletons (foraminiferids). Amongst these were the fusulinids which reached the peak of their development in the Permian. The fusulinids were unusually large for

Diagrammatic sections of the genus *Fusulinia* show the complex internal character of this fusulinid foraminiferid. Changes in the shape of the shell, and in the form of the elongate plates (septa) which lie parallel to the axis are but two of the important evolutionary trends that take place within fusulinids.

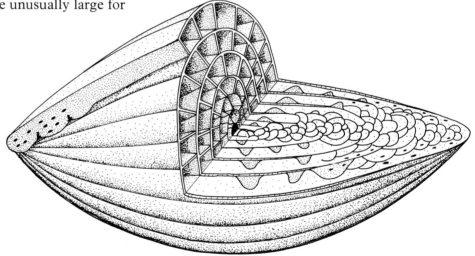

foraminiferids with the largest shells reaching 60 millimetres in length. The shells were generally cylindrical in shape and tapered at both ends. Internally they were rather complex, with these structures rapidly changing in character during the last 60 million years or so of the Palaeozoic era. Numerous genera and species of fusulinids are known and in general they were thought to have lived in shallow, off-shore environments. In some regions of the United States some limestones are made up almost entirely of fusulinid tests.

The rapid evolution and wide distribution of the fusulinids makes them extremely useful as zone or index fossils in the Upper Carboniferous (Pennsylvanian) and Permian periods of Eurasia and the central and western regions of the United States. Geologists have discovered that the distribution of certain genera and species provides evidence of distinct faunal provinces within the Pacific and Tethyan Oceans during the Permian. Migration routes for particular species have also been established.

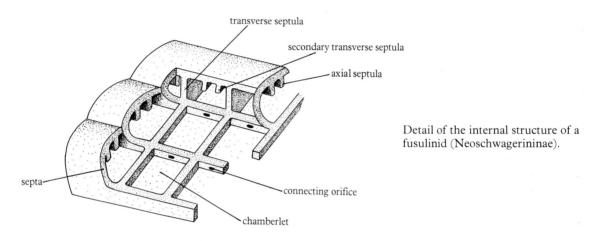

Detail of the internal structure of a fusulinid (Neoschwagerininae).

The evolution of the fusulinids in the Upper Carboniferous (Pennsylvanian) and the Permian is extremely complex. Our 'family tree' shows only the major types that existed during those times, in spite of its conservatism it does provide information on ancestral ties, stratigraphic distribution and structural variation.

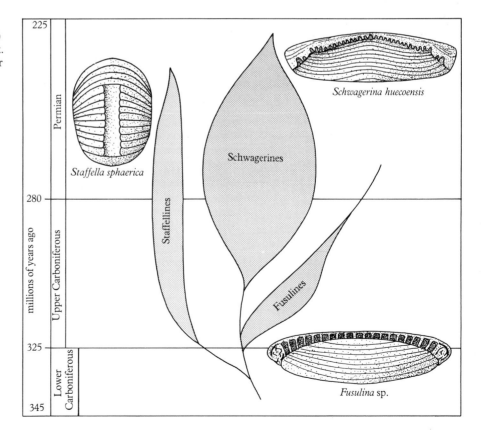

Barrier reefs and enclosed basins

The restorations are of three communities that occurred during the Permian. They represent different environmental conditions found when moving from a land-locked basin into a lagoon and finally onto a barrier reef. Communities such as these were typical of several regions. In the land-locked basin the waters were highly saline due to evaporation and the fauna was restricted to those animals that could tolerate such conditions. The shallow lagoons

Land-locked basin communites have been recorded from North America and Europe. The waters were of high salinity and the fauna restricted to bivalves, gastropods, ostracodes and foraminiferids. The largest of the bivalves was *Schizodus*, an early relative of the well-known Jurassic

form *Trigonia*. *Schizodus* was rather trapezoidal in shape and is known to have burrowed into the sediment. The bottom-dwelling bivalve *Bakevellia* was the most common organism in some communities. Both *Schizodus* and *Bakevellia* are known from mid continental America and Europe.

The lagoonal side of the Permian reefs was characterized by sands made up of the skeletal fragments of algae, molluscans, bryozoans and foraminiferids. These organisms lived on the slopes at the back of the reef where sheets of algae bound the sediments together. The fauna was dominated by bivalves and gastropods although, brachiopods, tolerant of a relatively high salinity were also abundant. The terebratulid brachiopod *Dielasma* was such an animal. The representative of the nautilods was *Peripetoceras*.

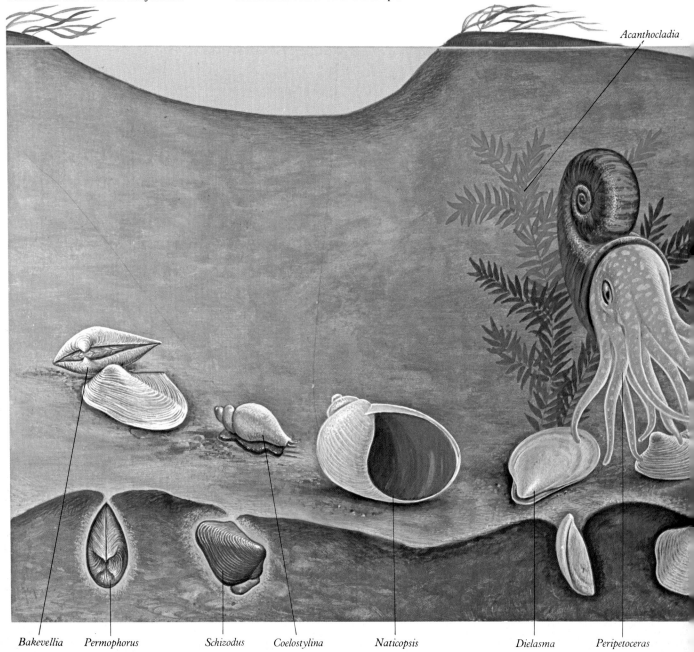

Acanthocladia

Bakevellia   *Permophorus*   *Schizodus*   *Coelostylina*   *Naticopsis*   *Dielasma*   *Peripetoceras*

106

were also subject to high evaporation but constant replenishment from the sea would have kept the overall salinity lower than that in the land-locked area. As a result the fauna on the inland side of the reef itself was relatively diverse. More normal marine conditions prevailed over the reef and the frequent exchange of water with a high oxygen and plankton content positively encouraged the growth of many organisms.

On the reef stromatolitic and red algae together with bryozoans acted as the binding agents. Large productids, bivalves and, in some areas, siliceous sponges encrusted the surface. In the El Capitan reef of the Guadalupe Mountains in Texas, the productids were often bizarre in character and they appear to represent the last 'fling' of a group destined for extinction by the end of the Permian period. The spiny *Cooperoceras* was one of several nautiloids that lived in close proximity of the reef.

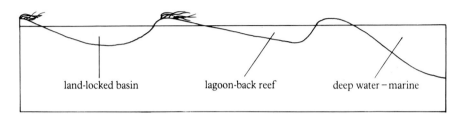

land-locked basin   lagoon-back reef   deep water – marine

Synocladia   *Peripetoceras*

Bakevellia   *Horridonia*   *Fenestella*   *Parallelodon*

Permian amphibians

Reconstruction of an Early Permian fauna

Cacops

Seymouria

Eryops

The early Permian amphibian faunas appear to bear close resemblance to those of the Late Carboniferous. Several well-established stocks remained, whilst others that had made only a minor contribution to life in the Carboniferous undertook considerable expansion. *Archeria* continued the swamp-dwelling habits of its relative *Eogyrinus* and a few rather eel-like nectridians still swam in ponds and lakes. Strange flat-bodied and grotesquely horned nectrideans such as *Diplocaulus* had also appeared. In terms of numbers, however, these amphibians were insignificant and the Lower Permian is noted more for the expansion of the seymouriamorph and rhachitome stocks.

Of the rhachitomes, *Eryops*, a swamp dweller, is the best known. It was rather sturdily built with a flattened skull and individuals grew to over 1·5 metres in length. *Eryops* was a fish-eater; the structure of its body suggesting that it roamed the swamp margins rather than swam in open waters. *Cacops*, a close relative of *Eryops*, had developed armour plates over its back and the indication is that it was more terrestrial in its habits than its

amphibious cousin.

The seymouriamorph amphibians, named after *Seymouria*, from Seymour in Texas, were also more truly terrestrial than earlier forms. Numerous species existed in the Lower Permian and *Diadectes* was so highly specialized that it probably challenged the early reptiles for the right to rule over its terrestrial realm. For an amphibian *Diadectes* was huge having a maximum length of just over 3 metres. Other seymouriamorphs were very small and *Discosauriscus* probably fed on insects. The structure of *Seymouria* and its relatives, is so similar to that of some early reptiles that many palaeontologists believed that these amphibians were the link between the two groups. This question of ancestry is dealt with more fully on the opposite page. By the Upper Permian, however, even the seymouriamorphs could not withstand the combined challenges of the reptiles and the changing climate and although individuals, such as *Kotlassia*, remain the importance of the stock and of the amphibians as a whole was to decline dramatically.

Amphibian or reptile

The form of the long bone in the forelimb (the humerus), the number of bones in the hand and the shape of the shoulder girdle of *Seymouria* and *Diadectes* support the classification of these animals with the reptiles. Other characters suggest that they passed through an aquatic larval stage and this would link them unquestionably with the amphibians. Such is the fine balance between amphibian and reptilian characters that for a long time *Seymouria* was classified with the more advanced of the two groups. It was also considered to be the ideal 'missing link', tying the evolution of reptiles with the labyrinthodont amphibians.

Unfortunately *Seymouria* and its relatives were too late as they did not appear until the Upper Carboniferous – Lower Permian, some tens of millions of years after the true ancestor had actually evolved. The skulls of juvenile seymouriamorphs provide the clues of a larval stage, whilst those of adults show that the slot-like otic notch, which occurs on both sides at the back of the skull, is similar to that found in advanced reptiles. In early reptiles the notch is missing and it is unlikely that a primitive creature such as *Hylonomus* could have arisen from such an advanced stock.

It therefore appears that the seymouriamorphs were specialized amphibians. Some were predators but in others the palate and cheek teeth suggests a plant-eating mode of life. The move towards more terrestrial habits necessitated changes such as a shortening of the jaw, the development of an otic notch and of strong limbs and vertebrae. In making these modification the seymouriamorphs paralleled the reptiles, but they were too set in their own specialized ways to provide the link palaeontologists seek. For this it is likely that we shall have to look at the more primitive labyrinthodonts or even the lepospondyls.

Skeleton of *Seymouria*

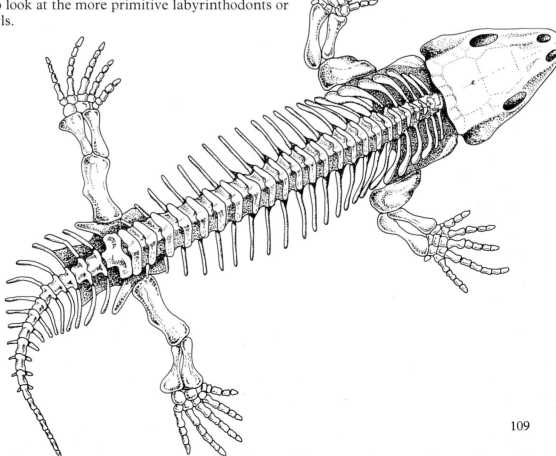

Reptiles dominate the food pyramid

Edaphosaurus, like *Dimetrodon* was a sail-backed synapsid. Its teeth were less differentiated and some were placed on the palatal surface. *Edaphosaurus* was a herbivore that lived on the shore line of lakes and swamps.

Seymouria and *Diadectes* were specialized amphibians that spent much of their life on land.

The sediments of the Lower Permian, Arroyo formation of North America has yielded many vertebrates and sufficient data exists for the reconstruction of a detailed ecological system. Several of the animals discovered in this formation are already known to us, with *Seymouria* and *Diadectes* being truly amphibious in habit. They were the middle-men of the community, for on land the true rulers were the sail-finned reptiles, whilst in the waters *Eryops* fed on a variety of crossopterygian fishes. *Eryops* was essentially a shallow water dweller, the truly aquatic amphibians being the horned *Diplocaulus* and primitive rhachitome *Trimerorhachis*.

In the reconstruction we can recognize four environments ranging from fully aquatic to terrestrial. As in modern community studies it is also possible to recognize various links in the food chain with each link or step being termed a trophic level. The plants were the primary producers within the Arroyo formation community, as they are in most; the various plant-eating invertebrates and vertebrates often acting as primary consumers. The next steps involve the meat-eaters with the sailed *Dimetrodon* ruling as the top predator. Many of the ideas expressed in this illustration are based on the work of the American palaeontologist Everett C. Olson.

Xenacanthus, a fresh-water shark.

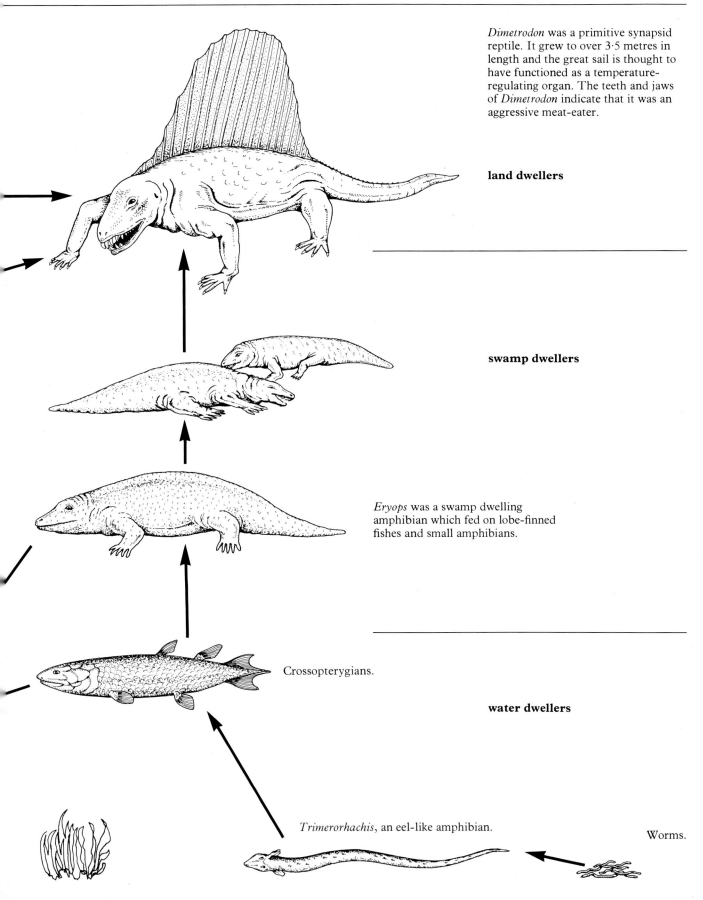

Dimetrodon was a primitive synapsid reptile. It grew to over 3·5 metres in length and the great sail is thought to have functioned as a temperature-regulating organ. The teeth and jaws of *Dimetrodon* indicate that it was an aggressive meat-eater.

land dwellers

swamp dwellers

Eryops was a swamp dwelling amphibian which fed on lobe-finned fishes and small amphibians.

Crossopterygians.

water dwellers

Trimerorhachis, an eel-like amphibian.

Worms.

The Triassic – a changing world

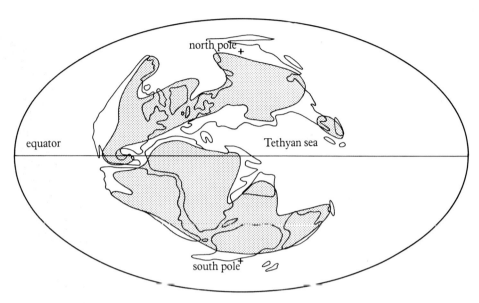

The Triassic was the first of the three Mesozoic periods, the others being the Jurassic and Cretaceous. It lasted approximately 35 million years, beginning 225 million years ago. The supercontinent Pangaea existed for much of this time but by the end of the period the first stages of its break up were well under way. The Triassic was also to witness the return of the shallow continental seas to many regions, although even at their maximum they were still restricted to only two-thirds of the coverage they enjoyed at the beginning of the Permian. The Equator and South Pole had migrated south of their Permian positions and many regions within 30° of the Equator were characterized by deserts and evaporitic basins. Coal-forming forests existed over much of northern Eurasia and southern Gondwanaland and reef knolls bordered the Tethyan sea. Overall the climate of the Triassic was warm and dry and red beds and dune-bedded sandstones are frequent deposits. Unlike the Permian there are no glacial deposits recorded from the Triassic period. Northern Europe experienced minor marine transgressions during mid and late Triassic times but these were essentially overshadowed by scenes of mountains, deserts and playa lakes. Shallow seas surrounded much of western and southern North America and the western shoreline of Tethys stretched from the eastern edge of the Pyrenees down into North Africa.

The Survivors

The persistence of continentality, i.e. Pangaea, during the Early Triassic was to have the effect of restricting the variety of marine organisms during that time. Individual species had survived and a number had taken advantage of the lack of competition to spread throughout the world. Members of many groups of invertebrates were extremely rare, however, and some like the stony corals were not represented. The main survivors of the Permian extinctions were to be found amongst the bivalves and brachiopods although a distinct continuity is also found between Permian and Triassic nautiloids. Amongst the fishes the acanthodians had vanished at the end of the Palaeozoic but both the cartilaginous and lobe-finned fishes, minus the crossopterygians, survived in reduced numbers. The shark *Hybodus* was one cartilaginous fish that existed in both Permian and Triassic periods. Ray-finned fishes continued their dominance of fish faunas from the Upper Palaeozoic into the Triassic. Several amphibian stocks also 'crossed' over the Palaeozoic–Mesozoic boundary and, according to many experts, the reptiles paid scant attention to this significant stratigraphic event.

In the Triassic the conifers and ginkgoes were to continue the evolutionary trends initiated by the cordaitales, none of which were to survive the passing of the Palaeozoic. In the continental lakes algal mounds similar to those of the Precambrian flourished in highly saline waters. Labyrinthodont amphibians such as *Parotosaurus* and *Metoposaurus* continue the line of a once great stock, whilst *Triadobatrachus* is the earliest known representative of the frogs and toads. Terrestrial floras of the Triassic were dominated by the 'naked-seed' plants with the cycads, bennettitaleans, caytonia-ceans and taxaleans all making an appearance by the end of the period.

Phylloceras

During the Triassic a strange group of reptiles, the placodonts, evolved to fill the role of mollusc-eater. They were rather turtle-like in character with the more specialized forms *Placochelys* and *Henodus* having their short bodies encased in a bony shell. The head of the placodonts also showed considerable specialization with the enormous flat teeth covering the inside of the lower jaw and the surface of the palate. The jaws were powerful and in *Placochelys* they were extended as robust pegs which were probably used to prise shells off the sea bottom. In *Placodus* the limbs were little modified but those of *Placochelys* were very similar to the broad paddles of the marine turtles.

New forms of life

The Triassic saw the appearance of many new forms in both marine and terrestrial environments. In the seas the clams and gastropods diversified with the oysters and cockles, limpets, periwinkles and predatory moon-shells becoming common in bottom communities. The cephalopod molluscs in the form of the nautiloids and ammonoids also increased in both numbers and variety; the number of ammonoid genera increasing from nine in the lowest Triassic to over 130 by the beginning of the second half of the period. Amongst these were representatives of a new major ammonoid stock, the phylloceratids. A new group of stony corals, the scleractinians or hexacorals, also appeared during the Triassic. On land the new forms of life were to include both the mammal-like, therapsid reptiles and the archosaurs in the form of the tooth-in-socket thecodontians and their descendents the crocodiles, pterosaurs and dinosaurs. True mammals were also to appear by the end of the period. The struggle for supremacy on land was to be a somewhat frenetic affair with first the therapsids, then the thecodontians and, finally, the dinosaurs ruling terrestrial dynasties. So fierce was the competition that many reptiles became adapted to an aquatic mode of life, with a large number of peg-like teeth arranged along the line of the jaws.

Ammonoids with a goniatitic suture line had virtually disappeared by the dawn of the Mesozoic Era. Their successors were the ceratite ammonoids in which the suture line was characterized by the subdivision of the lobes. The ceratites dominated Upper Permian and early Triassic cephalopod stocks but by the end of the latter period their position had been usurped by more advanced forms with an ammonitic suture line. Such cephalopods had first appeared in the Permian and were characterized by the subdivision of both lobes and saddles into second order folds. The earliest representatives of a major group of ammonites, namely the phylloceratids, appeared during the Triassic, the group takes its name from the genus *Phylloceras*.

The nothosaurs were one of the earliest groups of marine reptiles with their slim bodies resembling those of the plesiosaurs. The skulls were still rather short. Few nothosaurs exceed 1 metre in length and most retained some features of land-dwelling creatures.

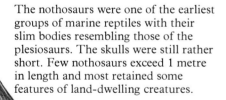

Triassic plants

Araucaria araucana the familiar Monkey Puzzle Tree, is a living representative of the ancient araucaracean pines that flourished during the Mesozoic Era. Many restorations of Triassic and Jurassic floras suggest that the Monkey Puzzle Tree actually lived during that period.

The popular view of arid and bare landscapes as the major feature of the Triassic is essentially true, but it is equally likely that areas of luxuriant vegetation existed in the southern and northern areas of the supercontinent Pangaea. In these regions vestiges of the great *Glossopteris* and Angaran floras survived, with the main elements consisting of gymnosperm genera. Horsetails and lycopods also persisted and it is probable that the southern floras contained representatives of the first flowering plants. Within the gymnosperms, the fern-like fronds, seed-bearing organs and pollen-bearing structures of pteridosperms have been discovered in South Africa, Australia and Argentina and it is probable that the genera to which these belonged were the ancestors of all later cycadopsids (cycads, bennettitaleans and caytonaceans). The last pteridosperms occurred in the Upper Triassic but by the time of their extinction all of their descendant stocks were well established.

The conifers, ginkgoes and yews represent a different line of evolution to that of the cycadopsids. And the persistence of the long ranging araucariaceans and of *Ginkgo biloba* is a testimony to their survival potential. The araucariaceans are represented today by such trees as the Norfolk Island Pine and the Kauris. If the latter is anything to go by, then the Triassic forests were marvellous sights, for the trunks of these great trees form a solid shaft of timber over 60 metres in height. The trunks do not taper and the branches occur towards the top of the tree. Geographically both the Kauris and Araucarian Pines are known only from the Southern Hemisphere and it is likely that their ancestors also preferred warmer climates. Inevitably man has interfered with the normal patterns of distribution and the species *Araucaria araucana*, the Monkey Puzzle tree, is a common sight in many European gardens. The araucariancean trees are thought to represent the most primitive condition amongst the pines although the other five living families have fossil records that date back to the Mesozoic. *Ginkgo biloba*, the Maidenhair Tree, was not the only ginkgoalean of the Triassic and *Sphenobaiera* is more likely to represent the ancestral condition. In this plant the leaves were branched and somewhat rounded in cross-section and the ovules, or female organs, were borne on short branching shoots in the axil of the leaf. At the present time the Maidenhair Tree is cultivated in China and Japan for its edible seeds and one wonders if such plants were not the ideal food source for the herbivorous

dinosaurs that were to emerge in the Middle and Late Triassic. The yews were the last group of conifer-type trees to appear in the Triassic with the genus *Palaeotaxus* being identified by the presence of large single ovules on the end of a female shoot.

Amongst the cycadopsid plants, cycads and bennettitaleans are the best known and, although they both have Triassic representation, they reached their acme during the Jurassic. The cycads of 200 million years ago were supposedly like those of the present day with reconstructions of *Palaeocycas* displaying a crown of leaves at the top of a stout trunk. *Palaeocycas* possessed leaves of a rather simple structure, which were approximately 1 metre in length and 20 centimetres in width. Superficially the leaves of certain cycads and bennettitaleans are similar but closer investigation reveals that the latter have several unique characteristics. *Williamsonia*, known from the Triassic, was approximately 2 metres in height with the leaves occurring in clusters on unevenly distributed branches. The leaves were subdivided into leaflets and in many ways this early bennettitalean resembled its pteridosperm ancestors.

Mammalian ancestors and the first mammal

The family tree of the synapsid reptiles has its roots set in the Carboniferous. At first, groups such as ophiacodants and edaphosaurs were typically reptilian but by the Triassic many therapsids were very similar to their mammalian descendants.

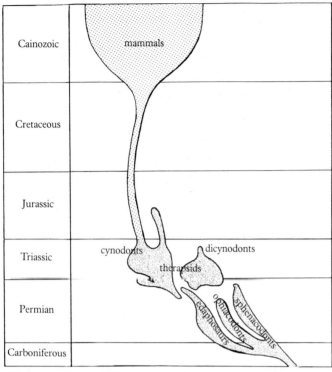

The ancestors of the mammals were synapsid reptiles, the first of which appeared approximately 300 million years ago. The first synapsids are called pelycosaurs and they are well known through the remains of *Dimetrodon* and *Edaphosaurus*. 'Sailed' reptiles were not the sole representatives of the group, however, and *Varanosaurus* and *Ophiacodon* represent the more normal, if somewhat primitive, condition. It is rather interesting that both *Dimetrodon* and *Edaphosaurus* should develop sails, as they belonged to different pelycosaur families and, as

Cynognathus a mammal-like reptile is now thought to have had a furry coat and to have been warm-blooded.

we have seen from our reconstruction of the Arroyo community, had different feeding habits. The sail was a temperature regulation device and its development suggests that both animals represented an experimental stage in the control of body temperature. In life the sail would have been turned 'in the early dawn' towards the sun, and the body temperature and metabolic rate would have risen on the absorption of heat. At mid-day or when the sun was hottest, the animal would place its body in line with the sun's rays and therefore the sail, like a large radiator, would tend to lose heat. The functional benefits of this device would have resulted in a higher rate of activity throughout the day.

The dentition of *Dimetrodon* exhibits greater differentiation than most pelycosaurs and the presence of highly specialized cheek teeth and sharp incisors would indicate the development of a biting and chewing mechanism. This is a character usually associated with mammals, who need to obtain the maximum amount of energy out of their food in the shortest possible period of time. The differentiation of teeth is a feature inherited by the various reptiles that developed from the pelycosaurs. These animals also experimented with the control of their body temperatures, but their control mechanisms were more sophisticated than those of the 'sail-backs'.

The pelycosaurs were replaced in the mid-Permian by the more advanced mammal-like reptiles, the therapsids. In these animals the overall structure of the skeleton is more 'refined' than that of their pelycosaur cousins. The organization of the limbs and of various muscles further

The remains of *Lystrosaurus*, a Triassic dicynodant, have been found in South Africa, Antarctica, Bengal and China. The discoveries are evidence that the continents were once part of the same land mass.

indicates that they had greatly improved upon the primitive sprawling gait of their ancestors. In several genera the skull was rather dog-like in appearance and a further differentiation of teeth was related to an improvement in food processing. Jaw muscles also showed a considerable increase in size and the presence of a secondary palate in the more advanced cynodont and bauriamorph therapsids enabled the individual to feed and breathe at the same time. *Thrinaxodon, Cynognathus* and *Bauria* were meat-eating representatives of the therapsid line. Other genera such as *Dicynodon* and *Moschops* were plant-eaters and, as is often the case in animals of that kind, they were larger than their carnivorous cousins and possessed several dental innovations that enabled them to fully exploit the lush vegetation. In *Dicynodon*, the beak-like jaws were activated by muscles sited forward of the jaw joint and the action was slow and powerful with some rotation that enabled the animal to chew its food over and over again.

The improved mechanics of the limbs and jaws of the therapsids provides evidence of their evolutionary status. Whilst modifications to the ear and reductions in the number of teeth and in

the bones of the hands and feet further indicate their ancestral link with the mammals, these changes are structural, in the sense of skeletal modifications, and provide little evidence as to the way in which the animals controlled their body temperatures. They do, however, suggest a higher metabolic rate. It has been recorded recently that some carnivorous therapsids such as *Thrinaxodon* have small 'whisker' pits on the sides of their snouts. Such pits occur in the mammals, which are, as we know, covered in hair, and therefore it is possible that some therapsids were also furry and warm-blooded. This last point is a mammalian character and is the most refined method of temperature control. The boundary line between the therapsids and mammals is a difficult one to draw and it seems likely that the ability to suckle young was a critical factor.

The first mammals appeared in the Upper Triassic. Surprisingly they were tiny and rather insignificant creatures, the skeletons of which are so delicate, they are rarely well preserved. *Megazostrodon*, one of the first mammals, is well known, however, and the presence of elaborate cusps on the cheek teeth, and of limbs drawn beneath the body, clearly separate it from the therapsids.

Megazostrodon, one of the first mammals

The age of reptiles

The Triassic as a period was notable for the origin and radiation of many reptile families. The dawn of this, the first of the Mesozoic periods, was heralded by the expansion of the mammal-like therapsids but by its close several waves of reptiles had come and gone, and the great dinosaur radiation was well under way. At first the reptiles were either semi-aquatic or terrestrial in habit but soon new stocks were to invade the seas and take to the air.

The end of the Permian period was marked, in terms of vertebrate history, by the extinction of many of the stem reptiles and the pelycosaurs. Only one group of the primitive stem reptiles survived into the Triassic and then only for a limited period of time. The pelycosaurs had been effectively replaced by the more advanced therapsids before the end of the Permian, and the latter group was to flourish, in the absence of competition, for almost 40 million years. The climate of the Triassic was tropical to subtropical throughout most areas, and these conditions were ideal for reptilian life and promoted their diversification.

It is likely that the dominance of the advanced mammal-like reptiles in the early Triassic forced other groups to adopt new modes of life. The Triassic saw the evolution of various euryapsid reptiles including the ichthyosaurs, nothosaurs and placodonts. The term euryapsid applies to the skull and denotes the condition in which a single opening is found high up on each temple. Many euryapsids exhibit a variety of adaptations to aquatic modes of life and their evolution enabled the reptiles to exploit the great food resources of the seas. Other euryapsids evolved to occupy terrestrial and semi-aquatic niches, with the strange long-necked *Tanystropheus* living and feeding like some demented angler along the shorelines of shallow inland seas.

The ancestors of the living *Sphenodon* also

Tanystropheus, a long-necked, rather grotesque euryapsid reptile from the Triassic of Europe and Australia.

Kuehneosaurus, a flying lizard, was an ancient representative of the living 'scaly' reptiles, the snakes, lizards and *Sphenodon*. The latter is the sole survivor of an ancestral stock which flourished in the early part of the Mesozoic era.

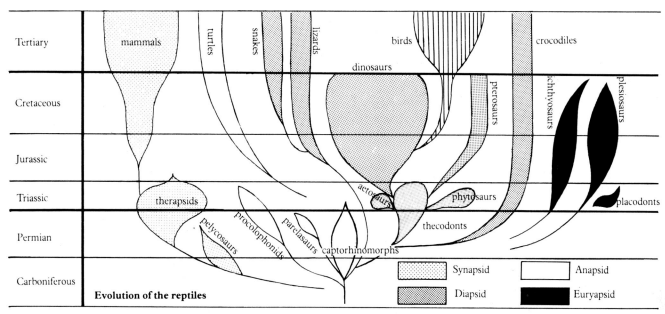

Tertiary	mammals	turtles	snakes	lizards	birds		crocodiles	
Cretaceous				dinosaurs		pterosaurs	ichthyosaurs	plesiosaurs
Jurassic								
Triassic	therapsids			aetosaurs	phytosaurs			placodonts
Permian	pelycosaurs	procolophonids	pareiasaurs	captorhinomorphs	thecodonts			
Carboniferous								

Evolution of the reptiles

Synapsid		Anapsid	
Diapsid		Euryapsid	

appeared in the early Triassic and some forms such as *Kuehneosaurus* were obviously adapted to a gliding mode of life. Others like *Scaphonyx* possessed beak-like jaws and it is likely that this creature fed on hard-shelled seeds and roots. In comparison with other reptile stocks the ancestral 'scaly' lizards were of limited significance in Triassic faunas.

By the Middle Triassic the therapsids and 'scaly' lizards were under the threat of extinction for the beginning of this sub-period witnessed the radiation of several diapsid stocks. These included the 'tooth in socket' thecodonts, which had first appeared in the Upper Permian, and their descendants the dinosaurs, the crocodiles and the pterosaurs. The appearance of these stocks ensured that reptiles dominated vertebrate communities for the next 140–150 million years.

Scaphonyx, a plant-eating rhynchosaur from the Middle Triassic of South Africa. The rhynchosaurs flourished briefly during this time in many areas of the southern continents.

The 'tooth-in-socket' reptiles

The thecodontians are commonly known as the 'tooth in socket' reptiles. They first appeared in the Late Permian; the earliest representatives living in water and having an entirely carnivorous diet. Many of the early thecodontians were rather crocodilian in appearance and the organization of their limbs suggests that they still possessed a 'sprawling' posture, with the limbs outspread and the trunk held close to ground. By the Lower Triassic small thecodontians such as *Euparkeria* had appeared. It had strong hind limbs and an elongate tail indicating that it had drastically improved its posture and adopted a bipedal stance. The improvement of limb posture was to occur in both bipedal and quadrupedal thecodontians. It was to prove such a great advantage over the mammal-like reptiles that by the end of the Middle Triassic the thecodontians, the first of the archosaurs, dominated vertebrate communities throughout the world.

Ornithosuchus was a heavily built, bipedal thecodontian from the Upper Triassic of Scotland, which had a protective cover of thickened plates across its back. The structure of its skull and limbs has led some palaeontologists to describe it as the first of the meat-eating dinosaurs, whilst others believe that it represents an evolutionary peak of thecodontian development.

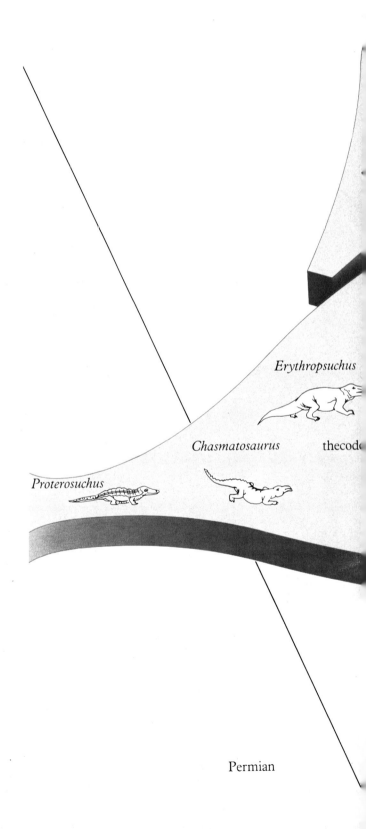

Erythropsuchus

Chasmatosaurus   thecod

Proterosuchus

During the Late Triassic the thecodontian expansion went unchecked for millions of years and two subgroups, namely the phytosaurs and aëtosaurs were to diverge from the main line. The phytosaurs were large crocodile-like creatures which were specialized to an aquatic mode of life, whilst the aëtosaurs were very heavily armoured land dwellers.

Permian

120

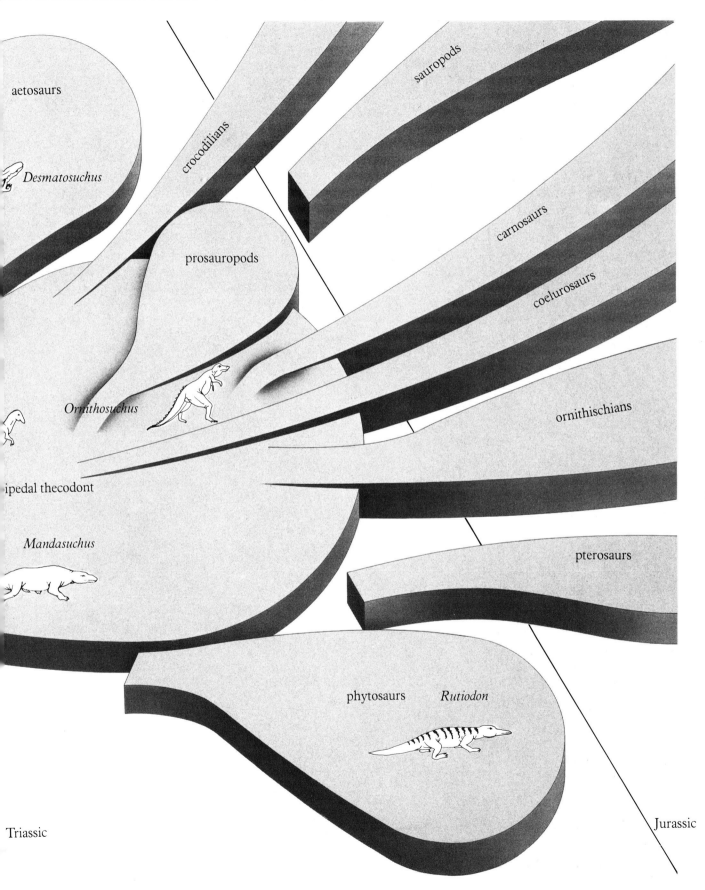

aetosaurs

Desmatosuchus

crocodilians

sauropods

prosauropods

carnosaurs

coelurosaurs

Ornithosuchus

ornithischians

ipedal thecodont

Mandasuchus

pterosaurs

phytosaurs   *Rutiodon*

Triassic

Jurassic

Replacements

The diversification of life that took place during the Triassic period succeeded the major Permian extinctions. Many of the new groups that arose, evolved from unspecialized or conservative ancestors that had been able to withstand the great changes that had taken place within the environment. Some new stocks arose to fill vacated niches and their appearance as successors exemplifies what is known in evolutionary terms as ecological replacement. A specific example of this was the appearance of the scleractian corals in niches formally occupied by members of the Tabulata and Rugosa.

In some cases the replacement was achieved very rapidly but in others it was a long drawn out process. Not all replacements are the result of adaptation to fill vacated niches, for in many cases replacement or displacement, as it is best termed in this particular case, follows a period of competition. In this instance the successful group was obviously adaptively superior to the loser and the fossil record of two groups would necessarily overlap. The phenomenon of displacement is also well documented in the Triassic, with the eclipse of the mammal-like therapsids being attributed to the more adaptively advanced thecodonts. Displacements can be recognized throughout the geological record with the demise of the relatively primitive Devonian ostracoderms and the Tertiary marsupials being attributed to the placoderms and placentals respectively. Ecological replacement, is also recognized elsewhere other than in the Triassic, with the appearance of the mammals as the ecological successors of the dinosaurs ranking as the classic example.

Our reconstruction of a Middle Triassic scene is an attempt to illustrate the phenomenon of displacement in visual terms with the adaptively superior thecodont *Mandasuchus* feeding from the carcass of a mammal-like therapsid. In this example the improved posture of thecodonts was to give them an advantage in the competition for food and the fortunes of groups such as dicynodonts and cynodonts were waning rapidly during the Late Middle and early Upper Triassic. At the end of the Triassic the thecodonts themselves were displaced by their dinosaurian descendants.

Mandasuchus, a Triassic thecodont feeding on the carcass of a mammal-like therapsid.

Chart showing some major faunal replacements and displacements

The first dinosaurs

It is odd to think that great success may ultimately lead to extinction, but this line of thought is certainly true in the case of the thecodontians. In the Middle Triassic and the early part of the Upper Triassic, they seemed to have few rivals and their voracious meat-eating habits were satisfied by the constant cropping of the herbivorous dicynodonts and rhynchosaurs. All the thecodontians were meat eaters, and as no herbivores evolved within their own lineage, the pressure on the existing herbivores increased dramatically. Middle and Upper Triassic communities show a rapid demise in non-thecodontian stocks, including some of the mammal-like carnivores, and the impression is that the thecodontian successs had destroyed its only source of food. The communities also reveal the presence of animals with a 'fully improved' limb posture and it seems likely that these, the first dinosaurs, had begun to evolve in the upper part of the early Triassic. Their emergence was probably linked with the extremely competitive nature of their thecodontian ancestors, with proto-dinosaurs being forced into new niches. Some of these became much larger in order to avoid predation, others took to the swamps and still others moved into the unoccupied upland regions. In time these proto-dinosaurs were in a position to challenge their own ancestors; their specific adaptations proving too much for the often smaller and more primitive thecodontians.

Dinosaur remains have been discovered in late Middle Triassic sediments in South Africa and South America. The South African fauna contains evidence of the earliest saurischians or lizard-hipped dinosaurs, such as *Melanorosaurus*, a prosauropod, and small nimble coelurosaurs. In South America the fauna includes the remains of prosauropods, coelurosaurs and ornithischians. *Pisanosaurus* from the Argentine is one of the earliest recorded ornithischian or 'bird-hipped' dinosaurs. By the uppermost Triassic the importance of the dinosaurs had increased considerably and faunas have been recorded from many parts of the world.

Melanorosaurus, a large prosauropod from the Middle Triassic of South Africa.

Lesothosaurus, an ornithopod from the Late Triassic of southern Africa.

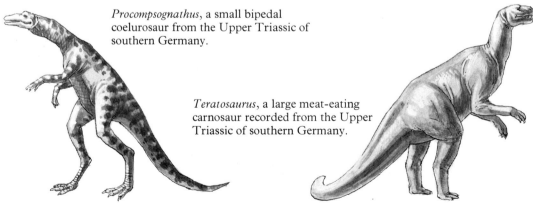

Procompsognathus, a small bipedal coelurosaur from the Upper Triassic of southern Germany.

Teratosaurus, a large meat-eating carnosaur recorded from the Upper Triassic of southern Germany.

What is a dinosaur?

To most of us, the dinosaurs were simply gigantic creatures that, because of their great size, died out million of years ago. In part this idea is correct, although size alone is not a criterion by which we should either judge the success of the group or characterize its membership. The fossil record shows that the dinosaurs were an enormously successful group in which numerous species specialized to different modes of life.

The eggs of the horned dinosaur, *Protoceratops*, and scaly skin of the duck-billed genus *Anatosaurus* prove that the dinosaurs were reptiles. Two temporal openings on the sides of head subsequently refer them to the diapsid line and a definite relationship with the crocodiles, pterosaurs and thecodontians. The dinosaurs can therefore be described as archosaurian or 'ruling reptiles'. Amongst these dinosaurs are the only group of archosaurs to universally achieve a 'fully improved' or erect posture. This involved the drawing of the limbs beneath the body and resulted in an increase in the efficiency of both bipedal and quadrupedal forms. The 'fully improved' posture is reflected in the shape and arrangement of the limbs and girdles, and it is through these that we can identify the dinosaurs as being a unique group in the evolutionary history of the reptiles. Within the family of dinosaurs the structure of the pelvic girdle is an important clue in the recognition of saurischian or ornithischian types.

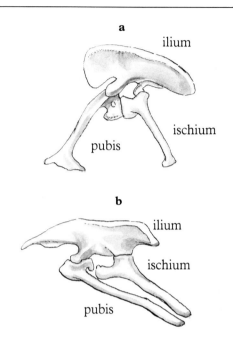

Pelvis of (a) a saurischian dinosaur; (b) an early 'bird-hipped' ornithischian dinosaur. (c) a later type of ornithischian showing forward extension of the pubic bone

The improvement of limb posture in various reptile groups is an important factor in their evolutionary success. The drawing of the limbs beneath the body aids energy conservation and is critical to the development of true bipedality.

(a) sprawling condition – as in the lizards

(b) semi-improved condition – as in the thecodontians

(c) fully-improved condition – as in dinosaurs and mammals

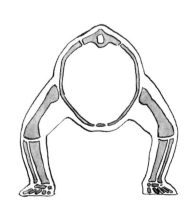
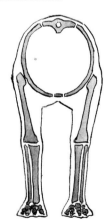

Dinosaur classification

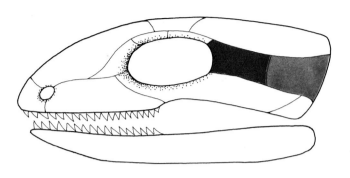

anapsid

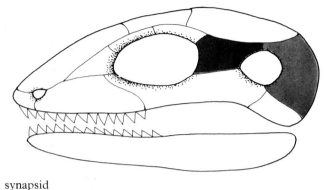

synapsid

Throughout the account of the evolution of the reptiles the terms anapsid, synapsid, euryapsid and diapsid have been used to describe the basic types of skull pattern. The diagrams clearly illustrate the arrangement of the temporal openings which occur on the side of the skull, behind the eye.

After the great radiation of the dinosaurs in the Upper Triassic–Lower Jurassic, successive waves of saurischian and ornithischian dinosaurs were to dominate vertebrate communities for the next 130 million years. In the Jurassic the major groups appeared to have developed in harmony with their environment and in most cases the basic form of the individuals referred to each group remains consistent throughout its evolution.

Modifications of the basic plan do occur at family and generic level, but overall it would appear that the designs were right first time.

In the Upper Jurassic the herbivorous faunas were dominated by the great sauropods and the stegosaurs; the major predators being *Allosaurus* and *Megalosaurus*, both giant carnosaurs. The small coelurosaurs and the flying pterosaurs filled the roles of scavengers and nest robbers.

During the Cretaceous the importance of the sauropods declined and the ornithopods and ankylosaurs were to become the dominant herbivores. The diversification of the ornithopods during the Upper Cretaceous provides a dramatic contrast to the conservatism shown by the sauropods. This is also true for the coelurosaurs for during the Cretaceous several new stocks evolved to fill different ecological niches. Once again the carnosaurs filled the role of the dominant predator.

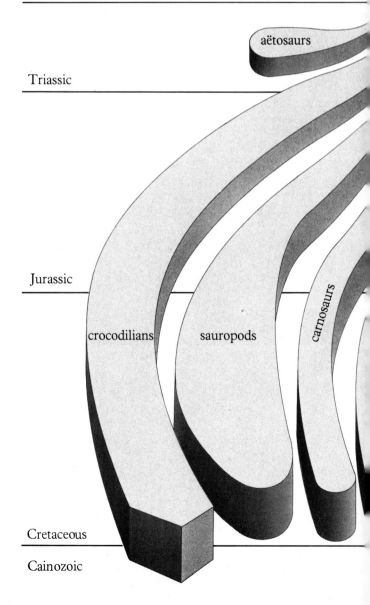

Permian

Triassic

aëtosaurs

Jurassic

crocodilians   sauropods   carnosaurs

Cretaceous

Cainozoic

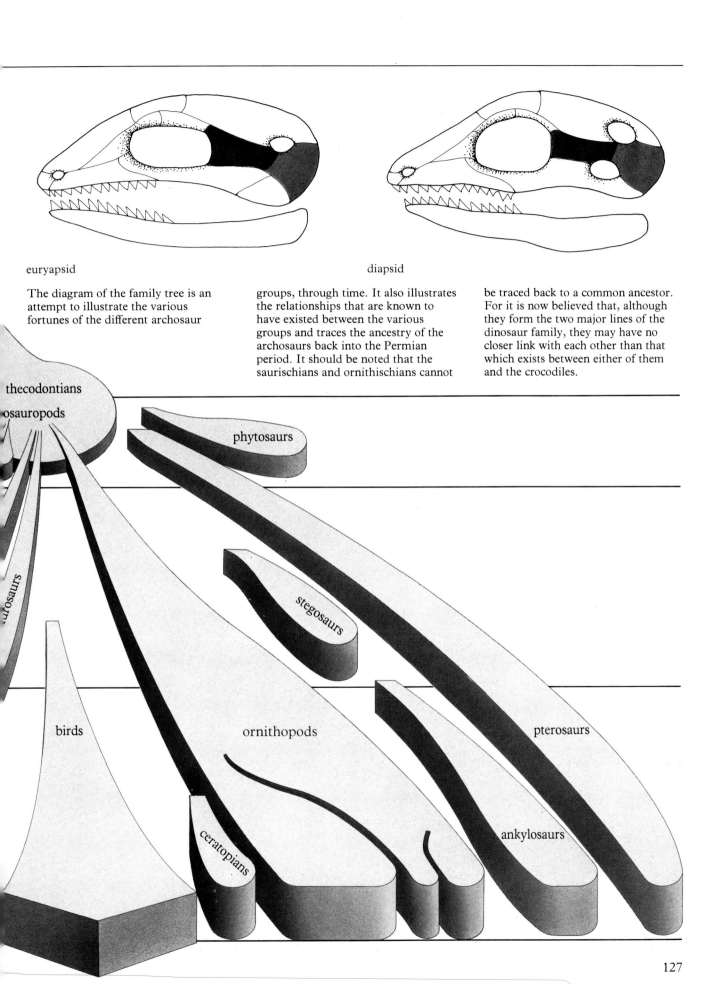

euryapsid

diapsid

The diagram of the family tree is an attempt to illustrate the various fortunes of the different archosaur groups, through time. It also illustrates the relationships that are known to have existed between the various groups and traces the ancestry of the archosaurs back into the Permian period. It should be noted that the saurischians and ornithischians cannot be traced back to a common ancestor. For it is now believed that, although they form the two major lines of the dinosaur family, they may have no closer link with each other than that which exists between either of them and the crocodiles.

thecodontians

osauropods

phytosaurs

stegosaurs

birds

ornithopods

pterosaurs

ceratopians

ankylosaurs

Triassic landscapes

During the latter half of the Triassic period a number of dinosaur families appeared to have a cosmopolitan distribution. Several communities have been discovered in different continents but in each case the membership includes representatives of the prosauropods, coelurosaurs and possibly the carnosaurs. The communities flourished in lowland areas bordering river estuaries and swamps where the landscape was covered with ferns, club mosses and horsetails. In the more arid regions beyond the river banks cycads, ginkgoes and conifers heralded the advance of the seed plants.

The two communities illustrated on this spread provide us with an insight into Late Triassic landscapes in South Africa and Germany. In South Africa the prosauropod *Melanorosaurus* was the most significant animal, it was 12 metres long and its heavy body was supported by four massive limbs. In many respects *Melanorosaurus* appeared to be the ideal ancestor to the great sauropods of the Jurassic and Cretaceous periods. Small coelurosaurs and carnosaurs lived in the same area as *Melanorosaurus* as did representatives of the rhynchosaurs, mammal-like tritylodonts and thecodonts.

a carnosaur

Melanorosaurus

a coelurosaur

South Africa

On the lowland plains of southern Germany the large prosauropods were represented by *Plateosaurus*, which was smaller than its South African counterpart and capable of both bipedal and quadrupedal locomotion. The coelurosaurs were known by the presence of *Procompsognathus* and the rhynchosaurs by that of the type genus *Rhynchosaurus*. The first turtles had appeared in the lowland lakes and amphibians such as *Gerrothorax*, a larval-like temnospondyl, still lived at the water's edge.

The grouping of the continents during the late Palaeozoic enabled the various reptile stocks to migrate freely. It is likely that representatives of both the mammal-like reptiles and the archosaurs radiated outwards from the southern hemisphere to occupy new lands during the Triassic.

Plateosaurus

Coelophysis

Rhynchosaurus

Procompsognathus

southern Germany

The basic plan is right first time

The first turtles are known from the Upper Triassic of Germany. They are primitive in that they possess teeth and short ribs on the vertebrae of the neck, but other than that they are instantly recognizable. No obvious ancestors have been identified, although a link with the procolophonid stem reptiles is now favoured. From the start the turtles were encased in a bony sandwich, consisting of a dorsal carapace and ventral plastron. Uniquely the limbs and girdles have moved inside the ribs and the latter are usually intimately involved in the production of the bony shields of the carapace. The adoption of a shell necessitated changes in the apparatuses involved in locomotion, respiration and reproduction but it also provided a form of protection unrivalled in the majority of vertebrate stocks. Since the Triassic few modifications have really taken place in the general structure of the shell and few were needed as it is only recently that a major threat to their existence has evolved. The threat is from man. Early turtles lacked the ability to protect the head by drawing it back into the shell, but in the Cretaceous even this problem was overcome with the evolution of pleurodiran and cryptodiran stocks. In the pleurodires the depressed or flattened skull is withdrawn sideways under the lip of the carapace whilst in the seemingly more specialized cryptodires the withdrawal of the head is effected by an S-shaped flexure in the vertical plane.

The genus '*Triassochelys*' is known from the Upper Triassic of Germany, it is one of the earliest turtles and unlike later forms possessed teeth, cervical ribs and a larger than normal number of bones around the edge of the dorsal carapace.

In the pleurodiran turtles the neck is simply drawn sideways into the shell with the main flexures of the neck occurring between vertebrae two and three, five and six and between number eight and dorsal vertebra one.

The withdrawal of the head in the cryptodires is achieved by the bending of the neck downwards and backwards, with the main flexures taking place between vertebrae five and six and between number eight and dorsal vertebra one.

In the Cretaceous the turtles underwent a considerable radiation with numerous families of both pleurodiran and cryptodiran affinities appearing throughout the world. At the present time the pleurodirans are confined to the Southern Hemisphere.

A scute from the upper part of the shell of *Trionyx*, a freshwater turtle, which has been discovered as far back as the Triassic.

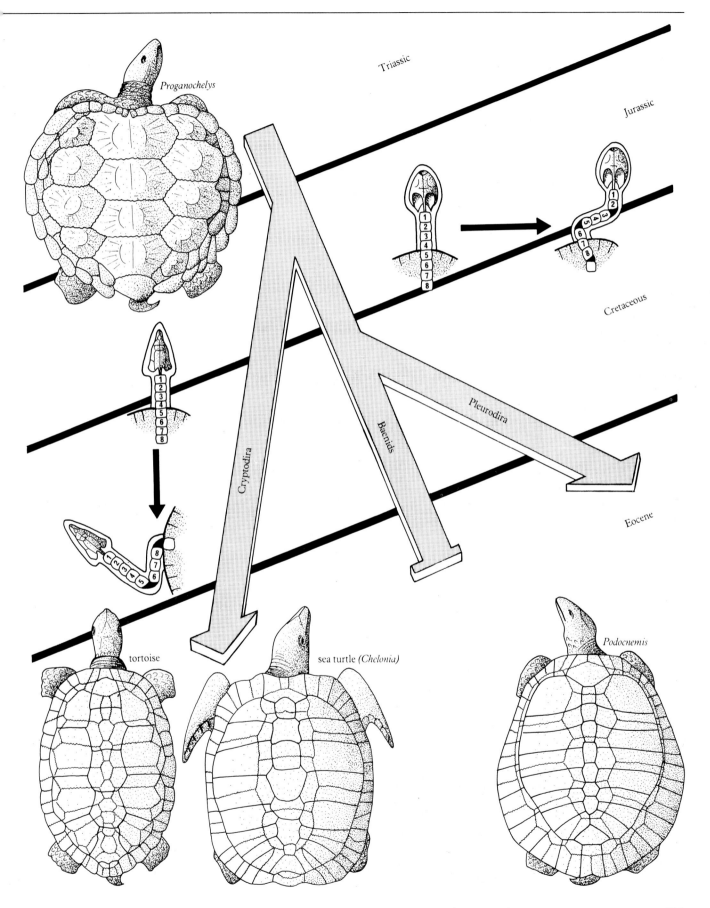

Proganochelys

Triassic

Jurassic

Cretaceous

Cryptodira

Baenids

Pleurodira

Eocene

tortoise

sea turtle *(Chelonia)*

Podocnemis

The Jurassic

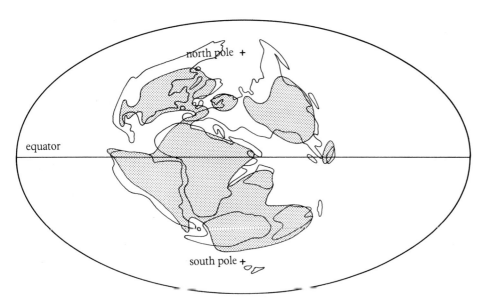

from the Indian/African plate in the Upper Jurassic. The break-up of Laurasia had also been initiated although numerous migration routes were to persist between major continental areas until well into the Cretaceous and even beyond. The Jurassic world was much more hospitable than that of the Triassic, and a major marine transgression at the beginning of the period served to increase the humidity over land areas. No glacial deposits are recorded from the Jurassic, and tropical, subtropical and temperate forests occupied much greater areas than during the Triassic. The forests grew to within 10° to 20° of the poles and in many regions they fringed the shallow seas that now covered a greater area than at any time since the Lower Carboniferous. The shallow waters and new coastlines offered many vacant ecological niches and these were soon occupied by a host of invertebrate animals.

The break-up of Pangaea which had begun in the Late Triassic was to continue during the Jurassic. By the dawn of the new period North America had already split from Gondwanaland and other divisions or separations were in progress, with South America, Antarctica and Australia moving away

The Jurassic equator lay across northernmost South America and in Africa could be traced from Ghana in the west to the central Red Sea area in the east. Southern Europe and the southern region of North America lay in tropics whilst the British Isles and Newfoundland were at a latitude of approximately 40° north. In the Lower Jurassic the deep waters of Tethys separated Eurasia from Africa and formed a geographic barrier which limited the migration of many shallow water organisms. Free swimming and planktonic creatures were abundant in these open waters but bottom-dwelling forms were extremely restricted . To the north of Tethys, shallow shelf seas which were rich in carbonates, covered much of southern Europe and structured communities including plants and many invertebrates thrived in their warm waters. Around the northern land masses the seas received a greater influx of sandy materials as a result of erosion and areas such as Great Britain are characterized by the deposition of rather mixed sediments with pure limestones having a limited presence. In North America the seas bordered much of the continent and a sand dune topography covered large areas of the continental interior.

In the Middle Jurassic significant changes in palaeogeography occurred in many regions. The shallow waters of the Sundance Sea advanced over a large area of the western interior of North

America, whilst in northern Europe uplift resulted in the formation of large deltas in the north Yorkshire area. Moving southwards, in England, the environments changed first to lagoons and then into open shelf seas which also covered much of France and central Europe. In southern Europe the break-up and widening of Tethys brought deeper waters to areas once characterized by thick limestones. This change was also reflected in the faunas with shallow shelf communities being replaced by open sea swimmers and floaters. The faunas of the Middle Jurassic sub-period can, as in most of the Jurassic and Cretaceous, be divided into northern boreal and southern Tethyan groupings, with a number of ecological factors, including temperature, salinity and substrate, exerting control over the distribution of specific faunal elements. Boreal and Tethyan faunas are recognized in Europe and North America. In the boreal fauna the diversity of organisms was restricted due to possible seasonal changes, whilst in Tethys conditions were more stable and the variety of organisms correspondingly greater.

Several fluctuations in sea level affected northern Europe and North America during the Upper Jurassic. In the British Isles a sequence of marine advances and withdrawals is indicated by the deposition of deep water clays and shallow water limestones and, as in North America, a major withdrawal or regression took place in the final stages of the period. In several areas of Europe the Upper Jurassic was a time of reef-building and in southern Germany the famous Lithographic Stone was deposited in a tropical lagoonal environment. Deeper water conditions prevailed over much of southern Europe, although several sea floor mounts were to act as centres for the deposition of ammonite rich limestones.

Jurassic plants

The general improvement of the climate suggested earlier, is supported by evidence drawn from Jurassic floras. In general these exhibited a greater variety than those of the Triassic and their distribution was much more widespread. The gymnosperms were by far the dominant group of plants, with the ginkgoes being more common in the Siberian region and the cycads essentially restricted to the floras of the subtropics. Conifers were also more abundant in lower latitudes, than they were in the north and, together with numerous species of subtropical and tropical ferns, they gave rise to many regions of luxuriant growth. Individual trees such as the primitive pine *Araucarites* were present in both northern and southern hemispheres but for the most part the floras were distinct, with Tethys acting as a barrier to migration. The Jurassic period has previously been referred to as the 'Age of Cycads' but in fact these plants were outnumbered by their close relatives the bennettitaleans. This is particularly true for the first half of the period when numerous genera including *Williamsonia* were present in large numbers. Of the ancient gymnosperms the caytoniales reach their acme in the Jurassic with *Caytonia* being widely distributed in the northern hemisphere and *Sagenopteris* having an even more cosmopolitan distribution. In wetland areas the horsetails persisted in limited numbers and evidence also exists for the widespread presence of liverworts and mosses in this type of environment.

Araucaria, cones.

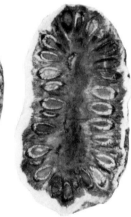

Ginkgo, leaves.

Williamsonia, the 'flower' consists of a discoid base from which large petal-like stamens are produced which curve inwards and upwards.

Pterophyllum, note the fern-like leaves.

Sediments control the variety of life

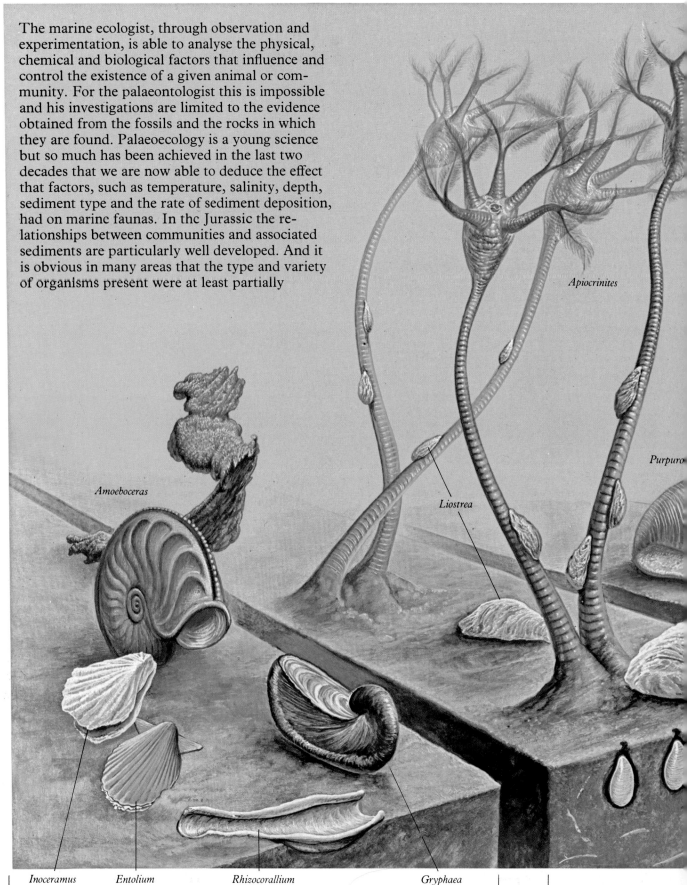

The marine ecologist, through observation and experimentation, is able to analyse the physical, chemical and biological factors that influence and control the existence of a given animal or community. For the palaeontologist this is impossible and his investigations are limited to the evidence obtained from the fossils and the rocks in which they are found. Palaeoecology is a young science but so much has been achieved in the last two decades that we are now able to deduce the effect that factors, such as temperature, salinity, depth, sediment type and the rate of sediment deposition, had on marine faunas. In the Jurassic the relationships between communities and associated sediments are particularly well developed. And it is obvious in many areas that the type and variety of organisms present were at least partially

Apiocrinites

Purpuro

Amoeboceras

Liostrea

Inoceramus   *Entolium*   *Rhizocorallium*   *Gryphaea*

deeper water environment

firm seabottom environm

controlled by the sediment that formed the sea floor and by the rate at which deposition took place. Naturally control by the substrate is essentially confined to bottom-dwelling organisms but a major influx of sediment, due to the continued erosion of a land mass, may restrict the migration of free-swimming and floating forms into the area in question.

In our restorations the environments range from coastal lagoon to relatively deep open sea and the sea-bottom sediments vary accordingly. In the lagoon environment salinity was also a major control factor but the stable muds of the sea floor provide an ideal substrate for colonization by both burrowing bivalves and fixed bottom-dwellers such as oysters, brachiopods and corals. Beyond the lagoon the environment illustrated is the equivalent of the shallow water, high energy conditions that exist around the Bahamas today. The waters were super-saturated with aragonite

and small concentric, laminated spheres called ooids were precipitated to give rise to oolitic limestones. These were frequently mobile and the unstable conditions resulted in a restricted fauna. In areas where the substrate was firm, due to cementation, numerous organisms could fix themselves to the sea bottom or bore below its surface. Such an environment is depicted in the third of our restorations and the firmness of the substrate coupled with normal marine conditions has resulted in a more diverse yet specialized community. In deeper waters sediments are often finer grained and the rate of deposition is slower than in areas close to the shore. Food supply in such areas is often limited and therefore the community is often dominated by mud ingestors, scavengers and filter feeders. In the Jurassic this was true of muddy sea floor communities although some bivalves, such as *Gryphaea dilatata*, adapted to the prevailing conditions.

Oysters

Isastrea

cerithid

Liostrea

Modiolus

Pygaster

Lucina

shallow water high energy environment

lagoonal environment

Traces of life

Trace fossils are the result of biological activity and they provide the geologist with an *in situ* record of the burrows, borings, tracks and trails created by animals in their everyday life. Often it is impossible to associate traces with a given organism but this does not detract from their usefulness. In general terms the complexity of traces increases with depth, with the simple vertical burrows of shallow water inhabitant being gradually replaced by the elaborate horizontal traces of sediment feeders in deep water environments. Traces not only reflect the functions of the animal but also its relationship to the environment and, as with body fossils, it is possible to recognize distinct groupings or communities. In some areas they are the only indication of past life and therefore their presence takes on an even greater significance. Trace fossils are best preserved in sediments of a sandy, often calcareous, nature and particularly where these and shale layers are inter-bedded. Shallow marine sandstones and shales are typical of many Jurassic horizons and exceptionally well preserved traces provide vital clues as to the conditions that prevailed over 136 million years ago. Depth, sediment type and the energy levels that prevailed within the area were amongst the most important factors that control the distribution of traces, with the animal involved being concerned with matters such as protection, and food availability. In very shallow waters or in a beach environment, animals need to protect themselves against such factors as dessication and exposure. Vertical burrows are therefore necessary and in the Jurassic the traces of *Skolithus* are an indication of these conditions. In a less turbulent environment, with a constant cover of water, the single tubes of *Skolithus* may be associated with the U-shaped burrows of *Arenicolites* and *Diplocraterion*. Further out to sea the burrows become oblique and eventually horizontal and the indication is that the major concern of the animal is the search for food. Horizontal burrows include those of *Rhizocorallium* (U-shaped) and *Thalassinoides* (branched) with the latter varying in diameter relative to the degree of turbulence. In areas of finer-grained sediments elongate sinuous *Rhizocorallium* burrows may dominate and the genus *Teichichnus* is also a useful indicator of deeper water. It is likely that no sharp distinctions occur between communities but one

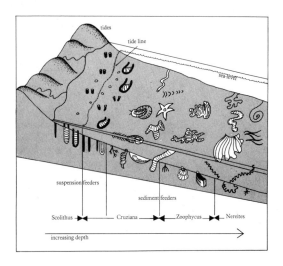

The various trace fossils of the Jurassic, like those of other geological periods, can be grouped into communities based on their distribution related to depth. This distribution is illustrated and an indication is given as to predominance of suspension or sediment feeders in given areas. In geology the term *facies* is applied to a rock unit with particular features that reflect specific environmental conditions, the features include fossils and several facies have been established on trace fossil content.

Thalassinoides is well known from various periods of geological time, particularly the Jurassic. The trace has been linked with the crab *Callianassa*, the elongate, repeatedly branched burrows sometimes containing crustacean droppings and scratch marks.

is fairly safe in claiming that *Teichichnus* and *Zoophycos*, with its elaborate tracings, represent those communities that occur further from land.

In some areas *Diplocraterion* burrows are noted for the presence of spreiten (lines which indicate the former position of the burrow) above and below the bend at the base of the burrow. This indicates fluctuating rates of deposition and removal of sediment, with the animal moving up and down relative to the sea bottom. The action is similar to that of a certain toy and the species is aptly named *Diplocraterion yoyo*.

137

Sediments that tell a story

The cliffs along the Dorset coast of southern England display many sections of rocks of Jurassic and Cretaceous age. At Lulworth Cove the outer more resistant rocks of the Jurassic have been breached and the sea has carved a beautifully symmetrical bay in the less resistant Cretaceous strata. The Jurassic rocks of Lulworth Cove represent the last two stages of the Upper Jurassic subperiod. Limestones of the older Portlandian stage form the lower cliffs with the more variable sediments of the Purbeck overlying. The Portland limestones can be divided on grain size and faunal content and the story they tell is of a gradual shallowing of the marine environment. Sponges and bivalves were abundant in the lower limestone communities but in time these were replaced by intertidal and very shallow water faunas and floras, with gastropods, sea urchins, bivalves and algal material as the main constituents.

Shallow water conditions persisted into the Purbeckian although in this stage various stratigraphic levels provide information of shallow marine, lagoonal and even terrestrial conditions. Dirt beds and algal limestones near the base of the sequence are good indicators of sub-aerial and intertidal conditions whilst overlying limestones and marls, rich in ostracodes and gypsum, are indicative of a rather fetid, evaporitic lagoonal environment. The fossil forest of Lulworth Cove is very famous, and its presence along with that of a dirt bed are evidence of truly sub-aerial conditions. The upper part of the Lower Purbeck at Lulworth provides further evidence of fluctuating environments, with beds rich in gypsum and moulds which indicate the former presence of halite cubes being common. These types of deposits and environments occur today along the shorelines of the Persian Gulf and we can therefore infer that during the Upper Jurassic similar conditions prevailed along the Dorset coast.

salt pseudomorphs

gypsum

Swimmers – floaters – bottom scavengers

The appearance of ammonites belonging to the suborder Phylloceratina during the Triassic period, marked the beginning of one of the most explosive phases of evolution recorded in the stratigraphic column. For by the Middle Jurassic two other suborders had arisen and approximately fifty families of ammonites were to have some representation during the Jurassic period. Amongst these families various species were to evolve to occupy particular niches and we are able to witness a great diversity of forms.

The types of shell ranged from tightly coiled and smoothly ornamented to loosely spiralled and coarsely ribbed. Between the two the variety is legion and one can infer that this is an indication of many different modes of life. Many ammonites look rather similar to the living *Nautilus*, and sophisticated studies related to the positions of their centres of gravity and buoyancy suggest that their position in the water was similar. In *Nautilus* the centres of buoyancy and gravity are set well apart and although this limits its ability to change its position readily, it does provide stability.

Dactylioceras, on the other hand, was more 'open' in its coiling than *Nautilus* and its centres of buoyancy and gravity lie very close together. In terms of stability this was a negative step but it greatly improved the animals ability to change its position. Like *Nautilus*, *Dactylioceras* was probably a good swimmer but it is likely that it lived in shallower waters. The best swimmers, however, were the flatter more streamlined and tightly coiled forms such as *Oxynoticeras*, in which the outer whorls overlapped the inner ones. Uncoiled

fossil forest, Lulworth, Dorset

oolitic limestone

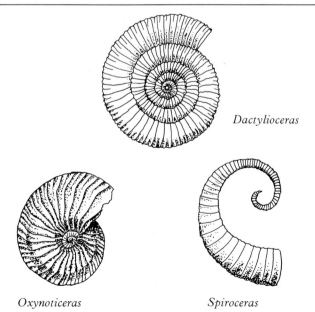

Dactylioceras

Oxynoticeras

Spiroceras

genera were seemingly more specialized for either floating or bottom-crawling modes of life. In many floaters the apertures were directed upwards and the centre of buoyancy was set well away from the centre of gravity.

Bottom-dwellers were often more irregular in shape and the aperture could even face sideways. The suture lines between chambers were also simpler in the bottom-dwelling forms. In life the sutures are thought to have borne tissues connected with the fluid/gas exchange essential for buoyancy control and it is believed that a reduction in the surface area covered by the tissue conforms with more sluggish benthonic habits. The ribs and spines of the more ornamented ammonites were linked with shell strength and camouflage.

Bivalves adapt to different niches

It is now thought that the first bivalves (clams) lived on the surface of the sea floor and that the development of a two-valved shell helped in the control of feeding currents and with the general stability of their internal environment. The shell also offered protection against predators and may originally have been developed by animals with a crawling mode of life. During the Palaeozoic several evolutionary bursts took place within bivalve stocks and many adapted to shallow burrowing. A major development in the Palaeozoic was the secretion of horny threads, collectively termed the byssus, which enabled the animal to attach itself to the substrate. In some ways this paralleled the development of the pedicle in brachiopods, but as the byssus was regenerative it was now possible for a detached bivalve to reattach itself. This was considered a major advance in the ability of the group to occupy niches denied the brachiopods.

However, the real radiation of the bivalves was to take place during the Mesozoic when many stocks perfected the development of siphons and modified the form of shell to suit various modes of life. The siphons enabled these animals to burrow more efficiently and is thought, as is the development of cementation in the oysters and free-swimming habits in the pectinids, to be linked with the avoidance of predation. This is probably true, as many clam eaters and grazers, including certain sharks and rays, spiny lobsters, starfishes and gastropods, arose in the early Mesozoic. Adaptations to different modes of life within the bivalve family are reflected in the structure of the shell, with variations in the muscle scar patterns, the dentition and the contour line which marks the marginal limit of the mantle (pallial line), providing vital clues. The diagrams of *Venus*, a burrower, and of a fixed oyster, clearly illustrate the differences in shell form, musculature and dentition that can be linked with various life styles.

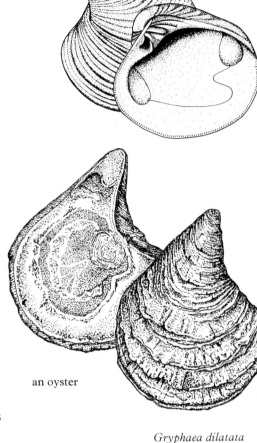

Venus

an oyster

Gryphaea dilatata

Gryphaea incurva

In the Jurassic, the coiled oysters of the genus *Gryphaea* lived on the surface of the sea-floor. They preferred a silt-clay or muddy-sand substrate and fed from currents developed by the movement of a large gill structure and by the gentle flapping of the upper valve. It would appear that the species *Gryphaea dilatata* with its greatly expanded lower valve was adapted to a softer substrate than *G. incurva*.

Pholadomya is a shallow burrowing bivalve which appeared during the Triassic. It has a strongly biconvex shell which is ovate to subtrigonol in outline. The valves are of equal size, with the posterior greatly extended. A noticeable for the siphons occurs between the two valves and the shell possesses a strong ornament. *Pholadomya* would appear to be perfectly adapted to its chosen mode of life and although living species occur in deep waters, Jurassic forms lived in relatively shallow environments.

Pholadomya

Plagiostoma

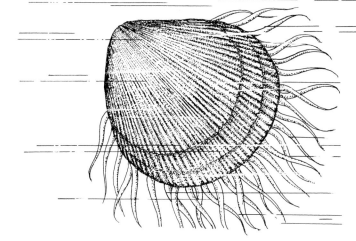

The free-swimming clam *Plagiostoma (Lima)* also appeared in Triassic but reached its acme during the Jurassic period. It was of medium to large size with the shell having a rather weak external ornament. Internally *Plagiostoma* possessed a large elastic ligament and a large single muscle placed in a central position. Living relatives of *Plagiostoma* swim by flapping their valves, with the muscle and ligament providing the 'drive' and control.

Although boring clams have been recorded from the Palaeozoic, forms such as *Lithophaga* did not flourish until Jurassic times. The shell of the living *Lithophaga* is elongate, cylindrical and tapered posteriorly and it conforms beautifully with the habits of the animal. *Lithophaga* excavates a cylindrical boring by means of chemical solution, with the secreted mucous dissolving the limestone around the base of the shell. As the boring increases in width and depth, the shell grows and soon it becomes impossible for it to vacate its permanent home. It is also impossible for the majority of organisms to attack it. *In situ* remains of *Lithophaga* are commonly associated with the Jurassic hardgrounds and firm substrate communities.

Lithophaga

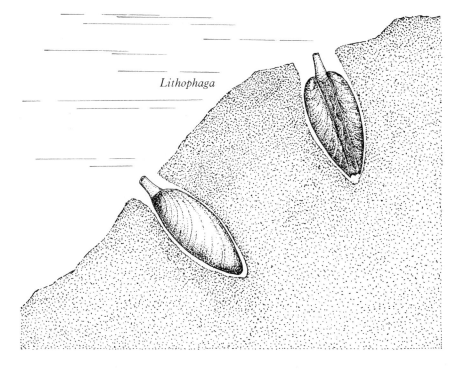

Giant bivalves

During the Middle and Upper Cretaceous the Tethyan Ocean extended from Mexico in the west, through the Mediterranean to Japan in the east. The central deeper waters of this great ocean were occupied by free-swimming animals such as the ammonites, but along its shores bottom-dwelling communities, including great stretches of reefs, flourished. Algae and corals were common in most reefs at this time, but the greater proportion of reef construction was attributable to a group of rather bizarre bivalves named the rudists. Unlike most bivalves the rudists were often strongly inequivalve, although the variety of shapes witnessed within the group differed considerably. The rudistids were suspension feeders which lived in shallow seas characterized by low rates of sediment deposition. They preferred rather coarse substrates and are sometimes found associated with submerged atolls or volcanic sea mounts.

The most spectacular rudists belong to coral-like genera such as *Hippurites* and *Radiolites*, individuals of which exceeded 30 centimetres in height. These animals secreted a thick porous skeleton in which the large right valve was partially buried in the substrate. The upper, left valve was lid-like with large teeth that were modified to allow only for vertical movement. These animals fed on small organisms or pieces of debris suspended in the surrounding waters, although like the corals they probably obtained some food from having a symbiotic relationship with the algae called zooxanthellae. The structure of rudist reefs was looser than the more typical coral-algal associations and it is thought that the reason for this lay in the secretion of some fluid that deterred the attachment of secondary organisms on the outside of the shell. This prevented the large shells from being bound together and as a result the rudist reefs were less durable. Studies of rudist reefs indicate that individual genera occupied different zones within the community, with the larger upright and barrel-shaped forms such as *Hippurites* and *Radiolites* occupying the upper reef slopes and the more exotic curved forms occupying the reef top and the inner lagoon areas.

A rudistid colony (after P. W. Skelton, 1979)

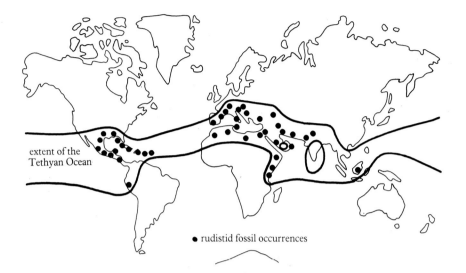

The reef-building rudistids are one of several fossil groups that are used by palaeontologists to define the palaeogeography of the Tethyan oceanic area. Rudists are particularly useful as their colonies were built up on the edges of the lime rich seas that bordered the ancient shore lines.

extent of the
Tethyan Ocean

• rudistid fossil occurrences

Why the rudists died out

The rudists died out suddenly at the end of the Cretaceous and the role of reef builders returned to the corals and algae. The replacement, in itself, is an obvious one but the extinction of the rudists is one of considerable interest. According to some palaeontologists the tolerant rudists were able to exist in areas of fluctuating temperatures, salinity and oxygen levels and that this ability enabled them to occupy niches denied to other organisms. This may be true, but it has also been postulated that the environments that persisted during the Middle and Upper Cretaceous lacked a high level of turbulence and a fast rate of sedimentation. The continued drift of the continents, together with the uplift of the lands around Tethys and a change in currents probably resulted in changes in these factors. It is likely that the rudists had no effective mechanism of ridding themselves of the falling sediment and that their loose formations could not withstand a continued high level of water turbulence.

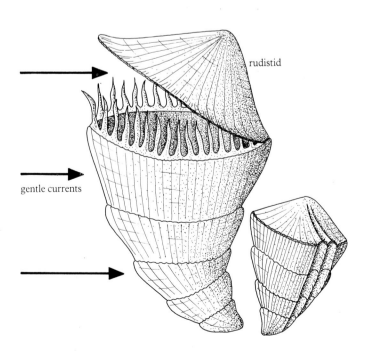

rudistid

gentle currents

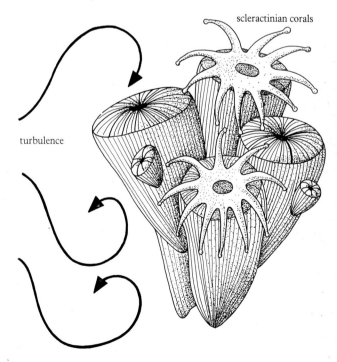

scleractinian corals

turbulence

Jurassic marine reptiles

By the beginning of the Jurassic period marine reptile faunas had undergone considerable change. The primitive nothosaurs and the armoured shell-eating placodonts had disappeared and the seas of the world were ruled by the ichthyosaurs and the newly evolved plesiosaurs. Both of these groups were highly adapted to an aquatic mode of life and the plesiosaurs exhibited many improvements over their nothosaur cousins. The remains of both ichthyosaurs and plesiosaurs are most often discovered in clays and muddy limestones deposited under off-shore conditions, and the indication is that the two were open sea dwellers. In the case of the ichthyosaurs the fish-like body was perfectly adapted to the role of hunter-killer, and the discovery of the gut remains of various individuals provides evidence of a diet of fish and cephalopods.

The plesiosaurs, by way of contrast, were less

Ichthyosaurus

fish-like in character and the head was set at the end of an elongate, flexible neck. In some genera the neck accounted for more than half of the body length, but in others, namely the pliosaurs, it was comparatively short and robust. The variation in the length of neck is likely to represent adaptation to different modes of life. It has been argued that the short-necked pliosaurs were not as manoeuvrable as their long-necked cousins and that they were essentially long-distance swimmers. This may be true, but it is equally likely that whilst the short-necked pliosaurs fed at depth, that is, below the surface, the long-necked plesiosaurs literally fished over the surface waters.

How did the plesiosaurs swim

There is little doubt that the plesiosaurs were good swimmers and that their paddles were also robust enough to drag the animal over land to its nesting site. However, some controversy does exist as to the way in which the paddles performed their primary function – that of swimming. Until recently, many scientists believed that the long-necked varieties rowed themselves through the water with a backwards and forwards motion, and that the pliosaurs adopted a penguin-like motion with a downwards and backwards movement. The different functional interpretations were based on the difference in the length of the long bones of the two groups, with the pliosaurs having the larger, long bones of the two. Recent research on the limbs and girdles, however, has modified these theories, and the accepted view is that both groups swam in a manner similar to the large sea turtles. In these the paddles are moved through a low figure of eight with the downward and backward part of the action providing the necessary propulsion. If this is true, then plesiosaur movement, could, in the terms applied to the sea turtles, be described as 'flying' through the water.

iosaurus

Geosaurus

Jurassic coelurosaurs

As in the Triassic, the meat-eating, saurischian dinosaurs (theropods) of the Jurassic were divided into two groups, the coelurosaurs and the carnosaurs. Size was again a major factor in distinguishing between the two, with the small coelurosaurs bearing a close resemblance to their Triassic forebears. Some were slightly larger but others such as *Compsognathus* were amongst the smallest dinosaurs known. It was no larger than a small turkey, measuring between 60 and 70 centimetres in length. Both the neck and tail were long and the small head had a rather pointed snout. Numerous sharp teeth lined the edges of the jaws. The animal was strongly bipedal with long hind limbs, in which the lower leg bones were considerably longer than the thigh bones. The fore limbs were reduced in size with three functional fingers on each hand. *Compsognathus*, translated means 'pretty jaw' and in many ways it resembles a bird stripped of all its feathers. There is little doubt

that it was a predator-scavenger and it is possible that it fed on small lizards, insects and even the first bird *Archaeopteryx*.

Some recent texts have shown a species of *Compsognathus* as a semi-aquatic animal, its fore limbs modified to form paddles. As interesting as this reconstruction is, there is little evidence in the fossil record to support it. Unlike the 'true' *Compsognathus* the 'paddle-equipped' species was supposedly a swimmer and diver, which fed off shrimps and other invertebrate organisms that lived in the lagoons that characterized southern Germany during the Upper Jurassic.

In the Upper Jurassic, Morrison Formation of North America, the genus *Coelurus (Ornitholestes)* was the representative coelurosaur. It was larger than *Compsognathus* with individuals growing to just over 2 metres in length. *Coelurus* is often depicted as a scavenger, stealing meat from the carcass of a recently killed herbivore. In the

The diagram illustrates the possible ancestral links between the 'normal' coelurosaurs and the ornithomimids, the dromaeosaurids and the birds. In some recent works the dromaeosaurids are thought to belong to a separate group.

Segisaurus

Procompsognathus

'ostrich-like coelurosaurs'

Ornithomimus

dromaeosaurids

thecodont ancestor

Deinonychus

Saurornithoides

'normal' coelurosaurs

Velociraptor

Coelophysis

birds

Archaeopteryx

Millions of years ago

225   Triassic   195   Jurassic   136   Cretaceous   65

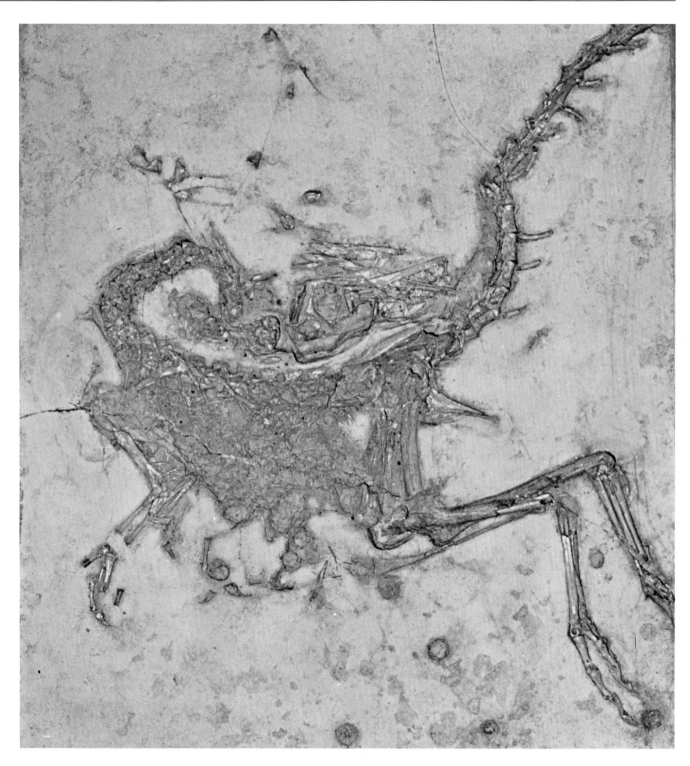

Morrison Formation the remains of *Coelurus* are found with those of the giant sauropod *Apatosaurus*, the ornithischians *Stegosaurus* and *Camptosaurus* and the large meat-eater *Ceratosaurus*. In view of the enormous size of these creatures, the role of scavenger or small scale predator represents the perfect niche for *Coelurus*.

During the Jurassic it is likely that the normal line of coelurosaurs, represented by *Coelurus* and *Compsognathus* gave rise to several important stocks. These included the dromaeosaurids and ornithomimids, two highly specialized groups of small bipedal theropods and the first representative of the birds.

Great Jurassic meat-eaters

In the Jurassic several types of great carnosaurs ruled over the dinosaur communities. In Europe the 'big lizard', *Megalosaurus*, roamed the lowlands of southern England and France. It grew to just over 6 metres in length and 3 metres in height, with large individuals weighing approximately 2 tonnes. The success of *Megalosaurus* as a major predator is reflected in the fact that it was represented in European communities for well over 50 million years. Elsewhere, other carnosaurs filled the same ecological niche, with the strange two crested *Dilophosaurus* occurring in the Lower Jurassic of Arizona. In the Upper Jurassic *Allosaurus*, a huge carnosaur appeared to replace *Dilophosaurus* in North America; adult allosaurs measured some 10 metres in length and 4 metres in height. *Allosaurus* was considerably larger than its contemporary the 'horn lizard', *Ceratosaurus*, in which bony thickenings on the snout and above the eyes are thought to have offered protection during battle.

All of the Jurassic carnosaurs were typically

The evolution of the carnosaurs is traced back to a thecodontian ancestry. The great meat-eaters were well represented throughout the whole of the 'Age of Dinosaurs'. The form *Spinosaurus* is thought to represent a specialized side-branch that evolved in the Cretaceous.

In life *Allosaurus*, the 'strange lizard', was the great predator of the Upper Jurassic. It lived in North America and fed on the sauropods, *Brachiosaurus*, *Apatosaurus* and *Diplodocus*, and ornithopods such as *Camptosaurus*. *Allosaurus* may have hunted in small groups, tracking and ultimately killing their giant prey. When *Allosaurus* had finished feeding it is possible that the smaller carnosaur *Ceratosaurus* or the even smaller coelurosaurs scavenged from the carcase.

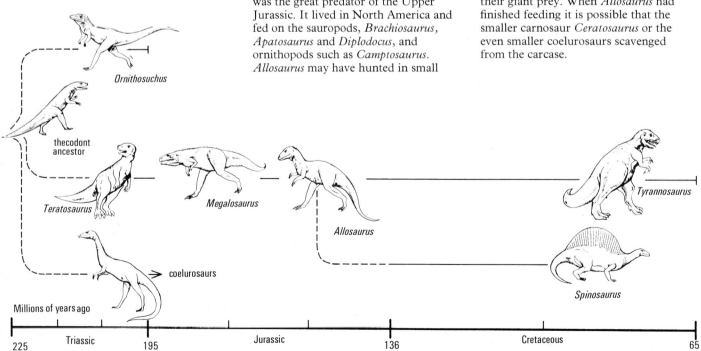

Ornithosuchus

thecodont ancestor

Teratosaurus

Megalosaurus

Allosaurus

coelurosaurs

Tyrannosaurus

Spinosaurus

Millions of years ago

| 225 | Triassic | 195 | Jurassic | 136 | Cretaceous | 65 |

bipedal with their long muscular tails helping the animals maintain their balance whilst running or feeding. The huge jaws and large sharp teeth were ideally suited for the task of killing, and then tearing the carcass apart. In most of the Jurassic communities the carnosaurs hunted and killed the great sauropods and it has been claimed that the ratio of carnosaurs to their prey was very similar to that which exists on the great plains of Africa between the great cats and the herds of zebra and other grazers.

The huge teeth of the carnosaurs are slightly curved and both edges are serrated like those of a sharp steak-knife. Numerous teeth lined the upper and lower jaws and their function was to tear and slice the flesh of the victim into conveniently sized lumps. The teeth illustrated are those of a *Megalosaurus* from the Upper Jurassic.

Sauropods – lizard-hipped giants

Unlike the other major groups of dinosaurs, ie. the coelurosaurs, carnosaurs and ornithischians, the sauropods are known only from rocks of Jurassic and Cretaceous age. The first representatives are found in Lower Jurassic communities and until recently it was thought that they were simply a continuation of the Late Triassic prosauropod lineage. In fact, the two groups have many similarities and it was assumed that the sauropods were just bigger and heavier forms of the same model. However, new studies have cast doubt on this belief and some scientists now believe that the prosauropods represent an older side branch of the family tree.

The Jurassic is really the age of the sauropods, for by the end of the period they were to account for almost half of the plant-eaters in various communities. Numerous species appeared during the Jurassic and various animals referred to the group can be safely described as the largest, longest and heaviest creatures ever to have walked on land. In the lower part of the period the sauropods were represented by *Rhoetosaurus* from Australia. This form was an early relative of the huge *Brachiosaurus* of the Upper Jurassic and characteristically it possessed long front legs and shorter back legs. This condition is diagnostic of the camarosaur sauropods whereas the opposite short front limbs, long hind limbs – is typical of the atlantosaurs such as *Diplodocus* and *Dicraeosaurus*.

The difference in limb proportions represents an adaptation to different modes of life, with the long front legs of the camarosaurs enabling them either to feed off higher levels of vegetation or to live in the deeper areas of swamps or lakes. These alternatives are emphasised deliberately, as several theories exist concerning the modes of life of the sauropod dinosaurs.

One theory, of long standing, suggested that these huge creatures lived most of their life in water, with only their nostrils peeping above the surface of the lake or swamp. This mode of life offered them protection against marauding carnosaurs and was, according to many experts, the only way they could support the great weight of their bodies. However, life at depth would have caused serious problems with breathing, and many of the features of the sauropod skeleton support a more land-based existence. This hypothesis is based on the depth of the body, which in the sauropods is more like that of an elephant than say, the water-dwelling hippopotamus. The limbs of the sauropods were also quite narrow and

Brachiosaurus one of the largest sauropods, known from the Upper Jurassic of North America and East Africa.

hardly likely to give a sound footing in muddy conditions. Further evidence is drawn from the massive construction of the limbs and girdles which would have to support the great weight of the animal in life. Unfortunately even the land-based theory has its faults and some scientists have proposed a compromise in which the great sauropods lived on the edges of swamps with the water rarely higher than shoulder height.

In the Upper Jurassic both the camarosaurs and atlantosaurs were common and *Brachiosaurus* the 'arm-lizard' known from North America and East Africa, grew to 12·6 metres in height and weighed approximately 80 tonnes. *Diplodocus* lived in the same community and although lighter and shorter than its camarosaur cousin was, at 26 metres long, the longest of all the sauropods. An even larger sauropod dubbed 'Supersaurus', discovered in 1972, is estimated to have reached over 30 metres in length and to have weighed over 100 tonnes. Giants were the norm for the Jurassic sauropods, although the discovery of a 32 millimetre sauropod-like dinosaur in 1977, has provided us with the remains of the smallest animal referable to the group. The animal is a juvenile and its discovery, together with that of an egg, from sediments straddling the Triassic-Jurassic boundary in Argentina, is an exciting clue to sauropod growth and evolution.

The family tree of the sauropods traces the ancestry of the group back to the prosauropods, other scientists believe that this is unlikely and that the prosauropods were an early side branch which arose from a common ancestor during the Triassic.

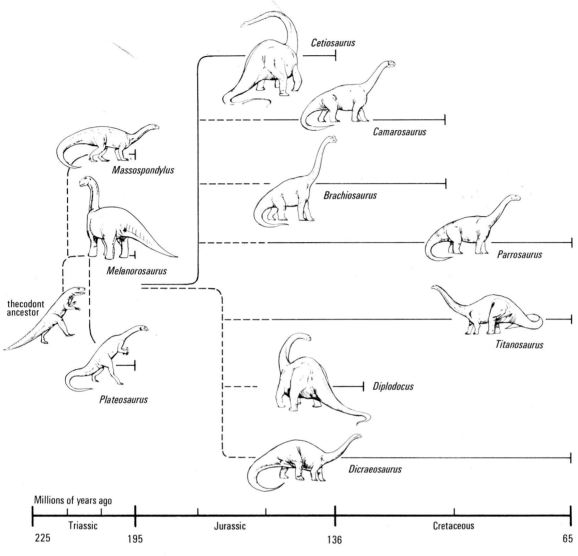

Cetiosaurus

Camarosaurus

Massospondylus

Brachiosaurus

Melanorosaurus

Parrosaurus

thecodont ancestor

Titanosaurus

Diplodocus

Plateosaurus

Dicraeosaurus

Millions of years ago

Triassic	Jurassic	Cretaceous
225	195	136	65

Apatosaurus the 'deceit lizard' is known from the Upper Jurassic of North America.

Diplodocus, at 26 metres it was one of the longest sauropods.

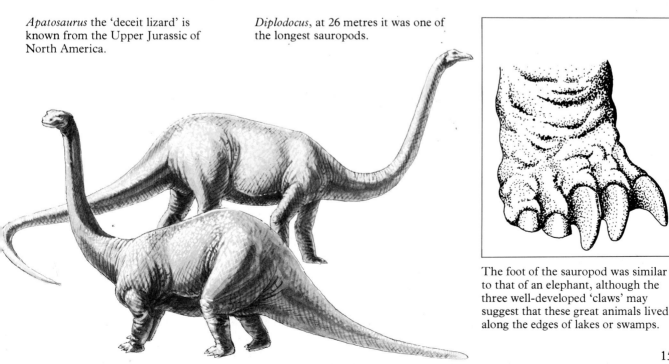

The foot of the sauropod was similar to that of an elephant, although the three well-developed 'claws' may suggest that these great animals lived along the edges of lakes or swamps.

151

Plant-eating bipeds and plated quadrupeds

Kentrosaurus, a plated dinosaur from the Upper Jurassic of East Africa.

The ornithischians of the Jurassic period included the plated quadrupeds, *Scelidosaurus*, *Stegosaurus* and *Kentrosaurus* and the bipedal ornithopods such as *Camptosaurus*. Plated dinosaurs are known from North America, England and East Africa and it is likely that they occupied the niche of low-level grazers. *Stegosaurus*, the 'roof lizard', was a rather strange looking beast, with a small, narrow head and a body that was topped by two rows of extremely large bony plates. It had a brain the size

Camptosaurus, a 'normal' or 'ordinary' ornithopod from the Upper Jurassic of North America. In life it lived alongside the great sauropods, *Diplodocus* and *Brachiosaurus*, the plated-lizard *Stegosaurus*, and the theropods *Allosaurus* and *Coelurus*.

152

Stegosaurus, the great plates along the length of its back are now thought to be linked with the control of its body temperature.

of a golf ball and it is unlikely that it was a very active individual. Various theories have been put forward to explain the presence of the great plates, with those of defence and heat-regulation receiving considerable support. *Stegosaurus* lived in North America, and in East Africa its place in Upper Jurassic communities was taken by the 'prickly lizard', *Kentrosaurus*. The latter was slightly smaller than its plated relative and at 5 metres in length weighed approximately 1 to 1·5 tonnes. The plated lizards are unknown in rocks of Cretaceous age.

The ornithopod, *Camptosaurus*, represented the so-called normal line of ornithopods during the Late Jurassic. Individuals grew to 5 metres in length and weighed up to 3·5 tonnes. The 'bent-lizard' was typically bipedal and it is probable that small herds of these animals fed in the open areas beyond the swamps and forests.

Across a Jurassic landscape

A detailed analysis of the sediments and the fossils of the Morrison Formation of the western part of the United States of America, has enabled palaeontologists to reconstruct the environment and community that existed during the Late Jurassic times in that region. The landscape was one of low lying lands, marked by patches of swamp and with undulating hills in the near distance. Horsetails, ferns and cycads bordered the swamps whilst conifers, ginkgoes and cycads gave rise to areas of denser vegetation. The great sauropods *Brachiosaurus*, *Diplodocus* and *Apatosaurus* fed on the higher levels of terrestrial vegetation, although some also waded into the swamps to crop the soft vegetation that grew close to the banks. Away from the swamps the ornithischians *Camptosaurus* and *Stegosaurus* grazed on ferns and palm-like cycads, always alert to the approach of the carnosaurs, *Allosaurus* and *Ceratosaurus*. At times the recently killed carcase of an ornithopod or a sauropod would litter the ground, with the carnosaurs and small coelurosaurs returning to scavenge the corpse. The coelurosaurs would be second in line in the feeding queue, although some may have attempted to snatch pieces of meat when the carnosaurs attention was distracted. Other scavengers may have

Stegosaurus

Ceratosaurus

154

included small pterosaurs, similar to *Rhamphorhynchus*, the long-tailed form, from East Africa, as well as lizards and crocodiles.

As in our reconstruction of the Arroyo community of the Lower Permian the great meat-eating reptiles topped the food pyramid. In this case *Allosaurus* was the last link in the food chain with the cycads, ferns and conifers as the primary producers of energy. Insects and marsh turtles probably occupied the roles of minor herbivores within the Morrison community. The climate of the time was warm temperate to sub tropical and little or no seasonal change occurred to affect the stability of the environment.

Apatosaurus

Brachiosaurus

Camptosaurus

Reptiles of the air

Although the pterosaurs are thought to have evolved from the small gliding archosaur, *Podopteryx*, during the latter half of the Triassic period, no remains of these flying reptiles have been discovered in rocks older than the Lower Jurassic. The first pterosaur skeleton is that of *Dimorphodon* which lived in the skies over southern England. *Dimorphodon* was a rather unspecialized form with a large, short snouted head and a long tail. This last was a characteristic feature of the majority of early pterosaurs, with *Rhamphorhynchus*, from the Upper Jurassic of East Africa, retaining the feature. *Rhamphorhynchus* possessed an elongate skull in which the sharp teeth sloped forwards. This is an indication of specialized feeding habits and it is likely that this small pterosaur fed on fish and insects that lived in or around the coastal lagoons of Europe and Africa. In the Upper Jurassic the short-tailed pterodactyls appeared in many areas and these longer winged flyers soon replaced the

Rhamphorhynchus

archaic rhamphorhychoids. It is likely that the new form, *Pterodactylus*, competed for the same food with the doomed *Rhamphorhynchus*. In Russia at this time the hairy *Sordes pilosus*, a long-tailed pterosaur, ruled the skies. The furry covering of its body has been discovered intact in the rocks near Chimkent in the Soviet Union, and it suggests that these pterosaurs were warm-blooded fliers.

The largest pterosaurs lived along the tops of coastal cliffs or on the edges of inland plateaus. From these heights they would launch themselves into the air and be lifted skywards on upwelling air currents. On the ground they were rather awkward, shuffling over the ground with their leathery wings held up and over their backs.

It is probable that some of the smaller pterosaurs hung on branches or rocky ledges in much the same way as do the bats of the present day.

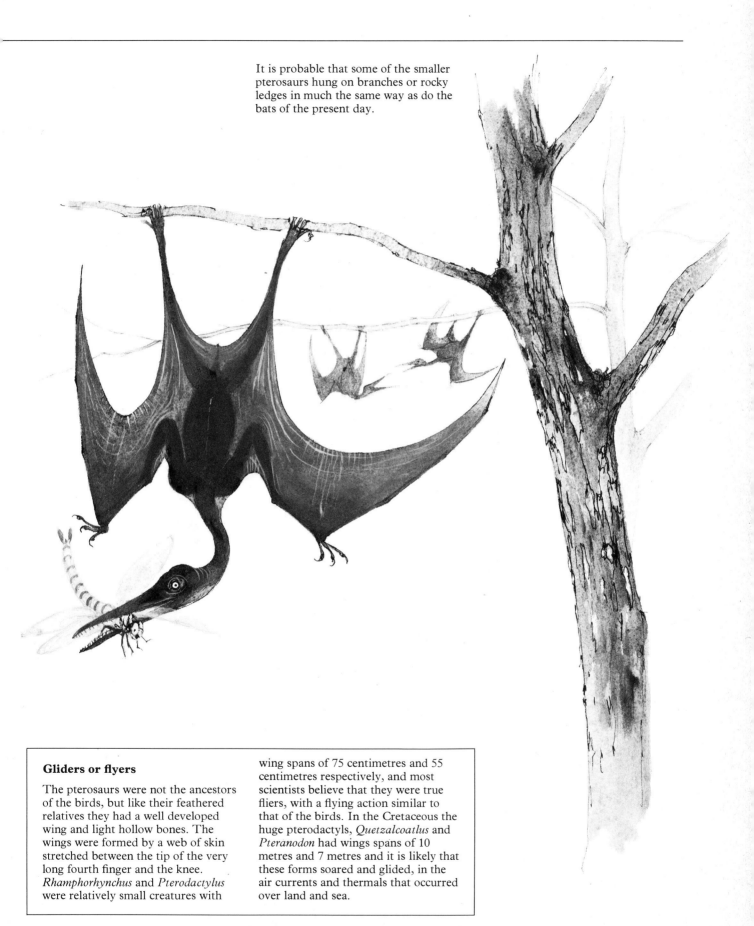

Gliders or flyers

The pterosaurs were not the ancestors of the birds, but like their feathered relatives they had a well developed wing and light hollow bones. The wings were formed by a web of skin stretched between the tip of the very long fourth finger and the knee. *Rhamphorhynchus* and *Pterodactylus* were relatively small creatures with wing spans of 75 centimetres and 55 centimetres respectively, and most scientists believe that they were true fliers, with a flying action similar to that of the birds. In the Cretaceous the huge pterodactyls, *Quetzalcoatlus* and *Pteranodon* had wings spans of 10 metres and 7 metres and it is likely that these forms soared and glided, in the air currents and thermals that occurred over land and sea.

The first bird

This specimen of *Archaeopteryx* was found near Eichstatt in southern Germany in 1951. The specimen is smaller than either of the other two complete specimens now housed in the Natural History Museums of London and Berlin.

Five fossils from the Upper Jurassic, Lithographic Limestone of Solnhofen in Bavaria, southern Germany mark the appearance of the birds in the fossil record. The fossils belong to *Archaeopteryx*, the 'ancient feather', and their independent discoveries rank amongst the more important finds in the history of palaeontology. Three of the specimens are of exceptional quality and provide us with detailed evidence of the skeleton and the feathers of this incredible animal. The skeleton in some ways is extremely reptilian, with many characters warranting direct comparison with those of the small, agile coelurosaurs. For example, it has a long bony tail and the fore-limb has three fingers as in *Compsognathus*. The bird characters of *Archaeopteryx* include the feathers, a wishbone, and obviously, the well-developed wing.

Many theories as to the origin of the first bird have been put forward but few people now question that it was possible for *Archaeopteryx* to have evolved from the coelurosaurs. One of the main objections was that *Archaeopteryx* possessed a wishbone and that dinosaurs had lost theirs, therefore evolution from these animals would have been impossible. Fortunately, the coelurosaurs have two collar bones, and these could have fused to form the wishbone of the first bird.

In life *Archaeopteryx* lived in the same region as *Compsognathus* and *Pterodactylus* and it is probable that it occupied the roles of small predator and insect eater. *Archaeopteryx* was relatively small with the overall length being slightly longer than that of *Compsognathus* (30 centimetres).

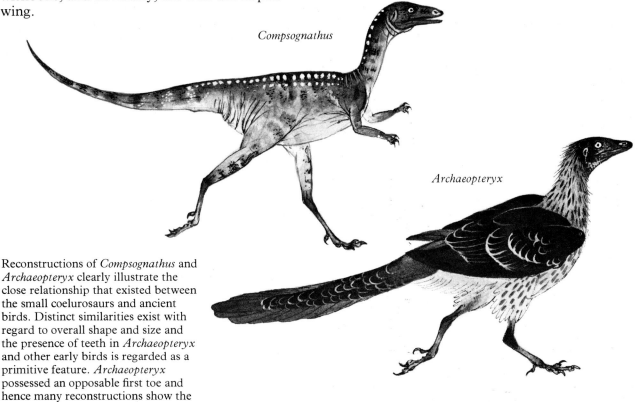

Compsognathus

Archaeopteryx

Reconstructions of *Compsognathus* and *Archaeopteryx* clearly illustrate the close relationship that existed between the small coelurosaurs and ancient birds. Distinct similarities exist with regard to overall shape and size and the presence of teeth in *Archaeopteryx* and other early birds is regarded as a primitive feature. *Archaeopteryx* possessed an opposable first toe and hence many reconstructions show the bird perched on the branch of a tree.

Another Jurassic bird?

The discovery of two thigh bones of Jurassic age from the Dry Mesa quarry of eastern Colorado, has cast some doubt on whether *Archaeopteryx* is really the first bird. The bones are more like those of modern birds, in that they lack the well-developed knob-like head that articulates with the hip socket in *Archaeopteryx* and the coelurosaurs.

According to their discoverer, Dr James Jensen, this is indication of a good flyer, but other scientists have reservations as to their taxonomic status and stratigraphic position.

Do feathers make a flyer?

Although *Archaeopteryx* has wings with feathers, and although the feathers have the same arrangement and structure as those of modern birds, the question of flight in the first bird, is still the subject of considerable debate. Internationally famous scientists have put forward several theories of how *Archaeopteryx* lived and whilst some claim that it was an active flyer, others see it as a glider or ground-dwelling carnivore. The various theories are based on the different characters present in the *Archaeopteryx* skeleton; the intermediate nature of which was bound to cause many problems when it came to a functional interpretation.

The scientists who see *Archaeopteryx* as a pre-flight creature, emphasize the presence of a primitive forelimb and shoulder girdle and the lack of a large bony breast plate. Nor say the supporters of the pre-flight argument, did *Archaeopteryx* have feathers that were firmly attached to a skeleton. Pre-flight theorists envisage the first bird as a fast running, ground dweller which probably used its wings as stabilizers or even to catch insects:

As a glider and percher, *Archaeopteryx* would have used the sharp claws on its hands and feet to climb trees. It could then have perched on a branch with the aid of its strong feet and opposable first toe, and in the last stage of this cycle it would glide to earth with the aid of its feathered wings and tail.

Support for the theory that *Archaeopteryx* was an efficient flyer have usually floundered on the absence of an ossified breast plate, which is necessary for the attachment of the powerful muscles needed for flight. In 1979, however, the American palaeontologists Storrs Olson and Alan Feduccia claimed that the breast plate or sternum was not really necessary and that the strong furcula of *Archaeopteryx* provided a 'suitable point

of origin' for the muscle that provided the power stroke of the wing. Olson and Feduccia concluded that there was nothing in the structure of the shoulder girdle of *Archaeopteryx*, that would preclude its having been an active flier!

It is possible that all the theories proposed for *Archaeopteryx* have something to contribute and it may be that the animal, in life, was deliberately unpredictable. Perhaps it did run along the ground, but it may also have launched itself into the air like some archaic chicken or sought refuge amongst the lower branches of trees. Its unpredictable nature could be interpreted as an escape mechanism, which in the long run, was to lead to true flight.

Unrivalled preservation

The Solnhofen Limestone of the Upper Jurassic of southern Germany outcrops over a broad area just to the north of the River Donau, between Regensburg in the east and Donauwörth in the west. The limestone is famous for its use in the manufacture of lithographic plates and, perhaps, more so as it is the sediment that has yielded such fossils as *Archaeopteryx lithographica*. The rock is extremely fine-grained and compact, and can be easily split into manageable slabs. A microscopic study of the limestone reveals that is composed of minute calcareous discs, that in life covered the outer envelopes of the planktonic organisms called coccolithophores. Blooms of these small organisms were common during the Jurassic period and their remains were often deposited in the sheltered waters between reef and shore. The accumulation of these organic materials gave rise to a carbonate – rich mud, which was not suitable for colonization by sedentary organisms. Fine laminations within the various outcrops indicate fluctuations in the type of sediment deposited; whilst relatively rare but diverse fossils provide information on both prevailing marine and terrestrial communities. The fossils are extremely well preserved, rapid burial in the soft muds preserving for posterity even the most intricate details of the soft parts of individual organisms. The muds must have been anaerobic as little or no organic disintegration has occurred in most specimens. Solnhofen has yielded fossils of many organisms including dinosaurs, birds, ammonites, belemnites, echinoderms, insects and hosts of arthropods. Their beauty is almost unrivalled in the fossil record and are extremely valuable.

Fossils from the Lithographic Limestone were recorded before the start of the last century and the first bird remains were recorded in 1820. In 1861 the first of the four major *Archaeopteryx* skeletons was found. It was discovered near Langenaltheim to the west of the village of Solnhofen and was eventually sold to the British Museum along with a number of other specimens for the 'princely' sum of £700. At the present time, experts believe that the London *Archaeopteryx*, on its own, is worth well over £1 000 000. *Archaeopteryx* is perhaps the 'unique' fossil of the Solnhofen limestone but other specimens are equally important in terms of the data they provide on both anatomical and palaeoecological matters. The skeleton of the small dinosaur *Compsognathus* is, in itself, a very beautiful specimen and its exceptional preservation has allowed palaeontologists to research fully the question of a coelurosaurian ancestry for the birds. Other vertebrate fossils include the remains of various pterosaurs which reveal details of the wings and, in some cases, the tail. It has been suggested that most of these animals died when the mudflats were uncovered by water and buried before either they could be scavenged or decay could truly set in.

In the case of the invertebrates the fauna is dominated by swimmers and bottom crawlers. It is possible that these organisms were stranded at low tide, although it is equally likely that they died during one of the phases when blooms of coccoliths poisoned the waters of the lagoon.

The two king crabs illustrated are remarkably similar, the lower one is a fossil from the Solnhofen limestone whilst the one on the left is the living *Limulus*. The similarity between the specimens is both an indication of the unchanging character of the 'sword tails' and an 'advertisement' for the kind of conditions that prevailed during the preservation of the fossils of the Lithographic Stone.

Below
Cyclocaris, a lobster-like decapod from the Solnhofen Limestone.

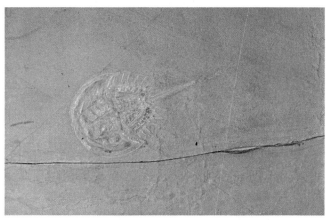

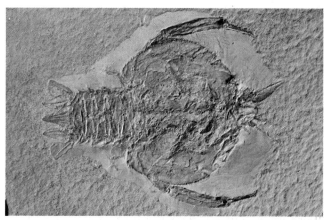

Numerous shrimps and shrimp-like crustaceans are recorded from the Solnhofen Limestone. They include the twisty shrimp *Aeger tipularis* and the beautiful *Acanthochrinus cordatus* (shown right).

Left
The limestone quarries of the Altmühl-Alb of the Southern Franconian Jura in south Germany were for many, many years an important source of the Lithographic Stone used in the printing industry. The limestone is of Kimmeridgian age (Upper Jurassic) and occurs in relatively thin layers. When it was being exploited, craftsmen split the limestone blocks along natural laminations and infrequently their work revealed exquisite fossils like those illustrated.

Well adapted to a life in water

The sharks, ichthyosaurs and dolphins are often used as classic examples of convergence, where three animals from totally unrelated stocks have developed similar characteristics. In the three groups in question the fish-shaped body is the most obvious feature of comparison and whilst one can argue that this a natural characteristic of sharks, in the ichthyosaurs and dolphins it represented an adaptation to a new environment. The environment is a positive control over evolution and therefore animals with similar habits can be expected to look alike. Naturally the modifications are mainly superficial and both the ichthyosaurs and dolphins retained the majority of their respective reptilian and mammalian characters. All three types of animal are, or were, extremely active hunter-predators in which the main organ of propulsion is the tail. In the shark and the ichthyosaur the tail movement is from side-to-side whilst in the dophin it is up and down. Speed is an essential pre-requisite of the hunter and it is possible that the ichthyosaurs, like the dolphins were capable of exceeding 15 or even 20 kilometres per hour. Apart from the fish-shaped body many other features of the ichthyosaurs indicated that they alone amongst the reptiles were totally adapted to a marine life. This included giving birth to live young.

The skull of the ichthyosaurs possessed a long narrow snout and the nostrils were placed far back on the sides of the head to allow the animal to feed and breathe at the same time. Ichthyosaurs had huge eyeballs which suggest good sight and if the size of the bony elements of the inner ear (stapes) are considered then they had also excellent hearing.

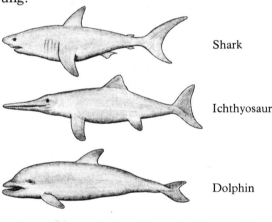

Shark

Ichthyosaur

Dolphin

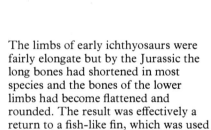

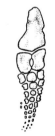

The limbs of early ichthyosaurs were fairly elongate but by the Jurassic the long bones had shortened in most species and the bones of the lower limbs had become flattened and rounded. The result was effectively a return to a fish-like fin, which was used for steering.

The eyeball of an ichthyosaur was strengthened by a ring of bones (the sclerotic ring) which curved backwards around the area outside the pupil. In life the ring prevented distortion of the eyeball when the animal was diving. Similar rings occur in many other reptiles including the duck-billed dinosaurs, in which the bones of the ring overlapped slightly. Some experts believe that in this case, the ring kept the eyeball at a constant size as an aid to focussing.

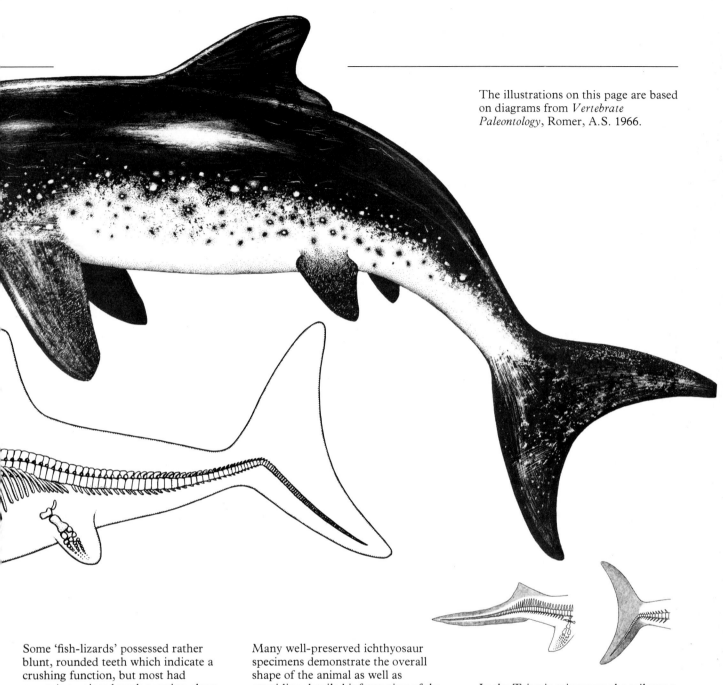

The illustrations on this page are based on diagrams from *Vertebrate Paleontology*, Romer, A.S. 1966.

Some 'fish-lizards' possessed rather blunt, rounded teeth which indicate a crushing function, but most had numerous pointed teeth running along the length of the jaws. Throughout the life of the animal worn teeth were constantly replaced by new ones.

The fossilized gut contents of various ichthyosaurs indicate that the animals in question fed mostly on fish and ammonites.

Many well-preserved ichthyosaur specimens demonstrate the overall shape of the animal as well as providing detailed information of the form of the skeleton. In these specimens it is possible to observe the outline of a large dorsal fin which helped the animal maintain an even keel whilst swimming.

In the Triassic mixosaurs the tail was a rather long, straight structure with ribbon-like fins above and below. This represented the primitive condition for in the more advanced stocks the tail was similar to that of a shark. The support for the lower part of the tail was provided by the backbone which was strongly downturned at the beginning of the tail region.

The Cretaceous

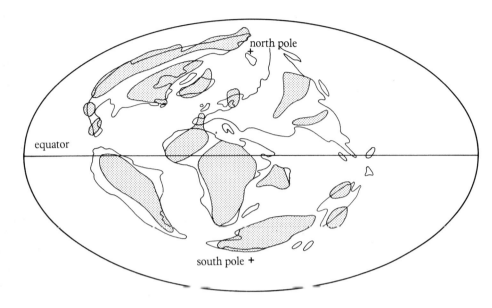

The Cretaceous period began 136 million years ago and finished approximately 71 million years later. During the period the opening of the Atlantic was to adopt an increasing significance and the break between Antarctica and Australia was probably initiated. At first the Cretaceous climate was equable like that of the Jurassic, but a gradual change towards increased seasonality was to mark the latter half of the period. Coal forests covered large areas of western North America, Alaska and Siberia and limited areas of South Africa and Australia. Reef building occurred along the shores of Tethys, the Caribbean and the western coastline of South America. Desert lands covered much of Mongolia and China. The Cretaceous was a period of dinosaurs, huge sea lizards, ammonites and rudists. It was the last period of the Mesozoic Era and its end was marked by the mass extinctions of many organisms.

One of the most significant events of the Cretaceous was the emergence of the flowering plants, or angiosperms, as a major component of world floras. The word angiosperm means 'enclosed seed' and the evolution of the group was as important as that of the mammals and birds. Angiosperms developed the unique feature of double fertilization in which two nuclei derived from the pollen grain enter into the ovule. One fertilizes the ovum, whilst the other fuses with the two polar nuclei that lie close to the ovum, and these three then divide to form the food store, or endosperm, of the seed. The seed, consisting of embryo and foodstore is protected by a seed coat and a fruit which provide a double protection. The fruits and seeds vary considerably and animals have become as important an agent of dispersal, as wind and water. Insects also help in pollination, with the colour and scent of the flowers attracting them to the plant. Many flowers have also developed complex mechanisms to prevent self pollination and these advances, coupled with improvements in woody tissues and in the variety and size of leaf, make the angiosperms the most advanced group within the plant kingdom.

Magnoliaceans are both evergreen and deciduous trees that were originally endemic to Asia and North America. Their large, colourful flowers possess a cone-like centre in which the carpels and stamens have a spiral arrangement. This is a primitive feature and in many ways is similar to the arrangement found in various gymnosperms. The actual structure of the carpels and the seeds is also less advanced than those of most recent

flowering plants and it is possible that the magnoliaceans represent a very early stage in the evolution of the flowering plants. Magnoliacean fossils have been recorded from the Lower Cretaceous and found in sediments of the Upper Cretaceous in association with species of oak, poplar, sycamore and maple.

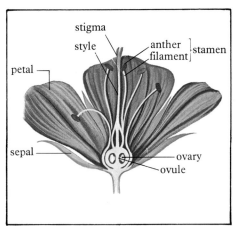

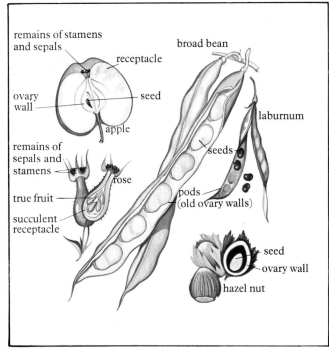

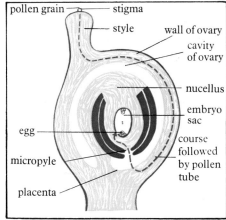

Top left
Vertical section through a flower to show the basic parts.

Top right
Some typical fruits and seeds

Above
Vertical section through an angiosperm carpel showing events following pollination, leading to fertilization.

Cretaceous vegetation

Below
The first undoubted angiosperm leaf-impressions are of Lower Cretaceous age, left is shown the impression of a leaf from the family *Laurus*, from this period.

The vegetation of the Lower Cretaceous comprised ferns, horsetails and gymnosperms such as cycads, ginkgoes and conifers. There was a fairly simple zonation into tropical and extra-tropical floras, and only the conifers showed distinct northern or southern affinities. Flowering plants, or angiosperms, which are known from the Jurassic, were insignificant, and it was not until later, in the Middle Cretaceous, that they became numerous. During the Upper Cretaceous, however, the angiosperms rose to dominance more or less everywhere. They achieved a remarkable modernization of the world's floras with a truly explosive radiation which defined many of the present-day families. The modernization was more complete in the northern hemisphere than in the southern, where ferns and conifers remained mixed in with the angiosperms up to the end of the Cretaceous.

Whilst the general picture is clear, the Cretaceous angiosperms nevertheless present some fascinating puzzles. When the first angiosperm leaf impressions make their sudden appearance in Lower Cretaceous sediments they are already essentially modern in aspect. For example, the poplar, fig and cinnamon genera can be recognized in the Lower Cretaceous of western Canada. Clearly, an earlier, undetected history is suggested. One palaeobotanist has argued that it may even extend back to the Carboniferous, and that the absence of fossils is due to the angiosperms having evolved in upland areas where preservation would not have been likely. Needless to say the absence of fossils has also led to competing claims for the place of origin, including northerly, equatorial and southern latitudes! Greenland was once regarded as the source, since in Cretaceous times it was linked to North America and Europe, and the oldest well-developed angiosperm floras occur on either side of the North Atlantic in supposedly contemporaneous sediments. The evidence for a tropical origin is twofold. In the northern hemisphere the first angiosperms are recorded in successively younger rocks going from equator to pole. This seems conclusive enough but unfortunately it is too soon to say whether the same applies to the southern hemisphere. The alternative support for a tropical origin is of a very different kind, namely that the greatest present-day concentrations of what may be regarded as primitive angiosperms live in south-east Asia, between Assam and Fiji. A possible southern derivation was referred to earlier and the justification is perhaps no less compelling. Basically it is

that 40 per cent of the major angiosperm families have modern distributions with a marked antarctic base and that many of them are exclusively confined to the southern hemisphere; just two very small families are confined to the northern hemisphere.

Turning now to the spectacularly rapid global dominance of the angiosperms in the Cretaceous, it is difficult to accept that it was achieved with the continents in their present position. Continental drift undoubtedly assisted in the widespread migration of the angiosperms, as the main families were established well before the fragmentation of the supercontinents was far advanced. This helps us to understand why the same four families – the grasses, sedges, legumes and daisies – are now amongst the six most numerous on every continent. Similarly it accounts for the fact that members of the same genus are today separated by vast oceanic distances. Thus the baobab trees grow in East Africa and Australia, whereas the southern beeches are found in the tip of South America and 10 000 kilometres away in New Zealand.

It is evident therefore, that the foundations of the modern floral kingdoms were laid in the Cretaceous, at the time when the angiosperms embarked upon a divergence that has left us with 225 000 living species.

Left
A plane leaf from the Cretaceous.
The Platanaceae were an abundant and
diverse group in the northern
hemisphere during this period.

Below left
A palm leaf from the Cretaceous
showing the parallel veining typical of
monocotyledons.

Below
Populus, this form was already present
in the Cretaceous.

Wealden shoreline

The low-lying coastal lands of the Early Cretaceous offered an ideal environment for the expansion of the ornithischian dinosaurs. In many ways the conditions represented a continuation of the Upper Jurassic, with the climate remaining warm and humid. Sauropods were still present in the form of *Diplodocus* whilst *Megalosaurus* retained the role of giant carnosaur and dominant predator. New herbivores had evolved, however, and *Iguanodon*, *Hypsilophodon* and *Polacanthus* were to herald the rise of the ornithischians to the position of the dominant herbivores during the Cretaceous period. The remains of *Diplodocus* are limited whereas those of *Iguanodon* and *Hypsilophodon* are relatively common and fairly cosmopolitan in their distribution.

In terms of numbers *Iguanodon* was the major herbivore of the Early Cretaceous. Individual animals grew to 9 or 10 metres in length and 5 metres in height. They were essentially bipedal, although a thickening of the forearms in older animals suggests that

Iguanodon is one of the best known dinosaurs, the first fossils of which were discovered by Mrs. Gideon Mantell in the spring of 1822. Between 1877 and 1880, thirty-one iguanodonts were collected from a fissure infill near the town of Bernissart in Belgium.

Hypsilophodon was once thought to have lived in the trees of the Lower Cretaceous, the length and structure of its limbs, however, indicate that it was a fast-running, ground dweller.

Polacanthus, an early ankylosaur from the Lower Cretaceous of England.

Hypsilophodon

Polacanthus

their great weight necessitated a quadrupedal stance. Evidence for herding amongst iguanodonts exists and it is conceivable that family groups of this large herbivore roamed the lowland plains. Herding afforded the animals considerable protection against predators, particularly as their only weapon of defence was the large spiky thumb on each hand.

Hypsilophodon looked like a smaller and more agile version of the large iguanodonts. It was a fast running biped; adult animals growing to just under 1·5 metres in length. Both *Hypsilophodon* and *Iguanodon* were ornithopods. They were very different to their distant relative the armoured, ankylosaur, *Polacanthus*. For *Polacanthus* was a slow moving quadruped with a dorsal armour of spines and plates. When attacked *Polacanthus* would not have been able to out run the great carnosaurs *Altispinax* and *Megalosaurus*, and therefore its defensive pose would have been to crouch low and present its tormentor with an almost impenetrable wall of bone.

Iguanodon   Hypsilophodon   171

Wealden lakes

During the Early Cretaceous terrestrial conditions covered Ireland, most of Scotland and western England. Northern and central France, Belgium and the London regions were also above sea level. In the south land flanked the coastal lakes and swamps of southern England, Paris and Holland whilst in the north it formed the shoreline of a shallow shelf sea. To the east and west, terrestrial conditions covered vast areas of Eurasia, Greenland and North America, with a southern shoreline from Newfoundland through Spain to India, marking the northern boundary of the great Tethyan Ocean. Throughout the Early Cretaceous the region of northern Europe fell within the so-called 'Boreal Realm' in which colder temperatures, differences in salinity and other ecological conditions produced very different communities to those of the warm, carbonite-rich waters of the Tethys. In the latter the coral-like rudistid bivalves grew to great sizes and many groups of ammonites flourished in the stable environmental conditions. Around the shores of southern Europe the scene was very different and the lakes and swamps supported a rather limited fauna of freshwater gastropods, bivalves and fishes. At times these freshwater communities would be exposed to an influx of saline waters from the northerly shelf seas and the change to brackish water or even marine faunas is well documented in the sediments of the Wealden basins.

Our reconstruction is of a freshwater Wealden community and the representative gastropod is *Viviparus* and a shallow burrowing bivalve known as *Pseudunio*. In the surface layers of the sediments millions of minute ostracodes thrived during Wealden times whilst the holostean fish *Lepidotes* swam in the upper waters of the lakes. *Lepidotes* was a long ranging and cosmopolitan form, with rather thick rhomboidal scales. The freshwater lakes were also the home of medium-size turtles, such as *Pleurosternum*, which fed on soft vegetation and soft-bodied invertebrates.

Along the edges of freshwater lakes the horsetails were still common although their size bore no comparison with that of Carboniferous species. Fragments of horsetails and conifers together with the decaying carcases of the dinosaurs *Iguanodon* and *Hypsilophodon* were transported into the lakes by rivers that frequently flooded the low-lying plains.

In some ways the landscape beyond the edges of the lakes was similar to that of the Florida Everglades, with the conifers forming a distinct canopy in the better drained areas. Flowering plants had appeared in numbers and various insects had evolved to collect their pollen.

Iguanodon and other dinosaurs were the major components of the vertebrate communities that lived along the edges of the Wealden swamps and lakes.

Equisetes, a horset

Viviparus, a small to medium-sized gastropod known from Jurassic to Recent sediments throughout the world. It is a good indicator of freshwater conditions.

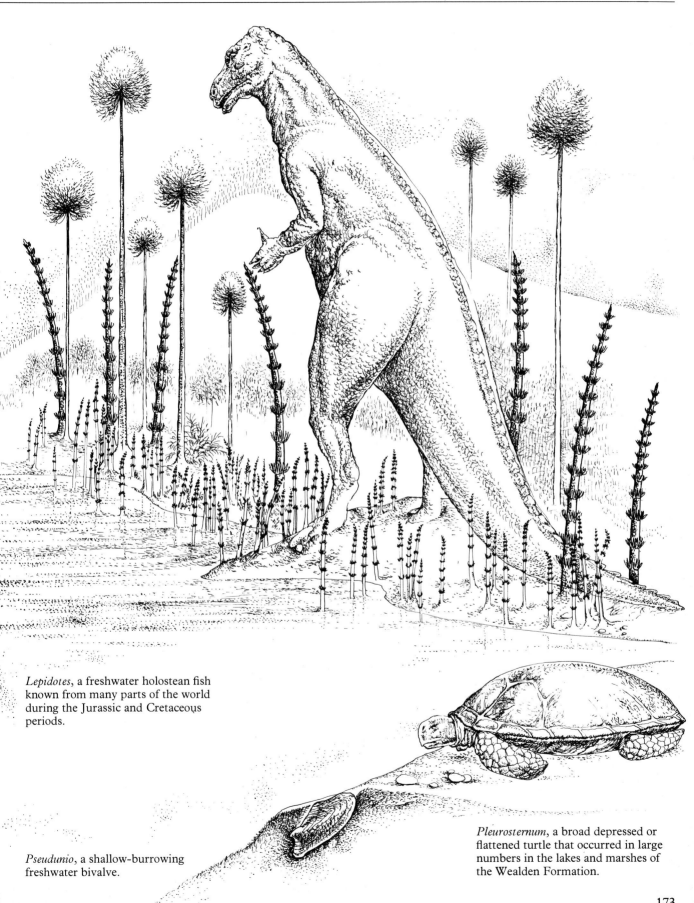

Lepidotes, a freshwater holostean fish known from many parts of the world during the Jurassic and Cretaceous periods.

Pseudunio, a shallow-burrowing freshwater bivalve.

Pleurosternum, a broad depressed or flattened turtle that occurred in large numbers in the lakes and marshes of the Wealden Formation.

Cretaceous hardgrounds

Calcareous hardground – Great Oolite; Cirencester, England.

The term *hardground* is used to describe ancient sea floors which became cemented to form a firm substrate. Hardgrounds and associated nodular beds are common throughout the statigraphic column, but those of the Cretaceous period and of the Chalk in particular, are possibly the best known. The formation of a hard ground proceeds most successfully in areas characterized by a low rate of sedimentation, which favours the precipitation of a binding cement. In the Chalk the initial cement was usually a magnesium-rich calcite but in other geological horizons the cements included phosphates and iron oxides. The preliminary stages in cementation may result in a nodular bed but in time a continuous hardground will appear. The latter was often formed just below the surface of the sea-floor and erosion would be necessary to expose the hardground prior to colonization. The firm substrate attracted organisms that attached themselves to the sea bed with encrusting animals such as bivalves, bryozoans, serpulid worms and small corals being well represented. Boring organisms, dominated by suspension feeders, would also inhabit the area.

In our example of an Upper Cretaceous hardground, it is noticeable that the substrate has been extensively burrowed. The burrows represent the activities of crustaceans and, like those of the Jurassic, are named *Thalassinoides*. They were formed before cementation occurred, and are often infilled with later sediments or fragments of shell material. In some hardgrounds the burrow infills provided homes for creatures that would normally inhabit a soft substrate. In the fixed or attached animal groups, bivalves such as the mussel-like *Septifer* and the large, concentrically ornamented, *Inoceramus* were dominant. The small solitary coral *Parasmilia* was also common and although living species exist at depths of up to 325 metres it is generally thought that the hardground community of the Upper Cretaceous developed in shallower waters. In some areas the hardgrounds were covered with algae and possibly sea grasses, and small gastropods were to be found attached to this vegetative cover. The sponge, *Entobia*, was also a member of the hardground community although it differed considerably from the other organisms in that it excavated hollow meandering galleries just below the hardground surface. Bivalves such as *Martesia* also bored into the surface for protection. The hardground community did not consist solely of attached and boring forms, as various free-living gastropods, bivalves and echinoids have been recorded. Other free-living creatures included the cephalopods, *Scaphites* and *Lewesiceras* and mollusc-eating sharks such as *Hybodus*. In times of increased sedimentation the hardground community would be buried and soft-bottom creatures including burrow-forming crustaceans would return.

Reconstruction of a Cretaceous
hardground (after McKerrow, 1978).

Kelp

Lewesiceras

Scaphites

Bostrychoceras

Inoceramus

Parasmilia

Modiolus

Coiled and uncoiled ammonites

For much of the Upper Cretaceous the seas of the world appear to have been warmer and generally more quiescent than today. This is emphasized by the widespread distribution of various genera and species of rudists, belemnites, ammonites and brachiopods. Numerous seaways carried warm water poleward from the Tethyan tropical region and many organisms were able to migrate fairly freely. Naturally in the circum-polar areas we can still recognize the existence of both northern Boreal and southern Austral provinces, and even determine the influence of cold water currents. But in the main the world was dominated by the warm equatorial influence of Tethys.

Of the various groups of animals noted above, the ammonites were persistently successful

Mantelliceras (after McKerrow, 1978)

throughout Tethys, whilst in the Boreal province the belemnites were the dominant cephalopod stock. Belemnites were also present in warmer waters but their fossil remains show little of the variety exhibited by their distant ancestors. The belemnites, like the squid and cuttle-fish, were free-swimming animals and their internal skeletons provided protection for the visceral organs and acted as a counterbalance to the weight of the anterior part of the body. The belemnites skeleton was ideally suited for these functions and although significant changes in shape occurred, the overall 'bullet-like' form is maintained throughout their history. Amongst Upper Cretaceous ammonites, both free-swimming and bottom-dwelling stocks can be recognized within a spectacular variety of

shells, indicating a high degree of habitat selection. Of the free swimmers *Mantelliceras* and *Acanthoceras* were widely distributed and it is thought that these normally coiled ammonites travelled the world feeding on the abundant food supplies carried by the oceanic currents. The same idea has also been put forward for, the essentially straight-shelled, *Baculites*. In this case it is thought the animal floated in a vertical position, as the shell had little or no weight to fully counterbalance the head and tentacles. Other floaters included the loosely-coiled *Scaphites* and *Hyphantoceras*, both of which show widespread distribution in the Upper Cretaceous. These loosely-coiled genera are often referred to as 'aberrant' forms or heteromorphs, and the climax

of these non-uniform types is seen in forms like *Turrilites* and *Nipponites*. The former had a cosmopolitan distribution and its high-spired, gastropod-like structure suggests that it either crawled or 'hovered' over the substrate. *Nipponites* was the ultimate non-conformist of the ammonite world and its intertwined shell is surely indicative of a bottom dweller. It has been recorded only from Japan and Siberia and the suggestion is that this rather grotesque form, had adapted to a fixed mode of life within a restricted environment. Normally coiled and 'aberrant' ammonites flourished until the end of the Cretaceous and little or no sign of their pending, total demise can be recognized within the stratigraphic record of that time.

Spiny skins

In the various references to the echinoderms we have established that various stocks such as the crinoids, blastoids and cystoids were well represented in Palaeozoic communities. The sea urchins (echinoids) and starfish (asterozoans), were also present and the fossil record of the 'spiny-skins' as a phylum supposedly dates back into the Precambrian. The majority of Palaeozoic echinoderms were fixed-bottom dwellers with the shift in emphasis towards the free-living echinoids and starfish, occurring only after the great Permian extinction. Of the fixed forms the blastoids, cystoids and many groups of crinoids failed to survive the Palaeozoic era. The crinoids of the Mesozoic and Cainozoic belong to the subclass Articulata with both stem-bearing and free-swimming forms being recorded. In the Jurassic the giant *Seirocrinus* grew to well over 6 metres with some experts believing that the animal floated in a hanging position attached to a log. In contrast the small stemless *Saccocoma* moved freely in the surface waters. Numerous specimens of this form have been found in the Jurassic Solnhofen Limestone deposits of southern Germany.

The Jurassic also saw the appearance of the first of the 'irregular' echinoids. These differed from their more ancient, 'regular' relatives in having a greater variety of shapes, due to the migration of the anus to the outside of the circlet of apical plates and the resulting loss of radial symmetry. Many 'irregular' echinoids were adapted to a partially or completely buried mode of life and as a result their preservational record since the Jurassic is good. In fact, it is much better than that of the 'regular' echinoids, who were and are mostly surface dwellers, whose tests are easily destroyed after death by current action or scavengers. The echinoids are gregarious animals and it is not unusual to find large numbers in a small, localized area. In the Jurassic 'irregular' genera such as *Nucleolites*, *Pygaster* and *Clypeus*, were important as were the 'regular' forms *Phymosoma* and *Palaeopedina*.

Amongst the asterozoans both starfishes and brittle stars are recorded from rocks of the Mesozoic but overall their fossil record from this era is very poor. Although as with other organisms characterized by a 'fragile' construction numerous individuals have been discovered in the Solnhofen Limestones.

Left
Hemicidaris, a small regular echinoid commonly found in shallow-water communities of the Upper Jurassic.

Right
Nucleolites, a small irregular echinoid which ranged from the Middle Jurassic through to the Upper Cretaceous. It is usually portrayed as a shallow burrower.

Seirocrinus, a gigantic crinoid from the Posidonia Shales of Germany.

Sea-going reptiles

By the Early Cretaceous the plesiosaurs were well on the way to being the dominant marine reptiles as the sea-going crocodiles and the ichthyosaurs were moving into steady decline. The crocodiles, of the two, had disappeared by the end of the Lower Cretaceous sub-period, but a limited number of ichthyosaurs persisted into the Upper Cretaceous. Amongst the plesiosaurs, both long and short-necked varieties thrived throughout the period, with one group, the elasmosaurs, having as many as seventy-six vertebrae in their long and extremely flexible necks. Their heads were relatively large indicating that the elasmosaurs had become specialists in feeding on the shoals of fishes that swam in the surface waters of the Cretaceous seas.

During the Upper Cretaceous the elasmosaurs were joined by the sea-going turtles and the voracious mosasaurs. The turtles belonged to several stocks, with the giant *Archelon* representing the archaic protostegids and *Allopleuron* the extant sea turtles –the cheloniids. Some evidence also exists for the appearance of the first leathery turtles and these together with the forms already mentioned indicate a significant diversification of the anapsid reptiles during the latter half of the Cretaceous. *Allopleuron* probably fed on the marine grasses that now flourished on the sea floor, whilst the protostegids and leathery turtles ate soft-bodied jellyfishes. All the groups were represented by powerful long distance swimmers. The feeding grounds of the *Allopleuron* were centered around islands in what is now the south-eastern part of Holland. Apart from sea-grasses, invertebrates were also abundant and the complex

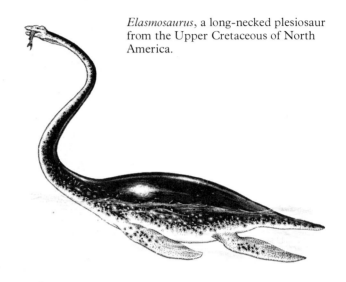

Elasmosaurus, a long-necked plesiosaur from the Upper Cretaceous of North America.

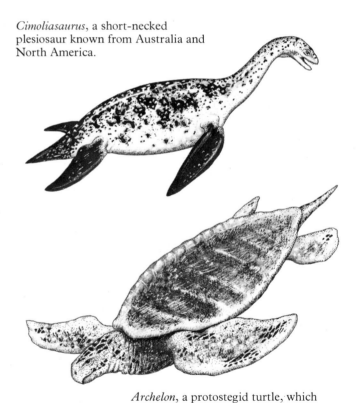

Cimoliasaurus, a short-necked plesiosaur known from Australia and North America.

Archelon, a protostegid turtle, which grew to almost 4 metres in length.

Miopterygius, an ichthyosaur from the Cretaceous of the Southern Hemisphere.

The huge jaws of the mosasaurs were highly effective in capturing their prey, such as marine turtles.

food chain was dominated by the predatory mosasaurs.

The mosasaurs were marine lizards fully adapted to an aquatic mode of life. They appear to have evolved from a group of semi-aquatic lizards, the first of which appeared in the Upper Jurassic. Unlike their ancestors, the mosasaurs were often extremely large and a long, rather eel-like tail was the main propulsive organ. The limbs consisted of reduced long bones and elongate digits, provided the animal with broad paddle-like structures, used as steering devices. Mosasaurs, such as *Tylosaurus* and *Clidastes*, were characterized by huge jaws and numerous large teeth that were set into deep pits. In *Globidens* the teeth were flattened and it appears that this mosasaur fed on the shell banks that bordered the Upper Cretaceous shoreline.

Voracious marine lizards

The first discovery of a mosasaur was made in 1770, when the huge jaws of a 'Meuse Lizard' were extracted from the Upper Cretaceous rocks of St. Peter's Mountain, Maastricht in Holland.

Reconstructed panoramic view of the appearance of insects in relation to the evolution of other animals and plants from the Carboniferous to the Jurassic Periods.

1 Blattodea – cockroach nymph; **2** Palaeodictyoptera – *Lithomantis carbonaria*; **3** Protodonata – *Meganeura monyi*; **4** Megasecoptera – *Corydaloides seudderi*; **5** Palaeodictyoptera – *Homaloneura ornata*; **6** Blattodea –

Phylloblatta carbonaria; **7** *Dictyomylaeris poipaulti*; **8** Protorthoptera – *Gerarus danielsi*; **9** Plecoptera – stonefly nymph under water; **10** Protoelytroptera – *Protodytron permianum*; **11** Plecoptera – *Lemmatrophora typica*; **12** Eryops – one of the first amphibians; **13** Ephemeroptera (mayfly) – *Protereisma permianum*; **14** Orthoptera (grasshopper) – *Metoedischia* spp; **15** Plectopera (stonefly) –

Triassic 200 million years ago ——————————→|←—————— Jurassic 150 million years ago ——————————

Permocapnia brevipes; **16** Protohemiptera (plant-sucking bugs) – *Eugereon böckingi*; **17** Odonata – blue darter dragonfly; **18** Neuroptera (lacewings) – *Megapsychops illidgei*; **19** Hymenoptera (sawflies) – *Symphyta* spp; **20** the first Archosaurs – *Scleromochlus* spp; **21** Mecoptera – scorpion flies; **22** Odonata – dragonflies; **23** Leaf-hopper; **24** Hemiptera: Homoptera – plant-feeding bugs; **25** Tricoptera – caddis flies; **26** Pterodactyls; **27** Hemiptera: Heteroptera (Pondskater) – *Chresmoda obscura*; **28** Hymenoptera: Symphyta (woodwasp) – *Pseudosirex* spp; **29** Archaeopteryx; **30** Dermaptera (earwigs) – *Semenoviola* spp; **31** Stegosauria; **32** Neuroptera – *Mesopsychopsis hospes*; **33** The Magnoliaceae – early flowering plants.

Cretaceous sauropods

The sauropods of the Cretaceous were fewer in numbers than those of the Upper Jurassic and none reached the incredible sizes attained by *Brachiosaurus* and '*Supersaurus*'. In the Northern Hemisphere the record of sauropods is extremely limited but on southern continents the continuation of more stable environmental conditions enabled these great saurischians to survive until the end of the period. Both camarasaurs and atlantosaurs occurred in the Early Cretaceous, but by the advent of the latter half of this period, the descendants of *Brachiosaurus* and the other 'high-shouldered' sauropods had, except for one doubtful recording, vanished.

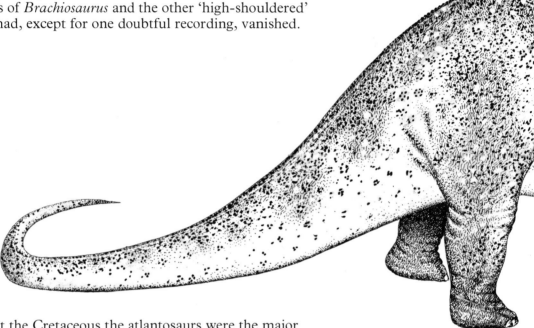

Alamosaurus, an atlantosaur from the Upper Cretaceous of North America.

Throughout the Cretaceous the atlantosaurs were the major sauropod stock. *Diplodocus* survived into the Cretaceous in the Northern Hemisphere, with a few individuals living in the same localities as *Iguanodon*. New forms on the northern continents included *Alamosaurus* and *Hypselosaurus*, of the Upper Cretaceous of North America and Europe respectively. *Alamosaurus* lived in the same communities as *Tyrannosaurus* and it is likely that the two were frequently involved in life or death struggles. *Hypselosaurus* is known from southern France and northern Spain and clutches of eggs only attributable to this sauropod have been found fossilized in the same Upper Cretaceous sediments. The eggs have a rough surface texture and a maximum length of approximately 25 centimetres.

In the Southern Hemisphere, atlantosaurs were quite common in the coastline communities of most of the individual continents, excluding Antarctica. *Titanosaurus* flourished in Africa and South America, whilst other genera, including *Aegyptosaurus*, were rently restricted to specific regions such as North Africa. The success of the atlantosaurs in surviving long after their camarasaur cousins was not due to the development of any new characteristics, for their body profiles were similar to those of their ancestors. Their brains were still extremely small and no new found intelligence had led these animals to migrate southwards away from the northern lands. The success of the atlantosaurs in the Southern Hemisphere is a puzzle, but then the warmer climes of these southern lands have frequently served as a living museum for rather primitive stocks.

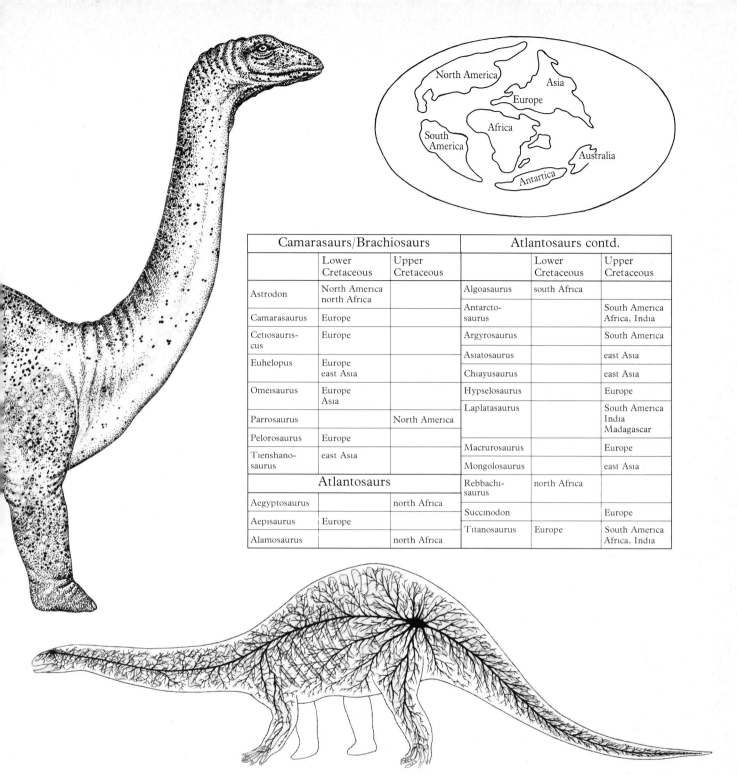

Camarasaurs/Brachiosaurs	Lower Cretaceous	Upper Cretaceous
Astrodon	North America north Africa	
Camarasaurus	Europe	
Cetiosauriscus	Europe	
Euhelopus	Europe east Asia	
Omeisaurus	Europe Asia	
Parrosaurus		North America
Pelorosaurus	Europe	
Tienshanosaurus	east Asia	
Atlantosaurs		
Aegyptosaurus		north Africa
Aepisaurus	Europe	
Alamosaurus		north Africa

Atlantosaurs contd.	Lower Cretaceous	Upper Cretaceous
Algoasaurus	south Africa	
Antarctosaurus		South America Africa, India
Argyrosaurus		South America
Asiatosaurus		east Asia
Chiayusaurus		east Asia
Hypselosaurus		Europe
Laplatasaurus		South America India Madagascar
Macrurosaurus		Europe
Mongolosaurus		east Asia
Rebbachisaurus	north Africa	
Succinodon		Europe
Titanosaurus	Europe	South America Africa, India

Many people believe that the great sauropods possessed two brains, one in the head and the other in the region of the hips. This is untrue, as the swelling in the pelvic region was simply an enlargement of the spinal cord which dealt with the relay of messages to the various nerves that controlled the movements of the huge back legs.

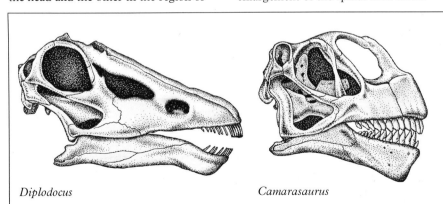

Diplodocus

Camarasaurus

The heads of different sauropods showed considerable variation as to the position of the nostrils and the arrangement of the teeth.

Fleet of foot – egg-stealers and predators

In contrast with the sauropods, the small agile coelurosaurs exhibited an enhanced cosmopolitan distribution during the Cretaceous. The new stocks that had branched off the 'normal' line during the Jurassic were now firmly established, with individuals showing different adaptations to particular modes of life. In the Early Cretaceous the 'normal' line of coelurosaurs was represented by *Coelurus*, which had persisted since Upper Jurassic times. By the Upper Cretaceous *Velociraptor* had evolved and this genus was to represent the 'normal' predatory lineage until the end of the period. *Velociraptor* roamed across the open lands

Ornithomimus, the 'bird imitator' was an 'ostrich-like dinosaur', which lived during the Upper Cretaceous from approximately 100 to 70 million years ago

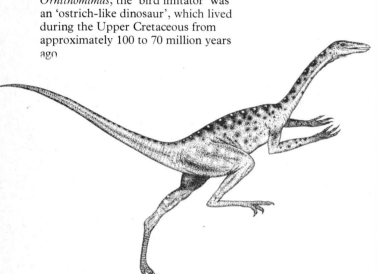

Right
In 1971 the remains of *Protoceratops* and *Velociraptor*, locked together in a death struggle, were discovered by a joint Polish-Mongolian Expedition to Mongolia. (see 'Horned dinosaurs')

Below right
Saurornithoides was an extremely agile dromaeosaur from the Upper Cretaceous of Asia and North America. It grew to just under 2 metres in length.

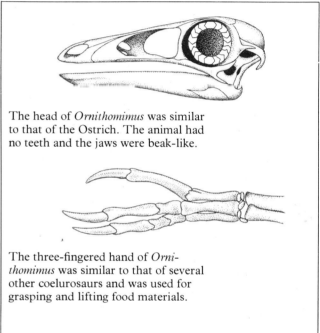

The head of *Ornithomimus* was similar to that of the Ostrich. The animal had no teeth and the jaws were beak-like.

The three-fingered hand of *Ornithomimus* was similar to that of several other coelurosaurs and was used for grasping and lifting food materials.

of Asia and possibly North America. It fed on the hatchlings of various dinosaurs and the carcases left by *Tyrannosaurus* or *Tarbosaurus*. *Velociraptor* had strong jaws, sharp teeth and a highly flexible wrist which indicated that the hand played an important role during feeding. Although a fast runner, *Velociraptor* could hardly match the speeds attained by its relatives the so-called 'ostrich' dinosaurs. *Ornithomimus*, the 'bird imitator', was a typical representative of these specialized forms, having a small head with toothless, beak-like jaws. The ornithomimids grew to approximately 4 metres in length. They robbed the nests of other dinosaurs and hunted for small lizards, mammals and insects. Their fore-limbs were often longer than those of most other coelurosaurs and they were used to grasp and lift food towards the mouth.

The Cretaceous also saw the appearance of the highly specialized dromaeosaurs which included *Deinonychus* and *Saurornithoides*. These dinosaurs apparently possessed an intelligence similar to that of the birds, with the large brain accounting for a thousandth of the body weight. They were extremely agile creatures, the fast-running *Deinonychus* having an enormous sickle-shaped claw on the second toe of its hind foot. The claw was used in the kill, with *Deinonychus* effectively stabbing its prey to death with a backwards kick. The tail of the 'terrible claw' dinosaur was sheathed in rods of thin bone and, in life, it was held high and rigid to give perfect balance during running. *Saurornithoides* was smaller than *Deinonychus* and probably more fleet of foot. It had a large brain and big eyes that provided an excellent 'all round' vision. *Saurornithoides* was a hunter, but, unlike its forebears, it hunted at night and fed on small nocturnal mammals.

Bipedal meat-eaters

Triassic carnosaurs were big, Jurassic forms were bigger but those of the Cretaceous were the biggest of all! In the early Cretaceous the long surviving *Megalosaurus* occupied the top spot in various terrestrial dynasties. *Megalosaurus* the 'big lizard' stood between 3 and 4 metres tall and was 6 metres in length. At 2·5 tonnes it was approximately twice the weight of its Jurassic cousin *Ceratosaurus*. The trend of an increase in overall size continued into the Upper Cretaceous with *Gorgosaurus*, *Tyrannosaurus* and *Tarbosaurus* representing a four or five-fold increase over their Triassic ancestors. The jaws of these huge creatures reached gigantic proportions with the teeth of *Tyrannosaurus* measuring 15 centimetres. Changes in the length of the neck, the size of the fore-limbs and the structure of the foot also took place, each modification improving the overall

ability of the animals to track and kill their prey.

In the Upper Cretaceous of North Africa and Europe huge carnosaurs such as *Spinosaurus* and *Altispinax* flourished. *Spinosaurus* was 11 metres in length and the long neural spines that rose from its back measured between 1·8 and 2 metres in length. The spines supported a sail which extended from the middle of the neck to a point just behind the pelvis. As in the pelycosaur *Dimetrodon*, the sail is thought to have acted as a heat-exchange device. From the geological evidence available it would seem that *Spinosaurus* lived on the edges of an arid desert region where temperature control would have been essential. Even *Spinosaurus* was small by comparison with the gigantic tyrannosaurs that flourished in North America and Asia during the closing years of the Upper Cretaceous.

Tyrannosaurus 'the largest flesh-eating animal that ever walked on Earth'. *Tyrannosaurus rex* the 'king of the tyrant lizards' is probably the best known of all dinosaurs.

The fore-limbs of *Tyrannosaurus* and its Upper Cretaceous relative *Tarbosaurus* were ridiculously small for such great beasts. Not only were they short in length but they possessed only two fingers on each hand. They were obviously of little use during an attack or even in feeding and it is difficult to link them with any reasonable function. However, the limbs were supported by large shoulder muscles and it is thought that *Tyrannosaurus* used its front legs whilst rising from a resting position. In this the front limbs would be pushed against the ground, the back legs straightened and the body raised by a backward, tossing movement of the great head.

Left
Spinosaurus, a sail-backed carnosaur, is known from the Upper Cretaceous of Egypt.

Tyrannosaurus rising

In the first stage of rising from the resting position the small front limbs were pushed firmly against the ground.

The back legs were then straightened, the small arms preventing the animal from sliding forwards.

A final toss of the head enabled the great predator to stabilize its centre of gravity over the legs and rise to its full height.

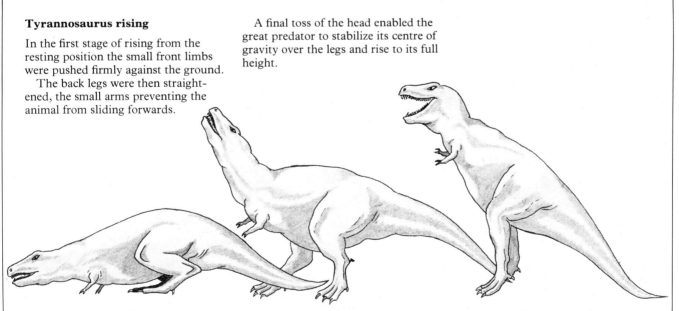

A story of discovery

In his original restoration of *Iguanodon* Dr Gideon Mantell portrayed the animal as a quadruped with a large spike on its nose. The spike was in actual fact one if its thumbs.

The first dinosaur bones and traces were attributed, in days of limited scientific knowledge, to giant men and to 'Noah's Raven'. The earliest recorded bone was described in 1676 by Dr Robert Plot, who thought it was the long bone of a giant's leg. In 1763 the same bone was figured by Brooks as 'scrotum humanum.' After Plot's discovery, early references to huge bones appear to be restricted to North America, with only a few specimens surviving the passage of time to be

subsequently identified as the remains of the coelurosaur *Anchisaurus*.

Only when Dr Gideon Mantell, a keen palaeontologist who lived and worked in Lewes in Sussex, insisted that some teeth discovered by his wife were those of a huge plant eater did the notion of giant land-dwelling reptiles really begin to germinate. At first, the teeth discovered by Mrs Mantell in Cretaceous rocks of the South Downs, were dismissed as those of large mammals, but

The concrete models in the grounds of the Crystal Palace, Sydenham, South London were created by Waterhouse Hawkins under the direction of Sir Richard Owen. The models were first shown to the general public in 1854. The restoration of *Iguanodon* is rather similar to that originally envisaged by Dr Gideon Mantell.

By comparison Gideon Mantell discovered that the teeth unearthed by his wife were like those of the living iguana lizard from Central America.

gradually further discoveries supported Mantell's argument and he named his great saurian *Iguanodon*, because of the similarities that existed between its teeth and those of the living iguana lizard of Central America.

Mantell's account of *Iguanodon* was not published until 1825, which was one year after the description of *Megalosaurus* by Dr William Buckland of Oxford University. Both authors made errors of judgement in their descriptions and Mantell's restoration of *Iguanodon* placed its spiky thumb on the tip of its nose. Mantell and Buckland, however, roused the palaeontological world into action and by the end of 1841 nine distinct genera had been recognized and Dr Richard Owen had, in a speech to the British Association in Plymouth established the suborder Dinosauria – the 'terrible lizards'.

Ornithischian ancestry and revolution

In terms of ornithischian history, the boundary between the Jurassic and Cretaceous periods is marked by the extinction of the stegosaurs. None of these spectacular creatures, known previously from North America, Europe and East Africa, survived into the new period and their absence from Lower Cretaceous landscapes seemingly encouraged the radiation of other ornithischian quadrupeds. These included the armoured ankylosaurs and the horned ceratopians. In evolutionary terms walking on all four legs, is regarded as a primitive character and one wonders whether this is not the case for each of these two groups. The common characteristic of quadrupedality does not necessarily mean that the groups were closely related and therefore the question of ancestry is worth investigating, especially as both types are so successful during the last period of the 'Age of Dinosaurs'. 'Missing links' are, by their very definition, rarities in the fossil record but although the evidence is limited it is possible to throw some light on the origins of both ankylosaur and ceratopian lineages. For the former we return to the Lower Jurassic and the presence of *Scelidosaurus*, which was once regarded as the earliest of all ornithischians. *Scelidosaurus* possesses some likenesses to both the stegosaurs and ankylosaurs and many scientists believe that it would make an ideal ancestor for both. Restorations of *Scelidosaurus*, the 'limb lizard', certainly bear comparison with early ankylosaurs and it is possible that a family link could be established through an Upper Jurassic intermediate. If this is the case then the quadrupedal stance of the ankylosaurs is a persistent primitive character, with the Cretaceous radiation of the group being linked closely with the demise of their stegosaurian relatives.

The ancestry of the ceratopians, on the other hand, is a different problem and as far as we can tell no link exists between the horned dinosaurs and either *Scelidosaurus* or the ankylosaurs. In fact, the ancestry of the ceratopians has been linked, as we shall see in our study of *Psittacosaurus*, with the ornithopods. If this is the case then quadrupedality in the horned dinosaurs is an acquired character, which enabled these animals to fill different ecological niches to those occupied by either the bipedal ornithopods or the armoured ankylosaurs.

Geological boundaries seemed to present no major problems to the 'normal' ornithopods and the line is represented in the Lower Cretaceous by *Iguanodon*, *Hypsilophodon* and *Psittacosaurus* are characterized by significant changes in structure, however, and it is likely that these, together with *Iguanodon*, represent the ancestral links with the specialized hadrosaur, pachycephalosaur and ceratopian stocks of the Upper Cretaceous. During the final 30 million years of dinosaur rule these ornithopods and the related ankylosaurs were to fill many of the niches open to plant-eaters and in many ways their diversification in the Upper Cretaceous parallels that of the herbivorous mammals in the Oligocene and Miocene.

Fleet-footed and armour-plated

If success is marked by variety alone, then the Cretaceous ornithischians must rank amongst the most successful groups of animals of all time. And if their variety is compared only with that of other groups of dinosaurs, then the word phenomenal is truly appropriate. The ornithischians of the

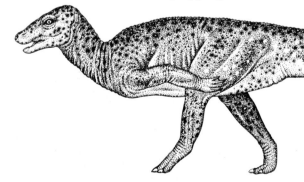

The ornithopod foot which in some animals is modified to form a hoof-like structure.

Anatosaurus, a duck-billed dinosaur, from the Upper Cretaceous of North America. This biped exhibits many of the characteristics that contributed to

the success of the ornithopods. *Anatosaurus* and its hadrosaur cousins possessed muscular cheeks and batteries of grinding teeth.

Although ornithischians are known throughout the 'Age of Dinosaurs', the radiation of the ornithopods during the Upper Cretaceous was a truly spectacular event. The family tree of the ornithopods suggests links between the more specialized stocks such as the duck-billed hadrosaurs and the 'normal' forms represented by *Iguanodon*. Some scientists now believe that the 'bone-headed' dinosaurs constitute a unique group totally separate from the ornithopods.

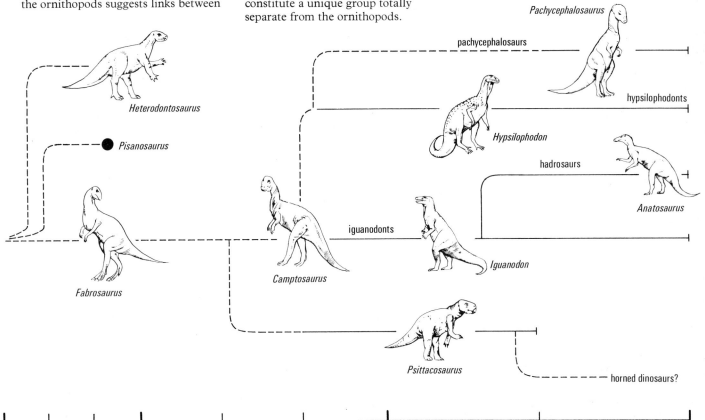

Heterodontosaurus

Pisanosaurus

Fabrosaurus

Camptosaurus

iguanodonts

Iguanodon

Psittacosaurus

pachycephalosaurs

Pachycephalosaurus

Hypsilophodon

hypsilophodonts

hadrosaurs

Anatosaurus

horned dinosaurs?

| 225 | Triassic | 193 | Jurassic | 136 | Cretaceous | 65 |

Cretaceous were to adapt themselves to a changing world and instead of living in areas where the great carnosaurs could not reach them they developed armoured shields, weapons of defence, formed into large herds and became fleet of foot. Size and weight were fairly important but none of the Cretaceous ornithischians were to reach the incredible proportions attained by the sauropods. In terms of speed, forms such as *Hypsilophodon* and, possibly, *Anatosaurus* were amongst the fastest plant-eating dinosaurs known to man, whereas *Euoplocephalus* and *Polacanthus* rank high amongst the most heavily armoured. Herding was a feature of ornithischian life and it has been estimated that herds of 5000 ceratopians once roamed the plains of the western States of North America. Vocal communication, territorial separation and male dominance structures have all been associated with various groups of Upper Cretaceous ornithischians. If these features had been developed, then the level of sophistication reached by the 'bird-hipped', plant-eaters, was much higher than that of any previous group that had walked on Earth. Geographically the major development of ornithischians in the Upper Cretaceous was to take place in the lands of the Northern Hemisphere.

Scolosaurus, an example of a heavily armoured ankylosaur from the Upper Cretaceous. It weighed 3·5 tonnes and grew to approximately 6 metres in length.

The ankylosaurs

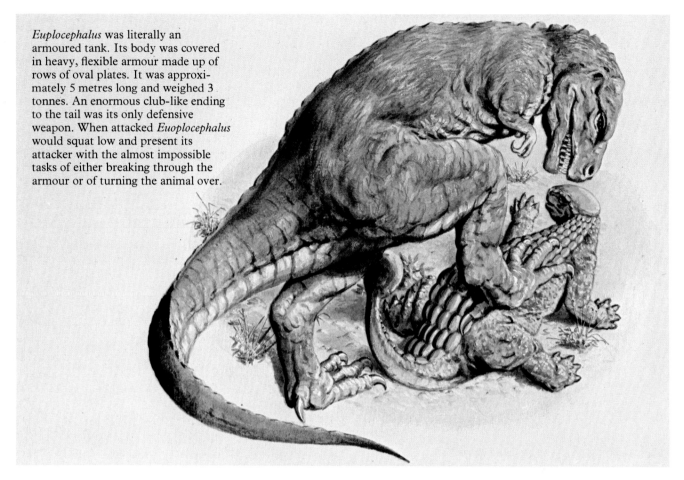

Euplocephalus was literally an armoured tank. Its body was covered in heavy, flexible armour made up of rows of oval plates. It was approximately 5 metres long and weighed 3 tonnes. An enormous club-like ending to the tail was its only defensive weapon. When attacked *Euoplocephalus* would squat low and present its attacker with the almost impossible tasks of either breaking through the armour or of turning the animal over.

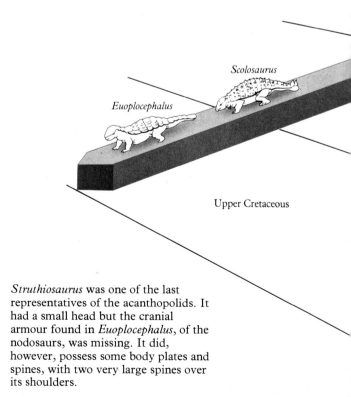

Scolosaurus

Euoplocephalus

Upper Cretaceous

Struthiosaurus was one of the last representatives of the acanthopolids. It had a small head but the cranial armour found in *Euoplocephalus*, of the nodosaurs, was missing. It did, however, possess some body plates and spines, with two very large spines over its shoulders.

The differences in the form of the body and in the amount of body armour they possessed, may indicate that the acanthopholids and nodosaurs lived in different terrains. The acanthopholids probably lived in the lowland regions, around lakes and the edges of forests, whilst the nodosaurs were more suited to life in open upland regions.

The quadrupedal ornithischian, *Scelidosaurus*, is possibly the ancestor of both the stegosaurs and the ankylosaurs. It measured some 4 metres in length and walked with a rather lumbering gait. The head was small with weak jaws and rather unspecialized teeth. Rows of solid bony plates extended along the whole length of the body, from the back of the head to the tip of the tail. The feet of *Scelidosaurus* were rather unspecialized and not hoof-like or padded like those of its descendants.

Lower Cretaceous ankylosaurs indicate that an early division had taken place within the group; the more primitive acanthopholid line retaining many of the characteristics of their ancestors. The acanthopholids were heavily built with rather massive hind limbs. Their bodies were protected by bony plates but in general they lacked the heavier body armour of their relatives, the nodosaurs which represent a more advanced line of ankylosaurs. Their heads were broader and flatter than those of the acanthopholids and the body was carried much closer to the ground. In some species the armour lay over the back like a thick protective blanket and the ribs were fused together to give greater protection.

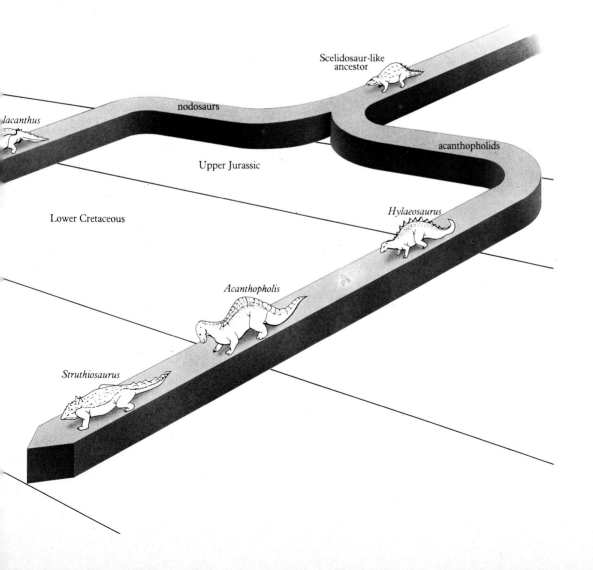

Scelidosaur-like ancestor

nodosaurs

lacanthus

acanthopholids

Upper Jurassic

Lower Cretaceous

Hylaeosaurus

Acanthopholis

Struthiosaurus

Duck-billed dinosaurs

It would be extremely difficult to show all the known species of duck-billed dinosaurs on any one diagram and therefore our family tree should be viewed essentially as an indication of the development of the group through time and of the relationships that existed between genera.

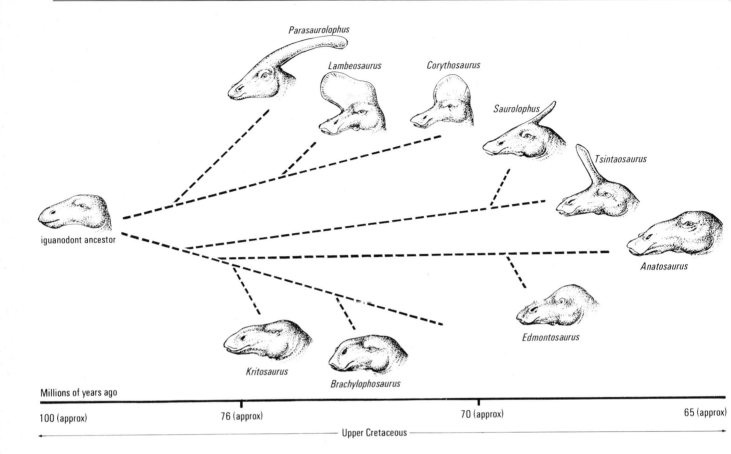

Parasaurolophus

Lambeosaurus

Corythosaurus

Saurolophus

Tsintaosaurus

iguanodont ancestor

Anatosaurus

Edmontosaurus

Kritosaurus

Brachylophosaurus

Millions of years ago

| 100 (approx) | 76 (approx) | 70 (approx) | 65 (approx) |

Upper Cretaceous

The great family of the hadrosaurs or duck-billed dinosaurs contained many of the most spectacular animals that lived during the Upper Cretaceous. The origins of the family rest in the Early Cretaceous with 'normal' iguanodonts providing a likely ancestor. *Bactrosaurus* from the Cretaceous of Mongolia is the earliest recorded hadrosaur, predating the North American genus *Claosaurus* by tens of thousands of years. Both forms were small compared with later hadrosaurs. The appearance of *Claosaurus* suggests that the migration of the group into North America was via the Bering 'land-bridge'. Approximately 75 million years ago two distinct types of hadrosaurs were recognizable and the majority of genera existed on the North American continent. Asian genera are well known, however, and isolated recordings from Europe and South America indicate a fairly cosmopolitan distribution. The two types of hadrosaurs noted above are distinguished by the presence or absence of a crest, with excellent collections from several North American localities allowing palaeontologists to reconstruct the complex family tree (see above). *Kritosaurus* and *Brachylophosaurus* were early 'flat-headed' hadrosaurs in which the characteristic duck-bill was surmounted by a facial

hump. The hump is thought to have been the equivalent of the thickened skull in the pachycephalosaurs, with large males pushing and butting each other in defence of their territory. In *Anatosaurus* and *Edmontosaurus*, the humps were missing but the front of the skull had broadened into a spoon-like beak. The function of the beak is difficult to interpret but one idea is that the resulting increase in the size of the nasal passages was linked with vocal communication. Social behaviour patterns are perhaps more pronounced in the hadrosaurs than in any other group of dinosaurs and it is now thought that the development of crests was linked with the demarcation of territorial boundaries and with mating. In some species inflation of the nasal region together with bright coloration could also have served as a display or intimidatory device. *Saurolophus* and *Tsintaosaurus* developed from a kritosaurian ancestor; their well-developed solid crests providing ideal visual signs by which individuals could recognize animals of their own kind. The crests of *Parasaurolophus*, *Lambeosaurus* and *Corythosaurus* were, to say the least, unusual and the variation in size that exists within these forms, gives some idea as to the ranking structure that existed within

Until recently several hadrosaur specimens had been identified as the remains of small even dwarf species. These specimens had been given their own names but these are now invalid as the actual animals were really the females and the young of *Cory-thosaurus*. The size of the crest varies considerably between the male and female of the species, whilst that of a juvenile is naturally smaller than both.

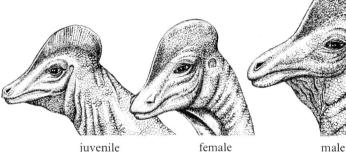

juvenile   female   male

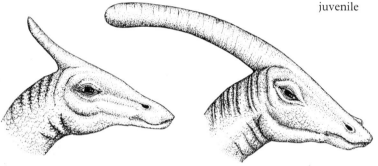

Saurolophus   *Parasaurolophus*

Saurolophus – The solid crests of the saurolophines enabled the animals to identify others of the same species.

The development of the hollow crest of *Parasaurolophus* was linked with an improved sense of smell but it also functioned as a visual display sign.

The development of the hollow crests as visual display or recognition structures was linked with an increase in the size of the nasal passages. This in turn was associated with an increase in the surface area of the lining membrane and ultimately with an increase in the sense of smell.

Modes of life

Except for specific details, the bodies of the hadrosaurs, unlike their heads, were rather similar in their overall structure. In this they resembled that of *Iguanodon*, although the presence of webbed fingers on each hand and of strong hoof-like feet does suggest specialization. The webbed fingers have been linked with swimming and the animals themselves with an aquatic or semi-aquatic mode of life. The line of reasoning is also supported by the lateral flattening of the tail, which presumably functioned as the main swimming organ. Unfortunately the hoof-like feet and the gut remains of number of mummified individuals, contradict this suggestion. The stomach contents include pine needles, twigs and fruits, hardly the diet of a swamp dweller! Furthermore the teeth of the hadrosaurs occur in batteries and resemble those of an elephant; the flattened surface being linked with the crushing of tough fibrous plant matter. The hadrosaurs were also good runners and it would appear from the evidence that they lived most of their lives on land moving into water only in times of danger.

hadrosaur herds during the Upper Cretaceous. Unlike those of *Saurolophus* and *Tsintaosaurus*, the crests of *Parasaurolophus* and its allies were hollow.

Function of the crest

The suggestion that the crests of the hadrosaurs had social significance is relatively new and if correct it replaces several theories of a more bizarre nature. First amongst these is the idea that the hollow crest was used to store air whilst the animal hid under water. The crest has also been linked with 'snorkelling' and has even been described as an area for muscle attachment or as the support structure for a large proboscis. Such theories can easily be disproved and their level of plausibility has always been less than acceptable.

The teeth rows of the hadrosaurs were closely packed together. Individual teeth overlapped each other and hundreds of teeth were united within a composite dental battery.

Parasaurolophus and Anatosaurus

Parasaurolophus

Left
Although the body of *Parasaurolophus* was similar to that of most other hadrosaurs, its crested head was unique. In *P. tubicens* the crest alone measured 1·5 metres, with the front facial bone, the premaxilla, forming the whole structure. As a fully aquatic mode of life has been ruled out for this animal, it is likely that the huge crest was linked with an increased sense of smell and/or the development of a 'voice'. *Parasaurolophus* was a herd-dweller and therefore good sight, hearing and smell would have been important attributes. It is possible that a broad frill extended from the tip of the crest to the base of the neck, in life this would have been used as a sex display feature or as a visual recognition symbol for members of the same species. The animal is unlikely to have used the delicate, hollow crest as a weapon, in the same way as the horns of a ram, and in times of danger the herd would have grouped and fled. *Parasaurolophus* is closely related to the two other hollow-crested hadrosaurs, *Lambeosaurus* and *Corythosaurus*. Its remains are recorded from the Upper Cretaceous, Belly River Formation of North America, the sediments of which were deposited approximately 70 to 75 million years ago.

Anatosaurus

Right
Anatosaurus was the last of the hadrosaurs. It grew to over 10 metres in length and weighed approximately 3 tonnes. Unlike *Parasaurolophus* it was a flat-headed hadrosaur, the most noticeable feature of which was the broad duck-billed snout. Adult animals possessed massive back legs and hoof-like toes on their feet. The tail was strengthened by bundles of ossified tendons and in life it would have been held horizontally to serve as balance when the animal was running. The mummified remains of *Anatosaurus* indicate that the skin was scaley, with minute tubercules and that the animal fed on pine needles and seeds. They also show that the animals had a small frill along its back and a web-like arrangement of skin between the fingers of the hand. *Anatosaurus* was a terrestrial herbivore and it is now thought that herds of thousands of these creatures roamed the Upper Cretaceous plains of North America approximately 65 to 68 million years ago.

The bone-headed ornithischians

The pachycephalosaurs or bone-headed dinosaurs are recorded from the Upper Cretaceous rocks of Europe, North America and Asia. They were bird-hipped plant-eaters but their relationships with other ornithischians are somewhat vague. Many palaeontologists link them with the ornithopods, with *Hypsilophodon* or its relative *Yaverlandia* as the possible ancestor. *Yaverlandia*, from the Lower Cretaceous of the Isle of Wight, England, was about the size of a turkey and although its skull was small it appears to show the first signs of the thickening of the skull roof. The actual evidence is slight and some scientists now believe that the dome-headed dinosaurs were not ornithopods but a separate group in their own right.

The earliest pachycephalosaur was *Stegoceras* which lived at the same time as the first of the triceratopians; their remains having been discovered in the sediments of the Upper Cretaceous, Edmonton formation of western North America. *Stegoceras* was a rather small dinosaur, its skull measuring only 19 centimetres in length. Surprisingly, the bone over the brain case was 5 centimetres thick, which is rather excessive when one realises that it was protecting a brain the size of a golf ball. In the later form *Pachycephalosaurus* the length of the skull had increased to 60 centimetres and the bony dome was 22 centimetres thick! Once again this would seem extravagant protection for such a small brain and one can only assume that there was another reason for this strange adaptation. Fortunately comparisons can be made amongst the hoofed mammals of today such as battling rams. It is likely that these dinosaurs roamed in upland areas with the large males dominating and protecting the herds.

Above
The skull of the dome-headed dinosaur *Pachycephalosaurus* from the Upper Cretaceous of Mongolia.

Left
Fighting rams – it has been argued that the thick dome of the pachycephalosaurs had a function similar to that of the horns of rams.

It is possible that the dome-headed dinosaurs lived in upland areas and that the thick domes were used mostly in territorial battles. The threat of an attack by a carnosaur was always a possibility and, in times of danger, the 'dome-heads' would have resorted to butting as a means of defence.

A link between families

During its life *Psittacosaurus* fed on several levels of vegetation, at times it would graze as a quadruped but it was also able to rise up onto its hind-legs and reach for delicate leaves and succulent fruits.

The remains of the beaked ornithopod *Psittacosaurus* have been discovered in the Lower Cretaceous of China and Mongolia. *Psittacosaurus* was a rather small animal, measuring between 1·5 and 2 metres in length. It had long hind-legs and presumably spent much of its life in a bipedal pose. The fore-limbs were strong, however, and although the hands may have still retained a gripping action, *Psittacosaurus* was capable of walking on all four limbs. The skull was narrow and rather deep, with the snout terminating in a sharp parrot-like beak. Few teeth are found inside the mouth and the holes for eyes and nostrils are placed high on the sides of the skull. A small flat crest is also noticeable at the back of the head and this, together with several of the features already mentioned, suggest a link between *Psittacosaurus* and the horned dinosaurs. In many ways, *Psittacosaurus* is a unique animal which is generally regarded as being a close relative of *Hypsilophodon*. As we know, the latter is a fast-running biped and if the ancestral chain from *Hypsilopodon* through *Psittacosaurus* to the ceratopians was ever proved conclusive, then it would support the argument for the horned dinosaurs being secondary quadrupeds. *Psittacosaurus* was a defenceless creature which spent most of its time grazing in forest areas beyond the reach of the huge carnosaurs. In time and through the process of evolutionary selection the descendants of the first 'parrot lizard' would have increased in both size and weight. The crest at the back of the head would also have developed, until it formed the solid frill typical of all ceratopians. The new animals would have been too big to live in forests glades and therefore would have gradually

The parrot-like beak and a small ridge at the back of the skull suggest that *Psittacosaurus* the 'parrot lizard' was closely linked with the ancestry of the ceratopians.

The skeleton of *Psittacosaurus*, a beaked ornithopod from the Upper Cretaceous of Asia.

migrated onto the open lands, where grouping or herding would provide a natural protection against predation. The change in size would have necessitated the adoption of a quadrupedal stance and by the appearance of the first ceratopian the grasping hand would have modified into a padded 'foot'. *Psittacosaurus* lived over 110 million years ago, approximately 20 million years before the appearance of the earliest horned dinosaur, *Protoceratops*. Obvious similarities can be identified but strangely closer comparison seems to exist between *Psittacosaurus* and the rather odd bipedal ceratopian *Leptoceratops*. It is possible that this last form represents the primitive condition and that unlike its huge contemporaries of the Upper Cretaceous it still dwelt within the same forest environment as its ancestor.

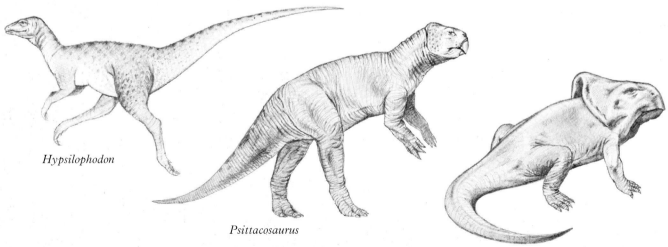

Hypsilophodon

Psittacosaurus

Protoceratops

Hypsilophodon, *Psittacosaurus* and *Protoceratops* represent the three important stages in the evolution from small ornithopod to the earliest ceratopian.

The horned dinosaurs

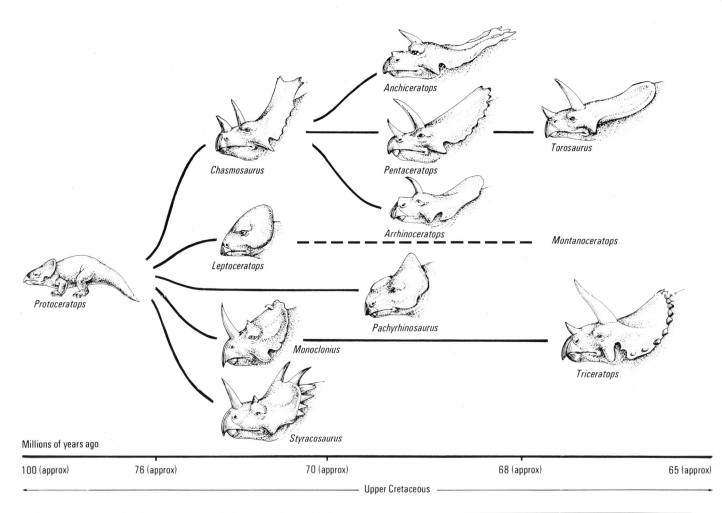

Millions of years ago

| 100 (approx) | 76 (approx) | 70 (approx) | 68 (approx) | 65 (approx) |

Upper Cretaceous

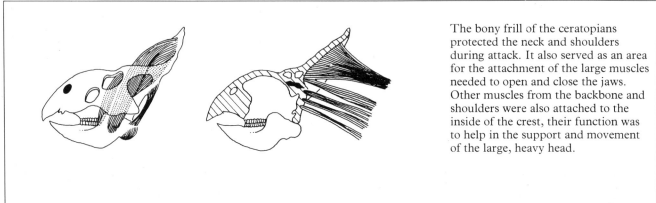

The bony frill of the ceratopians protected the neck and shoulders during attack. It also served as an area for the attachment of the large muscles needed to open and close the jaws. Other muscles from the backbone and shoulders were also attached to the inside of the crest, their function was to help in the support and movement of the large, heavy head.

The appearance of *Protoceratops* during the early part of the Upper Cretaceous marked the beginning of one of the greatest radiations amongst the ornithischian dinosaurs. We have seen that *Protoceratops* probably originated from the beaked ornithopod *Psittacosaurus*, but unlike its ancestor, *Protoceratops*, the 'first horned face', possessed a massive frill over its neck and shoulders. In size it measured approximately 2 metres in length and weighed a little under 200 kilograms. The head was exceptionally deep and narrow and the parrot-like beak was very pronounced in its development.

In time *Protoceratops* was to give rise to numerous descendants, some of whom grew to over 7 or 8 metres in length and weighed between 7 and 9 tonnes. Two distinct branches can be identified

Numerous nests, with eggs and even baby dinosaurs, have been discovered in the Upper Cretaceous of Mongolia. They are associated with the earliest horned dinosaur *Protoceratops*. The eggs measure 20 centimetres in length.

In 1971 members of a Joint Polish-Mongolian Expedition to the Gobi Desert, discovered the remains of the two dinosaurs *Protoceratops* and *Velociraptor* literally 'wrapped' in each others arms. The discovery is a convincing record of the death struggles that must of taken place during the 'Age of Dinosaurs'. It may also indicate that the nest robber, *Velociraptor* was actually caught in the act by a watchful parent.

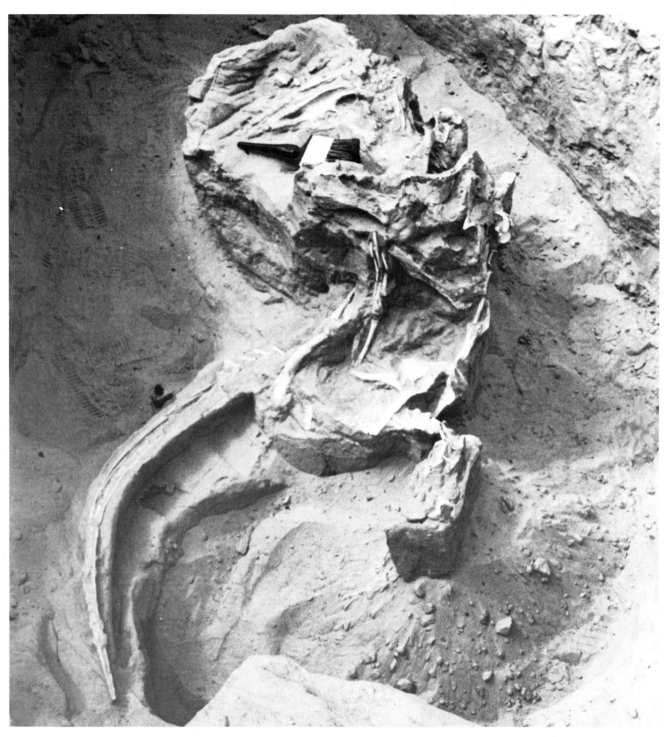

within the ceratopian family tree, with the basic division being made on the relative length of the bony crest. The so-called long-crested ceratopians include *Chasmosaurus, Pentaceratops, Torosaurus* and associated genera, whilst the short-crested forms include *Leptoceratops, Monoclonius Styracosaurus* and the great *Triceratops*. In terms of size the huge beasts of the latter part of the Upper Cretaceous, represent a four to five-fold increase in length and a nine-fold increase in weight over their ancestor. In a relatively short period of time the ceratopians were to exhibit several evolutionary trends, with changes in overall size, the width of the bony frill and in the facial ornament, all having some significance in the development of the group.

The triceratopians

An abundance of triceratopian fossils in the Lance Formation of western North America, has led palaeontologists to believe that huge herds of these horned dinosaurs once roamed the open lands of the region, 68 to 65 million years ago.

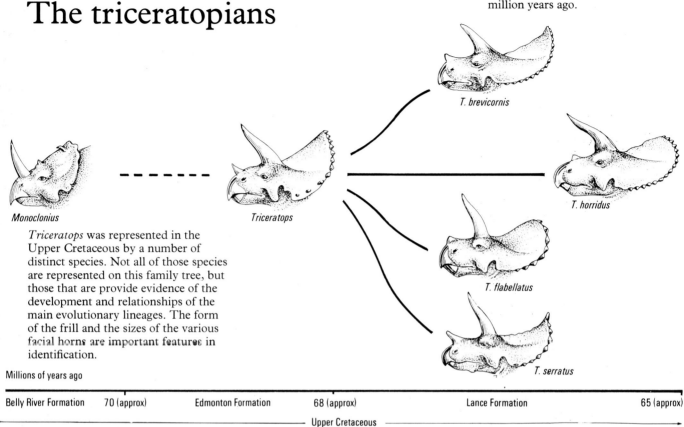

Monoclonius

Triceratops

T. brevicornis

T. horridus

T. flabellatus

T. serratus

Triceratops was represented in the Upper Cretaceous by a number of distinct species. Not all of those species are represented on this family tree, but those that are provide evidence of the development and relationships of the main evolutionary lineages. The form of the frill and the sizes of the various facial horns are important features in identification.

Millions of years ago

Belly River Formation	70 (approx)	Edmonton Formation	68 (approx)	Lance Formation	65 (approx)

Upper Cretaceous

Although many of the horned dinosaurs are spectacular creatures in their own right, none have caught the imagination quite as much as *Triceratops*. This may seem strange in view of the size of some of these creatures and the ornament developed in forms such as *Pentaceratops* ('five-horn faced'), *Styracosaurus* ('spiky lizard') and *Chasmosaurus* ('chasm lizard'). *Triceratops* rules supreme in our image of Upper Cretaceous ornithischians and the reason for this is that it has so often been illustrated in combat with its arch enemy *Tyrannosaurus rex*. The triceratopian usually illustrated is the largest of all the known forms and it should be noted that *Triceratops horridus* is but one of many species that existed between 70 and 65 million years ago.

The triceratopians evolved from the genus *Monoclonius* which lived in the Belly River region of western North America. *Monoclonius*, the 'single horn', measured just under 6 metres in length. The head alone measured 2 metres, and the facial ornament consisted of a long, single horn over the top of the nose and two short brow horns, one over each eye. In the descendants of *Monoclonius* the size of the brow horns increased dramatically, with some measuring a metre in length. The first triceratopian appeared in the Edmonton Formation of Canada and from this species, ten others were to evolve during the last three million years of the Cretaceous period. A

radiation that can surely be compared with any that has taken place before or since!

Within the group the evolutionary trends included an increase in overall size, of the skull in particular, broadening of the crest and an increase in the length of the brow horns. The evolution of the triceratopians was not along one single line and most palaeontologists recognize three main branches. Of these the broad-crested species such as *Triceratops horridus* and *T. eurycephalus* are thought to be the most advanced. In *T. serratus* the crest was relatively narrow and the nasal horn primitively long. In *T. horridus* and *T. eurycephalus* the brow horns were exceptionally large and had replaced the now stub-like nasal horn as the major defensive weapons. It is possible that the size of the horns and the width of crest represent sexual differences but no proof of this exists at the present time. Evidence does exist, however, of battles, for several of the great crests show evidence of wounding. These may have been inflicted by a hungry predator, but they may also be the result of territorial battles, in which the huge males fought to preserve selected females during the mating season. It is likely that huge herds of *Triceratops* roamed the open lands of western North America during the final stages of the Cretaceous period. The variation in the head shields could have been used by individual animals to identify members of their own species.

An American landscape

The record of terrestrial life from western North America during the uppermost Cretaceous is quite exceptional. Sedimentary formations in Alberta and Montana have yielded vast quantities of dinosaur bones and palaeontologists have sufficient data to reconstruct three distinct terrestrial communities. The period of time involved was approximately 20 million years. The earliest community was centred on the countryside of the Belly River and the fauna was dominated by the hadrosaurs, which accounted for just under 70 per cent of the entire plant-eating population. *Gorgosaurus* was the major predator. By 70 million years ago the Edmonton community was firmly established and hadrosaurs such as *Saurolophus* and *Edmontosaurus* occurred in great numbers. In fact the hadrosaurs now accounted for 80 per

Gorgosaurus

Torosaurus

Tyrannosaurus

208

cent of all herbivores with the ceratopians, *Anchiceratops* and *Pentaceratops*, playing minor roles within the community. The day of the ceratopians was to come, for in the Lance – Hell Creek community horned giants such as *Triceratops* and *Torosaurus* formed more than 50 per cent of the plant-eating population. *Anatosaurus* was now the dominant hadrosaur and *Tyrannosaurus* had

appeared as the major predator. The role of scavenger and egg-stealer was retained by *Ornithomimus* which was present in all three communities. Pachycephalosaurs had appeared by Lance – Hell Creek times and it would appear that they were ideally suited to the drier landscapes that now prevailed. The climate of the times was slightly less stable than that which had prevailed during the 'Age of

Dinosaurs' and the vegetation was dominated by the flowering plants and conifers. Times were changing and although the dinosaurs responded with the introduction of many new species and a variety of adaptations, their days were numbered and by the end of Lance – Hell Creek times they had vanished for ever.

Anatosaurus

Saurolophus

Triceratops

Ornithomimus

209

The Niobrara Seas

The Niobrara Chalk of Kansas, North America, was laid down
during the Late Cretaceous approximately 80–75 million years ago.
The chalky sediment is a typical open sea deposit and the fauna
entombed within its layers are evidence of a very diverse marine
community. Fish and invertebrates abounded and they provided a
rich source of food for both bird and reptilian faunas.

The major predators of the Niobrara
Chalk Seas were the huge, swimming
lizards – the mosasaurs – *Tylosaurus
dispar* grew to approximately 9 metres
in length.

Of the birds, *Hesperornis*, the 'dawn bird', was amongst the largest. It was a flightless form with diver-like habits.

The plesiosaurs were important members of the Niobrara community although long-necked genera such as *Elasmosaurus* outnumbered their short-necked cousins – the pliosaurs.

plesiosaur

Hesperornis

Cretaceous birds

Although *Archaeopteryx* had evolved during the Upper Jurassic, the fossil record of the birds is poor until the Upper Cretaceous, and even then it bears little relationship to the variety that probably existed within the world's avifauna. The record of Lower Cretaceous birds is essentially restricted to the grebe-like *Enaliornis* from the Cambridge Greensand of England and the supposedly goose-like *Gallornis* from France. A few feathers from the Lower Cretaceous of Australia and a possible thigh bone of *Ichthyornis* from the English Wealden Formation, complete the picture.

Ichthyornis, is also recorded from the Upper Cretaceous of North America and together with other birds from this sub-period provides us with a better understanding of avian evolution than those recorded from the preceding 60 million years. The 'fish-bird' resembled the living terns and was of a similar size. It was a good flyer and fed on small marine fishes. Another fish-eater was the grebe-like *Baptornis* which lived at the same time, and in the same area. It lived like the modern diving-birds and its wings were not so well developed as those of *Ichthyornis*. Birds with diver-like habits were seemingly common to the Upper Cretaceous of North America, for the 'dawn bird', *Hesperornis*, is also recorded from the

Hesperornis

Icthyornids

same strata as *Baptornis* and *Ichthyornis*. Unlike many of its contemporaries *Hesperornis* completely lacked the power of flight, as the wings and the keel of the breastbone, to which the flight muscles were attached, had been almost completely lost. *Hesperornis* was extremely specialized to a sea-dwelling mode of life and its short hind limbs and out-turned feet were the main organs of propulsion. In terms of evolutionary standing *Hesperornis* was primitive as it still retained several reptilian characteristics. These included the presence of teeth on both upper and lower jaws and more specific details of the skull structure. *Hesperornis* was much larger than either *Baptornis*

or *Ichthyornis* with individuals measuring some 2 metres in length.

Other birds recorded from the Upper Cretaceous include the flamingo-like scaniornids from Sweden and *Totorix* from Wyoming. These were shore or shallow water dwellers and unfortunately they are the nearest thing to a true land bird recorded from this period of time. Some scientific works have described early ratites and giant owls from Mongolia and Transylvania respectively. But such is the similarity between the bones of large early birds and their dinosaurian relatives that it is likely that these identifications are unfounded.

Baptornis

Icthyornids

Catastrophy

Until the middle of the 19th century the philosophies of catastrophism and of a special creation, guided the thinking of many famous scientists. Most had been brought up in a world which believed that the formation of the Earth was a very recent event and the two philosophies were the only means of explaining away great mountains and canyons or thick sequences of sediments and the masses of extinct organisms found in them.

William Buckland, the discoverer of *Megalosaurus*, believed that three great floods were responsible for the changes in the fossil content of the geological column, whilst Georges Cuvier, (1769–1832), the father of the 'catastrophic theory', claimed that the floods were the result of 'instantaneous rather than gradual' episodes of crustal deformation. The works of Darwin and others were to expose the naivety of these beliefs but strangely the idea

of catastrophic happenings has lurked persistently in the background of geological thought. Recently new theories and new discoveries have turned the spotlight back on catastrophism and the explosion of a distant star or supernova has donned the mantle once held by the great deluge or Noah's Flood.

The theory of an exploding supernova has been linked with the extinction of the dinosaurs and other organisms at the end of the Cretaceous. The disintegration of this far-off star would have resulted in a disturbance of the Earth's atmosphere, an increase in air turbulence and a frightening bombardment by lethal doses of ultraviolet light. A drastic drop in temperature could also be linked with this theory and, surely, say the catastrophists, this would be enough to cause the extinction of many organisms. Unfortunately no graveyards mark the sudden end of the dinosaurs but traces of the metallic element iridium recently discovered in limestones from the Gubbio district of Italy have resulted in the banner headline dinosaurs 'Killed by Star Rays'. The limestones are of Cretaceous age and apparently only an exploding supernova could have caused the appearance of this rare element within these rocks. Catastrophism is not dead!

Mass extinctions

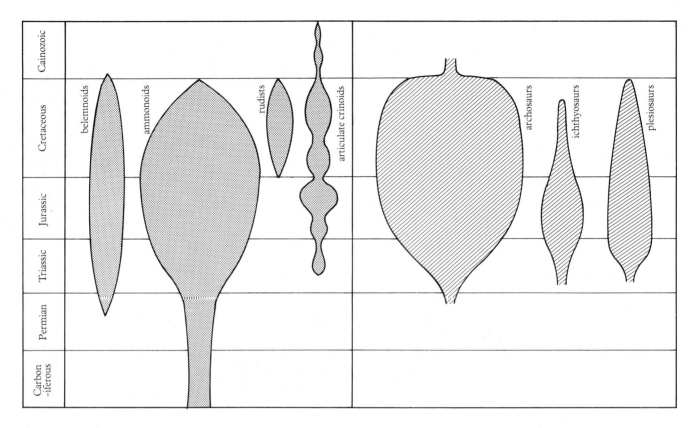

The Mesozoic Era ended approximately 65 million years ago, with a large-scale extinction decimating many groups of plants and animals simultaneously. Whole families and orders were eliminated, with both giants and microscopic creatures being shown no 'mercy'. The extinctions occurred at local and cosmopolitan level and affected land and sea dwellers alike. In scale, the mass extinction of the Upper Cretaceous rivalled those of the Late Permian with the disappearance of the dinosaurs, plesiosaurs, mosasaurs, ammonoids, belemnoids and rudists indicating the profound effect the extinction had on the world's biota. Other organisms eliminated included many planktonic foraminiferids and from the plant kingdom, caytonaleans as well as the bennettitaleans.

The question as to why so many organisms should die out, lacks a definitive answer and many palaeontologists would, in fact, argue for a gradual rather than a sudden disappearance. It may be that specific extinctions took place over several million years although, as we have seen, some theories would confine certain catastrophic happenings to periods which are insignificant in terms of geological time. In the case of the dinosaurs both gradual and catastrophic theories have been postulated. So have two or three dozen

The boundary between the Cretaceous and the Cainozoic is marked by the extinction of many groups of plants and animals. The possible reasons for the extinctions are discussed in the main text but this diagram provides a visual insight as to the significance of these events on the world's biota. Fortunately there were many survivors and from these arose the replacement stocks that were to inherit the world. Strangely Late Cretaceous extinctions amongst freshwater dwelling animals such as the turtles and crocodiles were extremely limited and one can only assume that their particular environments were generally unaffected by the major changes that took place at the end of the Mesozoic era.

others, ranging from the visits of little green men from Mars to that of no standing room in Noah's Ark. These are rather ridiculous, and totally unscientific, and one must look to more feasible theories for an explanation of why the dinosaurs and other groups vanished. Environmental change is a likely cause of extinction and if one looks at the stratigraphic record there is evidence to suggest that the transition between the Mesozoic and Cainozoic was marked by major changes, which were linked with plate movements.

As we have seen from our study of Permian extinctions the withdrawal of the sea from the land brought about changes in climate and reduced the number of niches available to marine organisms. It is known that a major regression also took place in the uppermost Cretaceous. This had the effect once again of changing the global climates and of disrupting the Tethyan equatorial current system, with the direct result that regions close to the equator experienced a considerable decrease in temperature.

The continued movement of the various plates also resulted in an increase in climatic seasonality in the lower latitudes. On land this affected both plants and animals. It led to the extinction of a significant part of the world's vegetation and in many areas *Sequoia* dominated forests were totally replaced by mixed broad-leaved plants. These changes probably eliminated the potential food supplies of many herbivores and initiated a series of breaks in long-established food chains. These were to prove irreversible as the alternative food supply, namely the angiosperms, is thought to have contained too many toxic chemicals for the reptilian herbivores of the Upper Cretaceous. In the marine realm the disruption of the Tethyan current system had a specific effect on the rudists and ammonites and the demise of the latter must have faced the ichthyosaurs and mosasaurs with insurmountable problems. Changes in temperature also affected the waters of the seas and oceans. This resulted in the extinction of many planktonic foraminiferids and in the inheritance,

albeit temporary, of the marine realm by the planktonic algae. The last was encouraged by the upwelling of colder waters from depth, and the often excessive concentrations of phytoplankton that developed were responsible for the phosphate deposits in such areas as Morocco, Tunisia and Jordan. The change from an animal to a plant dominated plankton must have had dramatic consequences including the possible poisoning of marine waters. When coupled with the regression of the seas and the intensification of competition for the remaining niches, it is perhaps less than surprising that many organisms adapted to the stable conditions of the Mesozoic era were unable to survive.

In conclusion the movement of the plates created a variety of effects, and geographic rearrangement linked with a regression of the seas and greater climatic differentiation were probably the major agents in the mass extinction of so many organisms.

Fossil skeleton of a *Plesiosaurus* discovered by Cuvier who believed that the world had undergone a succession of catastrophies after which a new 'creation' of plants and animals inherited the Earth.

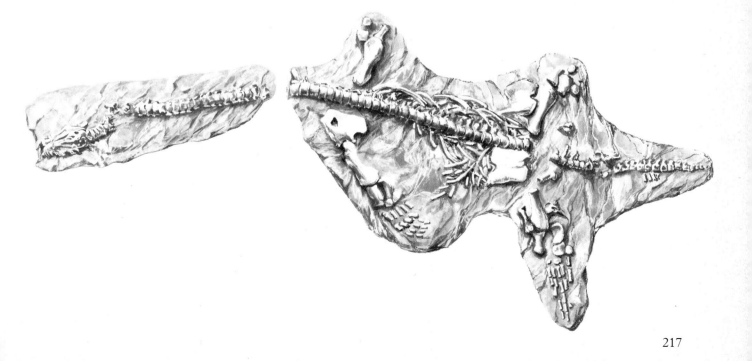

217

Cainozoic era

The Cainozoic era is the last of the three major subdivisions of the stratigraphic column and it began approximately 65 million years ago. It is divided into the Tertiary and Quaternary sub-eras. The former is often referred to as the 'Age of Mammals' and the latter should really be regarded as the 'Age of Man'. Mammals were not the only creatures to flourish during the Cainozoic, as numerous new families of birds and invertebrates also appeared for the first time. The flowering plants also diversified during this era and were eventually to occupy more habitats than any other group of plants. The successes of the angiosperms, the birds and the mammals are closely interwoven and the Cainozoic era added many new chapters to the story of life on Earth.

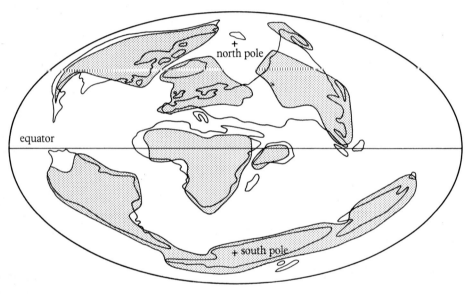

A reconstruction of the world during the Early Cainozoic.

By the beginning of the Cainozoic the geography of the various continents was similar to that of today, although the waters of Tethys still covered much of the Middle East. India was moving inexorably towards the Eurasian plate and Antarctica and Australia had begun to split. Countries like Chad and Niger were now on the equator whilst the British Isles were positioned approximately 40°N. In time the continents were to move into their present day positions and the climate generally was to cool quite considerably. Mountain building resulted in the formation of the Andes, the Alps and the Himalayas and also in the closing of the eastern Tethyan seaway. At the beginning of the Cainozoic the Atlantic Ocean was approximately 1000 kilometres wide and was to increase gradually throughout the era as the various plates moved away from the mid-oceanic ridge. During the Tertiary sub-era glaciation was to return to Antarctica, and in the Pleistocene the lands around the north pole were to experience the world's greatest glacial episode since the Permo-Carboniferous.

The Cainozoic era is divided into the Tertiary and Quaternary sub-eras and the former of these two is then further divided into the Palaeogene and Neogene periods. The Palaeogene is comprised of the Palaeocene, Eocene and Oligocene and the Neogene of the Miocene and Pliocene epochs. These subdivisions and the major events of the era are illustrated on this chart. The boundary between the Pliocene and Pleistocene epochs is based as much on faunal and floral evidence as it is on the advent of widespread glaciation. The Pleistocene is now thought to have begun approximately 1·8 million years ago and is thought to have ended 11 000 years ago. The boundary between the Pleistocene and Holocene epochs is rather an arbitrary one with various groups of stratigraphers using different lines of evidence. Four our purposes the boundary is drawn at the mid-point of the warming of the oceans, reflected in a significant increase in the abundance of planktonic foraminiferids and radiolarians. The Holocene is also referred to as the *Post-glacial* epoch.

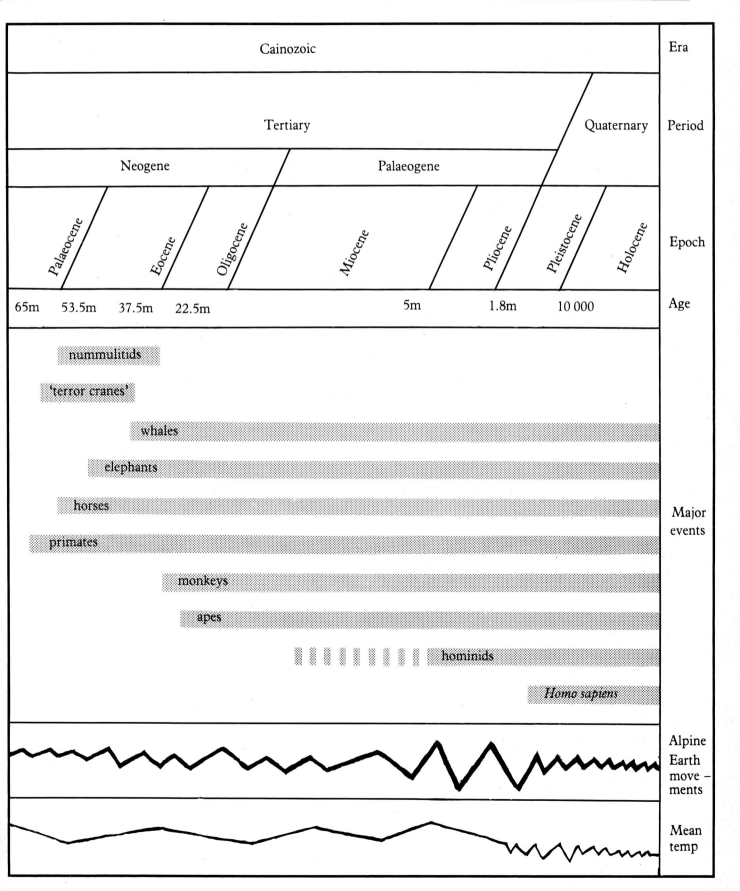

Cainozoic								Era
Tertiary						Quaternary		Period
Neogene			Palaeogene					
Palaeocene	Eocene	Oligocene	Miocene		Pliocene	Pleistocene	Holocene	Epoch
65m 53.5m 37.5m 22.5m			5m		1.8m	10 000		Age

nummulitids

'terror cranes'

whales

elephants

horses

primates

monkeys

apes

hominids

Homo sapiens

Major events

Alpine Earth move-ments

Mean temp

Birds of terror

The almost complete skeleton of *Diatryma steini* enables the artist to present an extremely accurate restoration. The diagram of the skeleton clearly illustrates the powerful build of the animal, its large bill and strong legs. It probably fed on small plant-eating mammals.

With the passing of the dinosaurs the terrestrial world awaited a new ruling class! The two contenders were the mammals and the birds and although the former ultimately proved to be the heirs, the early days of their rule were endangered by the appearance of a group of gigantic birds. These were the 'Terror Cranes' or Diatrymiformes, a group of flightless birds that lived in Europe and North America during the Upper Palaeocene and first half of the Eocene. Only a few genera are known but their size and a number of rather unique characteristics made them formidable enemies of the emergent mammals. Effectively the Diatrymiformes replaced their dinosaurian ancestors as the major predators, as no true rivals had yet appeared amongst the meat-eating mammals. The best known diatrymid is *Diatryma steini* from the Lower Eocene of Wyoming. It stood almost 2 metres high and bore some resemblance to the living flightless ratites, such as

A reconstruction of a Palaeocene avifauna.

the emu and cassowaries. *Diatryma steini* was powerfully built with long limbs and much reduced wings. The head was the most striking feature, however, with a maximum length equal to that of a modern horse. The bill was massive and the probability is that *Diatryma* was raptorial in habit, snatching and crushing its prey. In general, this is the accepted theory although some palaeontologists have indicated that many living birds with similar structures use them for slicing and shearing plant materials.

The long, strongly built legs of *Diatryma* belonged to a fast running animal. The femur was comparatively short but the tibia and metatarsal were very long. Overall the limb was similar to that of the dinosaurs with the huge clawed foot functioning as a weapon during a kill. The diatrymids probably lived in the more open areas of the early Cainozoic landscape. As stated above their appearance had been encouraged by the

absence of enemies such as the dinosaurs or meat-eating mammals and the development of powerful legs provided the animals with a more efficient method of catching food. In the presence of other predators the lack of flight would have been a liability but for the diatrymids and several other groups of large running birds it was energy-wasting and unnecessary. By the end of the Eocene the carnivorous mammals successfully replaced the diatrymids as the ruling predators, as several species had become larger and more suited to a life in open country areas.

Apart from the diatrymids the fossil record of Palaeocene birds is rather poor, although representatives of owls, vultures, terns and wading birds have been discovered. The true record of Cainozoic birds really begins in the Eocene by end of which time, ten orders of modern birds could be recognized.

Diatryma, a flightless bird from the Upper Palaeocene to Middle Eocene of North America.

Shark-infested seas

In many parts of the world marine sediments of the Early Cainozoic and, in some areas, of the Late Cretaceous contain evidence of a dramatic radiation amongst the sharks. Millions and millions of teeth bear testament to the great numbers of individuals that lived during this period. They also enable palaeontologists to identify large numbers of species. The upsurge in the shark population as a whole is probably linked with the extinction of the major marine predators, such as the ichthyosaurs, plesiosaurs and mosasaurs. Their demise left many marine niches unoccupied and it allowed the sharks to exploit food sources previously denied them. By the dawn of the Cainozoic both groups of modern sharks were well represented whilst the primitive hybodont sharks persisted only in reduced numbers. Of the two modern groups the galeoid sharks, characterized by the structure of the jaw and the presence of an anal fin, were the most numerous, with various genera occupying both deep and shallow water niches. Different fossil localities may yield different species but in many cases the generic composition is very similar and evidence exists for the widespread distribution of the sand shark (*Odontaspis*) and of the porbeagle shark (*Lamna*). In the former the teeth were slender and awl-shaped whilst in the latter they were broad and flattened. Nurse sharks (ginglymostomids) and hammerheads (sphyrnids) have also been recorded from the Early Cainozoic, and no account of the sharks would be complete without mention of the great white shark or *Carcharodon*. This genus originated in the Late Cretaceous and during the Tertiary some individuals had a mouth gape of almost 2 metres. *Carcharodon* was, and is, a huge fish, with teeth longer than 14 centimetres recorded from Tertiary strata. In the London Clay sea of the Early Eocene a number of deep water galeoid sharks have been recorded, and genera such as *Notorhynchus* and *Megasscyliorhinus* are known to have inhabited the 150 metre deep waters which once covered much of Essex and the Isle of Sheppey.

Of the other group of modern sharks the spiny dogfish (*Squalus*) and the angel shark (*Squatina*) have both been recorded from rocks of Tertiary age. Unlike the galeoids, living squaloid sharks lack an anal fin and the majority of forms appear to be adapted to a bottom-dwelling mode of life. And there is no reason to suspect that their mode of life has changed since Tertiary times.

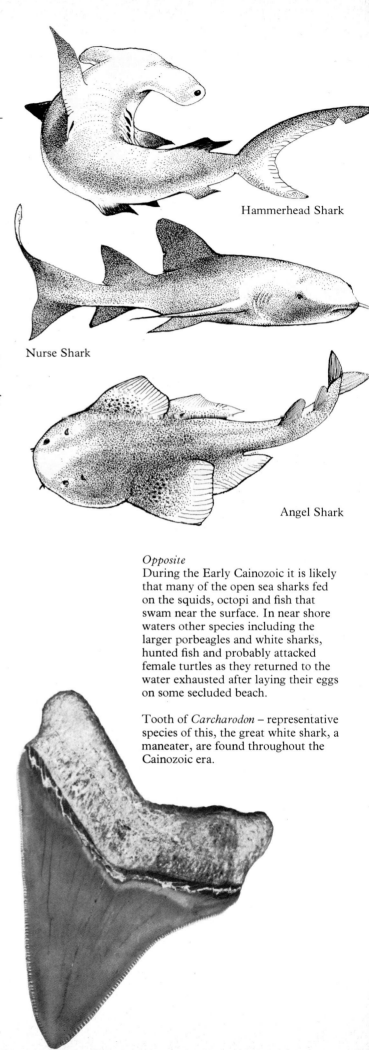

Hammerhead Shark

Nurse Shark

Angel Shark

Opposite
During the Early Cainozoic it is likely that many of the open sea sharks fed on the squids, octopi and fish that swam near the surface. In near shore waters other species including the larger porbeagles and white sharks, hunted fish and probably attacked female turtles as they returned to the water exhausted after laying their eggs on some secluded beach.

Tooth of *Carcharodon* – representative species of this, the great white shark, a maneater, are found throughout the Cainozoic era.

Turtles and tortoises

By the beginning of the Cainozoic the huge sea-going turtles, *Archelon*, *Protostega* and *Allopleuron* had vanished. In the Atlantic their niches had been occupied by the long surviving and rather primitive toxochelyids and the leathery turtle *Eosphargis*. The latter was a cosmopolitan form whose remains have been found as far afield as South Africa and Denmark. *Eosphargis* is also known from England and Belgium and it would appear that the northern sites represent feeding and/or nesting areas. Individuals of this genus grew to almost 3 metres in length and their great paddle-like fore-limbs pulled them through the water with a 'flying' action. *Eosphargis* was much larger than the toxichelyids that swam in the same waters and was to survive long after genera such as *Erquelinnesia* had become extinct. *Erquelinnesia* was in itself a unique animal as it possessed the most extensive secondary palate of any turtle. This structure shelved the roof of the mouth and enabled the animal to breathe and feed at the same time, and in *Erquelinnesia* the internal openings of the nasal passages were sited right at the back of the mouth. In the seas of the Anglo-Belgium basin, some 48 million years ago, *Eosphargis* existed alongside a number of small sea-turtles which appear to be the ancestors of the living Green and Ridley Turtles. (*Chelone mydas* and *Lepidochelys kempii*). Amongst the ancestral forms several genera can be identified and each would appear to have been adapted to a specific mode of life. Mostly they lived in coastal waters, with their feeding and nesting sites being in the regions of Sheppey and Bruxelles respectively. The genera *Puppigerus* and *Argillochelys* were to exist for almost 10 million years but it is unlikely that they ever ventured outside their northern province.

Along the shorelines of Europe during the Early Cainozoic side-necked and soft-shelled turtles flourished in marsh and river environments. The side-necked forms belonged to the pelomedusid family and although they were generally small to medium size in Europe, in North Africa and South America they grew to exceptional sizes and were capable of swimming far out to sea. Variation in size was also a feature of the soft-shelled trionychids and it is likely that the larger species were active predators. The largest trionychids of these times exceeded 1·5 metres in length but most were less than one third that size. Aquatic turtles were not the only representatives of this group, of essentially primitive reptiles, and evidence exists for the presence of a number of land-dwelling species. These were rather small and their humped-backed shells were quite distinct, compared with the depressed or flattened types characteristic of their aquatic cousins.

The species *Puppigerus camperi* is one of the best known sea-turtles of the Early Eocene of the Anglo-Belgium Basin. Large numbers of specimens have been found in the London Clay of the Isle of Sheppey and in the sand deposits of the Bruxelles district of Belgium.

Below
The restoration of *Eosphargis gigas* shows it to have had a similar form to the living species *Dermochelys coriacea*. Significant differences exist with regard to the structure of the shell but

it is believed that the fossil species was an open sea-dweller like *Dermochelys* and that it fed on soft-bodied creatures that floated in the Eocene seas.

Bottom
In coastal regions turtles and tortoises occupied many niches and their presence was an indication of the warm sub-tropical conditions that existed during the Early Eocene.

Eosphargis gigas

Puppigerus

land tortoise

Trionyx

225

Microfossils and faunal provinces

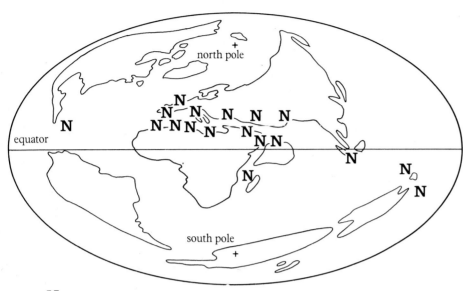

N nummulitids

The distribution of numerous nummulitid, alveolinid and disco-cyclinid species accurately charts the outline of the Tethyan Ocean that extended from Spain west, as far as India during the early Cainozoic. It is possible in palaeontological terms that this area could be identified as a faunal province.

The close of the Cretaceous period was, according to many experts, followed by a period during which cold waters from the north spread south-wards into the Anglo-Paris-Belgium Basin; the sea-floor communities being characterized by the presence of the bivalves *Artica, Tellina* and *Panopea*. At this time, the early Palaeocene, the foraminiferids were poorly represented in this area although a number of globular species (globigeri-nids) floated in the cool waters. In the west, the Atlantic Ocean was now over a thousand kilo-metres wide and the globigerinids flourished over large areas. The small foraminiferids were also common in Tethys and were to remain the dominant calcareous protozoans until the evol-ution of the large nummulitids, alveolinids and discocyclines of the Late Palaeocene – Early Eocene. This is not to say that the globigerinids diminished, in fact they continued to diversify, but their relative importance is completely over-shadowed by the rather dramatic appearance of the large bottom-dwelling forms.

The latter first appeared in Tethys and were essentially shallow-water dwellers which inhabited the protected waters between the shoreline and offshore reefs or bars. In the Tethyan Ocean the waters were warm and food supplies and the calcareous minerals needed for the construction of the shell were readily available. Of the three groups noted the nummulitids are the most spectacular with some species growing to over four centimetres in diameter. They evolved rapidly during the Eocene and Early Oligocene with a number of short-lived but widely distributed

In comparison with the fusulinids the structure of a typical nummulitid is relatively simple with a large number of chambers arranged around a spiral axis. Size and external ornament are important features used in their classification. The photograph opposite shows *Nummulites laevigatus* from the Isle of White, England.

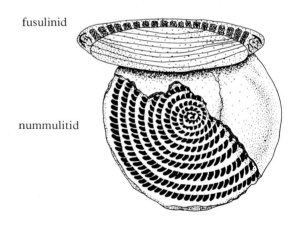

fusulinid

nummulitid

The globigerinids first flourished during the Cretaceous and although groups such as the globotruncanids died out at the end of that period some survived, and their descendants are still common today. During the Tertiary, globigerinids were prolific in many areas and short-lived species are used for the purposes of zonation. The distinctive globular shells of the group were ideally suited to a planktonic mode of life.

The alveolinids are almost as important as the nummulitids in the zonation of Eocene strata, particularly in the Tethyan region. Both rounded and elongate cylindrical forms are known and apart from being useful stratigraphically they provide information on the biogeography of the Eocene. The photograph shows a stained section of alveolinid limestone.

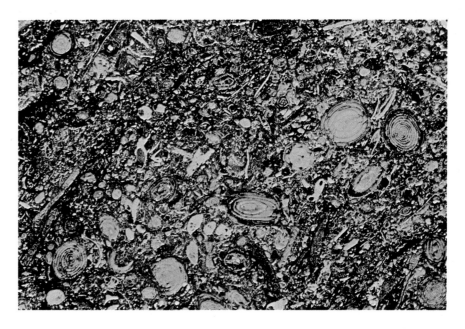

species serving as zone fossils. The first nummulite to appear in the Anglo-Paris-Belgium Basin was *Nummulites planulatus* which arrived in the area several million years after the earliest representatives had appeared in Tethys. Several waves of nummulitids were to enter Anglo-Paris-Belgium Basin from the south during a period of approximately 8 million years, their migration coinciding with the influx of warmer waters. In areas such as Fosses in the Paris Basin and Whitecliffe Bay on the Isle of Wight, nummulitids are abundant but they never rival the massive accumulations that characterize the Eocene rocks of many Mediterranean and Near East countries. Often the remains of nummulitids constitute 80 to 90 per cent of the rock and limestones packed with their remains form very prominent features over great stretches of barren landscape.

Shallow sealife

Borings in wood by *Teredo*, London Clay.

During the Early Eocene, from approximately 46 to 51 million years ago, the London Clay sea covered much of south-east England. In the region of the Isle of Sheppey the sea water was an estimated 150 metres in depth, whilst in Hampshire, which was nearer the western shoreline, the depth was an estimated 20 to 50 metres. The deeper water communities were rather restricted in terms of faunal content, although evidence exists for various species of gastropods, bivalves, echinoids, crabs and lobsters. The sea floor of the deeper water areas was also littered with the waterlogged fragments of trees which contained the borings of the bivalve *Teredo*. Turtles, sharks and bony fishes swam in the surface waters and nautiloids such as *Cimomia* drifted into the region from the Atlantic Ocean.

In the shallower water areas gastropods and bivalves still dominated the bottom-dwelling faunas. Some gastropods such as the high spired *Turritella*, were shallow burrowers whilst others including the gastropod *Aporrhais* were surface scavengers. *Aporrhais* often outnumbered most other species in these shallow water communities, although in some areas beds of surface-dwelling oysters or of shallow burrowing pinnid bivalves dominated the sea floor. The abundance of shellfish encouraged many rays into the area whilst other fishes were attracted by the debris that floated in the coastal waters and by the soft-bodied creatures that lived in the bottom muds. Sharks and turtles were infrequent visitors to the area and it is likely that their main feeding grounds lay to the northeast. The conditions that prevailed in the shallow-water areas were similar to those that now exist in many sub-tropical regions suggesting that deposition took place in a relatively low-energy environment.

The London Clay sea also covered areas of northern France, Belgium, Denmark and northwest Germany. Unfortunately the deposits of certain of these regions have been subsequently decalcified. Limited evidence, however, indicates mollusc-dominated communities somewhat similar to those of Sheppey or slightly deeper. In Denmark the evidence is of a very different story, as nearly 200 volcanic ash bands dominate the sediments of the Mo Clay Formation. Few bottom-dwelling organisms could exist on a sea floor subject to such a continuous bombardment of air fall materials. And in contrast to Sheppey the fauna of the Mo Clay is dominated by surface water dwellers and myriads of insects. The source of the ash material was a volcano or volcanoes situated in the present day area of the Skagerrak.

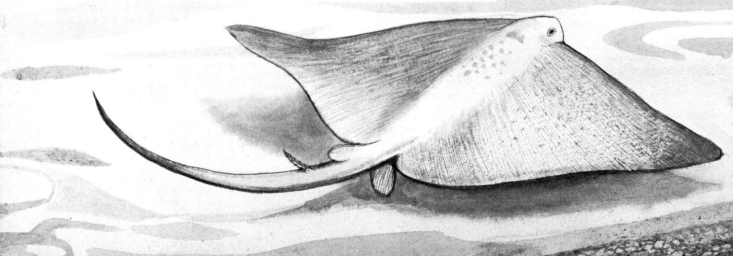

Glycyneris and serpulid worm tubes; London Clay.

Myliobatis teeth; a ray.

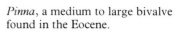

Pinna, a medium to large bivalve found in the Eocene.

momia

gastropod

Pinna

Ostrea

London Clay plants

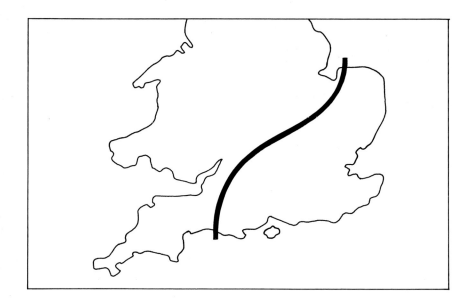

The flora of the London Clay reveals that the Thames Basin lay near the Lower Eocene shoreline, and that the Atlantic and Indian Oceans were connected by the Tethys Sea. The map shows the extent of the sea during the Eocene.

The London Clay of the Lower Eocene has long been famed for the rich flora of seeds and fruit which it yields in the cliffs of the Isle of Sheppey, near the mouth of the Thames. The London Clay is essentially a marine deposit and it seems that the seeds and fruit, along with much drift-wood, were deposited near the mouth of a great river. Significantly, analogous detritus was reported off the mouth of the Ambernoh River – the largest in New Guinea – by the Challenger Expedition, towards the end of the last century. The vegetation that the fossils represent was undoubtedly tropical in character, as the following analysis reveals.

The many thousands of specimens which have been collected are generally pyritized, though nevertheless well preserved. A total of 314 species of seed and fruit are present, and 234 of them have been identified. All but seven of the species are angiosperms; the exceptions being conifers. The species have been grouped into about 100 genera, three-quarters of which are extinct. The families to which the genera belong, however, are still with us, and so give a good idea of the climate which prevailed at the time concerned. Over 40 per cent of the families are almost entirely restricted to the tropics at the present time. Very roughly the same proportion are equally well distributed today in tropical and extra-tropical regions, whilst only about 10 per cent of the families are mainly temperate. A very similar breakdown is obtained, incidentally, from an analysis of angiosperm families living in the modern tropics. The implications then are clear: the London Basin in the early Eocene experienced a tropical climate. This conclusion is also corroborated by the London Clay fauna, which includes crocodiles and turtles.

The total flora bears a marked resemblance to that found today in south-east Asia, particularly on the Malaysian islands. More than a dozen species of palm are present, the most characteristic being *Sabal* and *Nipa*. They grew alongside other familiar plants such as cinnamon, magnolia and redwood. *Nipa* now flourishes in Malaysia and Australia and requires brackish water, so that it is restricted to shoreline environments. Its presence in the London Basin during the Eocene, therefore, suggests that it migrated along the northern shores of Tethys.

Evidently in London Clay times southern England lay 10–15° south of its present position. Yet even then, there is evidence that tropical vegetation penetrated farther north in this part of the world than it did elsewhere at similar latitudes. This means presumably that the proto-Gulf Stream was already in existence as the Atlantic Ocean was coming into being.

The Hordle flora of the Hampshire Basin shows that many of the London Clay species had disappeared from southern England in the late Eocene, as Britain moved northward into cooler latitudes. The affinities with present-day south-east Asia persist, but they are essentially with the floras well to the north of the Malaysian Islands.

Oncoba variabilis. This species was also commonly found in the London Clay deposits of the Eocene.

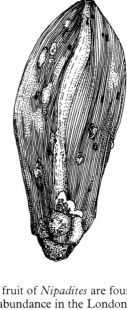

Fossil fruit of *Nipadites* are found in great abundance in the London Clay on the Isle of Sheppey, and are frequently pyritized.

One of the commonest London Clay species is the stemless palm *Nipa*, which today grows in brackish-water environments in Malaysia and Australia.

London Clay shoreline

Platychoerops (very similar to *Plesiadapis*, a lemur-like animal).

From our studies of the London Clay Formation we see that the various fossiliferous localities have yielded an enormous amount of data on both the marine and terrestrial conditions that prevailed. The shallow-water temperatures were approximately 16°c and the temperature on land has been estimated at between 20–30°c. Sharks and turtles were common in both deep and shallow water environments, and marsh turtles, tortoises and crocodiles inhabited various niches on land. The vegetative cover of the coastal region contained both angiosperms and gymnosperms. Birds were numerous and extremely diverse and from the presence of many land-dwelling species it has been suggested that the landscape included stretches of well-drained lowland as well as areas of dense tropical vegetation. In forest and forest glades, mammals were common with the first horse *Hyracotherium* living in the same region as various species of small primates, creodonts and archaic ungulates.

Oxyaena   *Hyracotherium*

Coryphodon, a plant-eating archaic ungulate from the Eocene. It was one of the earliest really large mammals and it is thought that it spent much of its time in water. The tusk-like canines were thought to have been used in the excavation of roots but now it is believed that they were either primitive display structures or weapons of defence.

The primates belonged to the primitive plesi-adapid family and were related to the type genus *Plesiadapis* of Europe (Menat) and North America. The London Clay genus is named *Platychoerops* and like its more cosmopolitan relative it was essentially a tree dweller. It resembled the living lemur but unlike *Plesiadapis* no evidence exists for the presence of a bushy tail in this London Clay genus. *Coryphodon* was by far the largest mammal of the region under consideration, with adults attaining lengths of over 2 metres.

They were quite heavily-built creatures with a large head and broad snout. Their teeth were those of herbivores with the cusp pattern indicating a specialization towards browsing feeding habits. It is unlikely that *Coryphodon* had any real enemies although the wolverine-like *Oxyaena*, of the creodont family, was quite a powerfully built carnivore. *Oxyaena* was about the size of a very large cat and it probably fed on small rodents, reptiles or even the first horses.

A restoration of a terrestrial environment

During the Early Tertairy the Massif Central in central France was an area of low mountains surrounded by tropical, red-soiled lowlands. The rocks of the region were mostly of Precambrian and Palaeozoic age with weathered granites forming distinct tors. The region was stable in the structural sense, with no evidence of the great volcanic activity which was to characterize later epochs. In the north of the region the mountain slopes were densely forested with redwoods (*Sequoia*), pines, cypresses and yews representing the gymnosperms, and oak, elm, poplar, the flowering plants. The undergrowth contained wild roses, rhododendrons and cinnamon and a

whole host of other shrubs and flowers. Numerous species of mushrooms also flourished in the more humid areas. In the area of Menat a small lake filled a depression in the ancient landscape and its waters were filled with tiny fish. The soft-backed turtle *Trionyx* swam in the surface waters of the lake and duck-like birds and waders frequented the waters edge. Insects of all shapes and sizes were abundant, with dragonflies and beetles being amongst the most common. The lake was a natural waterhole and small mammals drank along its shores. These included *Plesiadapis*, a small tree-dwelling primate that closely resembled the living lemurs and tarsiers of Madagascar and the East Indies. However, unlike the lemurs and tarsiers it possessed clawed hands and feet and large chisel-like incisors. *Plesiadapis* also had a strong bushy tail. The small primate fed on the nuts and fruits that littered the forest floor and hung from the branches of trees and shrubs. In the rainy season the waters of the lake were clouded with sediment and the remains of plants, insects and vertebrates were deposited in the fine muds at the bottom. These sediments can now be split into very thin layers and a fine colour banding suggests seasonal fluctuation in deposition. The amount of plant material preserved is extremely high and it suggests that the lake floor was rather fetid, and unlikely to support much invertebrate life.

A time of warmer waters

The Pliocene epoch represented the last 3 or 4 million years of the Tertiary sub-era. Terrestrial deposits are widely distributed throughout southern Europe, North America, China and Argentina and they mostly indicate an extensive modernization of mammalian and avian faunas. In Eurasia the horse, *Hipparion*, appeared along with many genera of cattle and antelopes but whilst *Hipparion* also flourished in North America, the cattle and true antelopes were unknown in that region. This indicates that no link between the two landmasses existed at this time, whereas the evidence for a re-establishment of the Panama land bridge is strong. Marine deposits of the Pliocene are recorded from many areas and the indication is that many communities contained between 50 and 90 per cent modern species. In general terms the indication is of warmer waters than those of today, with the limited Pliocene deposits of northern Europe being laid down in waters with temperatures within the warm-temperate range. The evidence for this comes from the fauna, of which a number of species exist today in warmer climes. In the Coralline Crag community of East Anglia and the southern North Sea, bryozoans and bivalves are the dominant groups with crustaceans, corals, brachiopods and others having a more limited representation. The community existed in waters not exceeding 40 to 50 metres in depth and on a substrate of rather coarse sand. Many of the bivalves were burrowers with *Venus*, *Glycymeris* and *Mya* being well known at the present time. Other 'in-sediment' dwellers included the sabellid worms who lived permanently in their distinctive U-shaped burrows. On the surface of the sediment the bryozoans and the branched and feather-like colonies of alcyonarian and gorgonacean corals gave the sea floor a garden-like appearance. Free-swimming bivalves such as *Chlamys* were common, as were the fixed 'lamp shells' or terebratulid brachiopods. Scavengers and predators were represented by the hermit crabs and by the moon shell, *Natica*. The cod, (*Gadus*) was also a common component of this community; its ancestry dating back to Late Cretaceous – Palaeocene times.

gorgonian coral

Chlamys

alcyonarian coral

sponge

cod-*Gadus*   echinoid   hermit crab

Insects flourish

A beetle from the bituminous varve-like deposits of Menat, France. (Ypresian-Lower Eocene).

We have already seen that the insects in the form of the earliest spiders and dragonflies were well represented in Palaeozoic terrestrial communities. In fact by the end of the Palaeozoic the insects had acquired a considerable diversity within their ancient orders, with numerous specimens having been collected from Carboniferous and Permian localities of the northern hemisphere. Strangely, apart from isolated horizons such as the Lithographic Stone of Bavaria, the record of Mesozoic insects is rather poor, with the Triassic and Cretaceous yielding few important specimens. This was due to the absence of suitable conditions for their preservation; the soft bodies of the insects disintegrating quickly if they were not rapidly covered by sediment. Insects obviously thrived during the Cretaceous and it is likely that many new species evolved in response to the expansion of the flowering plants. However, the fossil record of the insects does not improve until the Cainozoic when suitable conditions for preservation occurred throughout various epochs. In the Eocene insect populations have been recorded from Für in Denmark, Menat in France and the Green River beds of Wyoming, whilst in the Oligocene the number of specimens collected from the amber rich shales of the Baltic region has exceeded 150 000. Thousands of specimens have also been collected from the Miocene, Florissant Shales of Colorado and the record of Plio-Pleistocene material is almost as impressive.

From these localities the evolution of the insects can be charted with some accuracy, although the number of species recorded from the whole of the stratigraphic column is but a fraction of the 750 000 species known today. The early Cainozoic witnessed the appearance of the first termites, butterflies and moths and a dramatic increase in the number of beetles, flies and caddis flies. In the Oligocene the first fleas appeared and it is possible that they, and other groups such as the blood-sucking cooties and biting lice, evolved in response to the great diversification that had taken place amongst the mammals and birds. The cooties are first recorded from the remains of a Pleistocene squirrel whilst the biting lice have little or no fossil record.

Ancestors of the living grasshoppers, crickets, locusts, bees and wasps are all recorded from the Tertiary, and in several localities the insect faunas can provide valuable information as to the environmental conditions that prevailed. In certain mid-Tertiary limestones of the Massif Central in France, the abundance of caddis-fly larval cases is quite remarkable and the indication is that the sediments were deposited in a marshland environment. By the Quaternary many of the orders of living insects were well established throughout the world. In the northern hemisphere, beetles, weevils and flies are commonly found in sediments laid down during interglacials and together with mammals and plants, provide important information on the warmer conditions that prevailed during these stages of the Great Ice Age.

A spider and a 'harvestman' preserved
in fossilized resin – amber (Oligocene,
Europe).

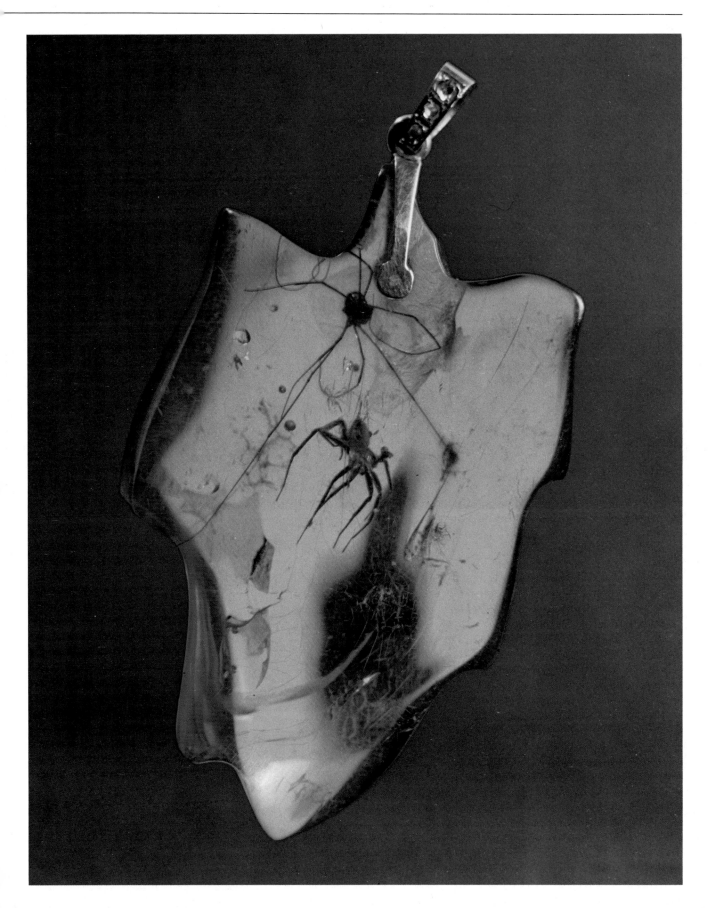

Tertiary volcanic areas

Map of the world showing the distribution of Tertiary and Quaternary volcanic centres.

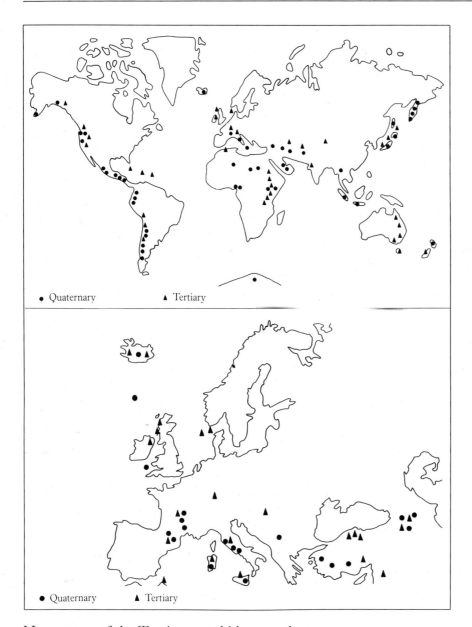

• Quaternary   ▲ Tertiary

• Quaternary   ▲ Tertiary

No account of the Tertiary would be complete without some mention of the igneous activity which occurred in so many parts of the world.

During the early part of the period centres of volcanic activity have been recorded from the Antilles, the North Atlantic area, Australasia, India and the ocean basins. Granite batholiths were also intruded in areas such as the Antilles and dyke-swarms and ring complexes occur in Northern Ireland and western Scotland. Igneous activity in later Tertiary times is just as prolific with examples to be found in central France, Catalunya, north-west Africa and South America. The activity was linked with the separation of the continents and with the building of mountain chains in areas of continental collision. In the

The Tertiary volcanic centres of . Europe and North Africa can be linked with crustal disturbances. Volcanoes in the North Sea basin were responsible for air-fall deposits in Denmark, Germany and East Anglia.

North Atlantic region plateau basalts poured out over great areas of central Greenland, Spitzbergen and northern parts of the British Isles, during the Early Tertiary. And much of this activity is directly linked with the opening of the ocean and the separation of Greenland from Europe. In Scotland and Ireland fossiliferous sediments occur within the volcanic sequences and leaves and pollen grains suggest that the flora was dominated by tropical and subtropical plants. Calculations

The Chaîne des Puys are a remarkable group of volcanoes which border the Limagne Basin of central France. The chain stretches north/south for approximately fifty kilometres and the majority of the cones are made up of ash and cinders. Most of the activity within the chain took place between 35000 and 3000 years ago and many lava flows were guided along pre-existing valleys.

Below
In areas such as the Massif Central very fine sediments composed essentially of volcanic particles formed the substrates of lakes and ponds. These fine muds were to prove an ideal medium for the preservation of plant and animal remains.

based on the sea floor spreading in the North Atlantic indicates that the separation of the land masses in this region began 50 to 60 million years ago. Iceland sits astride the mid-oceanic ridge and is itself an accumulation of Late Tertiary and Quaternary volcanics. Late Tertiary volcanism is beautifully illustrated in the Massif Central and Olot regions of France and north-east Spain, where numerous volcanoes erupted along the lines of weakness in the Earth's crust. As in Scotland and Ireland fossiliferous sediments occur within the volcanic sequences and at Perrier in the Massif the remains of mastodons, rhinoceroses, deer and carnivores have been discovered. In the Massif, the final volcanic episodes have been dated at less than 3000 years.

A leaf from the fine Ypresian deposits of Menat in France.

Great mountain chains

Cross-section of the Alps showing the folding that resulted from the collision of the European and African plates (after Holmes, A. 1965).

↖ direction of converging plates

north west   south east

European plate   African plate

The continued movement of the continental plates away from the mid-oceanic ridges during the Cainozoic, resulted in the widening of the Atlantic and Indian oceans and in a corresponding decrease in the size of the Pacific. It was also to result in the closure of the Tethyan seaway when the African and Indian plates collided with Eurasia. In both cases the plates involved were of the continental type, the majority of the oceanic crust descending into a subduction zone, examples of which, at the present time, are marked by the occurrence of oceanic trenches, lines of volcanoes, and earthquake foci. The collision of the Indian and Eurasian plates was to result in the formation of the Himalayas. The first episode took place in the Oligocene with the intensive folding of the sediments that had been deposited in the south eastern area of the Tethyan Ocean. Granitic rocks were also emplaced at this time. The movement of India under the Eurasian plate continued and a second major episode took place during the Miocene. This involved a great deal of folding and faulting and the thrusting of great sheets of folded strata southwards. The convergence of the two plates created a double layer of continental crust and this explains the elevated topography of the region. By the end of the Miocene the two continents were well and truly welded together. Apart from the Himalayas this collision was also to produce the highlands of the Tibetan Plateau.

The collision of the African and Eurasian plates also resulted in intense deformation during the Oligocene and Miocene. The result was the Alpine chain of mountains. Unlike India and Asia, Eurasia and Africa are not completely welded together and the oceanic crust remains in the form of the Mediterranean. Alpine mountains occur on both continents, along the northern and south-western shores of the Mediterranean sea. The Alps proper are the main product of the folding of the north-western region of Tethys. An almost continuous line of mountains marks the former northern shoreline of the once great ocean, with the European Alpine chain, the Zagros mountains and the Himalayas forming a formidable geographic barrier. This barrier has existed since the Pliocene and its effect on plant and animal migration, survival and speciation was of particular importance in Pleistocene times.

Mountain building during the Cainozoic was not confined to the old Tethyan region. In the south-eastern Pacific the oceanic plate converged with South America and this resulted in the formation of the Andes. The initial episodes in their construction took place at the end of the Middle Eocene, with further more major phases of activity occurring in the Oligocene, Late Miocene and Late Pliocene. Radiometric dating of the granitic rocks of the Andes indicates that they were emplaced during the Eocene and Oligocene phases. Unlike the Alps and the Himalayas, the Andes were less important as a geographic barrier during the Pleistocene. This was because of their north-south alignment, which ran parallel to, and not across, the main migration routes which led away from the advancing ice sheets.

An aerial photograph of the Alpine
chain.

An Eocene avifauna

The fossil record of the birds improves considerably in sediments of Eocene age and it is obvious that the limited number of discoveries made from Palaeocene rocks, bear small testament to the continued evolution and diversification that was actually taking place. Both land and sea birds are well known by the Early Eocene and during the 15 million years of the epoch, the overall trend was of a continual modernization of the world's avifauna. The descriptive history of Eocene birds began in the early years of the last century with accounts of the now famous genera *Halcyornis* and *Dasornis*. The former was a small, early relative of the barbets, kingfishers and rollers, whilst the latter was a large sea bird which exhibited a mixture of pelicaniform (pelicans, cormorants, gannets) and procellariform (albatrosses, petrels) characters. *Dasornis* was a close relative of *Odontopteryx* which was the size of a small cormorant. *Odontopteryx* had a long bill with tooth-like projections along the edges of the jaws to grip its food. Other sea-birds of the Eocene included the primitive tropicbird-like *Prophaeton*.

All of the genera noted above have been discovered in the London Clay Formation of south-east England, from which other finds provide evidence of both shoreline and inland dwelling forms. In the past, most palaeontologists have pictured the landscape of these times as being covered with dense tropical-subtropical vegetation. The evidence from an analysis of the bird fauna is, however, contradictory as the land-dwelling forms are dominated by small game birds, waders, herons, cuckoos and pigeons. This suggests that the landscape was more varied and that some areas were flat and comparatively well-drained. Of the gamebirds *Argillipes*, or 'Clay-foot', was a little smaller than the living grouse, whilst others like *Coturnipes* resembled the quails. The pigeons and cuckoos were very small, which is, perhaps, to be expected in species that represent early stages in the evolution of their respective families. The largest land birds of the London Clay avifauna included the 'walker rail' *Pediorallus* which grew to the size of the common pheasant, and the giant running bird *Gastornis*, which was of similar dimensions to the diatrymids

Prophaeton

Parvigyps

Odontopteryx

Coturnipes

or 'terror cranes'. To complete the avifauna of the London Clay one has to mention the presences of birds of prey with *Parvigyps*, a small old world vulture, being the best known.

Continued collection from the London Clay Formation is continually adding to our knowledge of the Lower Eocene avifauna. In some ways it is specialized, related to environment, and we should remember that many other families of birds were represented in other habitats throughout the epoch. Evidence exists for wetland avifaunas in both Early and Late Eocene times with water-dwelling rails, cranes and duck-like birds as the dominant groups. In North America the avifaunas included some New World Vultures which were adapted to a running mode of life whilst in Australia the remains of giant penguins represent the northern limits of Antarctic populations.

barbet

heron

Gastornis

Pediorallus

Argillipes

Oligocene, Miocene and Pliocene birds

The phosphate-rich deposits of Quercy in southern France are famed for their rich assemblage of fossil birds. Waders, ibises, owls, hawks, gamebirds, swifts and rollers have all been discovered and any attempt to reconstruct the palaeogeography of the region during the Oligocene has to take into account the diverse habitats that existed.

The modernization of the world's avifaunas continued throughout the Oligocene, Miocene and Pliocene epochs. By the Oligocene approximately 25 per cent of modern families were represented band from the Miocene into the Pliocene the percentage of modern genera increased from roughly 33 to 75 per cent.

In the Oligocene the appearance of the giant running phororhacids in South America appeared to parallel the evolution of the 'terror cranes' in the Eocene of North America and Europe; the absence of placental mammals in the southern landmass allowing the phororhacids to occupy the role of a major predator for approximately 35 million years. *Phororhacos* and its relatives were of rather similar build to the diatrymids, with long, strong legs and a large head. They stood at approximately 1·5 metres in height and weighed as much as a full grown man. Other giants of the Oligocene included the huge penguins of Australia and Antarctica, with the genus *Pachydyptes* representing a group that ranged from the Lower Eocene

through to the Miocene.

The giant penguins and phororhacids represent the more spectacular aspects of Oligocene bird life. They are rather specialized stocks and in themselves provide little information as to the general evolution of the birds as a whole. Such information is available from the Oligocene phosphate deposits of the Quercy region in France, from which some forty-six species of bird have been recorded. The species represent eighteen families with the majority being indicative of a tropical environment. As in the Eocene, rails, waders, herons and ibises were common along with owls, hawks, gamebirds and primitive swifts.

Many of these are also known from the Miocene of France when they were joined by representatives of the first wood hoopoes, and parrots. In other areas the first true grebes and woodpeckers have been recorded and crows and finches were now recognizable. Several types of flamingoes also flourished during this epoch with

Phororhacos

Pachydyptes

Palaeolodus from the Quercy phosphates representing a rather primitive stage in the evolution of the group. *Palaeolodus* had a shorter, straighter bill than living genera and thus differed from other Miocene species which possessed the normal downcurved, jaw structure. Of all the Miocene birds the 'bony-toothed' descendants of *Odontopteryx* warrant specific mention as the genus *Osteodontornis* from the west coast of North America had a wing-span in excess of 4 metres. The wings were narrow and it is likely that this bird spent much of its time gliding over the sea.

By the Pliocene the avifauna bore comparison with that of the present day and a number of living species have actually been identified from this epoch, and groups such as the ostriches, emus, rheas and tinamous appear in the fossil record for the first time during this epoch. Finally, it should be noted that the flightless auks also appeared during the Pliocene with two species of the genus *Mancalla* paralleling the evolution of the Great Auk of the North Atlantic which became extinct in recent times mainly due to exploitation by man.

Mancalla

emu

Pleistocene birds

The succession of glacial and interglacial stages that took place in the northern hemisphere during the 1·6 to 1·8 million years of the Pleistocene were to have a significant effect on the geographic distribution of many bird families. The cold stages were also the direct cause of many extinctions. Also it is probable that the patterns of migration that now exist were developed during this epoch. In Eurasia the southern migration of species during the cold stages would have been restricted by natural barriers such as the Himalayas and Alps and certain previously widespread species would have been forced to seek refuge in isolated areas. In times of warmer weather these birds would move north again but it is possible that during the period of isolation minor changes had occurred that would prevent interbreeding and lead to the development of a new species. Isolation could also result from the changes in sea-level that

went hand-in-hand with glacials and interglacials. In this case the effects were to extend into the Southern Hemisphere with coastal and island communities being affected.

At the beginning of the Pleistocene most modern bird families were well established although at species level living representatives accounted for only 25 per cent of known forms. Gigantism was still a common phenomena with huge swans, storks and vultures recorded from different parts of the world. These included *Teratornis* the condor-like vulture from the Rancho La Brea tar pits of California, which had a wing-span of over 4 metres.

As in the Pliocene the ratites were common to both northern and southern lands, with the ostriches in particular having a much greater distribution than they do today. The tinamous and rheas were confined to South America and the

tinamou

rhea   kiwi

Aepyornis

moas to New Zealand. In the case of the latter some species grew to just over 3 metres in height and rank amongst the largest known ratites. Other large ratites of the Pleistocene included the 'elephant birds' or Aepyornithiformes. Initially, during the Tertiary, these were distributed throughout North and West Africa but by the Pleistocene they were restricted to the island of Madagascar. This change in distribution was probably linked with climatic and predatory factors with genera such as *Aepyornis* crossing to the temporary safety of Madagascar via a possible 'sweepstake route'. The eggs of Aepyornithiformes were as spectacular as the birds themselves, with some specimens having a capacity of approximately a litre. Not surprisingly, both the 'elephant birds' and the moas attracted the attention of the men who were to invade their island refuges and both groups were to die out in recent times.

By the end of the Pleistocene over 80 per cent of modern bird species had representation in the fossil record and it is likely that new discoveries will, in time, push this figure even higher.

The flightless ratites are thought to be one of the most primitive groups of birds but as is often the case in the fossil record, the remains of these animals are not recorded until long after the appearance of many more advanced forms. It is unlikely that the various ratite families, which appeared simultaneously during the Plio-Pleistocene, evolved independently on separate continents and one must argue for a common ancestor prior to the separation of certain landmasses. The ancestor probably lived on Gondwanaland during the Upper Cretaceous and if one should picture a living tinamou with wings, this would closely resemble the earliest ratite.

moa

ostrich

More niches: a greater variety

The close of the Mesozoic saw dramatic changes in the distribution, relief and climate of the Earth's land masses. Pangaea, the old super continent, had already fragmented towards the end of the Palaeozoic era, to give Laurasia in the north and Gondwanaland in the south, separated by the Tethys Ocean. During the Mesozoic era Gondwanaland itself began to break up and North America started to drift away from Eurasia. Even so, well into Cretaceous times the rifts between the protocontinents were not so great as to prevent the essentially free spread of land animals. Nor were there high mountain chains or adverse climates to limit their movement. Hence the reptiles which ruled the Mesozoic world were more or less cosmopolitan or global in their occurrence. The vegetation too was rather uniform, with many gymnosperms such as conifers, cycads and ginkgoes, and numerous ferns. Whilst the first mammals had appeared in the Triassic and were well established in the Cretaceous, the scene was not yet set for their rise to dominance. The flowering plants or angiosperms, on the other hand, made a sudden debut in the lower Cretaceous fossil record, and by the late Cretaceous were nearly everywhere dominant over the gymnosperms. Their take-over was aided by an evolutionary burst in insects, which pollinated their flowers more effectively than the wind pollinated the gymnosperms. The late Cretaceous also witnessed extensive mountain building, as the continents drifted ever farther apart. Such profound geographical rearrangement led to greater climatic differentiation and general cooling. No doubt this was the underlying cause of the extinction of the dinosaurs and most other reptiles.

The Tethys Ocean was narrowest in the west, where there was probably a land bridge which permitted faunal exchange between Laurasia and Gondwanaland during the Mesozoic era. Thus, most of the twelve basic reptile groups of the Cretaceous period which are listed here inhabited both land masses.

chelonians

snakes

lizards

crocodilians

sauropods

carnosaurs

coelurosaurs

ceratopians

hadrosaurs

ornithopods

ankylosaurs

pterosaurs

The Mesozoic World

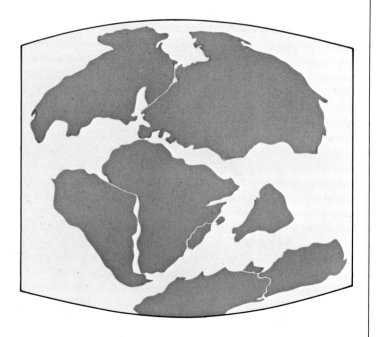

The niches vacated by the dinosaurs provided the stimulus for the long-delayed radiation of the mammals, at the dawn of the Cainozoic era. Unlike the Mesozoic setting, the more diverse world which the mammals inherited presented formidable barriers to their dispersal. Independent faunal provinces thus emerged on the new continental 'rafts'. Their distinctiveness varied with the degree of isolation of the continents in space and time. In Australia, one of the two island continents, the marsupial or pouched mammals filled almost all of the available niches, as it had become detached from Gondwanaland before the arrival of the placental mammals, i.e. those which give birth to more advanced young. Marsupials occupied the insectivorous and carnivorous roles in South America as well, but the herbivores were descended from primitive placental ancestors. This unusual fauna survived until the beginning of the Pleistocene, when North and South America were reunited, and the invasion of more highly evolved placental mammals from the north brought about the extinction of all except a few of their southern counterparts. Although part of the so-called world continent, Africa was similarly isolated early in the Cainozoic and functioned as another centre of mammal radiation. In the Oligocene epoch, however, Africa drifted into contact with Eurasia and faunal mixing ensued. The expansion of the Sahara desert at the opening of the Pleistocene restored its isolation, and allowed its entirely placental mammals to diverge once again from those to the north. Over the rest of the world continent, namely North America and Eurasia, faunal interchange was possible throughout much of the Cainozoic era, so that the mammals of the northern hemisphere have retained marked affinities to this day.

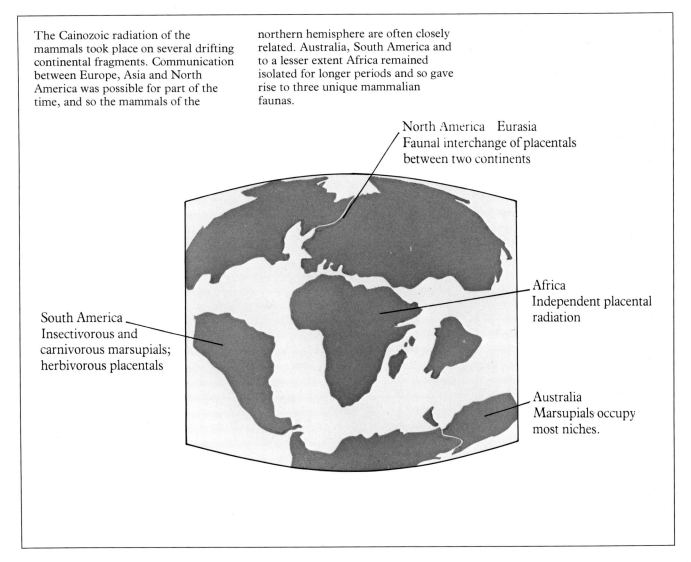

The Cainozoic radiation of the mammals took place on several drifting continental fragments. Communication between Europe, Asia and North America was possible for part of the time, and so the mammals of the northern hemisphere are often closely related. Australia, South America and to a lesser extent Africa remained isolated for longer periods and so gave rise to three unique mammalian faunas.

North America   Eurasia
Faunal interchange of placentals between two continents

Africa
Independent placental radiation

South America
Insectivorous and carnivorous marsupials; herbivorous placentals

Australia
Marsupials occupy most niches.

Mammalian all-sorts

Nearly 100 million years of mammalian history had already lapsed when the 'Age of Mammals' commenced some 60 million years ago, at the start of the Cainozoic era. The mammals had evolved from the predatory therapsid reptiles in late Triassic times, and subsequently diverged to give five distinct orders in the Jurassic. Of these, the triconodonts, symmetrodonts and docodonts – all probably carnivorous or insectivorous in their habits – became extinct in the Jurassic or early Cretaceous, although the docodonts may be ancestral to the monotremes of Australia. In fact, the only group that survived into the Cainozoic were the multituberculates, perhaps best described as pseudo-rodents. The remaining pantotheres were egg-laying insectivores of shrew-like appearance, and they also became extinct early in the Cretaceous. They are of great interest, nevertheless, as they gave rise to the marsupial and placental mammals.

The first Cretaceous marsupial resembled the modern American opossum, and it was from this base that a wide range of adaptive types was to evolve in later epochs, especially in Australia and the Americas. The earliest Cretaceous placentals were small insectivores, which before the end of the period had differentiated into several new orders. These included: the primates, to which man belongs; the meat-eating creodonts, which preceded and developed separately from the true carnivores; and the condylarths, which were primitive hoofed animals with an essentially omnivorous way of life. Compared with the variety, number and, above all, size of the contemporary reptiles, the new mammals remained insignificant.

With the passing of the 'Age of Reptiles', the mammals underwent a veritable evolutionary explosion to fill the empty niches. Experimentation was the keynote of the Palaeocene and Eocene scramble to adapt to the new meat-eating and plant-eating roles, both large and small. The multituberculates and creodonts flourished, and the condylarths radiated along lines from which many modern and extinct herbivores arose. Precisely how many new lines these 'old-stagers' initiated is not clear, yet so far as is known all the orders of mammals originating in the Cainozoic extend back to this early period. In the late Eocene and Oligocene the more archaic and often bizarre forms such as the taeniodonts, tillodonts and amblypods disappear, whilst the condylarths and creodonts dwindle. This 'weeding out' was due partly to continued climatic cooling and partly to intensified competition for similar niches. In the next epoch, the Miocene, the world took on a more familiar aspect, and recognisably modern mammalian types were by now well established. Their adaptive perfectioning reached a climax in the Pliocene, with a greater variety of advanced,

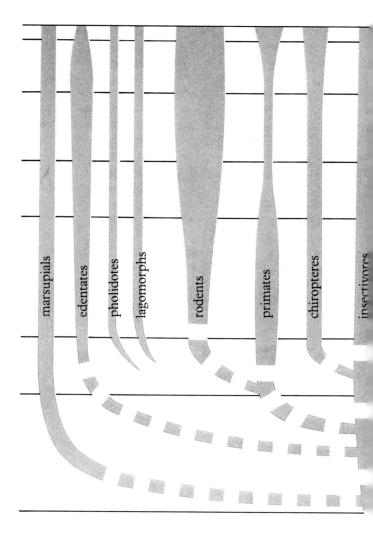

specialized mammals than ever before or since. Further evolutionary adjustments were achieved in response to the Pleistocene Ice Age, and produced the mammals we know to-day. Many, however, particularly the larger ones, vanished without replacement in a wave of extinctions between 60 000 and 1000 years ago, as human hunters spread across the globe. The 'Age of Mammals' is, in a sense, over: we have entered the 'Age of Man'.

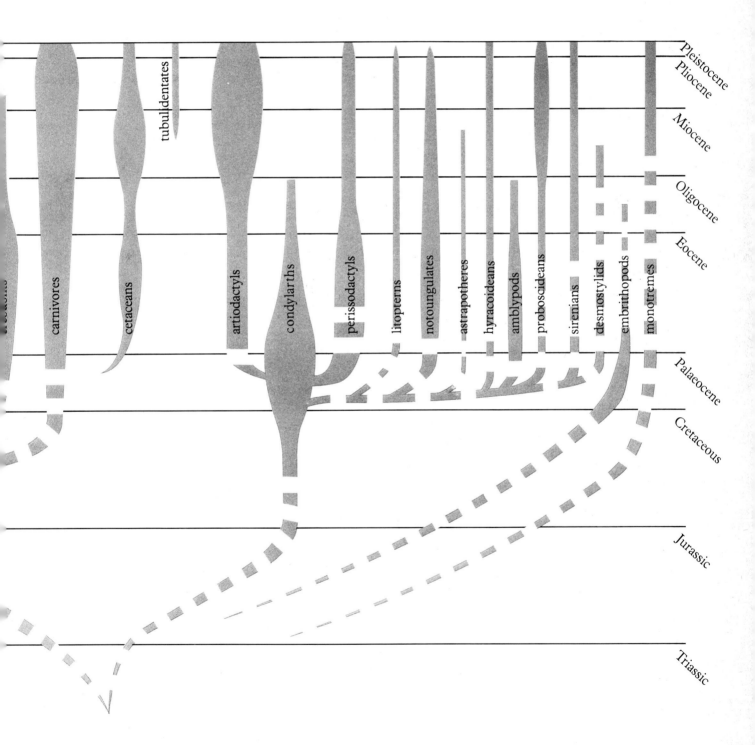

The evolution of monotreme, marsupial and placental mammals

Living mammals belong to three basic groups: monotremes, marsupials and placentals. That each represents a progressive stage in just one line of mammalian evolution is no longer accepted as correct. The monotremes, i.e. the Duck-billed Platypus of Australia and the spiny, ant-eating echidnas of New Guinea and Australia, have the more obscure ancestry, for they have no fossil record before the Pleistocene. Their general anatomy, however, implies an independent descent from the earliest Mesozoic mammals. Indeed, they retain to this day an intermediate position between the mammal-like reptiles and the higher mammals. For example, they lay eggs, and

Eodelphis, a Cretaceous marsupial which strikingly resembled the modern American opossum, *Didelphis*, so that the latter can rightly be regarded as a living fossil.

not only is their body temperature lower than that of other mammals, it also fluctuates with the environment. They conform most obviously to the mammal grade in having hair and suckling their young.

The marsupial and placental mammals are more clearly related, and apparently diverged from a common stock in the Cretaceous, for the first fossil teeth of both groups are of this age, and were even then diagnostically different. Apart from teeth, there are marked reproductive and skeletal contrasts, perhaps the most significant of the latter being the enlarged brain case of the placentals, which reflects their generally greater mental capacity. In modern marsupials the young are born as very small larval animals and immediately crawl into the mother's pouch. Here they become attached to teats and remain for several months as their development continues. Young placentals grow for a longer time inside the mother's womb and consequently are that much more advanced at birth. In some cases, such as the hoofed mammals and whales, the newly-born offspring are active almost immediately.

On balance the fossil evidence suggests that initially the marsupials were restricted to North America and the placentals to Asia. When they eventually spread and mixed it was usually to the detriment of the former. Thus, in North America and Europe the marsupials were extinguished during the mid-Cainozoic, and in all probability the superior intelligence of the placentals had proved a decisive factor in the struggle for survival. We have seen that the marsupials lived on only in Australia and South America. The massive extinction of the remarkable South American fauna at the end of the Pliocene produced yet further impoverishment, for, of the marsupial element, all except the opossums and rat opossums were eliminated. Ironically, the opossums have since extended their range back into North America, as far as Canada. In retrospect, this one anomaly hardly disguises the fact that the 'Age of Mammals' is more aptly named the 'Age of Placental Mammals'.

Uintatherium, an ancient hoofed placental mammal of Eocene age, included in the extinct order Amblypoda. It was as large as an African white rhinoceros.

255

Origin and evolution of carnivorous mammals

Meat-eating habits in mammals have been essentially restricted to just two marsupial and two placental groups. Each evolved similar teeth, namely strong incisors for nipping, dagger-like canines for stabbing and blade-like cheek-teeth or carnassials for slicing meat. They also developed the necessary intelligence, sensory faculties, power and agility for finding and catching a mainly vertebrate prey.

The extinct marsupial carnivores of South America, the borhyaenids, emerged from the didelphids in the Early Cainozoic. A range of types was produced, including the wolf-like *Borhyaena* in the Miocene, and the larger sabre-tooth 'cat' *Thylacosmilus* in the Pliocene. The native 'cats' and the Tasmanian Wolf or Thylacine of Australia arose from a different marsupial family, the dasyurids. Their numbers have been greatly reduced in the recent past, and in the case of the Thylacine probably to extinction.

Of the two placental carnivorous orders, the creodonts are the older and more primitive. Dating from the Cretaceous, they reached their zenith in the Early Cainozoic with the wolverine-like oxyaenids and the more varied hyaenodonts. The latter actually yielded sabre-tooth, dog-, cat- and hyaena-like forms, thus anticipating later differentiation in the other order, Carnivora. Except for the hyaenodonts, which seem to have been scavengers, the creodonts did not survive the Eocene. Their demise coincided with the major evolutionary advances in herbivorous mammals at this time, as the latter adapted for grazing and speed in the more open habitats then coming into existence. Greater intelligence was required to bring down these animals, and so the role of hunter passed from the creodonts to the true carnivores, with their larger brains.

The earliest carnivores, the weasel-like miacids, first appear in the Palaeocene and before their extinction at the end of the Eocene had initiated the two main lines of modern Carnivores – the Canoidea and the Feloidea. Two of the canoid families, the dogs along with the weasels and their kin, were already distinct at the Eocene-Oligocene transition. The weasel family subsequently radiated widely, whilst the otter branch of the family diverged in the mid-Cainozoic to give the true seals. The dogs have remained far less specialized, which is why today they are the most widely spread carnivores. However, several offshoots have developed from the central canid stock. These culminated in the amphicyons –

extinct dog–bears – the sea lions, the raccoons and pandas, and most recently, the bears. The last two families are notable in having omnivorous or even vegetarian habits.

The feloids comprise the old world civets, the hyenas and the cats. Most primitive are the civets, being little-modified descendants of the miacids. In Late Miocene times the hyenas evolved rapidly from the civets, and finally dislodged the last of

Palaeocene

Eocene

Oligocene

Miocene

Pliocene

Pleistocene

Hyaenidae   Viverridae   Felidae

the ancient hyaenodonts from the scavenging niche. The most completely specialized land-carnivores, the cats, broke away from civet-like forebears at an even earlier date, in the Late Eocene, and by the Early Oligocene were essentially modern in form. Thereafter two basic evolutionary trends are apparent: the sabre-tooths, adapted to killing large, slow-moving prey; and the more agile felids, better equipped for chasing faster prey. The sabre-tooths disappeared in the late Pleistocene, because of the catastrophic extermination of the animals on which they subsisted.

To conclude, mammalian predators were quickly on the Cainozoic scene. They were so efficient and diverse that the opportunity for other mammalian categories to become carnivorous simply did not materialize.

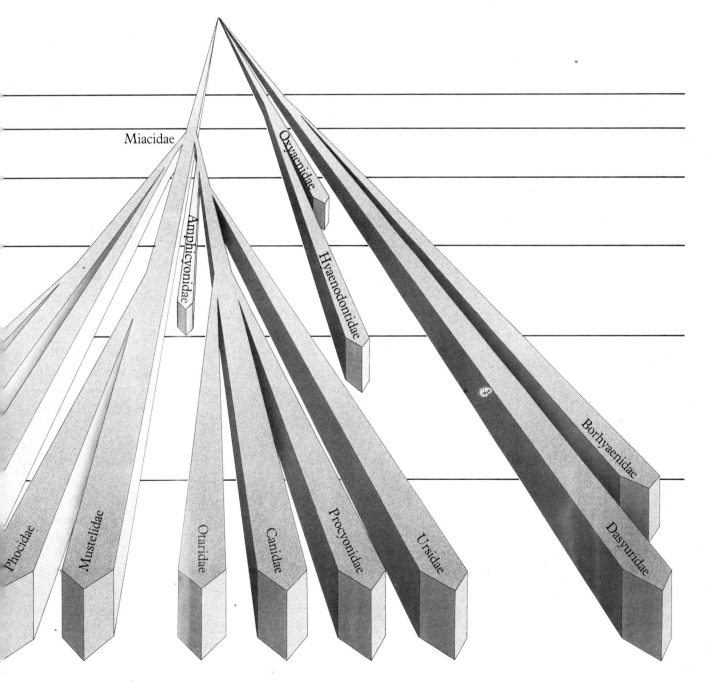

257

The first horse

Most modern hoofed animals or ungulates are grouped into two orders, the odd-toed Perissodactyla and the even-toed Artiodactyla. Horses are odd-toed and extend back in time for over 55 million years to the late Palaeocene. The earliest ancestor was no larger than a fox, and when first discovered was mistakenly linked with the small African hyraxes or dassies and named *Hyracotherium* accordingly. Later work established its true family connections and a new name, *Eohippus* or 'dawn horse', was given, but strictly this cannot have precedence over the original and so is used only in the vernacular.

Apart from being a prototype horse, *Hyracotherium (Eohippus)* possessed many features that place it close to the evolutionary stem or base of all perissodactyls. The immediate forebear was a condylarth, from which *Hyracotherium* differed mainly in respect of its teeth, feet, legs and somewhat larger brain. Thus certain of the molar teeth had developed a more distinct bunodont condition, i.e. a bubbly surface to the crowns, better suited to browsing on the leaves of trees and bushes. Grasses are more abrasive and did not become important in the diet of horses until they evolved true grinding teeth with high, ridged crowns. The canines of *Hyracotherium* were smaller than those of the condylarth predecessor, and a diastema or gap had appeared between them and the cheek teeth. Diastemas are much larger in more modern horses; they serve to collect food before it is passed backwards to the grinding teeth.

As for the feet of *Hyracotherium*, whereas the digits still ended in miniature padded hooves, their number had been reduced to three in the hind feet and four on the fore-feet, the fourth being largely non-functional. This reduction reflected developments in the joints of the legs and in the inter-relation of the small bones of the feet, which restricted lateral movement thereby concentrating thrust onto the central digits. As well as fewer digits, the lower leg bones had become longer and the effective length of the legs was further increased because *Hyracotherium*, unlike the condylarths, walked on its toes.

Such changes made *Hyracotherium* a more efficient browser and a faster runner than its condylarth equivalents. They were stimulated by pressures exerted by the predators of the time and explain the initial success of the perissodactyls as a whole and the subsequent decline of the less well-endowed condylarths.

Opposite
Hyracotherium lived from the late Palaeocene to the early Eocene and, in general appearance, more closely resembled a condylarth than a horse. No more than 50 centimetres long, it was a forest-dweller and lived on a diet of leaves.

In contrast to the condylarths, the small bones of the hind foot of *Hyracotherium* were interlocked and the lower part of the pulley-like joint or astragalus attached to them was relatively straight. The combined effect was to reduce lateral movement.

Hyracotherium was probably widely distributed throughout the northern hemisphere, but became extinct in Eurasia at the close of early Eocene times. From then on the evolution of the horse was largely confined to North America. Fossil evidence suggests that it originally migrated across from North America to Eurasia in the Early Eocene.

A classic case for evolution

From *Hyracotherium* to the modern horse *Equus*, a single, progressive line of evolution can be traced. The full picture is actually more complex, for after the Oligocene there were divergent branches. These were advanced in some respects yet old-fashioned in others, except for that which led to *Equus* (diagram partly based on Halstead, 1978).

The evolutionary stages from *Hyracotherium* to the sheep-sized *Miohippus* were exclusive to the New World. The toes on all four feet of *Miohippus* had been reduced to three, and the central toe had been further enlarged. Each toe remained functional, however, and still ended in a padded hoof. The pre-molar teeth had become fully molar-like to give a greater surface-area for chewing food. Moreover, enamel ridges had developed on the crowns of the cheek-teeth – the lophodont condition – which again aided the pre-digestive breakdown of plant food. Even so, the

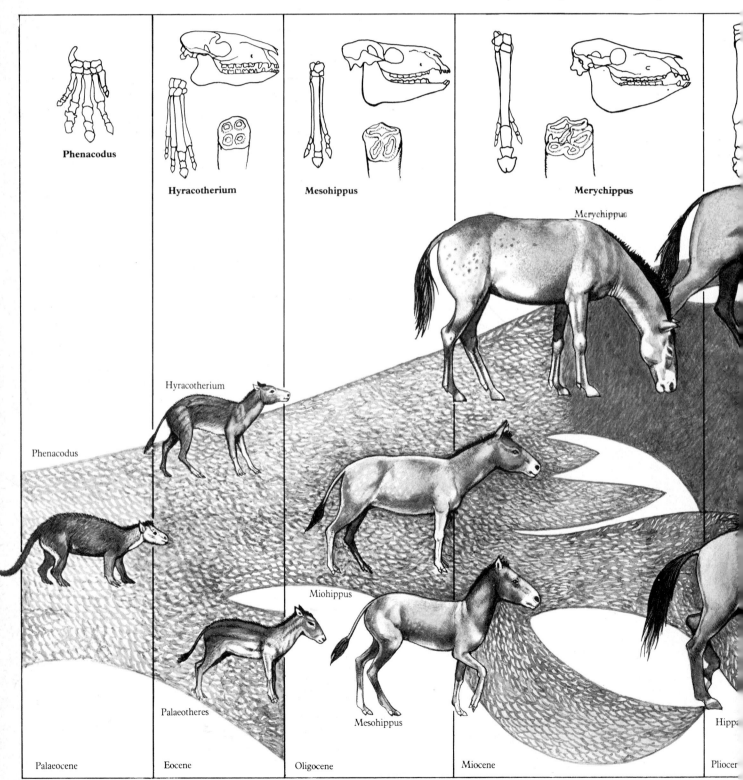

Phenacodus

Hyracotherium

Mesohippus

Merychippus

Merychippus

Hyracotherium

Phenacodus

Miohippus

Palaeotheres

Mesohippus

Hippa

| Palaeocene | Eocene | Oligocene | Miocene | Plioce |

crowns themselves had stayed low or brachydont; extra modifications were to be made before a diet of grass, as opposed to leaves and soft plants, could be tackled.

The horses diversified in Miocene times as habitats became more varied. *Archaeohippus* and *Anchitherium* continued in the browsing tradition of *Miohippus* with little significant structural change, although in the case of *Anchitherium* there was an eventual size increase to that of a modern horse. The latter subsequently gave rise to *Hypohippus* and at different times both crossed over the Bering land bridge into the Old World. In contrast to these browsers, a true plains horse, the pony-sized *Merychippus*, also arose from the ancestral *Miohippus*. This horse too inherited three toes, but differed from the others in that it walked on the central toe, which ended in a hoof without a pad. The foot had in addition developed a springing action.

Equus

ohippus

Equus

Pleistocene

Holocene

The adaptations for speed in *Merychippus* were complemented by advanced specializations of the teeth. There was a great increase in crown height to the hypsodont condition, the crowns became cement-covered, and the enamel ridges were folded into complex patterns. Thus as the teeth wore down, the ridges being harder stood above the cement and the dentine in the cores of teeth, to present a sharply crested surface on which to grind tough grasses. *Merychippus* was therefore well equipped for grazing and fast running on the early grasslands of North America.

From *Merychippus* there were several descendant lines, including the miniature horses *Calippus* and *Nannippus*, but in evolutionary terms *Hipparion* and *Pliohippus* were the most important. *Hipparion* retained three-toed feet and was later to migrate to the Old World, where it eclipsed the older brachydont horses and managed to survive until the Pleistocene. Conversely, in *Pliohippus* the lateral toes were reduced to mere splints of bone within the skin of the upper foot: it was in other words the first single-toed horse. From *Pliohippus* there evolved *Hippidion*, the extinct, short-legged mountain horse of South America, and *Equus*, which survived the Pleistocene, surprisingly enough, only in the Old World. The Spanish conquistadores re-introduced it to the Americas.

Odd-toed hoofed mammals: the perissodactyla

We have noted the anatomical features which set the first horses apart from their condylarth ancestors, and these features apply in a general way to all early perissodactyls. In the initial radiation of the order, three suborders were established: the Ceratomorpha – rhinoceroses, tapirs and several extinct forms closely related to the tapirs; the Hippomorpha – horses and the extinct palaeotheres and titanotheres; and the Ancylopoda – better known as the extinct chalicotheres, the most recent of which resembled large, clawed horses. Although several ancient types of perissodactyls, such as the horse-like palaeotheres and the massive titanotheres, died out in the Oligocene or earlier, the order enjoyed its heyday in mid-Tertiary times when they were the dominant ungulates over most of the world. Since then they have been steadily replaced by the more successful artiodactyls, and the order as a whole is moving towards extinction.

The following deals with the evolution of living perissodactyls excluding the horse; examples of extinct forms are illustrated. Of the living representatives, the tapirs are the most primitive, being little more advanced than *Hyracotherium*. Several extinct tapir families are known from the Eocene, including the isectolophids, helaletids and lophiodonts. The modern tapir family seems to have

The titanotheres appeared in the Eocene and reached their evolutionary peak in mid-Oligocene times as huge creatures over 2 metres high at the shoulder. Later forms, such as *Brontotherium* shown here, carried Y- or V- shaped bony protuberances on the nose. They became extinct because they failed to develop teeth suited to grazing, and the softer vegetation on which they fed became more scarce. Their rather primitive brain was probably another contributory factor.

The radiation of the odd-toed mammals (after Romer, 1966).

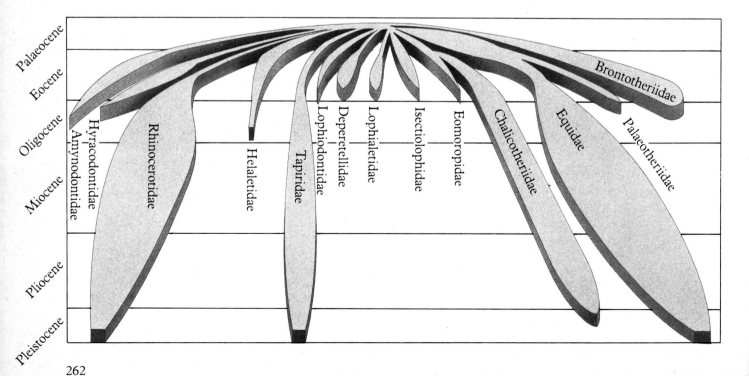

been derived from the lophiodonts and has hardly changed at all since it appeared in the Oligocene. As recently as the Early Pleistocene tapirs were widespread in the northern hemisphere, but thereafter their range was reduced to the tropics and today they survive only in Malaysia and Central and Southern America.

The closely related rhinoceroses arose from a tapiroid predecessor in the Eocene and subsequently branched along three main lines. The hyracodonts or running rhinoceroses were small, slender browsers which flourished in the Oligocene and became extinct soon after. Much larger and heavier were the amynodonts, probably water-lovers with hippopotamus-like habits. These, too, became extinct soon after the Oligocene. The third line, the rhinocerotids did not emerge until the Oligocene, apparently from hyracodonts. Various evolutionary directions were then followed. One led to *Baluchitherium*, the largest land mammal ever. Other lines developed horns. Thus the Oligo-Miocene *Diceratherium* was a small rhino with two horns side by side. Varieties with two horns one in front of the other also appeared in the Oligocene and survive to this day in Africa and Sumatra. The single-horned rhinos of India and Java came later, towards the close of the Miocene.

Baluchitherium, this hornless giant rhinoceros was probably a tree-top browser.

Moropus, a Miocene chalicothere. More successful than the titanotheres, the chalicotheres lived from the Eocene until the major extinctions of the late Pleistocene. They may have used their claws to bend down leafy branches, or their diet may have included roots and tubers unearthed by these claws.

Even-toed hoofed mammals: the artiodactyla

The radiation of the even-toed mammals (after Romer, 1966).

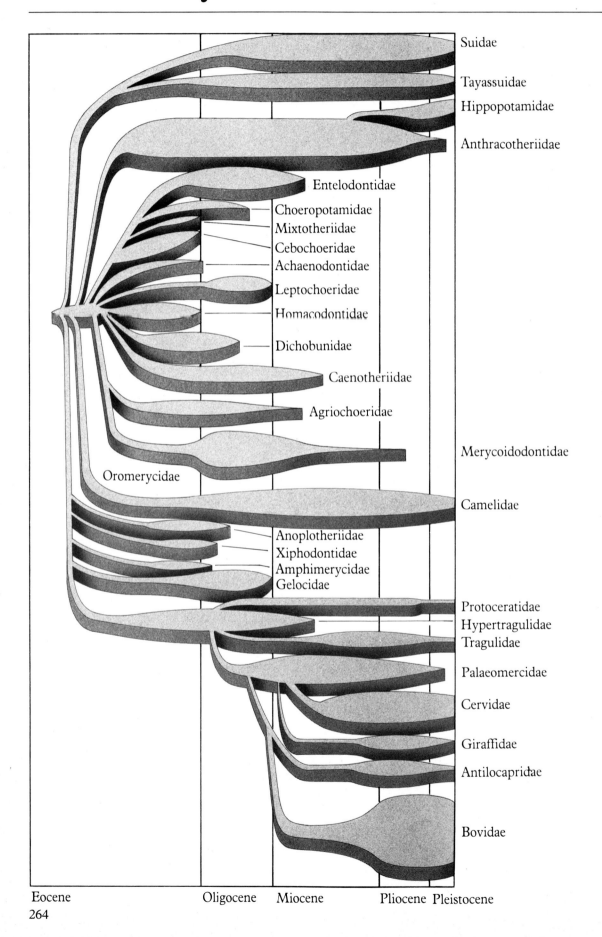

Suidae

Tayassuidae

Hippopotamidae

Anthracotheriidae

Entelodontidae

Choeropotamidae

Mixtotheriidae

Cebochoeridae

Achaenodontidae

Leptochoeridae

Homacodontidae

Dichobunidae

Caenotheriidae

Agriochoeridae

Merycoidodontidae

Oromerycidae

Camelidae

Anoplotheriidae

Xiphodontidae

Amphimerycidae

Gelocidae

Protoceratidae

Hypertragulidae

Tragulidae

Palaeomercidae

Cervidae

Giraffidae

Antilocapridae

Bovidae

Eocene

Oligocene   Miocene   Pliocene Pleistocene

Artiodactyls appeared in Eocene times along with many of the ancient perissodactyls. In this order, however, the digits are normally reduced to four or two, and the ankle-joint or astragalus is modified for leaping. Most artiodactyls are also ruminants, i.e. they regurgitate their food for further chewing. This allows hurried feeding but leisurely digestion, when the threat of attack by predators is passed. Perhaps this adaptation above all others explains the astonishing late Cainozoic success of the artiodactyls compared with the dwindling of the perissodactyls. Further ruminant specializations include crescent-shaped or sele-nodont ridges on the molar teeth and, in the more advanced ruminants, the replacement of the upper incisors by a hard cropping pad against which the lower incisors bite. Although camels have such a pad and chew the cud, they are not usually categorized as ruminants, for they have been quite separate from all other artiodactyls since their origin in Eocene times.

A very early artiodactyl was the small *Dia-codexis*, a contemporary of *Hyracotherium* and like the latter an immediate descendant of the con-dylarths. Characteristically it had the diagnostic astragalus and had lost the innermost toe on each foot. Interestingly the molar teeth of the animal reveal that it was not entirely herbivorous. This is significant for *Diacodexis* was a dichobunoid, the group ancestral to the essentially pig-like, non-ruminating artiodactyls, whose teeth suggest a varied diet. The initial radiation of the non-ruminants spanned the Eocene-Oligocene tran-sition and resulted in several distinct forms. There were enteledonts or 'giant pigs', true pigs and peccaries ultimately replaced them, and the anthracotheres, extinct forebears of the Hippo-potamus. The North American oreodonts may have been related to this broad group, except that their molars were selenodont implying that they

were, in fact, 'ruminating swine'. Other likely relatives are the hare-like cainotheres, which disappeared in the Oligocene, probably because of competition from predecessors of the real hares.

The ruminants comprise the more primitive tragulines and the advanced pecorans. Tragulines emerged in the Eocene as small rabbit-size creatures, similar in many respects to their modern Old World descendants, the mouse deer. From the main traguloid stem two North Amer-ican offshoots subsequently evolved: the equally small hypertragulids and the deer-size pro-toceratids, one of which, *Synthetoceras*, sported a Y-shaped nose-horn. The least advanced pecorans – the deer – diverged from the traguloids in the Oligocene, whilst the giraffes in turn branched away from the deer in the Miocene. By this time, incidentally, the ruminants had overhauled the pig-like artiodactyls in both number and variety. The bovoids were also present in the Miocene, but their radiation occurred in the Pliocene and later. It produced a truly staggering array of animals, namely the pronghorns, sheep, goats, musk-oxen, antelopes and cattle.

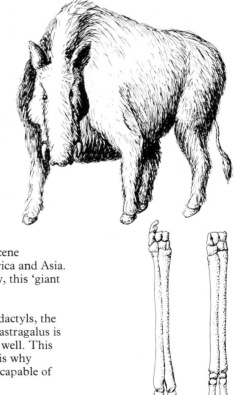

Archaeotherium, an Oligocene enteledont of North America and Asia. Although the size of a cow, this 'giant pig' was a fast runner.

Unlike that of the perissodactyls, the artiodactyl ankle-joint or astragalus is grooved on the bottom as well. This 'double-pulley' structure is why artiodactyls generally are capable of impressive leaps.

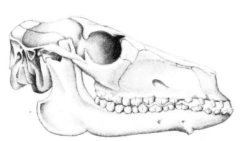

Skull of the primitive Oligocene camel *Poëbrotherium*. Camels evolved mainly in North America and produced a variety of large and small forms. Late

in the Cainozoic they crossed into South America and Asia, but became extinct in North America itself at the very end of the Pleistocene epoch.

Dinotheres, mastodonts and elephants: the proboscidea

Modern elephants are relics of a formerly more numerous and varied order – the Proboscidea – that colonized every continent except Australia and Antarctica. The oldest undoubted representatives, *Palaeomastodon* and *Phiomia*, are from the Lower Oligocene of Egypt. They were already specialized mastodonts, presumably descended from much earlier condylarth immigrants. *Phiomia* was the larger and approached the size of a small to medium present-day elephant. Both were unmistakably elephant-like in appearance, although all their incisors were developed into tusks. The upper two, which were relatively short and pointed downwards, probably served as weapons; whereas the lower two, which were shorter still and projected from an elongated lower jaw in a scoop-type structure, were no doubt used for digging. From the position of the nasal bones it is also evident that these animals had reasonably well-formed trunks.

When the next proboscideans are encountered, several million years later, in the Miocene, three distinct groups are apparent: the dinotheres, the long-jawed mastodonts, or gomphotheres, and the short-jawed mastodonts. The dinotheres are distinguished by an absence of tusks from the upper jaw, and by powerful down-turned tusks on the lower jaw – again, presumably an adaptation

Deinotherium, a Pliocene 'hoe-tusker', with a shoulder height of almost 4 metres. 'Hoe-tuskers' or dinotheres lived from Miocene times until the Pleistocene and are a good, if very unusual, example of a highly specialized mammalian type existing with little change over a number of geological epochs. An early palaeontologist, incidentally, believed the deinotheres to be river-dwellers and that their tusks were used to anchor themselves to the river bank whilst they slept in the water!

for digging. Apart from an increase in size to as much as 3 metres at the shoulder, the dinotheres remained remarkably unchanged until their disappearance in the general extinction of large mammals in the Pleistocene. The short-jawed mastodonts evolved independently and spread, not only to Eurasia as did the dinotheres, but to the Americas as well. They were browsers and the last of them – shorter and more heavily built than modern elephants – survived in North America until post-glacial times, as recently as 8000 years ago. The first gomphothere was merely a larger version of *Phiomia*. Various descendant lines then developed, the most novel being the Pliocene shovel-tuskers of Asia and North America. Here the lower tusks formed huge scoops or shovels, probably for digging, perhaps in shallow water.

True elephants are now believed to have diverged from the gomphotheres during Mio-Pliocene times in Africa, rather than from the very advanced Plio-Pleistocene mastodont, *Stegodon*, of Asia. Compared with mastodonts, they have higher skulls, shorter jaws and are taller with a slimmer build. The key difference, however, lies in the nature of the cheek teeth, for those of the elephant are far more complex and adapted for grazing. Two of the elephants which appeared are living today in Africa and India. A third, the straight-tusked elephant, evolved in the northern hemisphere of the Old World and was common in the earlier inter-glacials of Europe. Lastly come the mammoths, one of the many evolutionary responses of the mammals to the extension of the tundra habitat. *Elephas trogontherii*, the earliest mammoth, was the largest proboscidean of all time, standing up to 4·5 metres high at the shoulder. The later woolly mammoth was smaller, yet still of monumental proportions. Mammoths crossed to North America and gave rise to several indigenous species there, the largest being the imperial mammoth (*Mammuthus imperator*), second only in size to *E. trogontherii*.

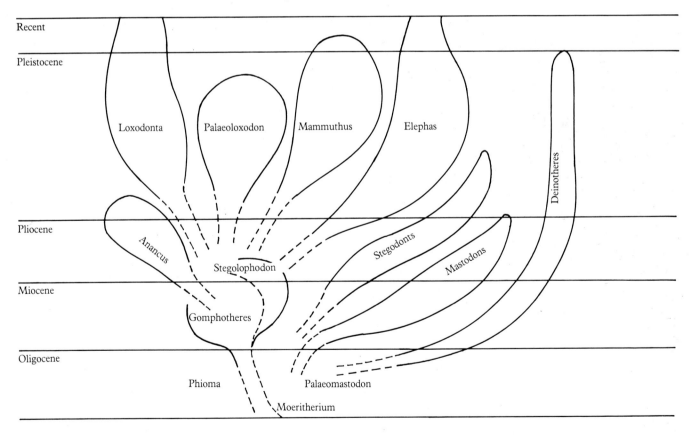

The radiation of the proboscideans.

Convergent evolution in mammals

During the Cainozoic era various mammalian groups evolved in isolation from each other and in the process of adapting to the same basic ways of life frequently developed very similar forms. This phenomenon, as shown in the case of the shark, ichthyosaur and dolphin, is called convergent evolution. A good example in living mammals is that of the anteaters: there are five types, belonging to five different orders, including the monotremes and marsupials.

On a grander scale, many elements in the mammalian faunas of the island continents, i.e. Australia and South America, have shown striking parallel developments and convergence of form with their world continent equivalents. Hence, in Australia there are marsupial counterparts of the true cats, mice, moles, rodents and squirrels. To these could be added in the recent past, a mar-

supial 'hippo' and the so-called marsupial lion *Thylacoleo*, which in reality was more likely to have been a herbivore! As described earlier, a marsupial 'wolf' also appeared in South America, together with a marsupial sabre-toothed 'cat'. Undoubtedly, however, the most impressive array of evolutionary convergence on this continent in Tertiary times occurred in the placental herbivores.

The extinct hoofed mammals of South America were probably all descended from the condylarths, and had differentiated into a full complement of adaptive types. The order Litopterna gave rise to the proterotheres – the horse-litopterns, and the macrauchenids – the camel-litopterns. The proterotheres reached their climax in the Miocene and Pliocene with extraordinarily horse-like forms, such as the three-toed *Diadiaphorus*, and

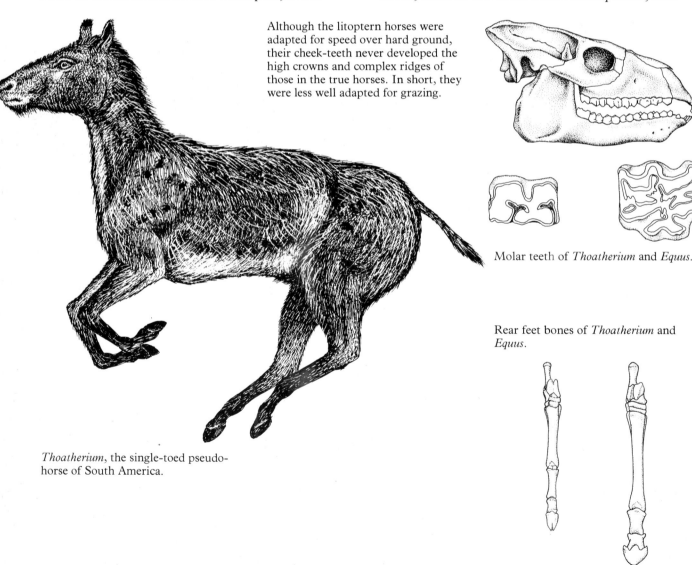

Although the litoptern horses were adapted for speed over hard ground, their cheek-teeth never developed the high crowns and complex ridges of those in the true horses. In short, they were less well adapted for grazing.

Molar teeth of *Thoatherium* and *Equus*.

Rear feet bones of *Thoatherium* and *Equus*.

Thoatherium, the single-toed pseudo-horse of South America.

the single-toed *Thoatherium*. *Diadiaphorus* was about the size of a pony, whilst *Thoatherium* was smaller and, perhaps, compared with *Nannipus*, the gazelle-horse from the Pliocene of North America. In *Thoatherium* the splint bones of the vestigial side toes were even smaller than those of the modern horse *Equus*. On the other hand, the teeth of the pseudo-horses remained low-crowned throughout and probably contributed to their extinction in the Pliocene, approximately at the time the first true horses invaded from North America, across the newly established Panama isthmus. The macrauchenids strongly resembled the camels of North America, except that they may have had a short tapir-like trunk. This last point is contested by some authorities for in the most advanced forms which survived into the Pleistocene, the peculiar nasal openings have

moved to the top of the head suggesting a life in water rather than one which involved a trunk. The toxodonts, of the order Notoungulata, initiated an even larger selection of convergent forms, including a number of rhinoceros-like types, the largest culminating in *Toxodon*. Another group of toxodonts, the homalodotheres, were very reminiscent of the chalicotheres, or clawed 'horses', whilst a third, the typotheres, may well have looked similar to rabbits. Finally there were the pyrotheres, a sub-order of the lumbering Amblypoda. These Eocene and early Oligocene animals so closely resemble the early mastodonts of Africa that they were formerly regarded by some palaeontologists as relatives of the proboscideans.

Pyrotherium, an Early Oligocene pseudo-mastodont of South America. It was about 2 metres high at the shoulder.

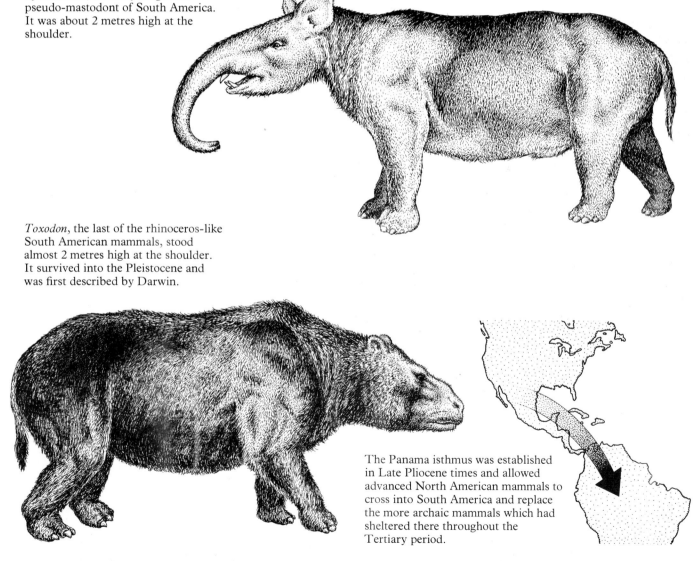

Toxodon, the last of the rhinoceros-like South American mammals, stood almost 2 metres high at the shoulder. It survived into the Pleistocene and was first described by Darwin.

The Panama isthmus was established in Late Pliocene times and allowed advanced North American mammals to cross into South America and replace the more archaic mammals which had sheltered there throughout the Tertiary period.

269

Marine mammals

The earliest marine mammals are recorded from sediments of Middle Eocene age with the first sea-cows and whales appearing over 20 million years after the dawn of the 'Age of Mammals'. The animals were primitive in comparison with later members of their respective orders but in terms of adaptation to an aquatic mode of life, they were already highly specialized. No obvious terrestrial ancestors can be identified for either type of animal, although many workers believe that the sirenians share a common ancestor with the elephants and the conies (*Hyrax*). It is obvious that the evolution of both the whales and sirenians began much earlier in the Tertiary period. *Eotheroides*, a sirenian from the Middle Eocene of Egypt is a likely ancestor of the dugongs or the 'mermaids' of the Red Sea and Indian Ocean. Unlike living dugongs it possessed a well-developed pelvis and small but well-formed limbs. But its incisor teeth and the cheek teeth were enlarged and the latter had begun to develop a rather bumpy crushing surface (like the bunodont molars of man or the pig). In true dugongs, such as *Halitherium* from the Oligocene, the pelvis was much reduced and the back legs had disappeared.

In the earliest whales the hind limbs were already reduced so that they did not project beyond the body. Elongation of the snout and the migration of the nostrils provide further evidence of aquatic specialization. The first whales possessed a primitive dentition and this together with their limited size, of between 5 and 6 metres in length, may indicate that they were inshore fish-eaters. Their descendants, the giant zeuglodont whales of the Upper Eocene,

The Upper Eocene whale *Basilosaurus* grew to approximately 20 metres in length and as living genera moved through the water with the aid of wave-like undulations of the body and horizontal rail. It is possible that *Basilosaurus* had already developed a thick layer of blubber around its body to protect it from excessive loss of heat.

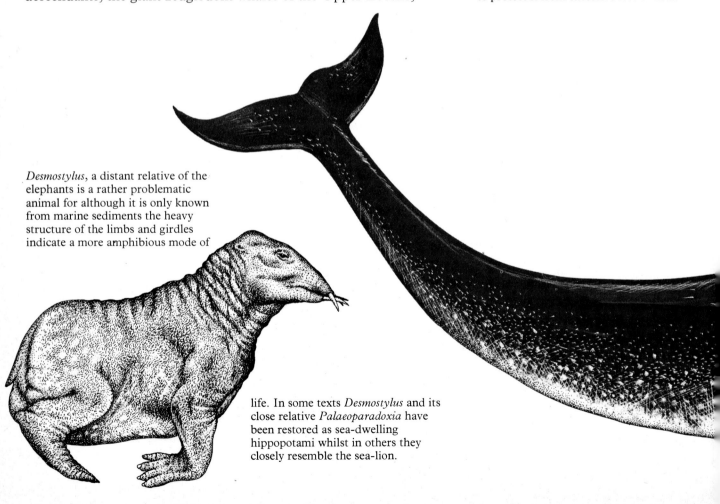

Desmostylus, a distant relative of the elephants is a rather problematic animal for although it is only known from marine sediments the heavy structure of the limbs and girdles indicate a more amphibious mode of life. In some texts *Desmostylus* and its close relative *Palaeoparadoxia* have been restored as sea-dwelling hippopotami whilst in others they closely resemble the sea-lion.

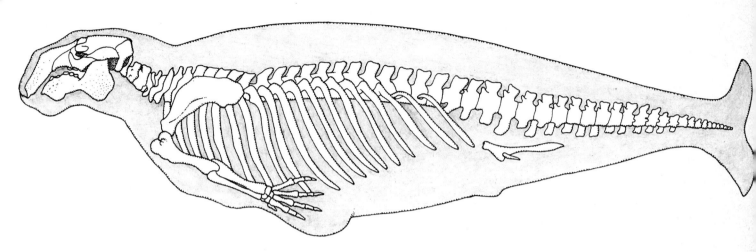

grew to over 20 metres in length and their elongate bodies resemble those of the Cretaceous mosasaurs. The earliest whales and the huge zeuglodonts are grouped together as archaeocetes and although the latter died out at the end of the Eocene, smaller forms persist into the Miocene. The archaeocetes were likely ancestors to the living whalebone and toothed whales, the first of which appeared in the Oligocene and Upper Eocene respectively. Toothed whales include the porpoises, dolphins, beaked and sperm whales, all of which are characterized by the presence of a single blowhole (combined nostrils) high up on the top of the skull. In the whalebone whales, the blowholes are double in structure and these giants of the seas have replaced their teeth with a system of 'hairy sieves'.

Apart from the sirenians and whales, the seals and walruses also represent a return of the mammals to a life in the sea. Unlike the other two they are carnivores and instead of using the tail as the main organ of propulsion, as do the whales, they use their modified hind limbs. The earliest seals and walruses can be traced back as far as the Miocene and it is probable that they share the same common ancestor as the dogs and cats.

The fossil dugong *Halitherium* grew to over 3 metres in length. It possessed evidence of a much reduced pelvis and the animal was figured by Darwin in a later edition of the *Origin of Species* as evidence of his theory of natural selection.

Early primates and the prosimians

Plesiadapsis, one of the earliest and most primitive primates, about the size of a squirrel.

Apart from their extinct Palaeocene and possibly Cretaceous ancestors, the primates include the prosimians – the lemurs, lorises and tarsiers – which arose in the Eocene, and the more advanced anthropoids – the monkeys, apes and men – which emerged from prosimian stock in the Oligocene. All the prosimian and anthropoid groups have living representatives and so in evolutionary terms have been successful. The reason for this success is their relative lack of adaptive specialization.

primates the eyes have moved to the front of the head. This and the fact that an acute sense of smell is not essential for an insect- or fruit-eating life in the trees, also accounts for the progressive reduction of both the nose and snout. Other related adaptations were longer and stronger arms, opposable first digits on the hands and feet, and the replacement of claws by nails. The last two in particular allowed branches to be grasped more firmly as well as objects to be manipulated. The

The primates originated from small insectivores very like the modern tree-shrews, indeed, some authorities regard the latter as primitive primates. At the outset of the Cainozoic, the primates were alone among the mammalian orders in that they stayed exclusively in the trees. The features which were eventually to set them so profoundly apart from other small tree-dwelling mammals were developed in response to increases in size. Unlike, say, a squirrel, a heavy animal could obviously not be supported on a slender branch or twig; it could only move about quickly in the tree-tops by jumping or swinging from branch to branch. Locomotion of this kind requires binocular vision for reliable estimation of distance, which is why in

need for rapid and effective coordination of movement and senses led in turn to a commensurate increase in brain-size.

The earliest primate, *Purgatorius*, is known only from isolated teeth which resemble those of insectivores and condylarths. In the middle Palaeocene three new primate groups appeared and from their chisel-like paired incisors it seems they occupied a rodent-type niche. The best known of these groups are the plesiadapids. They retained claws, a long snout and the eyes were still positioned somewhat laterally. These Palaeocene forms persisted into the Eocene when a further three primate groups – the adapids, anaplomorphids and the omomyids – with no trace of rodent-like teeth, make their entry in the fossil record. The adapids are clearly in direct line of descent to the lemurs and lorises. The small Eocene adapid *Notharctus*, for example, was very similar in general appearance to the modern lemurs, and like these primitive primates had much longer legs than arms and a rather fox-like muzzle. The anaptomorphids and omomyids were more progressive with larger brains, flatter faces and further advances in development. As in the case of the adapids, it is equally clear that these were the forebears of the tarsiers. The Eocene *Necrolemur*, for instance, although misleadingly named, would have looked much like its modern descendants, with their unusually large, close-set eyes. Finally, all these early prosimians were widely distributed over the 'world continent'. Due to a climatic cooling and competition from the higher primates, they have not survived outside the Old World tropics. In fact, lemurs occur only in Madagascar.

Necrolemur, an Eocene ancestor of the modern tarsier, from France.

Primate evolution

We have traced the Eocene radiation of the prosimians, which have remained primitive to this day. The higher primates probably emerged from the omomyids and underwent a second radiation, to give the monkeys, apes and men.

Within the monkeys, a distinction is made between the platyrrhines of South America and the catarrhines of the Old World. The names refer to nose shape, but there are other important contrasts which reflect a long period of separate evolutionary development. The platyrrhines appear first in Oligocene strata, descended presumably from earlier omomyid or possibly adapid immigrants from North America. Their marked resemblance to the catarrhine monkeys, therefore, has arisen through parallel evolution from the same genetic stock. Even so they are less advanced than their Old World cousins, and have a more primitive dentition together with, in most instances, a prehensile tail.

The first Old World anthropoids are also known from Oligocene sediments, namely those in the famous quarries of the Fayum depression in Egypt. Though desert now, the Fayum at the time in question was a region of woodland and forest-fringed rivers. The lowest and oldest sediments have yielded *Oligopithecus*, which apart from certain omomyid traits, has teeth that indicate that it was the forerunner of the apes. At a higher, and so younger, level in the quarries was found *Aegyptopithecus*, very likely a descendant of *Oligopithecus* and the ancestor of the undoubted Miocene apes, the dryopithecines. *Aegyptopithecus* was about the size of a gibbon, with a rather small brain case and a projecting snout. Two smaller Fayum primates, *Parapithecus* and *Apidium*, have teeth which imply that the Old World monkeys were already distinct from the earliest apes. This indicates, in other words, that the monkeys were not precursors of the hominoids – the apes and men – and that from their beginning they have progressed along a different path.

Evolutionary trends in apes have been towards a great increase in size of the body and brain, the enlargement of the canine teeth for fighting, and the development of longer, stronger arms for brachiating, i.e. swinging from branch to branch. The tail, which in monkeys is retained for balance when running on all fours and leaping, became unnecessary for 'two-handed' locomotion and consequently was lost. Partly or fully developed, these and certain other adaptations are common to the Miocene dryopithecines, which unlike their predecessors are found in Eurasia as well as

Africa. From these apes or a closely allied group arose *Ramapithecus*, with small canines and incisors, as in man, and, significantly, a flatter face. Whether this 'chimp'-size animal which appeared about 14 million years ago was itself an ape or actually a hominid – a member of the family of man – is debatable. There seems little question, however, that it belongs to the lineage which led directly to the first undisputed men.

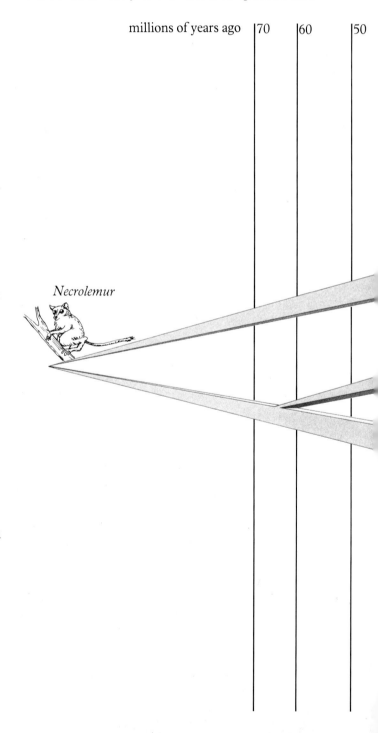

millions of years ago |70 |60 |50

Necrolemur

The dental innovations suggest a departure from a diet of fruit and leaves, and that *Ramapithecus* foraged on the ground for much of the time. Perhaps this change of life style resulted from a coincidence between an increase in body-size, which would have made movement through the tree-tops more difficult, and the relentless spread of drier climates, which reduced the extent of forest. Devoid of large canines, and having no other specialist means of defence, *Ramapithecus* may well have resorted to the use of sticks and stones and group strategies to discourage enemies encountered on open ground.

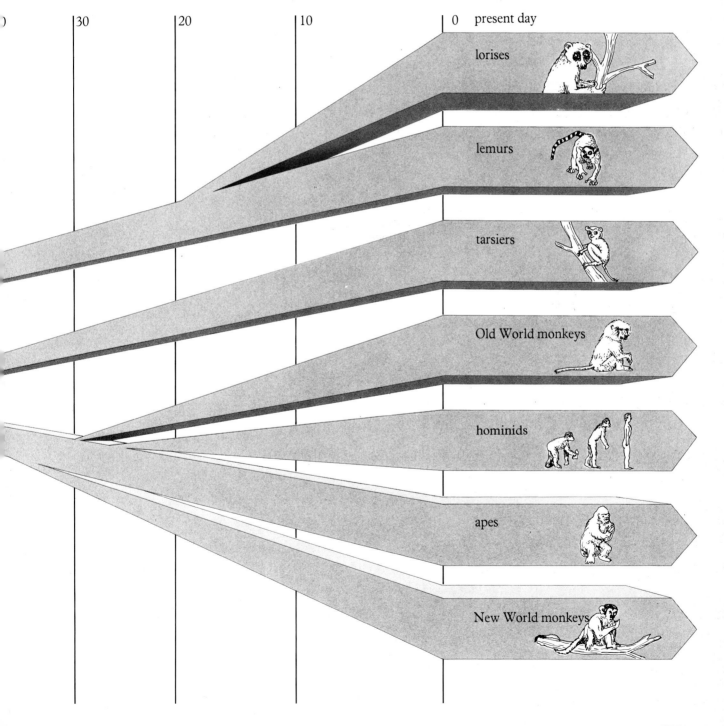

Ancient apes and their descendants

In contrast to the monkeys, relatively few apes have survived to the present day. They are the gibbons and the great apes or pongids, including the orangutan, gorilla and chimpanzee. Whilst the gibbons of south-east Asia have exceptionally long arms and are the most skilful brachiators, they are nevertheless the least advanced of the apes. As a type they can be traced back to the Miocene *Plio-pithecus* and possibly even to *Propliopithecus* in the Oligocene rocks of the Fayum depression. The great apes were differentiated much later, in Plio-Pleistocene times, after the dryopithecines and *Ramapithecus* had already diverged from the central hominoid stock. They are, then, the specialized descendants of the dryo-pithecines and differ from them in several respects. They have a bigger brain capacity, their bodies are generally much larger, and their arms and fingers are appreciably longer, so that when they walk on all fours they balance on their knuckles. They have also developed brow ridges over the eyes and a bony crest to the skull for the attachment of powerful jaw and neck muscles. The climat-ically induced reduction of forest habitats which restricted the radiation of the apes, has latterly been greatly accelerated by man. He has in addition killed and trapped apes, with the overall result that several of the species are now threatened with extinction.

Other evolutionary directions were followed from the early generalized apes and the best known of these led to *Oreopithecus* and *Gigantopithecus*. *Oreopithecus* was the size of a chimpanzee and lived in a swamp environment in the Lower Pliocene of Italy. It possessed long arms for brachiating, yet its broad pelvis and features of the spine testify to an erect or semi-erect posture. The

Dryopithecines were rather small, unspecialized apes with much shorter arms than their descendants, showing that they were not yet fully adapted for brachiating.

Chimpanzees are more acrobatic than the other great apes. They spend much of their time on the ground, but sleep in nests which they build in trees each evening.

As the name implies *Gigantopithecus* was a giant ape. From the nature of its teeth it seems that this animal had a more varied diet than modern apes, which are essentially vegetarian.

Gorillas are the largest of the great apes. Mature male gorillas are almost 2 metres tall and weigh as much as 140 kilograms. Gorillas are gentle creatures and, like the chimpanzee, are extremely intelligent.

skull and jaw similarly have primitive human affinities, as do the small canines and first pre-molars. Evidently as regards external appearance it may have been difficult to distinguish *Oreopithecus* from the proto-homonids. The monkey-like cusps of the molar teeth, however, give the game away, and reveal that here we are dealing with a remarkable, indeed the only, example of evolution parallel to that of man.

Gigantopithecus is known from the Pliocene of India and from the Lower and Middle Pleistocene of China, so that it still existed 500 000 years ago, when true men lived in this part of the world. Certain of the teeth are of hominid aspect, but the immense jaws are larger than those of a gorilla. Like *Oreopithecus* it has left no descendants, unless, as some people have speculated, it is the abominable snowman!

Towards modern man

The story of man's evolution from *Ramapithecus* is essentially one of further adaptation to savannas and grassy plains. Bipedal locomotion and erect posture were crucial in this development, as they freed the hands for making and using tools. When this stage was eventually reached, selection for increased brain-size was greatly accelerated and became the dominant trend in the succession of hominids leading to modern man – *Homo sapiens*.

The australopithecines were the probable descendants of *Ramapithecus*, and lived in Africa from at least 3 million to just over 1 million years ago. No more than 1·5 metres tall, they were ape-like in their small brain-size and skull shape, yet human-like in their upright stance and gait. Two forms of these pre-humans are known: the larger and less man-like *Australopithecus robustus*, and the more slender or gracile *A. africanus*. It has been argued that the latter gave rise to the first real men, of the genus *Homo*, about 1·75 million years ago. They have been given the species name *Homo habilis* or 'handyman', after the rudimentary shelter and pebble tools found in association with their remains in the Olduvai Gorge of East Africa. Their skulls and teeth, and also, perhaps, the bones of their hands and feet, are rather more progressive than those of the australopithecines. The opposing view is that 'handyman' is merely a variant, albeit a superior one, of the gracile australopithecines. More recent hominid finds from other East African sites, however, have revealed that tool-using representatives of the genus *Homo* co-existed with the australopithecines, possibly as much as 2·5 to 3 million years ago. Evidently this makes the evolutionary sequence of these early hominids somewhat uncertain, and final clarification must await additional discoveries.

The next generally agreed step towards modern man is represented by *Homo erectus*. This hominid lived in Africa and Asia between 1·5 and 1 million years ago, having arisen it seems from *Homo habilis*-type forebears. *Homo erectus* was about 1·5 metres tall with a skeleton very similar to that of modern man, but the brain-size was roughly 25 per cent smaller, and the skull possessed heavy

Homo sapiens

Neanderthal man

Controversy surrrounds all the important 'forks' in the evolution of modern man. Thus the presence of three early hominids in East Africa makes it unclear whether the australopithecines diverged to give robust and gracile forms, or whether the gracile form in fact diverged from the line which gave rise to modern man. Similarly some authorities have claimed that *Homo erectus* was an evolutionary 'dead-end' and that *Homo sapiens* is descended directly from *Homo habilis*.

278

Homo erectus

Homo habilis

Ramapithecus

Australopithecus africanus

Australopithecus robustus

eyebrow ridges and lacked a forehead. Associated with *Homo erectus* are the first signs of big-game hunting, sophisticated tools of standard design, including hand axes, and the use of fire. From these achievements it may be reasonable to assume that some form of speech had been developed.

There are some European skulls dating from the period 500 to 250 000 years ago, which seem to mark the transition from *Homo erectus* to *Homo sapiens*. From the last interglacial interlude of

Europe, between 200 and 100 000 years ago, there are skulls of even more advanced appearance. The problem is deciding if these are ancestral to the 'Neanderthal' men who inhabited Europe for much of the last glacial phase, or to the fully modern man who suddenly replaced them about 40 000 years ago. As we shall see, the matter is complicated by whether these two kinds of men can be regarded as belonging to the same species or not.

The habitats of early man: *Australopithecus*

A cave at the Sterkfontein site of *Australopithecus africanus*.

Skull of 'Mrs Ples', *Australopithecus africanus*.

The australopithecines were first known from limestone caves in the south of Africa, and there is no firm evidence that they ever existed outside this continent. The hominid remains from the caves at Taung, Sterkfontein and Makapansgat were of *Australopithecus africanus*, whereas those from the caves at Swartkrans and Kromdraai were of *A. robustus* only. The fossil animals associated with these australopithecines provide a means of relative dating, which suggests that the robust australopithecines are decidedly younger than the gracile forms. That the australopithecines actually occupied these caves is highly unlikely. Curiously, most of the hominid remains are skull fragments and neck vertebrae. They could well have been derived from the prey of leopards, for it is well known that these animals feed in trees, and then, as now, overhanging trees were probably common around the edge of cave shafts. Such a reconstruction is far from fanciful, for some of the hominid and other animal bones at Swartkrans bear teeth marks compatible with those of the canines of leopards which lived at that time.

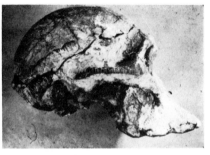

Apart from furnishing a relative age, the fossil animals also imply that the gracile australopithecines lived in an environment of bush and woodland, in contrast to their more robust relatives, who seemed to have roamed over dry, open grasslands. Their very different teeth and jaw dimensions further bears this out. In *A.*

Australopithecus african

280

robustus the incisors are comparatively small, but the cheek teeth are exceptionally large and often show signs of marked wear. Allied with the massive jaws and the bony skull ridges for the attachment of powerful chewing muscles, it is evident that this hominid largely subsisted on a tough diet of seeds, roots and tubers. Probably the grit introduced with such food contributed to the wear of the teeth. Except for the incisors, the teeth of *A. africanus* are much smaller, as are the jaws, reflecting a more mixed diet, including meat. From this it may be inferred that scavenging and small-scale hunting may have been undertaken, yet in this connection there is no reliable evidence that the gracile australopithecines made tools. The stone implements at Sterkfontein, for instance, are now known to have come from a younger layer than that which yielded the australopithecines. Then there are the numerous lower jaw bones and arm bone ends of antelopes at Makapansgat, which were at one time regarded as proof of the use of osteo-dento-keratic (bone, tooth and horn) tools. Comparative studies have shown that the frequency of such bones is precisely what might be expected in a leopard's lair.

A dominantly vegetarian role for the robust australopithecines is logical in one other respect,

Australopithecus robustus

for although there is doubt as to whether they were contemporaneous with the gracile forms, it is certain that they co-existed over a long period with *Homo habilis* and even earlier members of the same genus. These were tool makers and hunted animals, so that if the robust australopithecines occupied the same niche the competitive pressure would surely have made them extinct at a much earlier date than was in fact the case. This conclusion raises an interesting point. Specifically, if, as may ultimately prove to be so, the robust australopithecines diverged from the mainstream of hominid development at a very early date, it becomes difficult to see why, as vegetarians, they should have developed bipedalism. Looking over tall grasses for predators is hardly a satisfactory explanation.

The habitats of early man: *Homo habilis*

Reconstruction of *Homo habilis*, showing their primitive use of stone tools.

The habitats of early man: *Homo habilis*

Olduvai Gorge in Tanzania, where the remains of *Homo habilis* were found in 1964, is an offshoot of the great East African rift valley and lies on the edge of the Serengeti Plain. The stratified sediments in the 40 kilometre long gorge are about 90 metres thick, and accumulated in and around an ancient lake of which the nearby Lake Eyasi is a shrunken remnant. The strata revealed by the river which cut the gorge rest on a lava flow and have been grouped into Beds I-V, Bed 1, the oldest, being next to the lava.

In 1959 a hominid skull was found in Bed 1, surrounded by numerous pebble tools of the 'Oldowan industry' as well as broken animal bones. The skull was that of a progressive robust australopithecine, *A. boisei*, nicknamed 'Nutcracker man' on account of the impressively large cheek teeth and bony ridges for the attachment of heavy jaw muscles. Naturally it was assumed that this hominid was responsible for the tools. However, later finds from the same 'living floor' clearly belonged to a more advanced hominid, who thus seemed the more likely manufacturer. These new finds and others at higher levels in Beds I and II were referred to the genus *Homo*. As described earlier, because of the association with a primitive shelter and frequent stone tools, the new species was named *Homo habilis* or 'handyman'.

There is a complicating factor in this interpretation. Bed I and the lowest part of Bed II accumulated when the climate was relatively wet' whereas the succeeding part of Bed II formed when the lake had shrunk and become more saline. This change is reflected in the fossil faunas and also coincides with the appearance of more sophisticated Oldowan tools. Accordingly, some critics have asserted that the younger *habilis* fossils are really early forms of *Homo erectus* and that the older ones, below the faunal break, are of late gracile australopithecines.

Either way these hominids do seem to have been the toolmakers at Olduvai, trekking as much as 19 kilometres for certain kinds of suitable stone. The tools are sometimes found with partial skeletons and numerous, often broken, bones of various animals, in a manner suggestive of butchering or killing sites. The variety of animals represented, and the concentration of bones of small birds, lizards and chameleons in what are apparently fossilized human faeces, reveal that *Homo habilis* was by no means a selective hunter. The mode of life perhaps resembled that of existing stone age tribes in Africa, rather than that of later specialized hominid hunters. Though unlikely, the presence of tools near to the skull of 'Nutcracker' man may mean that he too was one of the hunted.

The wealth of remains attributed to *Homo habilis* at Olduvai, clearly differentiates it from the australopithecine sites of South Africa, where only hominid bones are definitely recorded. This seems to imply that the achievement of the *habilis* stage in human evolution was accompanied by significant cultural and technological advances. On the other hand since we know that the australopithecines were unlikely to have lived in the caves where their bones were found, the absence of tools and other possible indicators of life-style is not entirely unexpected.

The habitats of early man: *Homo erectus*

Homo erectus ranged more widely than the australopithecines and inhabited Eurasia as well as Africa. No doubt this territorial expansion was assisted by his increased intelligence and improved technology. Other helpful agencies perhaps were low sea-levels and the land-bridges these revealed, for vast quantities of water had become locked up in the newly formed continental ice sheets. Where he spread from is not entirely certain. The first remains were found in Java and were originally attributed to *Pithecanthropus erectus* – the erect ape-man. Later similar finds were concentrated in China – the legendary Peking man – and again in Java. All of them are now regarded as variants of *Homo erectus*, except for *Meganthropus palaeojav-* anicus – giant old Java man. The latter has in fact been correlated with *Homo habilis*, although it is later with an age of about 1 million years. With this emphasis on south east Asia, it was believed that *Homo erectus* originated there, and subsequently migrated to Europe and Africa. This had the merit of explaining, moreover, the abrupt appearance at Olduvai of hand-axes typically associated with this hominid in North Africa and Europe. Recent investigations, however, have largely discredited this theory. They revealed *Homo erectus* skeletal material analogous to that of Java and China, but which, significantly, is 1 million years older than the reliably dated Chinese specimens.

Reconstruction of a cave scene showing
how *Homo erectus* might have utilized
fire and clothes in the cooler
Pleistocene climate.

It seems, then, that *Homo erectus* evolved in
Africa. As he moved northward into the cooler
climates of Pleistocene Eurasia he took with him
the use of fire and possibly clothes. We know too
that he lived in caves. Those at Choukoutien – or
Dragon Bone Hill – near Peking, in which Peking
man was discovered, had obviously been occupied
for long periods. They have also provided the first
evidence of the use of fire. Huge piles of ash were
traced through about 5 metres of debris which had
accumulated on the cave floor. Evidently the fire
had been carefully tended, and apart from giving
warmth, light and heat for cooking, had dis-
couraged wild animals as well. The broken bones
of deer, elephant and rhinoceros, some of them in
large numbers, indicate that Peking man was a
successful hunter of big game. Some of the broken
bones burned in the hearth of the fire were
actually human, which together with the fractures
at the base of some of the human skulls, appear to
suggest cannibalism.

Successful big-game hunting implies cooper-
ation, and further proof that this occurred has

come from both Europe and Africa. At Olduvai,
and at Ambrona and Torralba in Spain, exca-
vations have shown that *Homo erectus* probably
drove animals onto swampy ground where they
were killed and butchered. At Ambrona, for
example, fires were apparently employed in the
drive, tools used for butchering trapped elephants
were left scattered over the edge of the swamp,
and the curious disposition of elephant leg-bones
points to the legs having served as stepping stones.

It is clear, furthermore, that some *Homo erectus*
groups made shelters. Remains of these have been
found at Latamne in Syria, together with more
elaborate affairs for communal use at Terra Amata
in the south-east of France. Those at Terra Amata
were erected on the floor of a cave and comprised
wooden poles and stones which had supported a
roof of branches or hides. They were seasonal
camps housing fifteen to twenty people. Each
possessed a hearth and a feeding area, and in one
of them it has been possible to show where a
toolmaker sat, from the distribution pattern of
flakes and cores which he chipped and discarded.

The habitats of early man: *Neanderthal man*

Homo erectus and the earliest forms of modern man were unable to survive in northern Europe during full glacial conditions. Although they possessed fire, their levels of cultural and technological achievement were inadequate for life in such a hostile setting. With the onset of the last glaciation over 100 000 years ago, however, onc group of people did not retreat southwards in search of more temperate climates. They stayed in northern Europe to hunt the plentiful game that grazed the tundra, including woolly mammoth, woolly rhinoceros, reindeer and steppe bison.

These hardy people were the Neanderthals.

They were short and sturdily built so that loss of body-heat was kept to a minimum. Although their cranial capacity on average exceeded that of living men, the classic Neanderthal skull was not yet fully modern. It was characterized by a prominent brow-ridge above high, circular, almost owlish eye-sockets. The forehead was flattened, the chin weak or absent, and there was a distinctive swelling of the back of the brain-case – the so-called occipital 'bun'. The cheek bones were swept back and lacked hollows, whilst the nose was large

modern civilized man

and protruding. These facial features seem to have been adaptations for reducing the risk of frostbite and for coping with the inhalation of cold, dry air.

In view of the climatic rigours, it is not surprising that Neanderthal man frequented caves. To gain vacant possession of them it was no doubt necessary to dispossess cave-bears, cave-lions and sabre-tooths! Inside the caves he built shelters of branches and skins, but there is evidence from Russia of camps having been erected in the open as well, with mammoth bones as part of their structure. The Neanderthals also carefully buried their dead in caves and from the frequent presence of grave goods it is clear that they believed in some kind of after-life. Elaborate rituals were performed too. At Teshik-Tash in Russia, for example, the remains of a young boy were found where the skull was surrounded by a circle of five pairs of goat horns stuck into the ground. It seems likely, moreover, that some of the ritual was associated with cannibalism.

The tools and implements of Neanderthal man were a key factor in ensuring his success. The stone tools were made from flakes struck off cores which had been specially prepared in advance, so that the shape of the flake could be better controlled. The flakes were then worked into hand axes, scrapers and triangular points with sharp edges which may have been hafted to form spears. In addition to these stone tools, which constitute the Mousterian culture, wooden spears were fashioned, along with, so it would appear, the bola, i.e. a missile of two or more balls of stone connected by leather thongs. The overall impression then, is of a hunting community and this is corroborated by the vast quantities of animal bones found at Mousterian sites. Limb bones predominate suggesting that carcasses were butchered at the scene of the kill rather than taken back to the camp. Flint blades were used to cut the meat, though from the innumerable scrapers, it is obvious that skins were greatly prized, for shelter, clothing and thongs.

Neanderthal man survived in Europe until 35 000 years ago, when he was replaced by Cro-Magnon or modern man, with his cave art and fine flint blades of the Upper Palaeolithic cultures. Whether the two kinds of men belong to the same species is a moot point. The consensus is that Neanderthal man is a subspecies of modern man – *Homo sapiens neanderthalis* – and that his distinctive features evolved in isolation from the more progressive human line, in response to a harsh periglacial environment. Precisely where *Homo*

sapiens sapiens developed after Neanderthal man split off in the last interglacial remains a mystery. A final imponderable is whether Neanderthal man was wiped out by Cro-Magnon man, either deliberately or as a result of competition, or whether Neanderthal man was assimilated into the Cro-Magnon population. The subsequent course of human history would suggest the latter, so that we may well carry some of Neanderthal man's genes.

287

Island faunas – giants and dwarfs

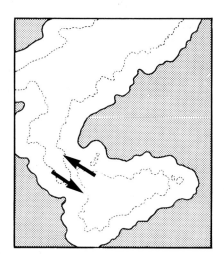
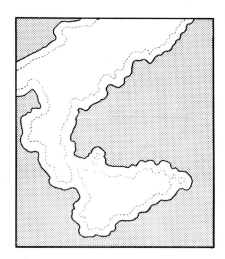
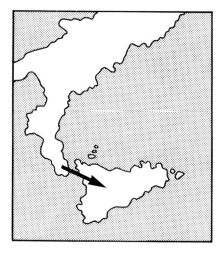

The diagrams illustrate the events that may have led to the development of many isolated island communities. In the first diagram the potential island is connected to the mainland and faunal exchange can take place freely; the second shows the island and parts of the mainland flooded due to a rise in sea-level and the third shows the island separated from mainland by a barrier of water. In the final diagram the arrow indicates that migration onto the island is restricted to those animals that can take advantage of the prevailing 'sweepstake route', by either swimming or floating to the island. Where they are able to develop beyond the reach of mainland predators.

Not unnaturally our record of the geographic distribution of organisms, in space and time, improves as we progress into the later epochs of the Cainozoic era. This is particularly true for both plants and mammals and during the Cainozoic we develop an increasing awareness of the effects of insularity or isolation on mammalian evolution. Geographic isolation may occur on continental masses when ecological and physical barriers confine a species or a group of species to a given area. It also occurs when areas linked to the mainland are cut off due to Earth movements or fluctuations in sea level, and when oceanic mounts appear, and are colonized by certain groups of animals. The island continents of Australia, South America and Madagascar are the classic examples used to explain the effects of isolation on endemic marsupial and placental mammals but small islands can yield as much, if not more, information on the mechanisms involved.

The study of the faunas of small islands has progressed greatly in recent times and much research has been centred on the Miocene, Pliocene and Pleistocene communities of the Mediterranean region. On some Mediterranean islands the content of the mammalian faunas varies considerably through time and it is possible that a given island may have a succession of 'normal' and 'abnormal' communities. The 'normal' or balanced communities were similar to those that lived on the mainland at the same time, whilst the 'abnormal' or unbalanced faunas were

known only from the island in question. This suggests that for periods of time the link between island and mainland was broken and that the endemic fauna developed in isolation. In some cases the island may have been 'drowned' by a rise in sea-level and as a result a gap would appear in the record of mammalian faunas. The subsequent reappearance of the island would result in its recolonization, which would have been selective if

The Pleistocene dwarf elephant, *Elephas falconeri* recorded from the island of Sicily was approximately one quarter of the size of its mainland ancestors. In our restoration it is drawn alongside its contemporary *Elephas antiquus* and it should be noted

that significant differences occur not only in size but also in the form of the head and in the position of the feet. These are the result of skeletal modifications related to the reduction in size and the development of a greater agility.

The giant hedgehog *Deinogalerix koenigswaldi* from the Miocene of Gargano, Italy.

it had remained isolated by a barrier of water. In this event the animals involved in the recolonization would have to have been good swimmers and many of the 'abnormal' faunas of the Mediterranean islands are dominated by deer, elephants and hippopotami. Small creatures such as rodents may have floated across to the islands on rafts of vegetation but large, poor swimmers such as the horses or the large carnivores were confined to their mainland niches.

The absences of major predators such as the cats eliminated the need for large size in the elephants and hippos and as a result dwarf forms were common to many island faunas. Size reduction helped to improve the general mobility of the animal and more obviously resulted in a decrease in the amount of food needed to live, and in the territory occupied. The predators of the island faunas were mainly birds and the prey mostly rodents. On some islands the birds grew to gigantic proportions, as did the hedgehog *Deinogalerix koenigswaldi* which grew to the size of fox within the Miocene island community of Gargano, Italy. In this case the hedgehog had abandoned its insect-eating habits and had turned carnivore as a result of the absence of any of the more accepted predators. Isolation and the lack of large mammalian predators may have resulted in over-population and on some islands, bone beds are an indication of mass extinctions, which were probably the result of overgrazing and the destruction of the vegetative cover.

Tarpit preservation

The tar pits of Rancho La Brea in the Wilshire district of the city of Los Angeles are essentially of Late Pleistocene age, although the discovery of some living species does suggest a continuing, albeit limited, accummulation through to the present time. Ages of between 20 000 and 6000 years have been published in connection with the Pleistocene materials, but radiocarbon dating on the remains of the camelid *Camelops* and the ground sloth *Nothrotherium* indicate that they were persistent in area around 10 000 to 8000 years ago. The range of material from the Rancho La Brea pits is truly spectacular and it allows the palaeoecologist to reconstruct both the environment and the community in some detail. The fossil plants and animals suggest a progressive change from an early humid climate to a warmer more arid one similar to that of the present day. The early climate was characterized by the presence of various pines and cypresses which were gradually replaced by oak, manzanita and elderberry.

The tar pits of Rancho La Brea were formed when oil seeped through to the surface and evaporated. Some pits still contain a sticky fluid but in others the tar has consolidated and palaeontologists are able to dig out the asphalt and retrieve the remains of an incredible variety of organisms. Specialists use xylene to separate the asphalt from the more delicate remains.

The fossil material collected from the tar pits of Rancho La Brea presents us with a somewhat biased view of life during the Late Pleistocene, as carnivores and large birds of prey clearly outnumber herbivores. The reason for this bias is illustrated, with dire-wolfs, and a pair of sabre-toothed tigers (*Smilodon*), all seeking food from the frame of a mammoth. Greed would have encouraged the meat-eaters to try and reach the carcase and it is likely that several would have failed and slipped into the

In the days of the Late Pleistocene, the fauna of the Rancho La Brea area included many large mammals, birds of prey and a large number of small amphibians and reptiles. The mammals were divided into herbivores and carnivores with the remains of the latter far outnumbering those of the plant-eaters. The large herbivores included herds of bison, horse and elephant which roamed over the nearby plains, and the ground sloths which fed on leaves and fruit within close proximity of the pits. The carnivores comprised sabre-toothed tigers and dire-wolfs. Over 1000 specimens of each of the meat-eating stocks have been collected from Rancho La Brea, and it is likely that the imbalance between predators and their prey, represented in the collections, is due to the fact that many predators would be attracted to the pits during the death struggles of a large herbivore. In their attempts to kill and feed from what would appear to be an easy victim, the predators would also be sucked down into the sticky tar. The herbivores may have ventured into the pits when the tar was covered with water and it is evident that numerous toads, frogs, lizards, skunks, snakes and pond turtles made the same mistake. As with the mammals, birds of prey such as eagles and scavenging types such as vultures form the greater percentage of the avifauna preserved at Rancho La Brea.

clinging tarry morass. In the background the giant sloth *Megatherium* is seen feeding on leaves and twigs and several horses are moving out of range of the carnivores. A huge imperial 'mammoth' elephant stands warily in the near foreground. The persistence of the sabre-toothed cats in North America until the Late Pleistocene was linked with the presence of the large, slow-moving and thick-skinned herbivores on which they fed.

A continental ark

We have noted that Australia remained isolated from early on in the 'Age of Mammals' and that as a consequence a unique, balanced, but almost exclusively marsupial fauna developed there. The story of this veritable continental ark can now be taken up more fully.

By mid-Eocene times, about 45 million years ago, Australia had finally broken free from Antarctica, which then was still in contact with South America. Already on the new continent were the ancestors of the present platypus and spiny anteaters, remnants presumably of the very primitive late Triassic and Jurassic mammalian stocks of Gondwanaland. It is probable, though by no means certain, that the first marsupial immigrants were present too. They almost certainly came from South America via Antarctica, yet it is not clear if, when they arrived, the overland route was still available and, if it was, why placental mammals did not follow. Alternatively it is just conceivable that a single pregnant female rafted on a floating tree could have given rise to the entire marsupial population of Australia!

Whether the journey was made by sea or by land there followed a diverse radiation of marsupial forms as Australia drifted north towards south-east Asia. Apart from the remarkable examples of convergent evolution described earlier, there also appeared entirely novel animals like the kangaroos and wallabies, which occupy the niche of the larger plant-eaters. Altogether three basic groups emerged. The dasyurids comprise such carnivorous types as the Tasmanian wolf, the Tasmanian devil and numerous native 'cats', as well as the wombats or anteaters, a 'mole' and various mice. Then there are the perameloids or bandicoots. These are generally small creatures with narrow, pointed snouts and long hind legs with which they hop like rabbits. Indeed, those with large, upright ears are called rabbit-bandicoots. Essentially bandicoots are insectivorous. Some of the most characteristic Australian marsupials are included in the diprodonts. There are the squirrel-like opossums, the monkey-like cuscuses, the koala 'bear' which eats nothing but certain kinds of eucalyptus leaves, the wombats which are badger-like with teeth resembling those of rodents and, of course, a great variety of kangaroos and wallabies. The latter are the herbivores of Australia and play the same roles as deer, antelopes and gazelle in other continents.

The southern hemisphere during (a) the Jurassic, (b) the Eocene and (c) recent time, showing the movement of Australia away from Gondwanaland.

Illustrated below is a Pliocene scene from Australia showing the marsupial 'lion' *Thylacoleo*, watching some giant Kangaroos, *Procoptodon*, bounding away in the distance.

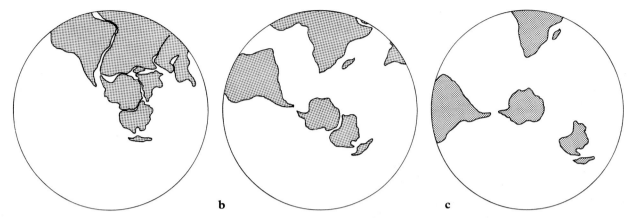

a   b   c

They account for 55 out of a total of about 170 marsupial species living in Australia today.

The total was once even greater for in addition to the extinct 'hippo' and so-called 'lion' which have already been referred to, there were giant versions of the kangaroo, wallaby and wombat. These vanished soon after men appeared in Australia nearly 30 000 years ago. The aboriginal men and later European settlers introduced placental dogs, cats and even the red fox, which through displacement and predation have further depleted the marsupial fauna. The classic case of displacement is that provided by the dingo, or native wild dog, which is descended from domesti-

cated forebears brought into Australia by the aborigines. The marsupial wolf or thylacine disappeared from the mainland at about the same time as the dingo became established. It survived only in Tasmania, an island that was never reached by the dingo.

However, not all the placental mammals in Australia arrived there with the aid of man. A third faunal stratum, far more recent than the monotremes and marsupials, was established by the chance migration of bats and rodents from south-east Asia during the Tertiary. They developed several distinctive forms in the new habitat they encountered.

A bridge through time: Beringia

Until relatively recently, significant similarities in the floras and faunas of land masses separated by sea or ocean were frequently explained in terms of land bridges. These were supposed to have existed in the past and to have subsequently become submerged. Now that it is realized that the land masses concerned have not always been in their present positions, the need for land-bridges has largely been dispensed with. One that really did exist, however, and which has already been referred to, was the Bering land-bridge between Siberia and Alaska.

It was utilized as an intercontinental highway in Cretaceous times, when the ceratopian dinosaurs, for example, spread from Asia into the western parts of North America. At this early date there seems to have been no restriction on the kind of animal that could make the crossing in either direction. Palaeontologists describe a migration route of this sort as a corridor. In the Cainozoic, conversely, it became a filter route, for warmth-loving animals were progressively unable to use it, especially so in the Pliocene and Pleistocene.

The bridge has linked two different continental patterns. Until the mid-Eocene, North America was still connected to Europe via what are today Greenland and Scandinavia. Europe, on the other hand, was separated from Asia by a seaway known as the Turgai Straits. Thereafter the North Atlantic was united with the Arctic Ocean as North America and Europe finally broke apart. At

The land surface which formerly united Siberia and Alaska has been named Beringia. Its climate was once sufficiently mild to allow dinosaurs to cross from Asia to North America.

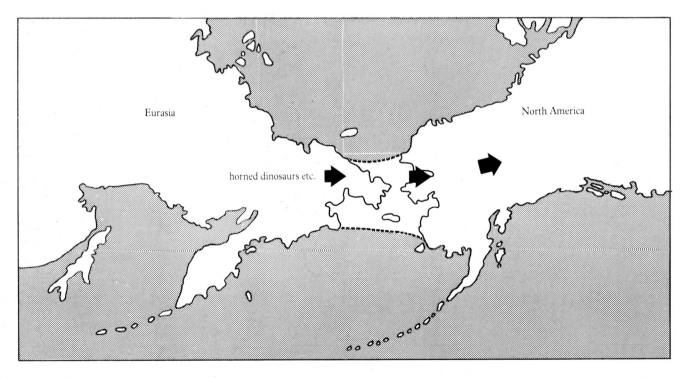

Eurasia

North America

horned dinosaurs etc.

about the same time the Turgai Straits dried up and allowed European faunas access to Asia. Whichever the pattern, the land-bridge was wooded for much of the Cainozoic, but during the Pliocene the woodland gave way to open country. Evidence for this is provided by the passage of the camel and one-toed horse from the New to the Old World.

During the Pleistocene the land-bridge seems to have existed in the glacial periods only, when sea-levels were lower. A fall of 100 metres, such as occurred at the height of the last glaciation, would expose a land connection roughly 1300 kilometres wide, whilst even a fall of 50 metres would reveal one about 400 kilometres wide. The majority of mammals that crossed in the glacials were of Eurasian origin, namely the mammoth, musk ox, reindeer, moose, red deer, bison, black bear, brown bear, polar bear, scimitar-tooth cat, sabre-tooth cat, wolf, wolverine, red fox and man. The mink is one of the few mammals which went in the other direction. Possibly the reason for this imbalanced exchange is that Alaska was generally cut off from the rest of North America by huge ice sheets whenever the land-bridge was available.

Clearly, then, the basic unity of the faunas of the northern continents results from the operation of the Bering land-bridge throughout most of the 'Age of Mammals'. This, and the fact that Eurasia and North America are essentially temperate and cold regions with similar habitats.

Beringia experienced a steady climatic deterioration during the Cainozoic, but woodland existed for much of the time and thus permitted an exchange of woodland faunas between the Old and New Worlds. Warmth-loving animals, however, were excluded, so that the apes and giraffes, for example, never entered North America.

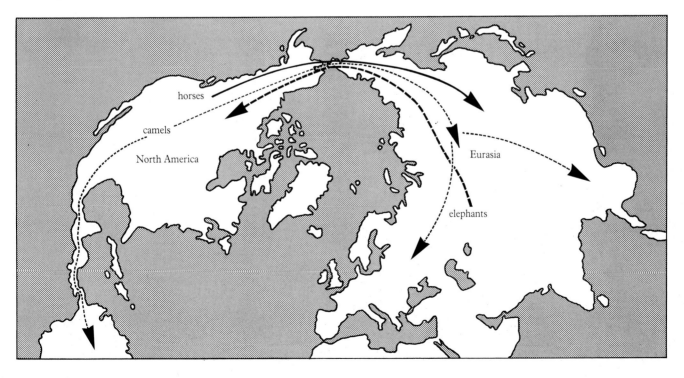

The Pleistocene ice age

Modern extent of the north polar glaciation.

the seed-bearing higher plants and of spores from the lower plants is frequently preserved in acid peats and lake muds. Thus the fossilized grains of pollen and spores recovered from different layers in such deposits are a more or less faithful record of the surrounding vegetation at the times when the layers were actually forming. In practice, the grains are extracted by destroying the materials in which they are preserved with chemical treatments. A high-power microscope is then used to identify the grains, and usually this can be done at the genus- or species-level. The results are portrayed as diagrams showing the frequency of the plants represented at the various depths or levels sampled, so that changes with time are at once apparent (e.g. Snowdonia).

Maximum extent of the north polar ice in the Würm glaciation.

At the height of the last glaciation ice-sheets covered enormous tracts of North America and Eurasia and in places were 3 kilometres thick.

Although sometimes different in detail, pollen diagrams for the glacial periods are basically the same. They all testify to the existence of treeless tundras over much of that part of Europe which was not ice-covered. Sedges, grasses and numerous herbs dominated the vegetation. Because of the lower latitude, the herbs were much more varied than those of the contemporary northern tundras. Relic populations of plants from the most recent of the mid-latitude Pleistocene tundras have managed to survive above the natural limit of tree growth on quite a number of British mountains.

Interglacial pollen diagrams are also alike in that they reveal a characteristic succession of vegetation types. As each interglacial opened the tundra was rapidly colonized by birch and pine woodland, which was in turn replaced by a forest of mixed deciduous hardwoods, especially oak, elm and lime. Later, as the soil and climate deteriorated, hornbeam and spruce invaded the forest, whilst the closing stages of the cycle saw a return to birch and pine woodland. The latter then thinned out as the spread of heathy vegetation heralded the onset of the next glaciation. By comparing postglacial pollen diagrams with the sequence of events just described, it is clear that we are perhaps two-thirds of the way through a typical interglacial period. The early appearance of moorland and heath is due to woodland clearance by man.

Since the start of the Pleistocene Ice Age about 1·6 million years ago, there have been some seventeen glacial phases separated by warmer inter-glacials of very much shorter duration. The ice-sheets expanded to as much as thirteen times their present extent and the vegetation belts were driven far south of their present latitude, often with considerable disruption and change. Polar deserts fringed the ice-sheets and were repeatedly veneered with accumulations of silt and sand. These were deposited by the cold winds which blew off the ice-sheets across the expanses of stony debris and waste dumped along their margins. Vast quantities of water were locked up in the ice so that sea-levels were over 100 metres lower than at present, and it would have been possible to walk from France to Britain and then on to Ireland.

The vegetation of Europe during the glacial and interglacial periods has been reconstructed by means of pollen analysis. The rain of pollen from

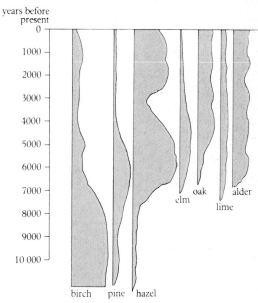

0

1000

2000

3000

4000

5000

6000

7000

8000

9000

10 000

oak

elm

alder

lime

birch   pine   hazel

percentage of tree pollen in samples

This pollen diagram is typical of those made from the lake sediments of Britain. It records the transition from the lateglacial Pleistocene tundra through to the early postglacial birch and pine woodlands and the eventual establishment of mixed oak forest. The reappearance of pollen of typical late-glacial plants of open habitats in the lake sediments, reflects the first forest clearances in the area, nearly 5000 years ago.

Until recently it was believed that valley glaciers like the one at Mont Blanc, Italy, shown left, descended onto lowland plains and merged to form the great continental ice-sheets of the Pleistocene. New research, however, has led to the 'snow-blitz' theory, which merely requires the coalescence of snow-banks over wide areas for the formation of an ice-sheet.

Glacial and interglacial periods

As the great continental ice-sheets repeatedly waxed and waned across Eurasia and North America, the tundra and forest belts were correspondingly displaced, along with their associated faunas. The successive tundra and forest faunas became progressively more modern as the Pleistocene advanced. Archaic forms were weeded out early in the Pleistocene, but a full complement of cold-adapted types was not established until the last glaciation. Even so, as the alteration of environments became more extreme in the Middle and Upper Pleistocene, evolution was speeded up, and new species appeared at a much faster pace than in the more stable African habitats.

The glacial faunas are well known, from frozen carcases in the permafrost of Sibera and Alaska, from their plentiful remains in cave deposits and from Palaeolithic cave-art. There were large herds of steppe mammoths, woolly mammoths and woolly rhinoceroses, all of which were hunted by stone-age men. The woolly mammoths had great curved tusks that were used to sweep snow off the grasses on which they fed, and the woolly rhinoceroses probably employed their long front horns in the same way. During times of lower sea-levels the mammoths crossed the Bering land bridge into North America, yet the equally hardy woolly rhinoceros seems not to have done so. Reindeer, musk-oxen and horses were also very numerous on the Pleistocene tundras, and although they still survive the musk-oxen have been eliminated from the greater part of their former range and the last wild horses – Przewalski's horse – are on the verge of extinction in their natural habitat.

The tundras on which the woolly mammoth and woolly rhinoceros grazed were unlike those of the arctic today. Because of their more southerly latitude the vegetation grew faster and large herds of animals could be supported, as well as the predators and stone-age hunting communities dependent upon them.

The herbivorous faunas of interglacial periods were similarly varied, particularly in comparison with those of the interglacial in which we now live. The imposing straight-tusked elephant inhabited the more open forests together with Merck's rhinoceros, woodland bison and the great ox or auroch from which modern cattle are descended. Several kinds of deer flourished as well, including the so-called Irish elk with magnificent antlers measuring up to 3·5 metres across. The latter actually persisted well into this interglacial and its remains are common in the peat bogs of Ireland. Hippopotamuses too spread along the river courses and judging from the enormous skeletons unearthed near Cambridge, they were even larger than living specimens.

Both the glacial and interglaical herbivores were preyed upon by an array of large, specialized predators. They included a giant cave-lion, a giant tiger, an enormous North American plains cat, big leopards, wolves and Asiatic wild dogs or dholes, and a cave hyena. Sabre-tooths had become extinct in the Old World by the middle Pleistocene, but the scimitar-tooth cat, possessed of sabres that were shorter, flatter and razor-sharp, lived on into the last glaciation, in England at least. No less awesome to Pleistocene men were the gigantic brown bears and the somewhat smaller European cave-bear, particularly the latter, with whom they competed for living-space. The cave-bear, however, was essentially a vegetarian, whereas the brown bear was, and still is omnivorous. Only the polar bear, one of the most recent additions to the high arctic fauna, is exclusively carnivorous.

Many of the animals that lived in Eurasia and North America during interglacial times are today associated with the tropics. Clearly their present distribution is merely a relic of their former range, due largely to the influence of man.

Prehistoric overkill

The dodo, a bird about the size of a turkey lived on the island of Mauritius in the Indian Ocean until 200 years ago. It was made extinct by visiting sailors who killed the dodo and stole its eggs for food. This fate was shared by many island birds which, in the absence of predators prior to the arrival of man, had lost the ability to fly.

Megatherium, the giant sloth of the Americas was nearly 6 metres long and larger than an elephant. It browsed on leaves and could reach high into trees to pull down branches. There is evidence that early men kept *Megatherium* in caves behind stockades. Probably they fed it until food became scarce, when it was killed and eaten.

The Late Pleistocene extinction of large mammalian herbivores and their ecologically dependent carnivores and scavengers reached a climax towards the end of the last glaciation. In all, about 200 genera were lost. The pattern of extinction was global, yet nowhere does the main wave of extinction pre-date the arrival of men with relatively advanced hunting cultures. Thus in Africa it coincided with the spread of the late Acheulian hand-axe cultures about 60 000 years ago, and only 70 per cent or so of the mid-Pleistocene African fauna remains today. In Europe, the extinction peak occurred later, around 30 000 to 10 000 years ago, as highly skilled hunters of the Cro-Magnon cultures moved across the continent. The North American extinction

event was more recent still, beginning roughly 11 000 years ago, and led to a decline of the order of 70 per cent in just over 1000 years! The extent and swiftness of the catastrophe probably resulted from the animals' lack of experience of modern men, whose entry into North America was very late. Most of the animals that survived, incidentally, were earlier immigrants from Eurasia, where they may have already been conditioned to man and as a result acquired appropriate flight responses. The extinctions on islands like Madagascar and New Zealand were delayed well into historical times, since islands were the last places

The glyptodonts, the heavily armoured, tank-like relatives of the armadillos originated in South America and succeeded in spreading into the southern parts of North America before becoming extinct in the Pleistocene. Some were 4 metres or more in length, hence the name 'giant armadillos'.

An example of extreme reduction of territorial range due to hunting by man and loss of habitat is that of the Asiatic race of the lion. Since the relict Iranian population is now believed to be extinct, the only representatives are restricted to the Gir Forest of India. From 'Crises in the History of Life', N. D. Newell, Copyright © 1963 by Scientific American Inc. All rights reserved.

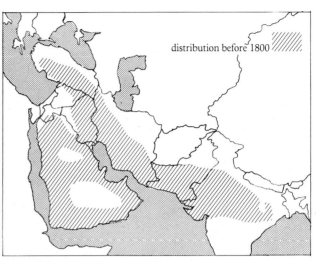

distribution before 1800

to be colonized by man. One further significant feature of these widespread extinctions which deserve mention is that unlike earlier extinction episodes in the fossil record, there were no replacements and niches have been left vacant – except insofar as they have been exploited by domesticated animals. This lack of evolutionary replacement again points to man as the prime cause of the extinctions.

Not unexpectedly, perhaps, other explanations have been advanced, usually stressing the role of climatic change. Yet had this really been the fundamental control it is difficult to see why the extinct camels and shasta ground sloths of North America should not have benefited from the spread of the interior arid lands, and how it was that all the extinct forms survived numerous similar climatic changes earlier in the Pleistocene.

Many of the survivors have subsequently undergone very extensive reductions in their territorial range and are generally much smaller than their Pleistocene predecessors. Predators have been persecuted regardless of whether they pose a threat to man and his animals, herbivores have been hunted for the resources they provide or merely for sport, whilst the destruction and deterioration of natural habitats has been unrelenting. As a consequence there are numerous threatened or endangered species. Those like the rhinoceroses, and certain of the whales and great apes belong to groups that were in eclipse before the advent of modern man. The majority, however, including some of the big cats, otters, several antelope and deer, to name but a few, belong to very diverse orders and owe their decline solely to man.

301

Geology – the founding fathers

Leonardo da Vinci (1452–1519)

The history of geological study dates back to Greco-Roman times with the observations of Xenophanes (540–450 BC) and Herodotus (485–425 BC). But their early studies had limited scientific merit and the title of 'first geologist' should be given to Leonardo da Vinci who in numerous references commented on the deposition of beach materials, argued against the great flood theory and wrote scientifically on the organic nature of fossils and the process of fossilization.

Georg Bauer (1494–1555)

Agricola or Georg Bauer of Saxony is known as the father of mineralogy and metallurgy. His major works included *De Re Metallica* and *De Natura Fossilium* with the former being ranked as one of the finest technical treatises ever written. Bauer was an expert on all aspects of minerals and metals including the practice and economics of mining them. His interest in mineralogy developed from his work as mining doctor in the Bleiberg (lead-hill) region of Saxony.

Niels Stensen (1638–1687)

Neils Stensen is the real name of the Danish physician, theologian and scientist Steno, who studied in Geneva, Paris and Padua, before he took the position of physician in the court of Florence. There Steno became interested in rocks and minerals and in 1669 he published a book entitled *De Solido intra Solidum naturaliter contento*. In this text he proposed several basic geological principles including those of *superimposition* and *original horizontality*. Steno is justly named the 'Father of Stratigraphy' but it should be emphasized that his work on minerals and 'the invariability of the angles between the faces of a crystal' were to provide a base for the work of the great crystallographer Haüy, published in 1800.

James Hutton (1726–1797)

Like Steno and Brauer before him, James Hutton was a doctor. He practised in Edinburgh and was one of a number of scientists and philosophers who earned the city the title of the 'Athens of the North'. Hutton published a paper entitled, *Theory of the Earth* in 1788, in which he argued that most geological phenomena were the products of the processes or forces

that continually act around us. He argued against both the catastrophic and neptunist schools of thought and placed his faith in constancy and his principle of *uniformitarianism*. Hutton's ideas were further elucidated by John Playfair in 1802 in his classic work, *Illustrations of the Huttonian Theory*.

William Smith (1769–1839)

William Smith lived in an age noted for great scientists with de Buffon (1707–1788), Cuvier (1769–1832), Lamarck (1744–1829) and Lyell (1797–1875) all making major contributions to the study of geology. Smith was a surveyor who worked on the construction of canals in the early years of the Industrial Revolution. He travelled throughout England and during his work noted that 'the same strata were found always in the same order and contained the same peculiar fossils'. His observations led to the *principle of faunal and floral succession* and were to be the basis for the hand-coloured geological map he published in 1815. William Smith, often called 'Strata Smith', is known as the 'Father of Geology' and his map is a remarkable testimony to his skills.

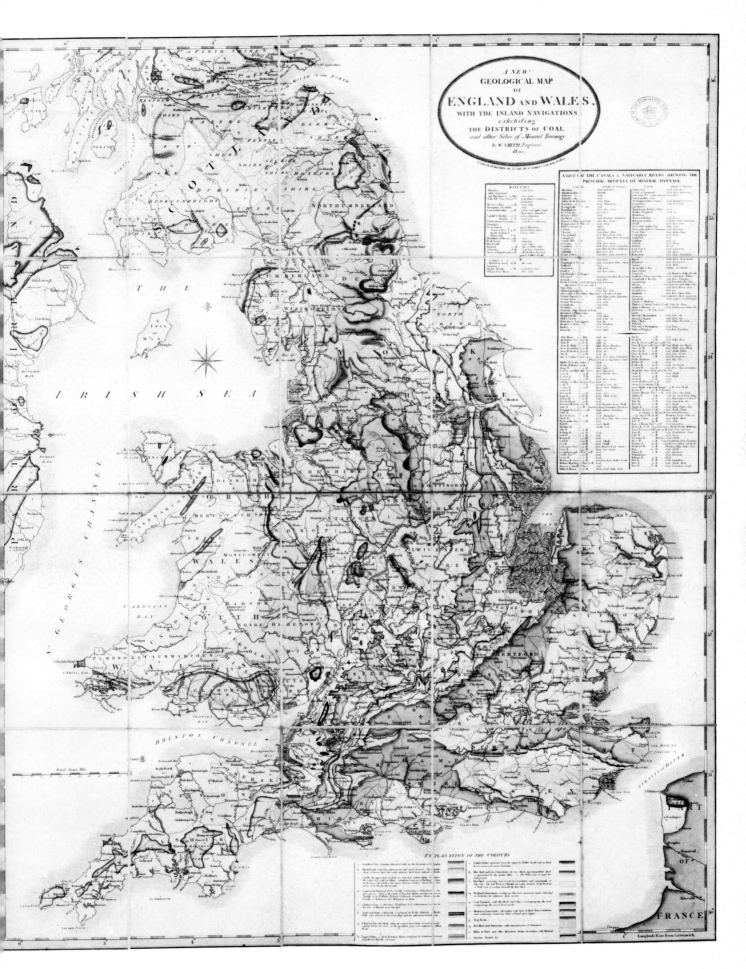

The early days of palaeontology

As with the history of geology, the earliest references to fossils come from works of the Greek and Roman philosophers. Da Vinci and other Renaissance artists, poets and scientists also mentioned them and the illustrations from *De Rerum fossilium* by Gesner in 1565 are thought to rank amongst the earliest known. In the 17th century illustrations of fossils and descriptions of 'cockle-like stones' were commonplace and the figures of a stigmarian root and a dinosaur thigh bone in Dr Robert Plot's *The Natural History of Oxforshire*, are well known, not for the accuracy of their identifications, but because they were at various times referred to as 'part of a carp or barbel' and as '*Scrotum humanum*'. Some of the illustrations from this period are truly magnificent and anyone who studies Hooke's *Discourse on Earthquakes* could not fail to be impressed by the accuracy of his observations. In the 18th century the study of palaeontology and evolution began to take on a new meaning when de Buffon wrote on the succession of faunas and floras and against the time limits postulated by the clergy of that time. The official church view followed the edict of Archbishop Ussher who claimed that the Creation had occurred at 9 o'clock in the morning on Sunday 23rd October, 4004 BC. Palaeontology as a science was further enhanced by the works of Cuvier, Smith, Lamarck and Owen (1804–1892) and through Darwin (1809–1882) with the *Origin of Species* published in 1859.

The science of palaeontology has attracted many people to its calling and not all of these have been trained scientists. In the early 19th century the interest in fossils had reached a new peak and many people had begun to set up private collections. In Lyme Regis a local carpenter named Anning searched for fossils along the cliffs and his daughter Mary often helped in the collection of specimens. After the death of her father, Mary collected to support her family and during her lifetime she collected the first articulated ichthyosaur, the first complete plesiosaur and the first British pterosaur. Mary Anning lived in Lyme Regis between 1799 and 1847 and from the age of 11 she ran a successful business selling the fossils she collected to visitors and collectors alike. Her Fossil Depot was once a major attraction of the region and although an amateur, Mary taught herself a great deal about the fossils she collected. Her customers included the King of Saxony and many of her fossils are now on display in the British Museum (Natural History) in London.

Richard Owen was one of the most eminent

Mary Anning   Sir Richard Owen

palaeontologists of the 19th Century. He was born in 1804 and initially trained as a doctor. His early career was spent as a specialized anatomist but he is best known for the work he did whilst he was superintendent of the zoological, botanical, geological and mineral collections of the British Museum. Owen's training as an anatomist helped in his career as a palaeontologist and he published many papers on the fossil vertebrates. Owen was often referred to as 'the English Cuvier' and in 1841 his claim to fame was truly established when he proposed that the name Dinosauria, derived from the Greek *deinos* – 'terrible', and *sauros* – 'lizard', be used in connection with the huge reptiles discovered by Mantell and Buckland. Owen was to be knighted for his work in palaeontology but unfortunately his final years were embittered due to the conflict over evolution between himself and the establishment and Darwin and Huxley.

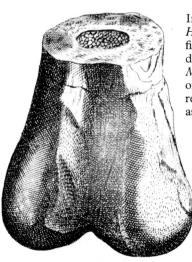

In his book, *The Natural History of Oxford*, Dr Plot figured the thigh bone of a dinosaur, probably *Megalosaurus* as the remains of a giant man. The bone was refigured by Brooks in 1763 as '*Scrotum Humanum*'.

This lithograph of fossils from the
Upper Chalk is reproduced from
William Smith's *Strata Identified by
Organised Fossils*, published in 1816.

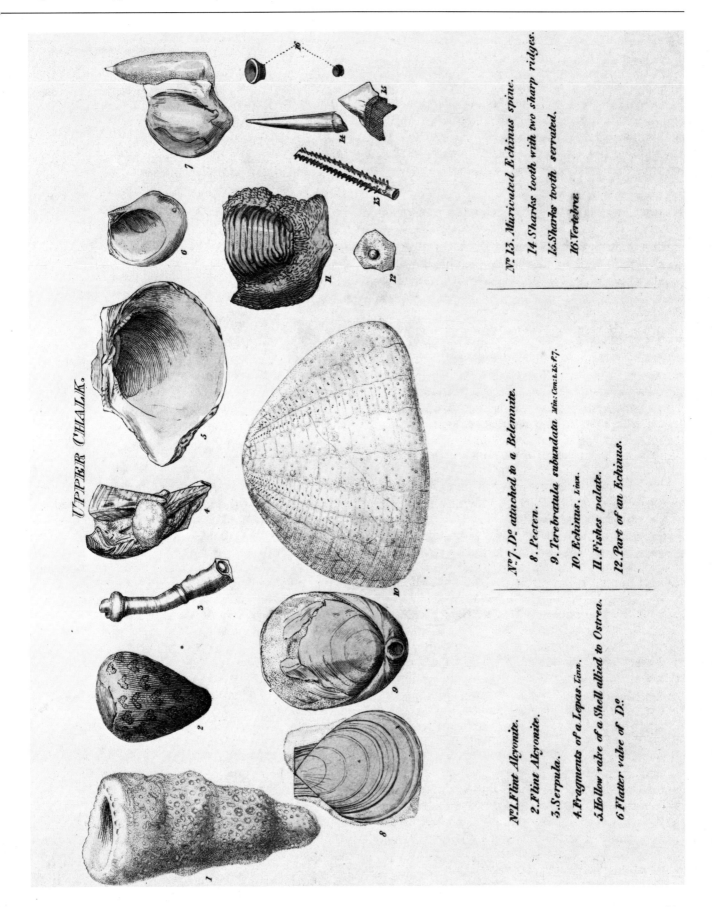

UPPER CHALK.

No 1. Flint Alcyonite.
2. Flint Alcyonite.
3. Serpula.
4. Fragments of a Lepas. Linn.
5. Hollow valve of a Shell allied to Ostrea.
6. Flatter valve of Do.

No 7. Do attached to a Belemnite.
8. Pecten.
9. Terebratula subundata. Min.Con:t.15.f.7.
10. Echinus. Linn.
11. Fishes palate.
12. Part of an Echinus.

No 13. Muricated Echinus spine.
14. Sharks tooth with two sharp ridges.
15. Sharks tooth serrated.
16. Vertebræ.

Lamarck, Darwin and evolution

The further we delve back into stratigraphic time the more obvious are the differences between ancient organisms and those that live at the present time. In these enlightened days we know that the differences are linked with the theory of evolution and that most living animals and plants have evolved from ancestral stocks by way of gradual change. Few people now believe that species were the result of special creation and that they persisted through time without change, but in the early part of the 19th century this was the accepted philosophy. Scientists like Cuvier were totally committed to this idea and linked the extinction of organisms with the waters of the great flood. An obvious opponent of the fixity of species was Jean Baptiste Lamarck, a palaeontologist whose writings included the *Mémoire sur les Fossiles des Environs de Paris* and a *Histoire Naturelle des Animaux sans Vertèbres*. Lamarck believed in the idea that given time and space animals would improve and diversify and he suggested that evolution was linked with the inheritance of acquired variations. In this Lamarck is associated with the idea that animals could improve themselves during their own lifetime and pass these new characteristics on to their young. The majority of scientists, past and present, have found these ideas unacceptable but a small minority still believe that Lamarck's theories have been misinterpreted. Lamarck was to die long before the catastrophic theory was itself finally laid to rest, although Charles Darwin, the first scientist to explain the mechanism of evolution, set out on his round the world voyage in the *Beagle* only two years after the death of the great Frenchman.

Darwin, like so many naturalists and palaeontologists before him, initially studied medicine and theology; his interests in biology and geology being fostered by new friendships with professional scientists. He was an ardent student of the revolution taking place in the science of geology and during the voyage of the *Beagle* he read and re-read Charles Lyell's *Principles of Geology*. Darwin was essentially an amateur geologist but he had worked in the field with the great Adam Sedgwick, and was to put this knowledge to work when he collected rocks and fossils during his travels. Darwin's attention to detail is legend and his fossil collection ranged from small invertebrates to the huge bones of giant armadillos. Many of the fossils were obviously linked with living forms and although Darwin appreciated that they were the product of

Jean Baptiste Lamark   Baron Georges Cuvier

change he was not to fathom the mechanism of evolution for some considerable time. Fossils provided Darwin with certain clues but his studies of the fauna and flora of the Galapagos Islands were to prove a greater influence in the development of the theory of natural selection.

The voyages of the *Beagle* ended in 1835 and on his return to England Darwin was soon to marry and retreat from the world to the quiet countryside of Downe in Kent. There he gathered new evidence and spent many years thinking and writing about his theory. As an author, Darwin was extremely meticulous and obviously concerned about presenting a text that would convince the scientific world. He saw no need to rush into print and only the knowledge that a young naturalist Alfred Russel Wallace had independently arrived at the same conclusions, inspired him to publish in 1858 and 1859. The first publication was in fact a joint effort with Wallace and credit for the discovery of natural selection is due to both. Wallace, however, was magnanimous and it was he who first used the word 'Darwinism' in relation to the theory of evolution. In 1859 the great work, *Origin of Species*, was published and although its main concepts were not, at first, universally accepted, Hewett Watson an eminent botanist wrote to Darwin saying, 'Your leading idea (natural selection) will assuredly become recognised as an established truth in science'.

Over the years Darwin recorded the variation that occurred within a species, the overproduction by organisms of more young than was necessary for survival and the elimination of the weaker or less well adapted during the competition for food and living space. Natural selection was for him the *survival of the fittest* with those organisms that had the ability to cope with a change, resist disease or

Thomas Huxley

Charles Darwin

predation surviving to raise a new generation. One of the main proponents of Darwin's theory was Thomas Huxley whose debate with Bishop Wilberforce at Oxford in 1860 caused a great furore. The articulate Huxley was to do much for the cause of Darwinism and was one of the first scientists bold enough to link man with the theory of evolution.

Skeleton and bones of a *Megatherium* which Darwin unearthed in South America during his voyage on the *Beagle* during the 1830s.

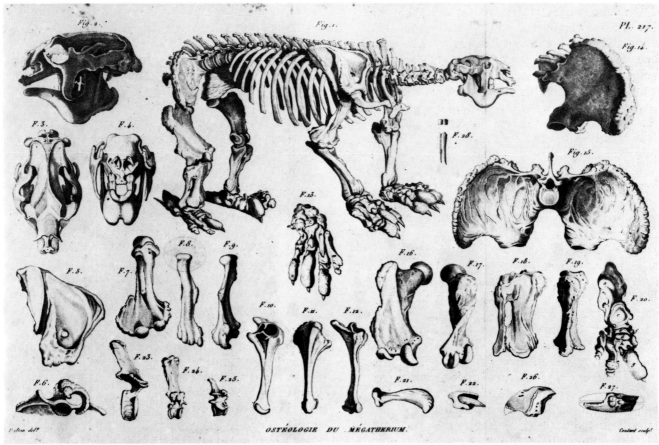

OSTÉOLOGIE DU MÉGATHERIUM.

Fossils and their uses

Geologists concerned with the exploration and exploitation of much needed fuels and other mineral resources rely heavily on fossils for the identification of rocks of different ages and of specific importance. In the drilling for oil or natural gas, errors cost millions of pounds and therefore core sections from rigs are continually analysed to establish the relationship between the depth of the hole and a zone of potential productivity. The core sections frequently contain micro-fossils such as foraminiferids, ostracodes and pollen and it is these organisms that provide the vital clues as to marker horizons within a given geological structure. Their use enables the geologist to correlate over wide areas and to make decisions regarding the continuation of drilling.

Apart from their value in stratigraphy and in the interpretation of past climates and communities, fossils are important economically, with fossil fuels such as coal, oil and natural gas forming as the result of the accumulation and decay of organic matter. Coal is a product of the accumulation and partial decay of plants in an anaerobic environment, and apart from being one of man's most important fuels it is also used as a source of the essential ingredients for drugs and cosmetics. Oil also has many by-products and, apart from petrol, contributes to the production of plastics and animal foodstuffs. Of the other important fossil products, limestones and phosphates provide man with much needed fertilizers. Limestones are also used in the production of cement and the construction of buildings.

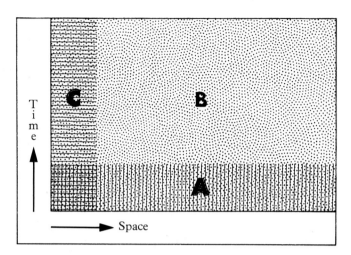

From the data set out in previous chapters it is obvious that fossils have an important role to play in our understanding of geological time, as well as in the investigation of past climates and in the correlation of strata throughout the world. They also provide information on the appearance and structure of past communities and reveal the evolutionary changes that have taken place in both plant and animal kingdoms. Groups such as the graptolites and ammonites show rapid evolutionary change and where individual species have a wide distribution and a limited time-scale they can be employed as zone or index fossils. In the diagram the ideal species that could be used as a zone fossil is A, for although B is widely distributed it is also long-ranging in time and C is to be found only in one area.

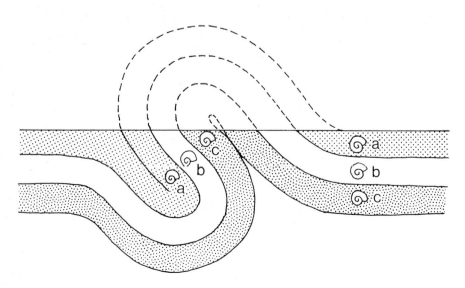

In the mapping of the Earth's surface and in the compilation of its geological history the correlation of strata is extremely important. To establish an orderly sequence of rocks in a given area the geologist will therefore select an undisturbed section and analyse the order in which various fossils occur. In our diagram the three ammonites A, B and C occur in chronological order within the undisturbed section, with A as the oldest species. Traced towards the south, however, we find that this order has changed and we can establish the rock units containing the three fossils have been overturned or inverted. In some areas the physical continuity of the rock units may be broken by faulting and fossils can again be used for correlation between outcrops

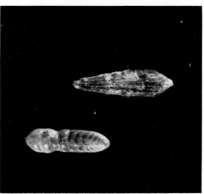

Above
Drill floor as seen from a derrick

Left
Frondicularia is a foraminiferid which is an important zone fossil.

Right
A sectioned drill rig core sample. The sections frequently contain micro-fossils such as foraminiferids and pollen which provide vital clues as to the geological structure.

Discovery and preparation

The contents of this book reflect the results of many years of collecting, preparation and analysis by both amateur and professional palaeontologists. Individual fossils may have been found by chance and represent a moment's climax in one's career, but most, especially those concerned with the detailed reconstruction of a community, are the result of careful planning and systematic collection. Many palaeontologists are experts in a specific group of plants or animals or specialists concerned with one particular period of geological time. When collecting they will have entered the field fully equipped with geological hammer, chisels, note-book, brushes, knife and handlers. They will also carry a selection of storage boxes, wrapping paper and other items vital for the protection of delicate or possibly unique discoveries. On major expeditions plaster of Paris, sacking plaster bandages and polyurethane foam will be carried by the palaeontologist concerned with the transport of large specimens over rough country. On site the palaeontologist should first record the extent and details of the section and establish a stratigraphic log of the various sedimentary horizons from which he is to collect. Having done this he will then be able to work systematically, relating each discovery to a specific level. In time this will prove invaluable for it allows him to establish an accurate range for each of the individual fossils discovered and enables him to analyse the succession that once existed with regard to communities. Most workers will also take detailed notes on the relationships that exist between the fossils and the sediment in which they are buried and record information related to sedimentary structures and texture.

The collection of fossils is often easiest in areas where they are weathered out and rest on the surface of an outcrop. However, these specimens may often be very delicate and expertise will be needed to lift and package the materials for their return to the laboratory. In the case of delicate specimens, photographs and field sketches should be made prior to removal. Each fossil should be carefully labelled and given a field log number which helps in separating similar specimens from different outcrops. On specific excursions one may discover a bedding plane crowded with fossils and in this case the field information should include accurate measurements regarding the orientation of the fossils. Where it is impossible to remove the specimen, photographs and distribution diagrams will help in the analysis of the fauna. Where possible bulk samples should be taken so as to

first find the specimen

remove it carefully from the rock

take notes

number the specimen

wrap it carefully

provide data on growth, variation and community composition. Time and care are the ingredients needed to obtain the best results and one should always be aware of the scientific merits of accurate sampling.

The removal of specimens from limestones, sandstones, phosphatic sediments or even shales can often involve one in many hours of patient, physical effort. In most cases it will be necessary to remove a large chunk of country rock along

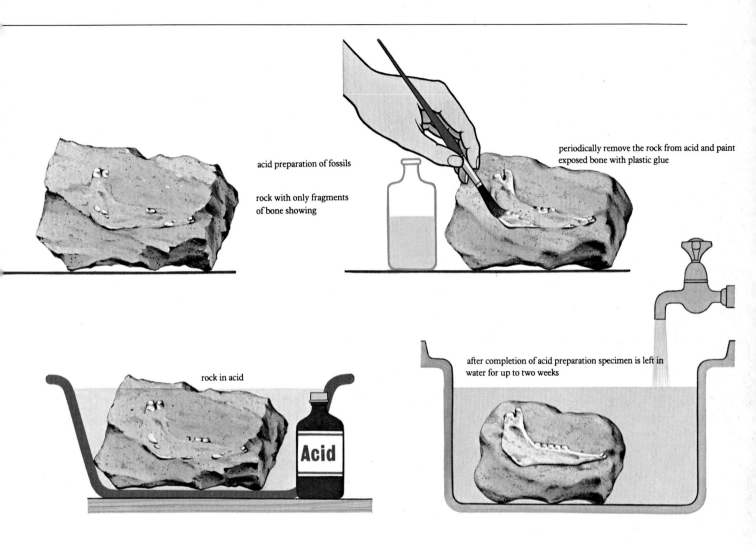

acid preparation of fossils

rock with only fragments of bone showing

periodically remove the rock from acid and paint exposed bone with plastic glue

rock in acid

after completion of acid preparation specimen is left in water for up to two weeks

with the fossil. To avoid fracture or damage the application of a plaster or polyurethane jacket is often essential and one should never set about the final preparation of a specimen under field conditions.

In the laboratory the specimens can be carefully extracted from their protective wrappings and an assessment made as to the best methods for preparation. Mechanical and chemical techniques may be then employed to reveal morphological details unseen during field work but often a good wash or soak will achieve excellent results. Mechanical techniques have been used by palaeontologists and skilled preparateurs for over 150 years and although we now use drills, air abrasives and air dents, instead of hammers and chisels, the method is essentially the same. It involves the removal of small flakes of sediment from around the edges of the specimen with care being taken not to damage the fabric of the fossil. Some protection against this can be obtained by the application of a plastic-based glue, which may

also be used to protect the specimen during chemical preparation.

For chemicals read acids, as dilute hydrochloric and acetic acids have in recent years become major 'tools' in the extraction of fossil materials. The method works well on fossils impregnated with silica or which have a chitinophosphatic skeleton and it involves the immersion of the specimen in acids of 2–10 per cent concentration. The periods in acid are limited to between two and six hours and after each one the specimen is removed and washed for a day or so in deionized water. It is then dried thoroughly and the newly exposed areas coated with a thin layer of the plastic-based glue.

Preparation of a large fossil vertebrate may take months or years of dedicated labour and the use of acids is not recommended to anyone in a hurry or who lacks the correct facilities. The results of this technique are often very beautiful and the data retrieved is a just reward for care taken during preparation.

Glossary

absolute age age of a rock or fossil measured in years before the present

agglutinated foreign particles, such as sand grains, bound together by a cement secreted by the animal

amber fossil resin

anaerobic bacteria minute organisms that can exist in the absence of oxygen

auricles wing-like growths of shell, in front and behind the beak (some scallops)

axial structure central structure in corallite (corals)

basal plates lower plates of theca that attach to stem (sea lilies and blastoids)

bipedal walking on two feet (e.g. birds and man)

bituminous shale fine-grained sediment, rich in oil-like minerals

body fossil preserved remains of skeleton or soft parts of animal

branching colony a colony consisting of a number of branch-like units

calcareous skeleton skeleton composed of calcium carbonate, $CaCO_3$

carapace shell of turtle or tortoise

carbonization fossilization method in which only the carbon content of the original organism is preserved

cartilage gristle-like substance forming skeleton (sharks and rays)

cast an impression obtained from a mould

cephalon head region of trilobite

chitin a complex organic substance made up of polysaccharides; forms external skeleton of arthropods

chitinophosphatic combination of chitin and phosphate, found in external skeletons of certain brachiopods

columella central column of shell (gastropods)

corallite solitary coral or individual of colony

cotyledons fleshy parts of seeds

crustal layer the outermost layer of the Earth, subdivided in two, sial and sima; sial 10–12 kilometres thick, sima 15–20 kilometres thick

cusps swellings on crowns of teeth (mammals)

Danian uppermost stage of the Cretaceous period

deltoid plates upper thecal plates (blastoids)

dicots plants in which seeds consist of two cotyledons

dissepiments minor horizontal to vertical divisions of corallites (corals)

encrusting moss-like growth form (corals and bryozoans)

evolute successive chambers resting on the inner ones without any overlap, as in ammonites

exoskeleton hard outer coating of body in crustaceans, etc

facial suture paired grooves running from front to back on the heads of many trilobites

facies those assemblages of fossils, structures or minerals that indicate the environment of deposition of a particular sediment

gape part of shell that has flexed margins and therefore stays permanently open (bivalve molluscs)

genal angle outer back region of head in trilobites

glabella central swelling of head in trilobites

glacial period time when ice sheets were extending during Ice Ages

Gondwanaland southern land mass that existed before the formation of modern continents and consisted of Africa, Australia, South America and Antarctica

hemisessile term used to describe an animal which spends part of its life in one spot but which may move in order to migrate or feed

hinge line region along which valves articulate (bivalve molluscs and brachiopods)

horizon geological time-plane recognized in rocks by means of fossils or a specific sediment

hydrospire respiratory structure in blastoids, developed parallel to ambulacral borders

ichnofacies facies characterized by the presence of a particular group of trace fossils, *see* facies

imperforate lacking pores

inequivalve with one valve larger than the other (brachiopods and some bivalve molluscs)

interarea flattened region of shell between hinge line and beak in brachiopods

interglacial period warm time when ice sheets had retreated during Ice Ages

intertidal zone area between high and low tides

involute the outer chambers of a shell overlapping those inside, as in ammonities

isotope one of two or more forms of a given element, each having a different atomic weight

keel ridge along outer face of ammonite

keratin organic, horny substance, found, for example, in some sponges

lamellate colony layers of skeletal material deposited one upon another

laminated layered structure

Laurasia northern land mass existing before the formation of modern continents and consisting of Europe, Asia and North America; *see* Gondwanaland and Pangaea

Lithographic limestone name applied to fine-grained carbonate rock used in print industry, the classic example being the Lithographic limestone of Bavaria, Germany

lobe backward projection of suture line (ammonites)

lophophore internal branching structure of brachiopod

magma molten fluid formed in Earth's crust, which may solidify to give igneous rock

massive colony large group of closely packed individual skeletons, as in corals

metamorphic rock the product of the interaction of metamorphic processes on a parent rock

metamorphism effect of agencies such as heat, pressure and chemically active fluids, including magmas, on rocks present within the Earth's crust

monocots plants in which seeds have only a single cotyledon

morphology scientific study of the form and structure of an organism

moss animals bryozoans

mould fossil resulting from the filling in of a cavity left after organic remains have decayed or dissolved

mudstone a sedimentary rock composed of fine-grained materials, similar to shale but more massive

notochord stiffening rod along back, present in the development of all chordates

ossicle a single calcareous plate of an echinoderm

outcrop exposed area of a particular rock type

Pangaea land mass that existed before Gondwanaland and Laurasia had separated

pedicle muscular attachment organ of brachiopod

petrification fossilization method in which animal or plant remains are impregnated with minerals that increase their hardness and weight

pleural regions side regions of trilobites

polyp soft parts of coral animal

pygidium tail region of trilobite

radial plates upper thecal plates (sea lilies); central or side plates (blastoids)

radioactive decay the breakdown of certain kinds of isotopes at a constant rate

ramp flattened region between shoulder and suture (gastropod)

replacement fossilization method in which original organic remains are replaced by minerals

saddle forward projection of suture line in ammonite

schizodont dental structure of certain bivalves (clams) in which two large, divergent teeth occur on right valve

sculpturing grooves, ridges, tubercles or swellings of shell surface

scutes bony plates forming carapace in turtles

seam line along which whorls meet in ammonites

sediment deposit formed from particles derived from the erosion of rocks or by the accumulation of organic materials

sedimentary rock consolidated sediment

selenizone ridge in sculpturing produced during the growth of some gastropods and indicating the presence of a 'slit' in outer edge of aperture

septate central cup area of skeleton being divided by radial partitions (coral)

septum vertical division of corallite (coral); wall dividing chambers (cephalopods)

shoulder strong swelling of shell near suture (gastropods)

silicified sediment a sediment with a high silica content, the silica taking the place of earlier materials

siphuncle narrow tube running through each chamber of cephalopod

slit deep notch in outer lip of aperture in some gastropods

spicular made up of numerous minute structures, *see* spicules

spicules skeletal elements having one or more axes, composed of calcite or silica, as in sponges, sea cucumbers and starfishes

spinose covered in spines or elongate projections

spiralium spiral support structure found in brachiopods

stipe the single branch of a graptolite colony

strata layers of rocks

stratigraphy the description, correlation and classification of bedded rocks, such as sediments and some volcanics

substrate rock surface or upper layers of sediment on which organisms live

suture line along which whorls join (gastropods); region where septum meets wall of shell (cephalopods)

symbiotic association the mutally beneficient relationship of two species

tabulae horizontal divisions of corallites (corals)

taxodont dental structure of certain bivalves (clams) where numerous comb-like teeth occur along hinge line

test the hard, calcareous wall of certain invertebrates such as echinoderms

thecal wall epitheca, outer wall of coral skeleton

trace fossil fossil giving indirect evidence of life (e.g. worm casts, footprints, burrows)

Further Reading

Ager, D. V. (1963) *Principles of Palaeoecology*. McGraw Hill.

Beneš, J. (1979) *Prehistoric Animals and Plants*. Hamlyn.

British Museum (Natural History) (1969) *British Palaeozoic Fossils*. London.

British Museum (Natural History) (1972) *British Mesozoic Fossils*. London.

British Museum (Natural History) (1971) *British Caenozoic Fossils*. London.

Charig, A. and Horsfield, B. (1975) *Before the Ark*. BBC Publications.

Charig, A. (1979) *A new look at the Dinosaurs*. Heinemann.

Clarkson, E. N. K. (1979) *Invertebrate Palaeontology and Evolution*. George Allen & Unwin.

Cox, C. B. (1969) *The Prehistoric World*. Sampson Low.

Colbert, E. H. (1962) *Dinosaurs – their discovery and their world*. Hutchinson.

Colbert, E. H. (1969) *Evolution of the Vertebrates*. E. H. Wiley Interscience.

Dury, G. H. (1970) *Face of the Earth*. Penguin.

Halstead, L. B. (1975) *The Evolution and Ecology of the Dinosaurs*. Peter Lowe.

Halstead, L. B. (1978) *The Evolution of the Mammals*. Peter Lowe.

Hamilton, W. R., Woolley, A. R. and Bishop, A. C. (1974) *The Hamlyn Guide to Minerals, Rocks and Fossils*. Hamlyn.

McKerrow, W. S. (1978) *The Ecology of Fossils*. Duckworth.

Moore, R. C., Lalicker, C. G. and Fischer, A. G. (1952) *Invertebrate Fossils*. McGraw Hill.

Moore, R. C. (ed) (1954) *Treatise on Invertebrate Palaeontology*. Geological Society of America and University of Kansas Press.

Moody, R. T. J. (1977) *A Natural History of Dinosaurs*. Hamlyn.

Moody, R. T. J. (1977) *The Fossil World*. Hamlyn.

Moody, R. T. J. (1978) *Hamlyn Nature Guides: Fossils*. Hamlyn.

Romer, A. S. (1966) *Vertebrate Palaeontology* (3rd edition). University of Chicago Press.

Wood, B. (1976) *The Evolution of Early Man*. Peter Lowe.

References cited in diagrams

Where appropriate, the source material for artwork has been acknowledged. However, in some of the drawings which have been derived from several disparate sources, acknowledgement has not been practical.

Cox, C. B. (1969) *The Prehistoric World*. Sampson Low.

Glaessner, M. F. (1961) 'Pre-cambrian Animals'. *Scientific American*. W. H. Freeman.

Halstead, L. B. (1978) *The Evolution of the Mammals*. Peter Low.

Holmes, A. (1978) *Principles of Physical Geography*. Nelson.

McKerrow, W. S. (1978) *The Ecology of Fossils*. Duckworth.

Newell, N. D. (1963) 'Crises in the History of Life' *Scientific American*. W. H. Freeman.

Romer, A. S. (1966) *Vertebrate Palaeontology* (3rd edition). University of Chicago Press.

Seyfert, C. K. & Sirkin, L. A. (1974) *Earth History and Plate Tectonics: An Introduction to Historical Geology*. Harper & Row.

The paintings by John Barber originally appeared in Charig, A. and Horsfield, B. (1975) *Before the Ark*. BBC Publications.

The drawing of *Anatolepis* scales on page 53 is based on a specimen from the Palaeontological Museum, Oslo.

Photographic acknowledgements

Heather Angel, Farnham 114; David Bellamy, Bishop Auckland 24; Biophoto Associates, Leeds 26 bottom, 27; British Museum (Natural History), London 300, 304 top left, 305, 307 bottom; Bruce Coleman, Uxbridge 97; Bruce Coleman – Jane Burton 94, 191 right; Bruce Coleman – J. A. L. Cooke 39 right; Bruce Coleman – Eric Crichton 166–167; Bruce Coleman – M. T. O'Keefe 254 bottom right; Bruce Coleman – Graham Pizzey 254 bottom left; Bruce Coleman – Leonard Lee Rue III 254 top; Bruce Coleman – Stouffer Productions 200 bottom; Diane Edwards, Cardiff 62; Trevor D. Ford, Leicester 21 right; M. Freudenthal, Leiden 289; Hamlyn Group Picture Library 16 top, 16 centre, 16 second from bottom, 16 bottom, 32 bottom right, 51 top, 53 left, 54 right, 98 right, 112, 130, 133, 168, 169 top, 169 bottom left, 169 bottom right, 177 left, 177 centre, 177 right, 222, 229 centre, 229 top right, 231 right, 304 bottom; Institut de Paleontologie, Paris – Denis Serrette 181; Institut für Geologie und Paleontologie, Tubingen 178–179; Institute of Geological Sciences, London 47 top right, 139 bottom left, 303; Jacana, Paris – Hervé Chaumeton 33 left; Jacana – P. Laboute 58; Jacana – N. Le Roy 32 bottom left; Zophia Kielan-Jarowska, Warsaw 200 top, 205; Mansell Collection, London 302 top, 302 bottom, 304 top right, 307 top left; Dr M. Muir 26 top; National Portrait Gallery, London 307 bottom right; NASA 12, 15; Natur-Museum, Senckenberg 35 bottom; Novosti Press Agency, London 35 top; Oxford Scientific Films – W. J. Kennedy 73, 174; RIDA, Norbiton – Donald Baird 39 left; RIDA – David Bayliss 16 second from top, 21 left, 29, 32 top left, 32 top right, 33 top right, 33 bottom right, 47 left, 47 centre top, 47 centre bottom, 51 bottom, 52 left, 52 top right, 52 bottom right, 54 left, 55 top left, 55 top right, 55 centre right, 55 bottom left, 55 bottom right, 57, 61, 85 bottom, 88 top left, 88 bottom left, 88–89, 89 right, 93 top left, 93 top right, 93 bottom, 136–137, 139 bottom right, 163 top, 163 centre right, 163 bottom, 178 top, 179 top, 227 top, 227 bottom, 228, 229 top left, 231 left, 238, 239, 241 bottom, 259, 266, 309 bottom left, 309 right; RIDA – Dick Moody 45, 47 bottom right, 53 right, 85 top, 115, 149, 190–191, 224, 240–241, 243, 295; RIDA – D. J. Taylor 309 top left; RIDA – C. A. Walker endpapers; RIDA – Peter Wellenhoffer 147, 158; RIDA – R. C. L. Wilson 25, 70, 138 left, 138 right, 139 top left, 139 top right, 162, 163 centre left; RIDA – Bernard Wood 280 top, 280 bottom; Roger-Viollet, Paris 11, 306 left, 306 right; Robert Würgler 98 left.

Artist acknowledgements

John Barber 90–91, 170–71, 210–11, 255–56, 290–91; Ray and Corinne Burrows 8, 164–65, 180–81, 184–85, 186, 192, 193 bottom, 202, 208–209, 255, 268–69, 270–71; Jim Channell-Linden Artists 128–29, 154–55; Thomas Crosby-Smith title spread, 123, 148–49, 187 top, 194; Peter Crump 16, 78–79, 92, 99, 102, 139, 204 bottom, 242, 292–93; Gordon Davies 10–11; Drawing Attention 120–21, 126–27, 175, 195, 252–53, 256–57, 262–63, 264–65, 274–75; Gay John Galsworthy 116–117, 118–119, 124, 125, 144–45, 150, 151 bottom, 152–53; Mary Lacey 198, 199, 203, 207; Kim Ludlow 22, 53, 56, 63, 65, 72–73, 75, 76–77, 80 top, 81, 95, 96–97, 113, 140–41, 197, 300–301; Jennifer Middleton 196, 204 top, 296; Tony Morris 66–67, 146, 148, 151 top, 188, 193 top, 201, 222–23, 225, 228–29, 232–33, 234–35, 236–37, 260–61, 272, 273, 276–77, 278–79; Oxford Illustrators 11 top, 17, 18, 28–29, 33, 34, 68–69, 80 bottom, 96, 108–109, 110–111; Pat Oxenham 298, 299; Sukhwinder Panesar 13, 94, 151 bottom right, 189, 226 bottom; Linda Parry 20, 36–37, 38, 40–41, 44, 45, 46, 48–49, 50, 54, 58–59, 64, 84 top, 98, 100, 101, 104–105, 112, 131, 132, 142–43, 166, 218, 226 top, 240; Eric Robson 182–83; Jane Scott 176, 216, 230–31, 288, 294–95; George Thompson 42–43, 60, 70, 71, 84 bottom, 86–87, 106–107, 134–35, 172–73, 214–215; Tudor Art 14, 19, 23, 27, 30, 31, 62, 82, 83, 103, 250–51; Maurice Wilson 156–57, 159, 160–61, 212–213, 220–21, 244–45, 246–47, 248–49; Michael Youens 187 bottom, 280–81, 282–83, 285, 286, 287.

Index